Collegiate Business Mathematics

5th Edition

Hyman Maxwell Berston, Ph.D.
Professor of Business

Paul Fisher, M.B.A., C.P.A.
Professor of Business

Both of the City College of San Francisco

IRWIN

Homewood, IL 60430
Boston, MA 02116

Sponsoring editor: Richard T. Hercher, Jr.
Project editor: Rita McMullen
Production manager: Ann Cassady
Cover Designer: Terri Ellenbach
Compositor: Interactive Composition Corporation
Typeface: 10/12 Frutiger
Printer: Van Hoffmann Press, Inc.

Library of Congress Cataloging-in-Publication Data

Berston, Hyman Maxwell.
Collegiate business mathematics / Hyman Maxwell Berston, Paul Fisher. — 5th ed.
p. cm.
Includes index.
ISBN 0-256-08028-3
1. Business mathematics—Problems, exercises, etc. I. Fisher, Paul. II. Title.
HF5691.B54 1990
650'.01'513—dc20 89–11014
CIP

Printed in the United States of America

1 2 3 4 5 6 7 8 9 0 VH 6 5 4 3 2 1 0 9

Acknowledgments

We thank the following business mathematics teachers, representing schools in all parts of the country, for their valuable suggestions and comments: John Casey, Robert delongh, Jack Dokey, Arnold Jacobson, Betty Johnson, Keith Kerr, Craig Kuhns, Louis Lindsey, James McConnell, Thomas Munro, Jack O'Shaughnessy, Irwin Phillips, Robert Plotkowski, James Poley, Gary Schaffer, Stephen Schneider, Marlene Stoner, Richard Szukalski, and Marian Terrell.

We also thank the instructors who worked with us on this 5th edition for their keen insight and useful advice: Ila Beaver, Stewart Bonem, Pat Farmer, Ron Faultisch, and Ken Ohm.

A very special thank you from Hyman Maxwell Berston to his wife Bertie, and children, Debbie, Marilyn, Susan, Emanuel, and Judith; and from Paul Fisher to his father Ernest, to his wife Dena, and children, Stephen and David, for their love, encouragement, and patience during the preparation of the manuscript.

HYMAN MAXWELL BERSTON
PAUL FISHER

To the Instructor

This text has been written for those students in community colleges, four-year colleges, adult schools, private business schools, trade and vocational schools, continuing education, and employee training who might need to refresh their understanding of basic arithmetic and then learn to apply these basic principles to problems encountered in common business situations.

The text is divided into 11 sections containing 38 instructional chapters. Chapters 1 to 11 present a brief review of basic arithmetic principles covering addition, subtraction, multiplication, and division in relation to whole numbers, fractions, decimals, and percent. Students *must* be able to perform these basic calculations before proceeding to the remaining 27 chapters, which deal with common business problems.

Our overall goal was to write a comprehensive business math book, using language that is easy to understand. We use an approach that has worked well in accounting. Each topic is introduced with a clear, concise explanation, followed immediately by supporting examples. From many years of teaching experience, we have found that students learn best by examples and illustrations.

The text offers an abundance of business math topics, so that, based on class time limitations, an instructor can selectively omit chapters, or even entire sections. Each chapter is self-contained so that the student will not be confused if some chapters are not covered.

For the instructor, answers are provided for all problems, with detailed solutions given for all word problems, saving the instructor time in reviewing assignments with the student.

When we started our teaching careers, each over 25 years ago, the business math textbooks were primarily math oriented, using business situations as a background. The material was fairly technical, with the goal being to challenge students mathematically. Students without a math background who were studying for a career in business and wanted an overview of the math problems encountered in the various business fields, were becoming discouraged. Our goal is to allow students to more easily understand and solve challenging business problems using arithmetic concepts.

Retained Features. In the 5th edition, the following techniques have been retained from the previous editions:

1. Two sets of exams, with and without solutions, are given to the instructor.
2. Plenty of space is provided between each assigned homework problem to let students solve and complete the problem without having to go to another page or work the problem on a separate piece of paper.
3. Assignments are prepared with the instructor in mind so that the instructor does not have to cover the entire chapter before assigning homework.
4. Detailed suggested solutions to all word problems are provided directly below the problem so that the instructor does not have to rework the problem or refer elsewhere when discussing the problem in class or during office hours. In addition, by use of an overhead projector, transparencies can be used directly as a teaching aid.
5. The homework problems are designed so that problems 1 and 2, 3 and 4, etc., are similar, with the answers to all odd-numbered problems provided in the back of the student edition.
6. The homework problems range from simple to moderately difficult to challenging, allowing the instructor flexibility, depending on the purpose of the course, number of class meetings, and backgrounds of the students.

New Procedures. There have been several substantive changes in the 5th edition, primarily to increase the student's comprehension of the course content.

1. A list of learning goals is presented at the beginning of each chapter which summarizes for the student what knowledge will be derived on completion of the chapter.
2. Student review problems are given at the end of each chapter before the homework problems. A cross-section of about five problems covering the contents of each chapter are provided as a review for the student prior to doing the homework assignment. Solutions and answers are provided on the back of the page. Based on a survey of students in several classes, this probably is the main improvement to help the students learn the new material and give them confidence to work each problem.
3. A mini practice set problem is provided that runs continuously at the end of each chapter throughout the book, beginning with Chapter 12. A college graduate goes to work for a company and, in each chapter, is assigned to solve a multitude of problems covered within the chapter. This concept has not been found in other business math books and, hopefully, will prove to be stimulating, challenging, and interesting to the students.
4. The three sets of exams per section, with and without solutions, are presented in a separate test booklet instead of in the teacher's edition. In addition, many test problems, ranging from relatively easy to challenging, are provided in the test booklet to allow instructors to vary

the tests each time, as well as to determine the number and type of test problems to be given.

5. Interesting statistics, covering a variety of topics, are presented in the margins of the text pages.
6. Transparencies are provided to assist the instructor in showing solutions to problems.
7. Supporting documents have been greatly expanded in the 5th edition.
8. Cartoons and cartoon characters are displayed throughout the book to lighten the reading.

New and Updated Material. The 5th edition contains the following new and updated material:

1. The banking chapter, which was briefly discussed in the 4th edition, is now quite comprehensive, with the introduction of many banking documents and a thorough review of the banking process, including the writing of checks, making bank deposits, and the preparation of a detailed bank reconciliation.
2. The payroll withholding taxes and tables are up-to-date at time of publication.
3. The new income tax MACRS rules for depreciation are introduced and explained.
4. The chapter on present value has been expanded to include a table for the present value of a series of equal payments or investments.
5. The loan repayment schedule has been expanded to include decreasing installment payment amounts with equal principal payments.

To the Student

The material presented in this text will let you review problems in everyday basic mathematics, if needed, and also learn to solve those problems typically found in business.

You will also review the various terms and phrases commonly encountered in the business world. To help you succeed in this course, the following suggestions are presented:

1. Starting with chapter 12, read the list of learning goals presented at the beginning of each chapter, which summarizes what you will learn on completion of the chapter.
2. Read the material in each unit carefully and pay particular attention to the examples provided, which demonstrate the solution to the problem material presented.
3. Before attempting to solve the homework assignments, work the student review problems presented at the end of the text of each chapter. Solutions and answers are provided on the backside of the page.
4. Before attempting to solve the problems given in each assignment, especially word problems, be sure to understand the facts and what you are being asked to determine.
5. Answers to each of the odd-numbered assignment problems are presented in the back of the book so that you may check the accuracy of your work. The problems are often designed so that problems 1 and 2, 3 and 4, etc., are similar. After completing each odd-numbered problem, you should check your answer before going on to the next problem.
6. Adequate space is provided on the assignment sheets for working out each problem.
7. Show each step in your calculations clearly so that your instructor can easily locate any error that you made.
8. After computing your answer, write it on the line provided for that answer.

9. Write your name at the top of each assignment sheet before submitting it to your instructor.
10. If you are confused or unclear regarding any material or problem covered in the text, do not hesitate to raise questions in class or see your instructor during office hours.
11. A Record of Student Progress is provided so that you may keep an account of your progress in the course.

Record of Student Progress

Section	Chapter and Assignment	Date	Score or Grade
1 Number Systems and Decimals	1–1		
	1–2		
	2–1		
	2–2		
	3–1		
	3–2		
	4–1		
	4–2		
	4–3		
	5–1		
	5–2		
2 Common fractions	6–1		
	6–2		
	7–1		
	7–2		
	8–1		
	8–2		
	9–1		
3 Percent	10–1		
	10–2		
	11–1		
	11–2		
	11–3		
	11–4		
	11–5		

Section	Chapter and Assignment	Date	Score or Grade
4 Cash and Payrolls	12–1		
	12–2		
	13–1		
	13–2		
	14–1		
	14–2		
	15–1		
	15–2		
	16–1		
	16–2		
5 Accounting Problems	17–1		
	17–2		
	17–3		
	18–1		
	18–2		
	18–3		
	19–1		
	19–2		
	20–1		
	20–2		
	20–3		
	20–4		
6 Simple Interest	21–1		
	21–2		
	22–1		
	22–2		
	22–3		
	23–1		
	23–2		
	23–3		
7 Compound Interest	24–1		
	24–2		
	24–3		
	25–1		
	25–2		
	26–1		
	26–2		
8 Consumer Purchases	27–1		
	27–2		
	28–1		
	29–1		
	29–2		
	30–1		

Section	Chapter and Assignment	Date	Score or Grade
9 Analysis of Financial Statements	31–1		
	31–2		
	32–1		
	32–2		
	33–1		
	33–2		
10 Business Organization	34–1		
	34–2		
	35–1		
11 Insurance	35–2		
	36–1		
	37–1		
	38–1		
Appendix Graphs and Tables	38–2 A–1		

Contents

Section III Percent

Section IV Cash and Payrolls

Section V Accounting Problems

Section VI Simple Interest

Section VII Compound Interest and Annuities

Section VIII Consumer Purchases

Section IX Analysis of Financial Statements

Section X Business Organization

Section 1

Number Systems and Decimals

Chapter 1

Number Systems

The three chief causes of divorce are men, women, and marriage.

Learning Goals

Upon completion of this chapter, you should be able to:

1. Read Roman numerals.
2. Identify place values.
3. Express amounts numerically and in word form.
4. Use rounding off and approximation.

Ancient Systems

Ancient people used certain symbols or marks to represent numbers and indicate amounts. Such a system could look like this:

/ = 1 one

= 10 ten

= 100 hundred

= 1,000 thousand

= 10,000 ten thousand

These symbols might be used as follows:

/// = 3

= 24

= 121

= 1,232

= 10,302

Roman Numeral System

The ancient Romans used letters of their alphabet to represent numbers, and this method is still used in certain countries even today. The Roman numeral system to express numbers is as follows:

I	V	X	L	C	D	M
1	5	10	50	100	500	1,000

The repetition of the letter repeats the value of the number. Thus,

XX = 20   CC = 200   MM = 2,000

***Average SAT Scores—1986**

	Male	*Female*
Verbal	437	426
Math	501	451

*Minimum score, 200; maximum score, 800. U.S. Bureau of the Census, *Statistical Abstract of the United States*: 1988 (108th edition) Washington, DC.

The value of the symbol following one of greater value is added to the value of the greater. Thus,

XV = 10 + 5 = 15
VII = 5 + 1 + 1 = 7
CXX = 100 + 10 + 10 = 120
MCXXIII = 1,000 + 100 + 10 + 10 + 1 + 1 + 1 = 1,123

The value of a symbol preceding one of greater value is subtracted from the value of the greater. Thus,

XC = 10 from 100 = 90   IV = 1 from 5 = 4
CCXC = (100 + 100) + (10 from 100) = 290

Hindu-Arabic or Decimal Number System

The number system most universally used today is known as the decimal system. It probably originated in India and was brought to Europe by the Arabs.

The digits 1, 2, 3, 4, 5, 6, 7, 8, 9, and 0 are called Hindu-Arabic numerals. This system is based on tens, and the starting point is indicated by a dot known as the decimal point.

Whole numbers are written to the left of the decimal point and increase by tens depending on the position of the numerals. Numbers to the right of the decimal point indicate amounts less than the number 1 and are also in groups of ten. The following table shows the names of the values and the places in the decimal system:

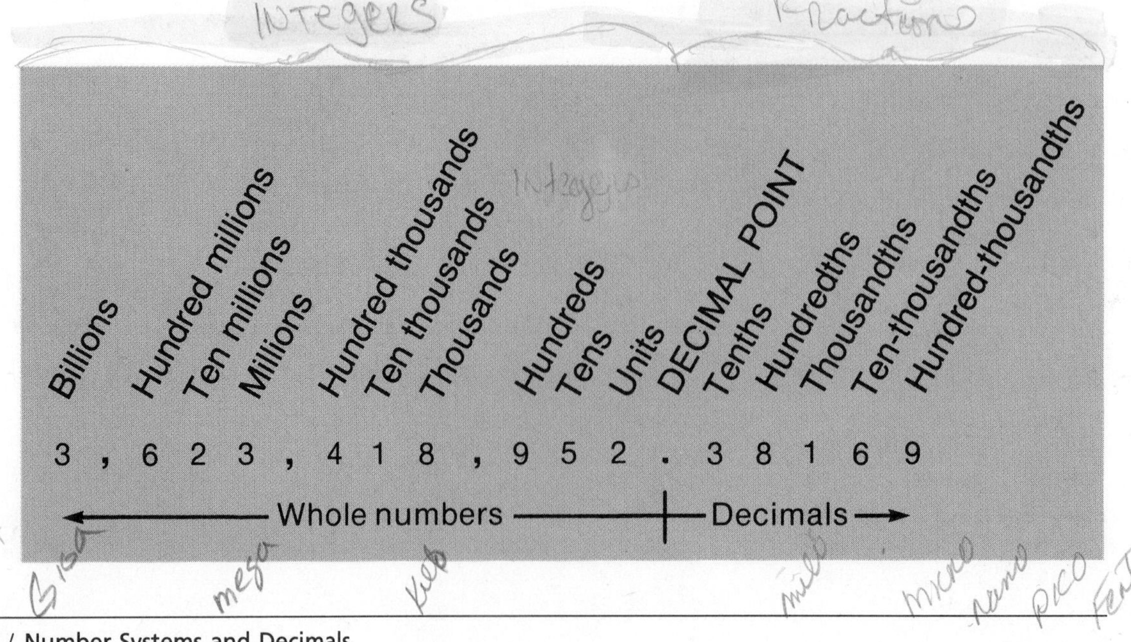

Each group of three digits to the left of the decimal point is generally separated by a comma.

The amount 283 would represent 2 hundreds, 8 tens, and 3 units. Another way to show this is that 283 equals:

$$\begin{array}{r l}
3 & \\
80 & \\
\underline{200} & \quad \text{or} \quad 200 + 80 + 3 = 283 \\
283 & \text{total}
\end{array}$$

The amount 637.5 would represent 6 hundreds, 3 tens, 7 units, and 5 tenths. This could also be shown as:

$$\begin{array}{r l}
.5 & \\
7. & \\
30. & \quad \text{or} \quad 600 + 30 + 7 + .5 = 637.5 \\
\underline{600.} & \\
637.5 & \text{total}
\end{array}$$

Numerals and Word Form

Amounts may be written numerically using numbers and may also be spelled out in word form.

Numerals	Word Form
3	three
27	twenty-seven
61.09	sixty-one and nine hundredths
862	eight hundred sixty-two
3,102	three thousand, one hundred two
27.3	twenty-seven and three tenths
826.126	eight hundred twenty-six and one hundred twenty-six thousandths

When writing a check, it is common to express the amount numerically and spelled out.

Bank of Trade

July 9 19 —

Pay to the order of Al Smith $ 100 00

One hundred and No/100 Dollars

Bill Johnston

Approximation and Rounding Off Numbers

In using arithmetic, there are many times that an approximation rather than an exact amount is used. In a great many situations the amount given is an approximation and for practical purposes is as good or better than an exact or precise amount.

If Smith purchases an automobile and the exact price is $8,988.73, he will most probably quote a price of $9,000 when asked how much the car cost him. A coat priced at $89.95 would be spoken of as a $90 coat, and a pair of shoes costing $48.50 or $49.50 would be referred to as $50 shoes.

The point is that quite often it is easier to approximate or round off to the nearest even amount than to try to recall an exact amount. In working out many basic arithmetic problems, it is a great help to be able to arrive quickly at a rough approximation before calculating the exact answer. Practice in developing such skills will often help to avoid serious errors, especially with problems involving decimals or money amounts.

The rounding off of a given number is quite simply the determination of its significant figures. If the population of a state is 3,172,421, such an amount would be easier to remember in general discussion if it is rounded off to the nearest even million, which in this case would be 3,000,000.

If Williams works 40 hours a week and is paid $9.73 per hour, the actual amount he earns before deductions is $389.20. However, in discussing his weekly earnings, Williams would probably say that he earns about $400 a week. The $389.20 has been rounded to the nearest even hundred, which makes it easier to remember even though it does not represent exact accuracy.

Rules for Rounding Off Numbers

1. First, determine the point of accuracy desired. It may be to the nearest hundred, thousand, unit, or decimal value, depending on the particular use or degree of accuracy needed or desired.
2. Underline the number appearing at the point of accuracy and look at the number immediately to its right.
3. If the number to the right is 5 or higher, increase the underlined number by 1 and change the remaining whole numbers to zeros.
4. If the number to the right of the underlined number is 4 or less, change the remaining whole numbers to zeros.

Since our number system increases by tens, a 5 would represent half or more of the amount we are rounding off to and therefore we increase the value of the underlined number to the next highest number.

Example: Round off 27 to nearest tens.

1. $\underline{2}7$ **The 2 is underlined since it is in the tens column.**
2. $\underline{2}7$ **Is the number immediately to the right 5 or more?**
3. 30 **The answer is yes, so we increase the underlined digit by 1 and change the 7 to a zero.**

```
               half
20 . . . .      |     . . . . 30
                    27——→
```

If we want to show 27 to the nearest even ten, then we must conclude that the answer would be either 20 or 30 since 27 falls between these even amounts of ten at either end. The number 7 in the units column represents more than half of 10, so 27 is nearer 30 than 20. Had the amount to be rounded off been 23, the answer would be 20 since the 3 would have represented less than half of 10.

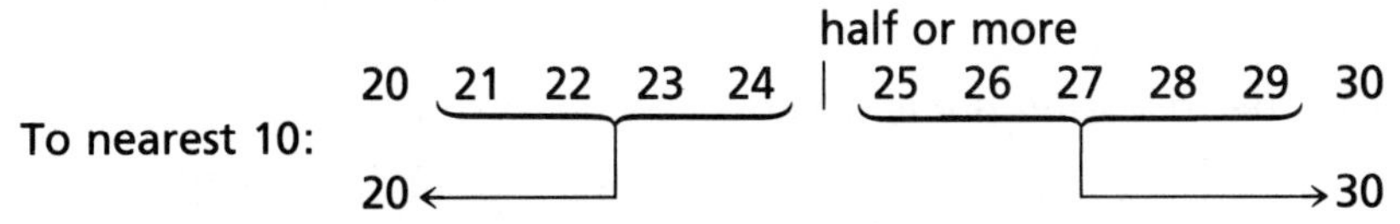

half or more

To nearest 10: 20 21 22 23 24 | 25 26 27 28 29 30

20 ← (21–24) | (25–29) → 30

Notice the following examples of rounding off numbers:

	Round off to tens:		Answer
1.	88	$\underline{8}8$	90
2.	62	$\underline{6}2$	60
3.	695	$6\underline{9}5$	700
4.	38,673	$38{,}6\underline{7}3$	38,670
5.	33.6	$\underline{3}3.6$	30
	Round off to thousands:		
6.	836,429	$83\underline{6},429$	836,000
7.	1,520	$\underline{1},520$	2,000
8.	26,821	$2\underline{6},821$	27,000
9.	921	$\underline{0},921$	1,000
10.	82,652.89	$8\underline{2},652.89$	83,000
	Round off to tenths:		
11.	.30157	$.\underline{3}0157$	.3
12.	27.261	$27.\underline{2}61$	27.3
13.	3.891	$3.\underline{8}91$	3.9
14.	863.98	$863.\underline{9}8$	864.0
15.	37.128	$37.\underline{1}28$	37.1
	Round off to units:		
16.	126.72	$12\underline{6}.72$	127
17.	8.3	$\underline{8}.3$	8
18.	2.1963	$\underline{2}.1963$	2
19.	83,762.99	$83{,}76\underline{2}.99$	83,763
20.	600.921	$60\underline{0}.921$	601

Quik-Quiz

Write the following numerically:

1. Seven thousand nine ____________

2. Sixty-three hundredths ____________

3. Two million ____________

Round off to nearest tens:

4. 875.6 ______

5. 9,824 ______

6. $329.49 ______

7. $19.70 ______

Round off to nearest hundredths:

8. 37.295 ______

9. .923 ______

10. 86.605 ______

11. 772.3907 ______

Round off to nearest units:

12. 1.9037 ______

13. 53,802.49 ______

14. 809.5 ______

15. 34,969.903 ______

Round off to nearest ten-thousandths:

16. .8427098 ______

17. 391.05099 ______

18. 39.888938 ______

1. 7,009; **2.** .63; **3.** 2,000,000; **4.** 880; **5.** 9,820; **6.** $330; **7.** $20; **8.** 37.30; **9.** .92; **10.** 86.61; **11.** 772.39; **12.** 2; **13.** 53,802; **14.** 810; **15.** 34,970; **16.** .8427; **17.** 391.0510; **18.** 39.8889.

Assignment 1–1

Number Systems

Name ______________________

Date ______________________

A. Write the following as arabic numerals:

1. LXXI — 71
2. MCM — 1900
3. LXIX — 80
4. DCC — 700
5. XCIX — 121

Write the following as roman numerals:

6. 250 — CCX
7. 1,206 — MCCVI
8. 18 — XVIII
9. 71 — LXXI
10. 310 — CCCX

In the amount 872, the 8 represents hundreds, the 7, tens, and the 2, units. In the following, tell what the underlined numeral represents:

11. 826 — Tens
12. 12,862 — Hundreds
13. 8.72 — Hundredths
14. 21,830.2 — 10 thousands
15. 37.721 — Hundred thousandths
16. 1,371,862 — millions
17. 82 — Units
18. 8.993 — Tenths
19. 623.712 — Hundreds
20. 121.003 — Tenths

B. Write the following numerically:

1. Seven hundred eighty 780
2. Thirty-three thousand five hundred forty-six 33,546
3. Seventy-three and ninety-one hundredths 73.91
4. Two million seven thousand sixty-one 2,007,061
5. One thousand nine hundred and fifty-two thousandths 1900.052
6. Six million three thousand seven 6,003,007
7. Seventy and two hundred fifty-eight thousandths 70.258
8. Nine million and two tenths 9,000,000.2
9. Two hundred twenty-nine and two tenths 229.2
10. Seventy-three hundred seven 7307
11. Three hundred sixty-nine and nine tenths 369.9
12. Eight hundred seven 807
13. Sixty-two and three thousandths 62.003
14. Twenty-seven thousand seven hundred fifty 27,750
15. Two hundred eighty-six thousand three 286,003
16. Eighty-four hundred 8400
17. Eighty-four hundredths .84
18. Ninety-one thousand 91,000
19. Ninety-one thousandths .091
20. Twenty-one and eighty-three hundredths 21.83
21. Three thousand seven hundred and seven tenths 307.7
22. Twenty-seven hundred and twenty-seven hundredths 2700.27
23. Ninety-three thousandths .093
24. Two hundred twenty-two and three thousandths 222.003
25. Fifty-six thousand eight hundred twenty-six 56,826

Assignment 1–2
Number System

Name ______________________

Date ______________________

A. Round off to nearest tens:

1.	272	200
2.	9.928	1
3.	3,876	3900
4.	$9.87	10.00
5.	$1,689.95	1 698.00

Round off to nearest hundreds:

6.	68.2063	69
7.	31,871.3	31,870
8.	38,452,121	38,452,100
9.	$239.82	200.00
10.	731.8056	780.

Round off to nearest units:

11.	206.84	207.00
12.	3.1762	3.0
13.	87,256.912	87,257.000
14.	80.542	80.000
15.	9,781.7	9,782.0

Round off to nearest thousands:

16.	2,876	3000
17.	33,874,621	33,875,000
18.	500.927	1000.927
19.	92,621.2	93,000.2
20.	99,187	99,000

B. Round off to nearest tenths:

1. .203718 ____________
2. 862.71 ____________
3. 6,384.064 ____________
4. 9.3170 ____________
5. 2,172.856 ____________

Round off to nearest thousandths:

6. .72168 ____________
7. 372.8107 ____________
8. 3.0062 ____________
9. 21,874.3264 ____________
10. 9.7996 ____________

Round off to nearest hundredths:

11. 107.842 ____________
12. .32268 ____________
13. 2.706 ____________
14. 33,841.556 ____________
15. 3.007 ____________

Round off to nearest ten-thousandths:

16. 37.17625 ____________
17. .720943 ____________
18. 3.17006 ____________
19. .003216 ____________
20. 612.62003 ____________

Chapter 2

Addition and Subtraction of Whole Numbers and Decimals

To err is human—but isn't it divine?

Learning Goals

Upon completion of this chapter, you should be able to:

1. Add and subtract whole numbers.
2. Add and subtract decimals.

Addition of Whole Numbers

Addition is the process of combining two or more numbers and arriving at a single total. The amounts to be added are called *addends* and the final result of the addition is called the *total, sum,* or *amount.*

The sign that represents addition is "+" and is called the plus sign. Thus, 7 + 3 + 9 is read as 7 plus 3 plus 9.

When adding whole numbers, those representing units, tens, hundreds, and so on are added separately and when each partial sum is totaled, the number of units of the next higher denomination is "carried over" to the next higher denomination column at the immediate left.

```
                 hundreds
                 | tens
                 | | units
                 7 8 9 } addends
   plus sign  +    6 3 } Augends
                 8 5 2   total or sum or amount
```

In the above example, when 9 and 3 are added, the sum 12 is separated into 1 ten and 2 units. The 2 is written under the units column and the 1 is carried over to the tens column. 1 plus 8 plus 6 equals 15.

Enrollment in 2-Year Colleges—1985

Public	4,270,000
Private	261,000
Male	2,002,000
Female	2,529,000

U.S. Bureau of the Census, *Statistical Abstract of the United States*: 1988 (108th edition) Washington, DC.

This represents 1 hundred and 5 tens. The 5 is written under the tens column and the 1 is carried over to the hundreds column. 1 plus 7 equals 8 and the 8 is written under the hundreds column.

The resultant sum is 8 hundreds, 5 tens, and 2 units, and is written as 852. A great number of calculations in business involve the process of addition. Practice makes perfect, and as individuals do more and more addition, they will increase their ability to immediately recognize the total of various combinations of numbers rather than having to count by ones.

There are various methods that will increase accuracy and help avoid errors in the addition of long columns of numbers:

a. Write the number being "carried" at the top of each column.

b. Break the column into parts and use subtotals.

c. Record the sum of each digit column separately and then find the total of the individual sums.

(a)	552
	372
	21
	8,460
	3,333
	861
	70
	926
	1,870
	68
	721
	8,462
	25,164

The numbers in the units column total 24. The 4 is written under the units column, and since the 2 is being carried over to the tens column, we write a small 2 at the top of the tens column. The ten column totals 56. We carry the 5 and write it above the 3 in the hundreds column. We repeat this procedure for the remaining column. If we are interrupted during the addition of any of the individual columns, we do not have to start at the beginning but can merely begin at the top of the particular column since we know the number being carried from the previous column.

Another method *(b)* used to add long columns is to divide the column into smaller groups and then add the subtotals obtained.

(b)			
	372		
	21		
	8,460	8,853	subtotal
	3,333		
	861		
	70		
	926	5,190	subtotal
	1,870		
	68		
	721		
	8,462	11,121	subtotal
		25,164	total

The addition of each digit column separately *(c)* is another simplified way to add a long vertical column. There are no numbers to "carry" since the total of each column is written in full.

(c)	372		372	
	21		21	
	8,460		8,460	
	3,333		3,333	
	861		861	
	70		70	
	926		926	
	1,870		1,870	
	68		68	
	721		721	
	8,462		8,462	
	24		24	units column
	54	sums of	540	tens column
	46	each column	4,600	hundreds column
	20		20,000	thousands column
	25,164	←total of the sums→	25,164	

Quik-Quiz

1. 29 62 53 144	**2.** 99 20 7 124	**3.** 3 90 27 120	**4.** 99 87 78 264	**5.** 34 70 90 194
6. 392 560 3,599 4551	**7.** 530 99 8,900 9529	**8.** 7,277 921 6,801 14999	**9.** 9,220 6,489 511 16220	**10.** 707 6,219 888 7814
11. 53 9 62 920 58 77 840 2019	**12.** 53,810 4,620 12,144 5,120 986 4,070 59,007 139757	**13.** 91 800 93 671 400 89 26 2170		

1. 144; **2.** 126; **3.** 120; **4.** 264; **5.** 194; **6.** 4,551; **7.** 9,529; **8.** 14,999; **9.** 16,220; **10.** 7,814; **11.** 2,019; **12.** 139,757; **13.** 2,170.

Subtraction of Whole Numbers

Subtraction is the process of finding the difference between two amounts. The number from which the subtraction is made is called the minuend while the amount being subtracted is called the subtrahend. The answer is the difference between the minuend and subtrahend and is called the remainder or difference.

The minus sign indicates subtraction.

	17	**minuend**
minus sign	−8	**subtrahend**
	9	**remainder, or difference**

Check for subtraction: Subtrahend plus difference equals the minuend. Thus, if 17 − 8 = 9, then 8 + 9 = 17.

The most common method of subtraction is to deduct one number from another.

Example:	368	**full amount we start with**
	−235	**amount to be deducted**
	133	**amount remaining**

To arrive at our answer, we begin with the units column and note that 5 from 8 equals 3. In the tens column, 3 from 6 equals 3; and in the hundreds column, 2 from 3 equals 1. We thus arrive at our answer, 133. To check, we add the amount taken away (235) and the amount remaining (133), and the answer is 368, the amount we started with.

At times, a number in the subtrahend is greater than the number above it in the minuend. In such cases, we must borrow in order to subtract.

$$\begin{array}{r} 91 \\ -7 \\ \hline 84 \end{array} \qquad \begin{array}{r} 80 + 11 \\ -7 \\ \hline 80 + \ \ 4 \end{array} = 84$$

In subtracting 7 from 91, we cannot subtract the 7 from 1 and therefore we must borrow 10 from the tens column and add it to the amount in the units column, making it 11. We now take 7 from 11 and the remainder is 4. The digit in the tens column was originally 9, representing 9 tens, or 90. Since we had to borrow 10 to add to the units column, the number of 10s in the tens column is reduced to 8 and we bring this down and write it next to the 4 for a remainder of 84.

The usual way in which borrowing is done is shown below. 7 from 11 is 4. Since we borrow 1 from the 9 it is now 8 and we bring the 8 down for a remainder of 84.

$$\begin{array}{r} 8\ \ \\ \not{9}1 \\ -7 \\ \hline 84 \end{array}$$

An example of a larger subtraction is shown below. 5 from 13 is 8, 3 from 8 is 5, 9 from 12 is 3, and 3 from 6 is 3.

$$\begin{array}{r} 7{,}293 \\ -3{,}935 \\ \hline 3{,}358 \end{array}$$

When a subtraction problem is set up in the usual manner, a quick check of the answer can easily be made. In the example below, we subtract (*b*) from (*a*) and arrive at answer (*c*). To check for correctness, add (*b*) and (*c*) and the answer should be the same as (*a*).

$$\begin{array}{ll} (a) & \$38.75 \\ (b) & \underline{-\ 23.50} \\ (c) & \$15.25 \end{array} \quad \left.\begin{array}{l} \\ \\ \end{array}\right\} = \$38.75$$

Quik-Quiz

1. $\begin{array}{r} 39 \\ -\ 21 \\ \hline \end{array}$ 18

2. $\begin{array}{r} 70 \\ -\ 19 \\ \hline \end{array}$ 51

3. $\begin{array}{r} 383 \\ -\ 92 \\ \hline \end{array}$ 291

4. $\begin{array}{r} 697 \\ -\ 208 \\ \hline \end{array}$ 489

5. $\begin{array}{r} 920 \\ -\ 777 \\ \hline \end{array}$ 143

6. $\begin{array}{r} 6{,}261 \\ -\ 970 \\ \hline \end{array}$ 5291

7. $\begin{array}{r} 9{,}390 \\ -\ 5{,}140 \\ \hline \end{array}$ 4250

8. $\begin{array}{r} 1{,}707 \\ -\ 618 \\ \hline \end{array}$ 1089

9. $\begin{array}{r} 33{,}920 \\ -\ 15{,}929 \\ \hline \end{array}$ 17991

10. $\begin{array}{r} 523{,}290 \\ -\ 91{,}040 \\ \hline \end{array}$ 432250

1. 18; **2.** 51; **3.** 291; **4.** 489; **5.** 143; **6.** 5,291; **7.** 4,250; **8.** 1,089; **9.** 17,991; **10.** 432,250.

Decimal Values

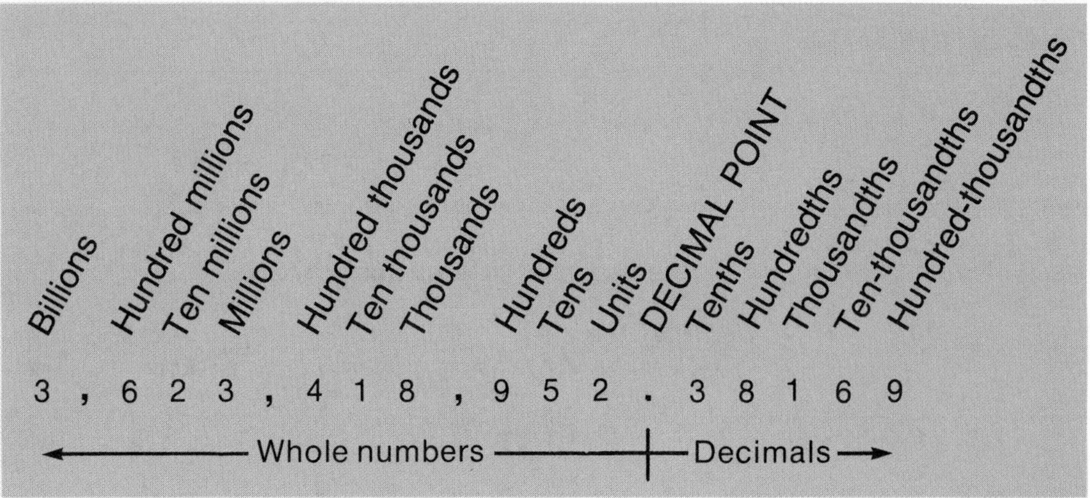

Addition with Decimals

When adding decimals, the decimal points of the amounts to be added must be placed in a straight vertical column before the addition begins.

Example 1. Add .75 + 38.627 + 3.7169.

(*a*)		(*b*)
.75		**.7500**
38.627	**or**	**38.6270**
3.7169		**3.7169**
43.0939		**43.0939**

The alignment of the decimal points in a straight vertical column is shown in the above examples. Although it is not necessary to do so, zeros may be added for better alignment of the numbers, as is done in (*b*) above.

Example 2. Add 387.2 + 86 + .79213 + 8.2.

387.2		**387.20000**
86.		**86.00000**
.79213	**or**	**.79213**
8.2		**8.20000**
482.19213		**482.19213**

Subtraction with Decimals

The same basic rule is followed in subtraction of decimals as in addition. The decimal points must be in vertical alignment. In subtraction each of the amounts must have the same number of decimal places and so it may be necessary to add zeros before beginning subtraction.

Ten Largest U.S. Metropolitan Areas—July 1, 1987

		(in millions)
1.	New York	18.1
2.	Los Angeles	13.5
3.	Chicago	8.1
4.	San Francisco	6.0
5.	Philadelphia	5.9
6.	Detroit	4.6
7.	Boston	4.1
8.	Dallas	3.7
9.	Washington, D.C.	3.6
10.	Houston	3.6

Example 1. Subtract 7.312 from 26.739.

$$\begin{array}{r} 26.739 \\ -\,7.312 \\ \hline 19.427 \end{array}$$

Example 2. Subtract 831.9 from 2,170.83.

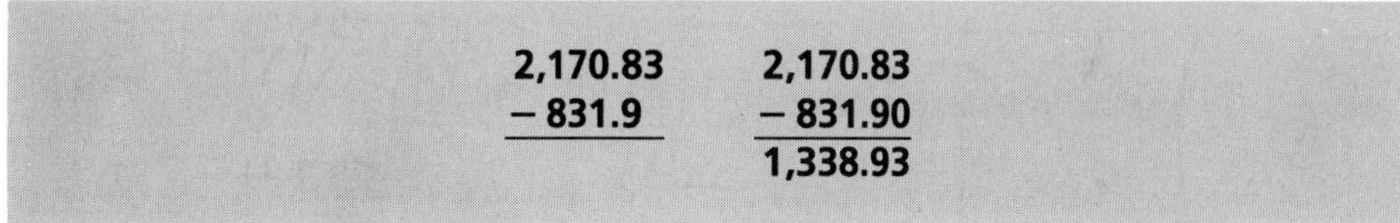

$$\begin{array}{r} 2{,}170.83 \\ -\,831.9 \\ \hline \end{array} \qquad \begin{array}{r} 2{,}170.83 \\ -\,831.90 \\ \hline 1{,}338.93 \end{array}$$

Example 3. 82.9 − 7.328 =

$$\begin{array}{r} 82.9 \\ -\,7.328 \\ \hline \end{array} \qquad \begin{array}{r} 82.900 \\ -\,7.328 \\ \hline 75.572 \end{array}$$

"Charles is alone with his memories."

From *The Wall Street Journal,* with permission of Cartoon Features Syndicate.

Quik-Quiz

Addition:

1. 32.8 + 62 + 5.823 100.623

2. 3.28 + 15.95 + 62.80 82,03

3. 33.810 + .821 + 9,343.521 9378.152

4. 73.286 + 623.5 + .86307 6976.64907

5. 874 + 52.25 + 7.7902 934.0402

Subtraction:

6. 32.726 − 4.25

   28.476

7. 956.726 − 830

   126.726

8. 73 − 5.211

   67.789

9. 724.9 − 5.7346

   573.466

10. 6,621 − 5,382.926

    1238.074

1. 100.623; **2.** 82.03; **3.** 9,378.152; **4.** 697.64907; **5.** 934.0402; **6.** 28.476; **7.** 126.726; **8.** 67.789; **9.** 719.1654; **10.** 1,238.074.

Assignment 2–1

Addition and Subtraction of Whole Numbers

Name ______________________

Date ______________________

A. Add the following:

1.	2.	3.	4.	5.	6.
3	11	2	6	58	621
70	2	18	12	129	80
7	9	17	29		

7.	8.	9.	10.	11.	12.
510	92	66	29	186	921
59	816	251	150	271	104

13.	14.	15.	16.
635	265	928	812
179	851	649	909

B. Add the following:

1.	2.	3.	4.
221	231	372	7,260
581	824	84	37
926	572	107	831
472	906	63	921
922	391	926	3,142

5.	6.	7.	8.
51	411,207	728	9,264
8	198	92	9
726	23,629	655	7,286
39	82	2,195	27
421	6,473	899	853
9	920	16,273	8
80	52	173	6,371
70	8,074	8,940	59
88	37	925	280
621	196	17,520	5,003
55	299	92	51
69	520	837,110	780
777	8,375	12,612	6,070
188	921	6,280	899
162	18	998	17

9.
35 + 18 + 98 + 73 + 37 + 86 + 99 = 446
19 + 53 + 77 + 81 + 93 + 17 + 10 = 350
21 + 36 + 43 + 83 + 70 + 62 + 96 = 411
33 + 16 + 94 + 72 + 52 + 21 + 47 = 335
36 + 73 + 41 + 53 + 26 + 18 + 72 = 319

10.
231 + 82 + 7 + 8,320 = 8,640
162 + 17 + 9 + 3,240 = 3,428
333 + 91 + 2 + 1,828 = 2,254
351 + 22 + 6 + 2,982 = 3,361
929 + 78 + 3 + 6,331 = 7,341

C. Subtract the following:

1. 56 − 38 = 18	**2.** 67 − 16 = 51	**3.** 93 − 46 = 47	**4.** 72 − 38 = 34	**5.** 53 − 33 = 20	**6.** 86 − 70 = 16
7. 624 − 191 = 433	**8.** 561 − 200 = 361	**9.** 362 − 82 = 280	**10.** 919 − 20 = 899	**11.** 3,261 − 876 = 2385	**12.** 6,289 − 4,021 = 2268
13. 80,248 − 16,562 = 63686	**14.** 906,872 − 501,640 = 405232	**15.** 756,000 − 206,890 = 549110	**16.** 318,742 − 60,910 = 257832		

D. Fill in the blanks:

De Iongh and Travers Custom Furniture Refinishing
1990 Report

Month	*Income*	*Expenses*	*Profit*	
January	$ 3,500.	$ 720.	2780	1
February	4,750.	865.	365	2
March	4,210.	820.	3390.00	3
April	5,688.	1,010.	4678	4
May	4,220.	790.	3430	5
June	3,619.	762.	2857	6
July	3,220.	769.	2451	7
August	2,875.	810.	2065	8
September	3,115.	829.	2286	9
October	5,860.	1,120.	4740	10
November	6,320.	1,273.	5047	11
December	5,219.	992.	4227	12
Totals	$52,596.00 (A)	$10,760.00 (B)	$38,316.00 (C)	

Assignment 2–2

Addition and Subtraction of Decimals

Name ______________________

Date ______________________

A. Add:

1. 37.1 + 826.763 = 863.863

2. 75 + .692 + 3,720.2 = 3795.892

3. 83.721 + .6107 = 84.3317

4. 8.921 + 7.263 + 9.439 = 25.623

5. 365.5 + 90 + 6.974 = 462.474

6. 673.002 + .93007 = 673.93207

7. 278 + 83.5 + 621.12 = 982.62

8. 1,279.26 + .38 + 97 = 1376.64

9. 3.7 + 4.08 + .99 + 16 = 24.77

10. 9,283.7619 + 728 + .0743 + 62.25 = 10,074.086

B. Subtract:

1. 638.9 − 16.7 =
2. 25.2 − 18.612 =
3. 61.748 − 32.9 =
4. 21,563 − 1,678.21 =
5. .3716 − .3129 =
6. 298.7 − 137.5 =
7. 198.3 − 7.9416 =
8. 25,856.502 − 16,841.99 =
9. 972.0072 − 8.75 =
10. 738.269 − 162 =

C. Solve the following:

1. Williams purchased vegetables for $6.79, fruit for $13.72, and $28.52 worth of chops and steaks. What is the total amount of the purchase?

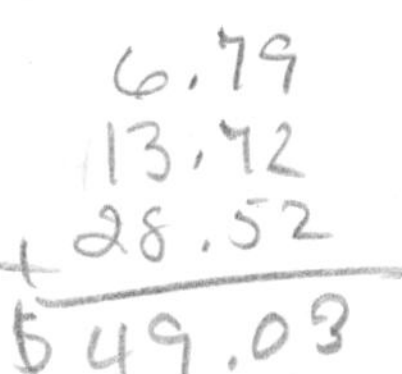

$ 49.03

2. Since coming to work for the ABC Real Estate Company, Brown has earned commissions of $3,500, $9,380, and $4,260. What is the total amount he has earned to date?

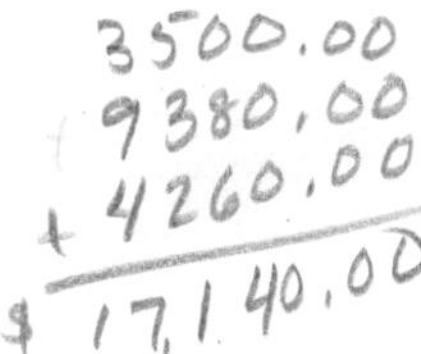

$ 17,140.00

3. If the Spencer Manufacturing Company purchases three stamping machines at a cost of $2,800, $3,200, and $6,350, what is the total cost of the machines purchased?

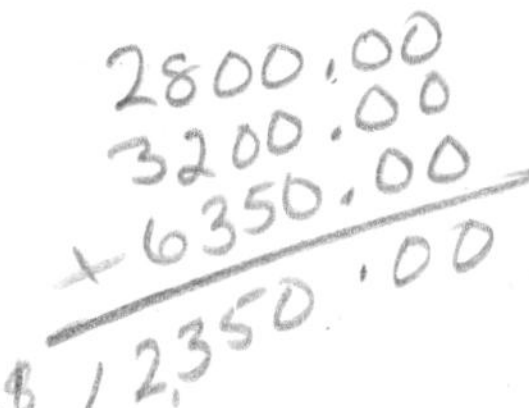

$ 12,350.00

4. Current state, county, and city taxes for the Lamont Corporation are $3,876.50, $5,312.70, and $12,821.00, respectively. What is the total amount due for taxes?

3,876.50
5312.70
+12821.00
$ 22,010.20

$ 22,010.20

5. Williams had $392.70 in his bank account and withdrew amounts of $221.50 and $37.58. What was the balance of his account?

392.70
−221.50
171.20
−37.58
133.62

$ 133.62

6. Johnson received rents from his apartment house totaling $16,350. During the same time, his expenses were $928.00 taxes, $296.25 insurance, $182.40 water, $527.60 maintenance and repairs, $825.10 gas and electric, and $192.70 garbage collection. What amount of rental income was left after payment of expenses?

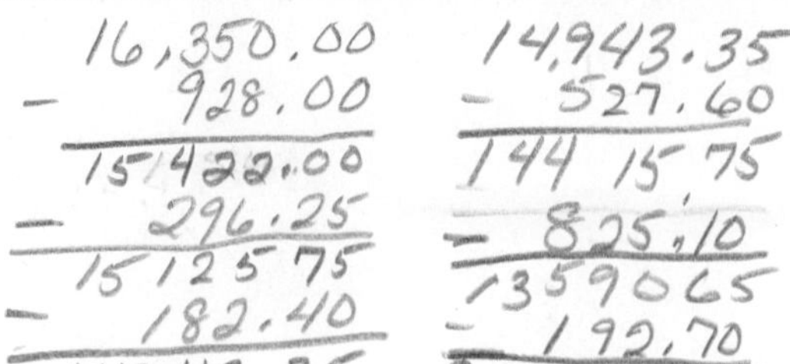

$13,397.95

7. Jordan made purchases at the Banner Hardware Store of $1.73, $2.90, $12.85, $7.40, and $1.28. He had a credit slip in the amount of $3.72 which the store owed him for an item previously returned. What is the total amount he owes the store?

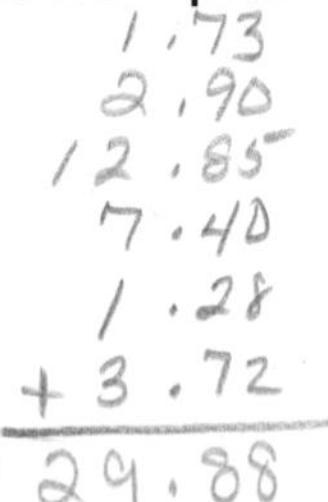

$29.88

8. The population of Central City is reported as 31,862 while that of neighboring Westville is 26,780. How many more individuals live in Central City than in Westville?

31,862
− 26,780
5,082

5,082

9. Builder Hawkins sold a house for $223,750. If the lot cost him $13,200 and the construction costs were $115,750, how much profit did Hawkins make?

223,750.00
− 13,200.00
210,550.00
− 115,750.00
94,800.00

$94,800.00

10. Taylor purchases five sets of rare stamps for $385, $2,125, $2,350, $175, and $3,318. A dealer offers $12,250 for the collection and Taylor accepts. What is Taylor's profit?

385
2125
2350
175
+3318
8353.00

12,250.00
− 8353.00
$3897.00

$3897.00

% − × + $ ÷ +

Chapter 3

Multiplication of Whole Numbers

I say that success is relative. The more success, the more relatives.

Learning Goals

Upon completion of this chapter, you should be able to:

1. Multiply whole numbers.
2. Multiply by powers of 10.
3. Use certain shortcuts in multiplying.

Multiplication is a form of repeated addition. $3 \times 4 = 12$ is the same as $4 + 4 + 4 = 12$, or $3 + 3 + 3 + 3 = 12$. The number multiplied is called the multiplicand, the multiplier is the number multiplied by, and the result of the multiplication is called the product.

	9	multiplicand
multiplication sign	×3	multiplier
	27	product

Selected Average Salaries Paid in Public School System—1987	
Superintendent	$64,580
Principals:	
Elementary	41,536
Middle	44,861
Senior	47,896
Classroom teachers	26,731
Counselors	31,132
Librarians	28,390
Secretarial	17,102

U.S. Bureau of the Census, *Statistical Abstract of the United States*: 1988 (108th edition) Washington, DC.

Multiplication is especially useful when larger numbers are to be multiplied. If we wish to find the product of 12 times 29, it would be very cumbersome to write 29 in column form 12 times and then add. Instead, we use multiplication, as follows:

(a)
$$\begin{array}{rl} 29 & \\ \times 12 & \\ \hline 58 & = 2 \times 29 \\ 290 & = 10 \times 29 \\ \hline 348 & \end{array}$$

(b)
$$\begin{array}{r} 29 \\ \times 12 \\ \hline 58 \\ 29 \\ \hline 348 \end{array}$$

When multiplying two numbers, the smaller is generally written directly beneath the larger. In the above example *(a),* we first multiply 2 times 29 and write the product directly below the line: 2 × 29 = 58.

The second figure of the multiplier is 1, which is in the tens column and represents 10 since the whole multiplier is 12.

10 times 29 is 290 and, if this were written under the first product, 58, the 0 would be under the 8, the 9 under the 5, and then the 2. The usual way, however, is to omit the 0 and merely write the 29 with the 9 directly under the 1 in the multiplier, as shown in example *(b).*

```
(c)        3 8 2
         × 8 7
        2 6 7 4 }
       3 0 5 6  }  partial products
      3 3, 2 3 4 = 33,234 product
```

In example *(c),* we begin by multiplying 7 times 382. 7 times 2 is 14. We write the 4 directly under the 7 and carry the 1.

7 times 8 is 56, plus the 1 being carried equals 57. We write the 7 and carry the 5.

7 times 3 is 21, plus the 5 equals 26. We now multiply by the number 8.

8 times 2 is 16. We write the 6 under the 8 and carry 1.

8 times 8 is 64, plus 1 equals 65. We write the 5 and carry the 6. 8 times 3 is 24, plus 6 equals 30.

We now add the partial products. Bring down the 4. Then 7 + 6 = 13. Write the 3 and carry 1. 6 + 5 + 1 = 12. Write the 2 and carry the 1. 2 + 1 = 3. Now bring down the remaining 3 and the product of the multiplication is 33,234.

The Zero in Multiplication

When multiplying by 10, 100, 1,000, or any other power of 10, simply add as many zeros to the multiplicand as there are zeros in the multiplier. If the multiplicand contains a decimal point, as is often the case with money amounts, then another way of stating this rule is to say that the decimal point in the multiplicand must be moved one place to the right for each zero in the multiplier.

Notice how the following amounts are multiplied:

10 × 28 = 280 10 × 726 = 7,260 10 × $3,290 = $32,900
100 × 23 = 2,300 100 × $7.25 = $725 100 × 9.2 = 920
1,000 × 87 = 87,000 1,000 × 876 = 876,000
1,000 × $1.98 = $1,980

Multiplying When Either or Both of the Numbers Ends in One or More Zeros

```
(a)   820      (b)   82  (0)
      ×12            ×12
     1640            164
     820             82
     9,840           984
```

984 plus one zero = 9,840

(c)	820	(d)	82 (0)
	×70		× 7 (0)
	57,400		574

574 plus two zeros = 57,400

Notice that in examples *(a)* and *(c)*, the zeros are included in the multiplication process. Examples *(b)* and *(d)* illustrate a shorter method. The ending zeros are omitted from the process of multiplication and are then added to the answer received after multiplying.

Multiplying When the Multiplier Contains a Zero

(a)	2761	(b)	3217
	× 702		×2003
	5522		9651
	19327		6434
	1,938,222		6,443,651

When a zero is contained in the multiplier, do not multiply by the zero but merely go on to the next number in the multiplier. In example *(a)*, 2 times 2761 is 5522. The next number in the multiplier is 0 so skip it and go on to the 7. 7 times 2761 is 19327. Remember, however, to begin writing the answer directly beneath the multiplier number being used.

In example *(b)*, we multiply by the 3 and then skip the two zeros and go on to the 2.

2 × 7 = 14. Remember that the 4 is written directly beneath the multiplier number 2. The two partial products obtained as the result of the multiplication are then added together to obtain the answer, 6,433,651.

Multiplying by 99 and 101

To multiply by an amount slightly more or less than 10, 100, 1,000, and other powers of 10, multiply by the nearest power of 10 and then add or subtract the amount of the multiplicand as necessary.

(a)	128	(b)	128	
	×99		×100	
	1152		12,800	(100 × 128)
	1152		−128	(minus 1 × 128)
	12,672		12,672	(equals 99 × 128)

128 may be multiplied by 99, as shown in example *(a)*. However, it is easier to use the procedure shown in example *(b)*. 128 is multiplied by 100 and then 128 is subtracted one time from the answer, which equals 128 multiplied 99 times.

To multiply 128 × 98, the proper procedure is 128 × 100 minus 128 × 2.

128	12,800	(100 × 128)
×100	−256	(minus 2 × 128)
12,800	12,544	(equals 98 × 128)

To multiply 12 × 826, merely multiply by 10 and add 826 twice.

```
  826    8,260  (10)
           826  ( 1)
  ×10     +826  ( 1)
8,260    9,912  (12)
```

Checking Multiplication

A simple method of checking multiplication is by transposing the factors. In the following example, 72 is multiplied by 23. The two amounts are then transposed and 23 is multiplied by 72. The answers must be the same.

```
   72       23
  ×23      ×72
  216       46
 144      161
1,656    1,656
```

Another check may be made by dividing the product by the multiplier. The resultant answer should be the same as the multiplicand.

```
  216  multiplicand        216
  ×32  multiplier      32)6,912
  432                     6 4
 648                       51
6,912  product             32
                           192
                           192
```

Quik-Quiz

1. $\begin{array}{r} 91 \\ \times 9 \\ \hline \end{array}$

2. $\begin{array}{r} 84 \\ \times 6 \\ \hline \end{array}$

3. $\begin{array}{r} 63 \\ \times 50 \\ \hline \end{array}$

4. $\begin{array}{r} 909 \\ \times 27 \\ \hline \end{array}$

5. $\begin{array}{r} 707 \\ \times 66 \\ \hline \end{array}$

6. $\begin{array}{r} 463 \\ \times 209 \\ \hline \end{array}$

7. $\begin{array}{r} 700 \\ \times 43 \\ \hline \end{array}$

8. $\begin{array}{r} 650 \\ \times 500 \\ \hline \end{array}$

9. $\begin{array}{r} 974 \\ \times 603 \\ \hline \end{array}$

10. $\begin{array}{r} 3{,}700 \\ \times 99 \\ \hline \end{array}$

11. $\begin{array}{r} 5{,}320 \\ \times 101 \\ \hline \end{array}$

12. $\begin{array}{r} 3{,}914 \\ \times 879 \\ \hline \end{array}$

13. $\begin{array}{r} 6{,}221 \\ \times 3{,}109 \\ \hline \end{array}$

14. $\begin{array}{r} 38{,}210 \\ \times 1{,}330 \\ \hline \end{array}$

15. $\begin{array}{r} 20{,}200 \\ \times 3{,}005 \\ \hline \end{array}$

1. 819; **2.** 504; **3.** 3,150; **4.** 24,543; **5.** 46,662 **6.** 96,767; **7.** 30,100; **8.** 325,000; **9.** 587,322; **10.** 366,300; **11.** 537,320; **12.** 3,440,406; **13.** 19,341,089; **14.** 50,819,300; **15.** 60,701,000.

Assignment 3–1

Multiplication of Whole Numbers

Name ____________________

Date ____________________

Multiply:

1. 53 × 7	2. 49 × 8	3. 83 × 3	4. 26 × 8	5. 51 × 9
371	392	249	208	459
6. 906 × 7	7. 998 × 4	8. 392 × 6	9. 781 × 7	10. 628 × 5
6342	3992	2352	5467	3140
11. 62 × 50	12. 21 × 10	13. 63 × 12	14. 81 × 32	15. 43 × 17
3100	210	756	2592	731
16. 29 × 80	17. 71 × 20	18. 49 × 19	19. 86 × 18	20. 72 × 16
2320	1420	931	1548	1152
21. 861 × 732	22. 658 × 502	23. 721 × 663	24. 970 × 351	25. 436 × 309
630252	330316	478023	340470	134724

26. 300×60

18000

27. 250×90

22500

28. 309×101

31209

29. 820×300

246000

30. 500×73

36500

31. 700×29

20300

32. $8{,}240 \times 700$

5,768000

33. $6{,}370 \times 80$

509600

34. 399×90

35910

35. $7{,}210 \times 10$

72100

36. $6{,}380 \times 505$

3221900

37. $1{,}246 \times 20$

24920

38. $72{,}900 \times 89$

6,488,100

39. $68{,}010 \times 83$

5,644830

40. $61{,}240 \times 826$

50,584,240

Assignment 3–2

Multiplication of Whole Numbers

Name ____________________

Date ____________________

Multiply:

1. William worked 36 hours and was paid at the rate of $5 per hour. What is the total amount he received?

   36 × 5 = $180.00

   $180.00

2. A theater contains 20 rows with 38 seats per row, 18 rows with 36 seats in each row, and 8 rows with 22 seats each. What is the total number of seats in the theater?

   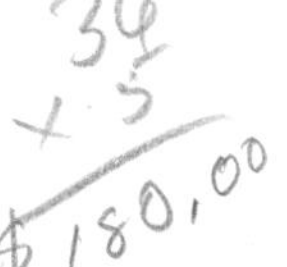

   20 × 38 = 760 + 648 + 8 × 22 = 176 = 1584

   1584

3. How man miles can a truck travel if its tank holds 70 gallons of gas and it averages 9 miles per gallon?

   70 × 9 = 630

   630.

4. Arthur purchases two dozen sacks of concrete at $6 per sack and 18 boxes of nails at $4 per box. What is the total dollar amount of the purchase?

   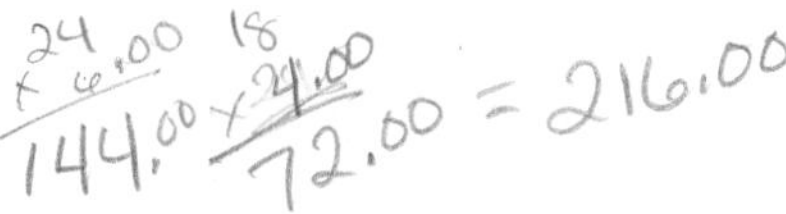

   $ 216.00

5. Henry borrows money from a bank and pays interest of $29 per month for 36 months. What is the total interest charge?

   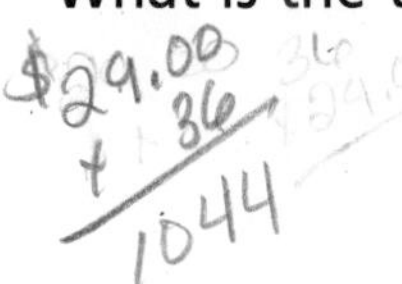

   $1044.00

6. If the enrollment at Monarch College is 629 students and 116 of them purchase a parking permit costing $13, what is the total dollar amount of permits sold by the college?

   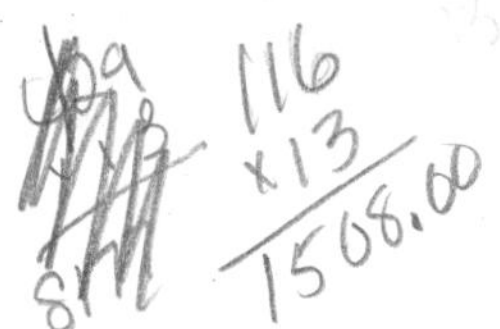

   $1508.00

7. The Thornton Men's Shop purchased 144 jackets at a cost of $30 each and resold them at $50 each. What amount of profit was made on the entire purchase?

$ 7200.00

8. 8,216 five-dollar tickets and 12,380 two-dollar tickets were sold for a football game. What was the total dollar amount of tickets sold for this game?

$ 65,840.00

9. An automobile dealer sold 28 cars to a taxicab company at a cost of $6,190 each. What was the total dollar amount of this sale?

$ 173,320.00

10. Elizabeth enrolled in college and signed for a 15-unit program. The charge was $33 per unit plus $10 for a parking permit and $282 for books and supplies. What is the total amount of money Elizabeth must have to meet these costs?

$ 787.00

11. Victor purchases a printing press, paying $1,200 cash and agreeing to make 36 monthly payments of $235. What will be the full cost of the press?

$ 9660.00

12. If Kuhns purchases 150 shares of stock at $23 per share, 200 shares at $32 per share, and 325 shares at $53 per share, what is the total purchase price of the stock?

$ 27075.00

Chapter **4**

Division of Whole Numbers

I want everyone working for me to tell the truth—even if it costs them their jobs.

Learning Goals

Upon completion of this chapter, you should be able to:

1. Use both short and long division as necessary.
2. Find a simple average or arithmetic mean in a group of numbers.

Division is a process of finding out how many times one number is contained in another number.

	3	quotient		3	quotient
divisor	$9\overline{)27}$	dividend	divisor	$9\overline{)29}$	dividend
	$\underline{27}$			$\underline{27}$	
	0	remainder		2	remainder

The dividend is the number being divided; the number by which the dividend is being divided is the divisor; the quotient is the result of the division and shows the number of times the divisor goes into the dividend; and the remainder is the amount remaining if the divisor does not go into the dividend an even number of times.

In the first example above, there is no remainder since 9 is contained in 27 exactly three times. In the second example, 9 is contained in 29 three times with 2 left over. $3 \times 9 = 27$ plus $2 = 29$.

The sign used to indicate division is ÷ and this is generally read as "divided by." Thus $63 \div 3$ is read as "sixty-three divided by three." In working out the problem, the symbol $\overline{)\quad}$ is commonly used and $63 \div 3$ is set up as $3\overline{)63}$.

Short Division

If the divisor is a small amount containing one or two numbers such as 5 or 12, the division may be easily accomplished by short division.

(a) $8 \div 2 = 4$ *(b)* $12 \div 6 = 2$

(c) $3\overline{)18}$ with quotient 6 *(d)* $15\overline{)60}$ with quotient 4

The above are simple enough so that the answer is readily apparent: 2 goes into 8 four times; 6 into 12 twice; 3 into 18 six times; and 15 into 60 four times.

Long Division

(a) $312 \div 12$ *(b)* $32,877 \div 125$

```
     26                263 r 2
 12)312          125)32,877
    24                25 0
     72                7 87
     72                7 50
      0                 377
                        375
                          2
```

In example *(a),* the following is the correct process of determining that 312 divided by 12 is 26:

The divisor 12 does not go into the first number in the dividend, 3. We move one number to the right in the dividend and now have 31. The divisor 12 goes into 31 two times. The numeral 2 is placed above the 1 in 31. Multiply 12 by 2 and place the answer, 24, directly under the 31. Subtract 24 from 31 to obtain 7. Since 12 does not go into 7 we bring down the 2 from the dividend and now have 72. We now estimate that 12 goes into 72 six times and place a 6 in the quotient. Multiply 12 by 6 and place the answer, 72, beneath the 72 below. 72 subtracted from 72 is 0 and thus there is no remainder and it is obvious that 12 is contained within 312 exactly 26 times.

In example *(b),* we estimate that 125 goes into 328 twice. 2 times 125 is 250, and 250 subtracted from 328 is 78. We bring down the 7 from the dividend and estimate that 125 goes into 787 six times. 6 times 125 is 750 and this is subtracted from 787 giving us 37. The remaining 7 is brought down from the dividend and we have 377. We estimate that 125 will go into 377 three times and enter 3 in the quotient. 3 times 125 equals 375, and 375 subtracted from 377 equals 2. We have used up each of the numerals in the dividend and have a quotient of 263 and a remainder of 2. We have thus determined that 125 is contained 263 times within 32,877 with a remainder of 2. This is shown as 263 *r 2.*

Checking Division

A simple means of checking the accuracy of division is to multiply the quotient by the divisor and add the remainder, if any. The answer should be the original dividend.

If $10 \div 2 = 5$ is correct, then 2×5 should equal 10, which it does.

Using the previous long-division examples:

$$\text{(a)}\quad 12\overline{)312}^{\;26} \qquad \text{(b)}\quad 125\overline{)32{,}877}^{\;263\ r\ 2}$$

check:

$$\begin{array}{r} 26 \\ \times 12 \\ \hline 52 \\ 26 \\ \hline 312 \end{array} \qquad \begin{array}{r} 263 \\ \times 125 \\ \hline 1\,315 \\ 5\,26 \\ 26\,3 \\ \hline 32\,875 \\ +2\ r \\ \hline 32{,}877 \end{array}$$

Simple Average

When a group of items are added together and the answer is divided by the number of items in the group, the result is called an average or arithmetic mean.

(a) What is the average of the numbers 21, 17, and 10?

$$21 + 17 + 10 = 48 \div 3 = 16$$

There are three items in the group, thus, 48 ÷ 3 = 16, which is the average or arithmetic mean.

(b) Four clerks reported daily sales of $625, $581, $861, and $389. What was the average amount of sales per clerk?

$$\begin{array}{r} \$\ 625 \\ 581 \\ 861 \\ 389 \\ \hline \$2{,}456 \end{array} \text{ total sales} \qquad 4\overline{)2{,}456}^{\;614} = \$614 \text{ average sales}$$

Pain-Relief Product Sales, September-October 1987

Aspirin-based	44.1%
Acetaminophen	36.3
Ibuprofen	19.6

The Wall Street Journal, 1/28/88
Nielsen Marketing

"Blood pressure's high, metabolism low, cholesterol high, blood sugar low—it all averages out pretty good."

From *The Wall Street Journal*, with permission of Cartoon Features Syndicate.

Quik-Quiz

1. $3\overline{)99}$

2. $7\overline{)67}$

3. $9\overline{)220}$

4. $5\overline{)900}$

5. $12\overline{)872}$

6. $11\overline{)187}$

7. $25\overline{)975}$

8. $63\overline{)890}$

9. $74\overline{)5,994}$

10. $125\overline{)9,000}$

11. $360\overline{)9,200}$

12. $223\overline{)7,805}$

13. $327\overline{)36,200}$

14. $1250\overline{)52,000}$

15. $2210\overline{)59,670}$

1. 33; **2.** 9 R 4; **3.** 24 R 4; **4.** 180; **5.** 72 R 8; **6.** 17; **7.** 39; **8.** 14 R 8; **9.** 81; **10.** 72; **11.** 25 R 200; **12.** 35; **13.** 110 R 230; **14.** 41 R 750; **15.** 27.

Assignment 4–1

Division of Whole Numbers

Name ______________________

Date ______________________

Divide by short division:

1. 3)69	**2.** 8)96	**3.** 7)28	**4.** 10)330	**5.** 5)90
6. 12)36	**7.** 4)208	**8.** 6)246	**9.** 11)22	**10.** 3)966
11. 4)804	**12.** 7)217	**13.** 8)800	**14.** 10)950	**15.** 2)972

Divide by long division:

16. 8)2,840	**17.** 12)2,592	**18.** 9)8,739	**19.** 25)7,275	**20.** 152)2,584
21. 235)6,580	**22.** 15)9,450	**23.** 71)16,685	**24.** 146)16,352	**25.** 297)26,433

Divide. If there is a remainder, show it to the right of the answer and preceded by an *r:*

26. 31)873

27. 83)969

28. 149)8,726

29. 67)6,839

30. 620)83,426

31. 820)29,312

32. 925)96,200

33. 1,920)117,263

34. 3,590)43,080

35. 3,250)682,500

Assignment 4–2

Division of Whole Numbers

Name ______________________

Date ______________________

1. What was the average monthly salary of a real estate salesman whose total earnings last year were $32,592?

   $2716.00

2. 280 scouts must be transported to a conference by bus. How many buses will be needed if each holds 35 passengers?

   8

3. A factory delivered 350 TV sets to a department store at a total cost of $45,675. What was the individual cost per set?

   130.5

4. During a week in which a taxicab was in use for five days, its mileage record indicated that it had been driven a total of 1,175 miles. What was the average daily mileage driven?

   235

5. A tanker delivered 21,880 gallons of kerosene to a refinery. How many five-gallon cans of kerosene can be produced as a result of this shipment?

   4376

6. How many cartons are shipped by the Calleja Manufacturing Company in filling an order for 468 bearings which are packed 18 to the carton?

   31.2

7. Brussell, Travers, and McConnell own a sporting goods store. Sales for the past 12 months totaled $258,000 and expenses were $195,000. If the 3 partners share profits equally, how much will each receive?

21,000

8. The sales of the Ace Auto Sales Company totaled $73,000 last month. If 4 salesmen are employed, what was the average amount of sales per salesman?

$18,250

9. If 26 students in a history class scored a total of 1,898 points on an examination, what was the average score per student?

73

10. The Johnson Engineering Company purchased a new piece of equipment at a cost of $1,290, and sold it after 3 years for $531. What was the yearly loss in value to the company?

253

11. What number of monthly payments will be necessary in order to repay a loan of $20,000 if the monthly payment is $250?

80

12. If Capps has a budget of $5,000 with which to purchase typewriters costing $583 each, Capps can order how many typewriters?

8.5763293

% − X + $ ÷ +

Chapter 5

Multiplication and Division of Decimals

My grandfather invented the burglar alarm. Unfortunately, it was stolen.

Learning Goals

Upon completion of this chapter, you should be able to:

1. Correctly place a decimal point in multiplication and division of decimals.
2. Use different ways to show a remainder in division of whole numbers and decimals.

Multiplication with Decimals

Decimals are multiplied in the same way as whole numbers. The only difference is the correct placement of the decimal point in the answer. This is done by counting digits to the right of the decimal point in the multiplier and multiplicand and then counting the same number of places from right to left in the answer and inserting the decimal point.

Example 1. 86.312 times 9.7

86.312	**3 decimal places**
× 9.7	**1 decimal place**
60 4184	
776 808	
837.2264	**4 decimal places**

States with Highest/Lowest Teachers' Average Salaries

Highest	(all in $000)
1. Alaska	$44.0
2. New York	32.6
3. Minnesota	31.5
4. California	31.2
5. Rhode Island	31.1
Lowest	
1. South Dakota	$18.8
2. Mississippi	19.6
3. Arkansas	20.0
4. Louisiana	21.3
5. Maine	21.3

U.S. Bureau of the Census, *Statistical Abstract of the United States*: 1988 (108th edition) Washington, DC.

Example 2. $126.83 × 72

```
 $126.83   2 decimal places
    × 72
 -------
  253 66
 8 878 1
 -------
$9,131.76  2 decimal places
```

Example 3. 8.712 × .00037

```
    8.712   3 decimal places
   .00037   5 decimal places
   ------
    60984
   26136
---------
.00322344   8 decimal places
```

Zeros must sometimes be added to the answer to obtain the required number of decimal places. In the third example, eight decimal places were needed; thus, two zeros had to be placed to the left of the 3.

Division with Decimals

In Division of Decimals, if the divisor is a decimal it must be changed to a whole number by moving the decimal point to the right. The decimal point in the dividend is then moved an equal number of places to the right. The decimal point in the answer is placed directly above that in the dividend.

Example 4. 352.675 divided by 2.5

```
2.5)352.675

      141.07
25)3526.75
   25
   ---
   102
   100
   ----
     26
     25
     ----
      1 75
      1 75
```

Example 5. **3760 ÷ 6.4**

```
6.4)3760.0

     587. = 587 32/64 = 587 1/2
64)37600.
   320
    560
    512
     480
     448
      32
```

At times, adding additional zeros to the dividend will cause the division to come out even without remainder.

Example 6. **3760 ÷ 6.4**

```
      587.5
64)37600.0
   320
    560
    512
     480
     448
      32 0
      32 0
```

Example 7. **67.280 divided by 20**

```
     3.364
20)67.280
   60
    7 2
    6 0
    1 28
    1 20
      80
      80
```

Since the divisor is already a whole number, no moving of the decimal point in the dividend is necessary.

Enrollment in Public and Private Schools—United States

	Percent
Nursery	4.3%
Kindergarten	6.7
Elementary	46.8
High School	23.9
College	18.4

U.S. Bureau of the Census, *Statistical Abstract of the United States*: 1988 (108th edition) Washington, DC.

Remainder in Division

A remainder in division may be expressed as a fraction, a decimal, or rounded off to a nearest given decimal place.

Example 1. Common fraction remainder:

390 divided by 12

$$\begin{array}{r} 32 \\ 12\overline{)390} \\ \underline{36} \\ 30 \\ \underline{24} \\ 6 \end{array} \quad 32 = 32\frac{6}{12} = 32\frac{1}{2}$$

Example 2. Decimal remainder:

390 divided by 12

$$\begin{array}{r} 32.5 \\ 12\overline{)390.0} \\ \underline{36} \\ 30 \\ \underline{24} \\ 6\,0 \\ 6\,0 \end{array}$$

Example 3. Divide 623 by 12, showing answer to nearest hundredths.

$$\begin{array}{r} 51.916 \\ 12\overline{)623.000} \\ \underline{60} \\ 23 \\ \underline{12} \\ 11\,0 \\ \underline{10\,8} \\ 20 \\ \underline{12} \\ 80 \\ \underline{72} \\ 9 \end{array} \quad 51.916 = 51.92$$

If instructions were to divide, showing answer to hundredths, the division would merely be carried out to two places past the decimal point and the answer would be 51.91. However, since instructions were to show answer to nearest hundredths, the division was carried out to thousandths and then rounded off to hundredths, giving an answer of 51.92.

"I find it rather difficult for the finite mind to grasp."

Quik-Quiz

Multiply:

1. 82.3 × 1.2 ______
2. 673.2 × .007 ______
3. 7.002 × 18.3 ______
4. 382.701 × .32 ______
5. 725 × .00378 ______

Divide, showing answer rounded off to nearest hundredths:

6. 62.382 ÷ 8.5 ______
7. 52 ÷ 8.3 ______
8. 32.6 ÷ .325 ______
9. 3780 ÷ 69.5 ______
10. .326 ÷ .9 ______

1. 98.76; **2.** 4.7124; **3.** 128.1366; **4.** 122.46432; **5.** 2.74050 **6.** 7.34; **7.** 6.27; **8.** 100.31; **9.** 54.39; **10.** .36.

Assignment 5–1

Multiplication and Division of Decimals

Name ____________________

Date ____________________

Multiply:

1. 63.7 × 1.2
1274
637
76.44

2. 372.8 × .008
2.9824

3. 1,688 × 7.2
12153.6

4. 8.09 × 1.53
12.3777

5. 2.009 × 13.6
27.3224

6. 21,750 × .00075
16.3125

7. 238.9 × .502
119.9278

8. 53.778 × 99.02
5325.0976

9. .0007338 × 813.9
.5972398

10. 19.51183 × 20.3
396.09015

11. 386.722 × 16.38
6334.5064

12. 53.0079 × 1.038
55,0222

Divide:

13. 7.5)62.25

14. .026)468

15. .03)79.8

16. 8.16)23,664

17. 83.2)15,808

18. 7.35)6,027

Divide, showing answer to nearest hundredths:

19. 72)81.25

20. 2.1)7.5332

21. 42)1,789

22. 5.06)82.9

23. 3.7)938.6

24. 53.8)921.7

25. 26.205)832.78

Assignment 5–2

Word Problems with Decimals

Name ______________________

Date ______________________

1. If the St. Charles Canal is 110 miles in length and the Castlerock Canal is 49.8 miles, how much longer is the St. Charles Canal?

   110 − 49.8 = 60.2

   Answer: 60.2

2. If the cost of a certain brand of marine gas is increased 3.5 cents per gallon, what is the additional cost of filling a 200 gallon tank?

   200 × 3.5

   Answer: 700

3. Thornhill had $250 to spend for clothing. He spent $135 for a sportscoat, $39.90 for slacks, $29.70 for shirts, and in addition had to pay $12.28 for sales tax. How much money does he have left?

   250.00 − 135.00 = 115.00; 115.00 − 39.90; 45.40 + 12.28 = 57.68

   Answer: $. 57.68

4. What was the original size of a parcel of land which has been divided into 28 lots of 2.25 acres per lot?

   2.25 × 28 = 63

   Answer: 63

5. In prerace tryouts, car A averaged 121.87 miles per hour while car B averaged 118.79 miles per hour. How much faster was car A?

   121.87 − 118.79 = 3.08

   Answer: 3.08

6. McNamara filled his gas tank and drove to the county fair and back, a total of 202.5 miles. When he refilled his gas tank, it took 12.5 gallons of gas. What was the average miles per gallon that McNamara received?

   12.5) 202.5

   Answer: 16.2

7. If 293 students spend an average of $3.92 in the school cafeteria daily, what was the total amount of money taken in by the cafeteria?

8. How many containers holding 9.8 gallons each can be filled from a 1,000 gallon tank car?

9. If an electric motor makes 1,800 revolutions per minute, how many revolutions will it make in 23.8 minutes?

10. What are the combined weights of three machine parts weighing 8.722, 1.36, and 1.91 pounds per part?

11. At $.255 each, what is the cost of eight dozen pens?

12. If 50 small transistor tubes transmit 825 watts of power, how many watts does each transmit?

Section 2

Common Fractions

% − × + $ ÷ +

Chapter 6

Introduction to Common Fractions

It's pretty embarrassing to watch the boss do something I said couldn't be done.

Learning Goals

Upon completion of this chapter, you should be able to:

1. Distinguish between a common fraction, improper fraction, and a mixed number.
2. Reduce a fraction to lowest terms.
3. Find a greatest common divisor.
4. Use rules of divisibility.
5. Raise a fraction to higher terms.
6. Change a mixed number to an improper fraction.
7. Change an improper fraction to a whole or mixed number.

Fractions are used to express amounts of less than a whole unit. The following are examples of fractions:

$$\frac{1}{2} \quad \frac{2}{5} \quad \frac{3}{10}$$

A fraction contains two terms, the numerator and the denominator. The number below the line is the denominator and represents the number of equal parts into which a whole unit has been divided. The number above the line is the numerator and represents the number of equal parts of the whole we wish to express. The line separating the numerator and denominator is also called a bar and indicates division. $\frac{7}{8}$ may be read as seven-eighths, seven divided by eight, or seven equal parts out of eight equal parts.

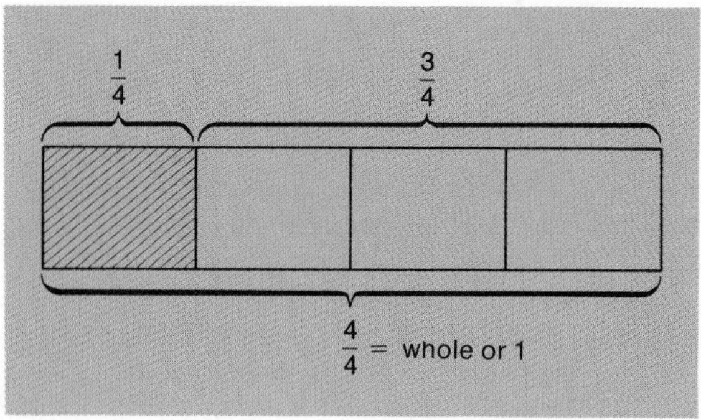

In the above example, we have divided a rectangle into four equal parts. There are four equal parts to the whole, which is represented by the fraction $\frac{4}{4}$. The shaded portion represents one part out of four and is shown by the fraction $\frac{1}{4}$. The unshaded portion represents three-fourths of the whole or $\frac{3}{4}$.

Proper Fractions, Improper Fractions, and Mixed Numbers

The three basic types of fractions are proper fractions, improper fractions, and mixed numbers.

In a *proper fraction,* the numerator is always less than the denominator and the fraction represents less than 1. Examples of proper fractions are:

$\frac{2}{3}$ two-thirds $\quad$ $\frac{7}{8}$ seven-eighths

$\frac{5}{6}$ five-sixths $\quad$ $\frac{11}{12}$ eleven-twelfths

When the numerator is more than the denominator, we are representing an amount larger than a whole unit and such a fraction is called an *improper fraction.* Examples are:

$\frac{4}{3}$ four-thirds

$\frac{9}{7}$ nine-sevenths

$\frac{11}{10}$ eleven-tenths

$\frac{23}{12}$ twenty-three-twelfths

A *mixed number* is a combination of whole numbers and a fraction. The following are mixed numbers:

$1\frac{1}{2}$ one and one-half

$3\frac{3}{4}$ three and three-fourths

$8\frac{1}{3}$ eight and one-third

$21\frac{2}{5}$ twenty-one and two-fifths

Reducing Fractions to Lowest Terms

Fractions may be reduced to lower terms or raised to higher terms without changing the value of the fraction. Generally, however, we reduce fractions to lowest terms. This is done by dividing both numerator and denominator by a common factor. A common factor is a number which will divide evenly into both terms of a fraction.

Thus, $\frac{2}{4}$ may be reduced to $\frac{1}{2}$ by dividing both the numerator and denominator by the common factor 2. Note the following examples:

	Fraction to Be Reduced:	Both Terms Can Be Divided By:	Reduced to Lowest Terms:
(a)	$\frac{2}{10}$	2	$\frac{1}{5}$
(b)	$\frac{5}{15}$	5	$\frac{1}{3}$
(c)	$\frac{8}{16}$	8	$\frac{1}{2}$
(d)	$\frac{6}{9}$	3	$\frac{2}{3}$

Finding the Greatest Common Divisor

To reduce a fraction to lowest terms with a single division, the number used to divide should be the largest number that will go into both terms of the fraction. Such a number is called the greatest common divisor of the fraction.

In example *(c)* above, we could have divided $\frac{8}{16}$ by 2, which would give us $\frac{4}{8}$. It is apparent that $\frac{4}{8}$ can still be further reduced if we now divide by 4 and obtain $\frac{1}{2}$. However, instead of dividing by 2 and then again by 4, we used the greatest common divisor 8, and thus reduced $\frac{8}{16}$ to $\frac{1}{2}$ with a single division.

When larger fractions must be reduced, the greatest common divisor is not always readily apparent. To find it, divide the numerator into the denominator, and then divide the remainder into the previous divisor. This process is continued until the remainder is zero and no further division is possible. The last divisor used is the greatest common divisor of the fraction and the largest number that will divide evenly into the numerator and denominator of the fraction to be reduced.

Projected U.S. Population

	1995	2000
	(in millions)	
Total	260	268
Male	127	131
Female	133	137
White	217	222
Black	33	35

U.S. Bureau of the Census, *Statistical Abstract of the United States*: 1988 (108th edition) Washington, DC.

1. Find the greatest common divisor of $\frac{96}{732}$ and reduce to lowest terms:

```
       7
   96)732
      672      1
       60  60)96
              60      1
              36  36)60
                     36      1
                     24  24)36
                            24      2
                            12  12)24
                                 ↗  24
greatest common divisor             0
```

$$\frac{96 \div 12}{732 \div 12} = \frac{8}{61}$$

2. Find the greatest common divisor of $\frac{107}{233}$ and reduce to lowest terms:

```
         2
   107)233
       214       5
        19   19)107
                95      1
                12  12)19
                       12     1
                        7  7)12
                              7    1
                              5  5)7
                                   5    2
                                   2  2)5
                                        4    2
                                        1  1)2
greatest common divisor               ↗     2
                                            0
```

$$\frac{107 \div 1}{233 \div 1} = \frac{107}{233}$$

The greatest common divisor in example 1 is 12, and division by 12 reduces $\frac{96}{732}$ to its lowest terms, $\frac{8}{61}$. In example 2, however, the greatest common divisor turns out to be 1, which means that the fraction $\frac{107}{233}$ is already expressed in lowest terms.

Rules of Divisibility

Skill in recognizing factors common to both numerator and denominator is very helpful in solving problems using canceling and also in reducing fractions to lower terms.

Numbers multiplied together to produce a certain number are factors of that number. If $2 \times 3 = 6$, then 2 and 3 are factors of 6. An exact divisor of a number is a factor of that number. Thus, 2 and 3 will divide evenly into 6 because 2 and 3 are factors of 6.

A prime number is a number that has no factors other than itself and 1. Numbers such as 1, 2, 3, 5, and 7 are examples of some prime numbers. Each is divisible without remainder only by itself and the number 1.

A composite number is a number that may be formed as the product of two or more factors other than itself and 1. Thus, 4, 6, 8, 9, and 10 are examples of some composite numbers, since $2 \times 2 = 4$; $3 \times 2 = 6$; $2 \times 2 \times 2$ or $2 \times 4 = 8$; $3 \times 3 = 9$; and $2 \times 5 = 10$.

The following rules of divisibility will make it easier to determine which numbers will divide evenly into another number or numbers.

A number can be divided without remainder by:

1, and by itself.

2, if the last digit is divisible by 2. Numbers ending in 0, 2, 4, 6, or 8 are divisible by 2. Amounts that end in even numbers are divisible by 2 without a remainder while amounts that end in odd numbers cannot be divided by 2 without a remainder.

3, if the sum of its digits is divisible by 3 without a remainder. Thus, 387 is divisible by 3 without a remainder because $3 + 8 + 7 = 18$, and 18 is divisible by 3 without a remainder.

4, if the number formed by the last two digits is divisible by 4 without a remainder. Thus, 232, 720, and 8,516 are divisible by 4 because the last two digits; 32, 20, and 16 are divisible by 4 without a remainder.

5, if the last digit is 5 or 0.

6, if the amount is an even number and the sum of the digits is divisible by 3 without a remainder. Thus, 5,718 and 8,190 are divisible by 6 because $5 + 7 + 1 + 8 = 21$, which is divisible by 3; and $8 + 1 + 9 + 0 = 18$, which is divisible by 3 without a remainder.

7, by simply using a trial and error method. There is no special rule for testing divisibility by 7.

8, if the number formed by the last three digits is divisible by 8 without a remainder. Thus 2,432 and 52,480 are divisible by 8 because 432 and 480 are divisible by 8 without a remainder.

9, if the sum of the digits is divisible by 9 without a remainder. Thus, 8,163 is divisible by 9 because $8 + 1 + 6 + 3 = 18$; and 18 is divisible by 9 without a remainder.

10, if the last digit is 0. Thus, any amount ending in 0 is divisible by 10 without a remainder.

Raising Fractions to Higher Terms

A fraction may be raised to higher terms by multiplying the numerator and denominator of the fraction by the same number. If we multiply each of the terms of the fraction $\frac{3}{4}$ by the number 2, we obtain the fraction $\frac{6}{8}$. The first fraction is expressed in fourths and the second fraction in eighths.

Multiplying the terms of a fraction by the same number does not change the value of the fraction. $\frac{6}{8}$ reduced to lowest terms returns to the fraction $\frac{3}{4}$.

1. Express $\frac{2}{5}$ as tenths. $\frac{2 \times 2}{5 \times 2} = \frac{4}{10}$

To change the denominator 5 to 10, we must multiply the 5 by 2. Thus, each of the terms of the fraction is multiplied by 2.

2. Express $\frac{3}{25}$ as hundredths. $\frac{3 \times 4}{25 \times 4} = \frac{12}{100}$

Since $4 \times 25 = 100$, each of the terms of the fraction is multiplied by 4.

3. Raise $\frac{7}{12}$ to a fraction with a denominator of 120.

$$12\overline{)120}^{\;10} \qquad 10 \times 7 = 70 \qquad \frac{7}{12} = \frac{70}{120}$$

Another method of raising a fraction is to divide the smaller denominator into the larger and multiply the numerator by the result of the division. Thus, 12 goes into 120 ten times, and 10 × 7 is 70. The new fraction is $\frac{70}{120}$.

Changing a Mixed Number to an Improper Fraction

A mixed number contains both a whole number and a fraction and is changed to an improper fraction by multiplying the whole number by the denominator and adding to this the numerator to form the new numerator. The denominator remains the same as the denominator of the mixed number.

1. Change $2\frac{2}{3}$ to an improper fraction.

   $3 \times 2 = 6$, and $6 + 2 = 8$. Thus, $2\frac{2}{3} = \frac{8}{3}$.

   Since the fraction is expressed in thirds, we know that $1 = \frac{3}{3}$.

   Thus $2\frac{2}{3}$ is actually $\frac{3}{3} + \frac{3}{3} + \frac{2}{3} = \frac{8}{3}$ or $1 + 1 + \frac{2}{3} = 2\frac{2}{3}$.

2. Change $12\frac{3}{5}$ to an improper fraction.

   $(5 \times 12) + 3 = 63$. The improper fraction is $\frac{63}{5}$.

Changing an Improper Fraction to a Whole or Mixed Number

An improper fraction is changed to a whole or mixed number by dividing the denominator into the numerator to obtain a whole number, and expressing any remainder as a fraction.

1. Change $\frac{15}{7}$ to a mixed number.

   15 divided by 7 equals 2 with a remainder of 1. The mixed number is thus $2\frac{1}{7}$.

2. Change $\frac{63}{5}$ to a mixed number.

   5 goes into 63 twelve times with a remainder of 3. Thus, $\frac{63}{5} = 12\frac{3}{5}$.

College Foreign-Language Enrollment	(in thousands)
Spanish	411
French	275
Italian	41
Russian	34
Latin	25

The Wall Street Journal
Chronicle of Higher Education

3. Convert the improper fraction $\frac{72}{10}$ to a mixed number.

$$\frac{72}{10} = 7\frac{2}{10} = 7\frac{1}{5}.$$

It is proper to show the fraction reduced to lowest terms, thus $\frac{2}{10}$ is reduced and shown as $\frac{1}{5}$.

4. Convert the improper fraction $\frac{27}{3}$ to a whole number.

3 goes into 27 nine times with no remainder, and thus converts into a whole number without any fraction: $\frac{27}{3} = 9$.

From *The Wall Street Journal,* with permission of Cartoon Features Syndicate.

Quik-Quiz

Reduce to lowest terms:

1. $\frac{7}{49}$ ___
2. $\frac{18}{81}$ ___
3. $\frac{21}{126}$ ___
4. $\frac{102}{969}$ ___
5. $\frac{325}{1,575}$ ___

Change to improper fractions:

6. $3\frac{1}{2}$ ___
7. $7\frac{11}{12}$ ___
8. $25\frac{3}{5}$ ___
9. $73\frac{8}{9}$ ___
10. $281\frac{2}{3}$ ___

Change to whole or mixed numbers:

11. $\frac{63}{3}$ ___
12. $\frac{126}{14}$ ___
13. $\frac{317}{82}$ ___
14. $\frac{926}{35}$ ___
15. $\frac{1,682}{365}$ ___

1. $\frac{1}{7}$; **2.** $\frac{2}{9}$; **3.** $\frac{1}{6}$; **4.** $\frac{2}{19}$; **5.** $\frac{13}{63}$; **6.** $\frac{7}{2}$; **7.** $\frac{95}{12}$; **8.** $\frac{128}{5}$; **9.** $\frac{665}{9}$; **10.** $\frac{845}{3}$; **11.** 21; **12.** 9; **13.** $3\frac{71}{82}$; **14.** $26\frac{16}{35}$; **15.** $4\frac{222}{365}$.

Assignment 6–1

Introduction to Common Fractions

Name ______________________

Date ______________________

Reduce to lowest terms:

1. $\frac{3}{6} =$
2. $\frac{14}{21} =$
3. $\frac{5}{15} =$
4. $\frac{4}{20} =$
5. $\frac{7}{49} =$
6. $\frac{9}{18} =$
7. $\frac{12}{24} =$
8. $\frac{10}{48} =$
9. $\frac{24}{98} =$
10. $\frac{21}{133} =$
11. $\frac{55}{120} =$
12. $\frac{32}{192} =$
13. $\frac{228}{924} =$
14. $\frac{325}{1{,}280} =$
15. $\frac{187}{275} =$
16. $\frac{183}{1{,}647} =$
17. $\frac{37}{180} =$
18. $\frac{117}{351} =$
19. $\frac{91}{190} =$
20. $\frac{59}{531} =$

Find *(a)* the greatest common divisor, and then *(b)* reduce the fraction to lowest terms:

1. $\frac{9}{81}$ **2.** $\frac{21}{49}$ **3.** $\frac{75}{105}$

4. $\frac{112}{336}$ **5.** $\frac{279}{558}$ **6.** $\frac{318}{1,166}$

7. $\frac{279}{465}$ **8.** $\frac{29}{203}$ **9.** $\frac{640}{8,260}$

10. $\frac{166}{581}$ **11.** $\frac{63}{357}$ **12.** $\frac{1,250}{9,000}$

1. *(a)* ______________
   (b) ______________
2. *(a)* ______________
   (b) ______________
3. *(a)* ______________
   (b) ______________
4. *(a)* ______________
   (b) ______________
5. *(a)* ______________
   (b) ______________
6. *(a)* ______________
   (b) ______________
7. *(a)* ______________
   (b) ______________
8. *(a)* ______________
   (b) ______________
9. *(a)* ______________
   (b) ______________
10. *(a)* ______________
    (b) ______________
11. *(a)* ______________
    (b) ______________
12. *(a)* 250
    (b) ______________

Assignment 6–2

Introduction to Common Fractions

Name ______________________

Date ______________________

A. Raise the following fractions to higher terms, using the new denominator indicated:

1. $\frac{7}{8} = \frac{98}{112}$

2. $\frac{9}{25} = \frac{36}{100}$

3. $\frac{5}{12} = \frac{75}{180}$

4. $\frac{15}{16} = \frac{120}{128}$

5. $\frac{5}{8} = \frac{125}{200}$

6. $\frac{11}{12} = \frac{275}{300}$

7. $\frac{14}{15} = \frac{\quad}{60}$

8. $\frac{21}{32} = \frac{\quad}{288}$

9. $\frac{3}{4} = \frac{\quad}{100}$

10. $\frac{9}{16} = \frac{\quad}{160}$

11. $\frac{23}{30} = \frac{\quad}{360}$

12. $\frac{11}{15} = \frac{88}{120}$

B. Change the following to improper fractions:

1. $2\frac{1}{2} = \frac{5}{2}$

2. $12\frac{5}{8} =$

3. $4\frac{11}{12} =$

4. $18\frac{9}{10} =$

5. $17\frac{9}{13} =$

6. $25\frac{3}{4} =$

7. $23\frac{7}{15} =$

8. $125\frac{3}{8} =$

9. $101\frac{7}{32} =$

10. $250\frac{1}{2} =$

C. Change the following to whole or mixed numbers:

1. $\frac{15}{4} =$

2. $\frac{38}{3} =$

3. $\frac{60}{5} =$

4. $\frac{365}{110} =$

5. $\frac{132}{12} =$

6. $\frac{183}{3} =$

7. $\frac{603}{8} =$

8. $\frac{1,250}{20} =$

9. $\frac{390}{126} =$

10. $\frac{3,185}{50} =$

11. $\frac{782}{143} =$

12. $\frac{429}{8} =$

13. $\frac{215}{12} =$

14. $\frac{636}{53} =$

15. $\frac{1,782}{99} =$

Chapter 7

Addition and Subtraction of Fractions

First my laundry called and said they lost my shirt—then my broker said the same thing.

Learning Goals

Upon completion of this chapter, you should be able to:

1. Find the lowest common denominator.
2. Add and subtract fractional amounts, using a lowest common denominator if necessary.

Addition of Fractions

In order to add fractions, they must have a common denominator.

1. $\frac{1}{5} + \frac{2}{5} = \frac{3}{5}$

2. $\frac{3}{16} + \frac{6}{16} = \frac{9}{16}$

3. $\frac{3}{8} + \frac{1}{8} = \frac{4}{8} = \frac{1}{2}$

The numerators are added together and placed over the common denominator. If an answer is capable of being reduced, as in example 3, this should be done and the answer shown in lowest terms.

Lowest Common Denominator

Fractions with different denominators are called unlike fractions and their denominators must be made equal before they can be added together. This is done by finding the lowest common denominator of the fractions. The lowest common denominator, commonly called the LCD, is the smallest amount into which the denominators will divide evenly.

1. Add $\frac{1}{4}$ and $\frac{2}{3}$.

$$\frac{1}{4} = \frac{3}{12}$$
$$\frac{2}{3} = \frac{8}{12}$$
$$\overline{\quad\frac{11}{12}\quad}$$

The LCD is 12; thus $\frac{1}{4}$ is raised to $\frac{3}{12}$ and $\frac{2}{3}$ is raised to $\frac{8}{12}$. With both of the fractions having a common denominator, the numerators are added and the result is $\frac{11}{12}$.

2. Add $\frac{1}{2} + \frac{2}{3} + \frac{5}{6}$

$$\frac{1}{2} = \frac{3}{6}$$
$$\frac{2}{3} = \frac{4}{6}$$
$$\frac{5}{6} = \frac{5}{6}$$
$$\overline{\quad\frac{12}{6} = 2\quad}$$

The LCD is 6 since it is the smallest amount into which 2, 3, and 6 will divide evenly. The fractions to be added are expressed in sixths and the numerators total 12. When an answer is an improper fraction, it should be shown as a mixed or whole number. In this case $\frac{12}{6}$ becomes 2.

When smaller fractions are to be added, the lowest common denominator is generally easy to determine by inspection. It may be the largest of the denominators or the result of multiplying the denominators together. The LCD of $\frac{1}{4}$ and $\frac{3}{8}$ is obviously 8, and although a common denominator can be found by multiplying the denominators together, it may not always be the lowest common denominator. Using $\frac{1}{4}$ and $\frac{3}{8}$, we could multiply $4 \times 8 = 32$ and use 32 as a common denominator. Our answer would have to be reduced to lowest terms however, since we did not use the lowest common denominator, 8.

1. $\frac{1}{4} + \frac{3}{8}$ using LCD 8.

$$\frac{1}{4} = \frac{2}{8}$$
$$\frac{3}{8} = \frac{3}{8}$$
$$\overline{\quad\frac{5}{8}\quad}$$

2. $\frac{1}{4} + \frac{3}{8}$ using 32.

$$\frac{1}{4} = \frac{8}{32}$$
$$\frac{3}{8} = \frac{12}{32}$$
$$\overline{\quad\frac{20}{32} = \frac{5}{8}\quad}$$

When fractions have large denominators, or where a number of fractions are to be added, the above methods are often difficult to use. In such cases, the following method is recommended.

1. Find the LCD and then add $\frac{5}{12}, \frac{4}{18}, \frac{7}{20}$, and $\frac{3}{40}$.

   (a) Set the denominators in a horizontal row.

   12 18 20 40

   (b) Divide by the smallest prime number other than 1 which will go evenly into at least two, or more, of the denominators. Usually a 2 or 3 can be used.

	12	18	20	40
2 /	6	9	10	20

   (c) The division is continued using the 2 as a divisor so long as it will divide into two or more of the denominators. Those amounts not evenly divisible by the divisor being used are merely brought down and written in the row of answers.

Divisor				
2 /	12	18	20	40
2 /	6	9	10	20
3 /	3	9	5	10
5 /	1	3	5	10
	1	3	1	2

   (d) After the second division, the 2 will no longer divide evenly into two or more of the amounts shown, and the smallest number that will divide into at least two of the amounts 3, 9, 5, and 10 is a 3. After dividing by 3, it can no longer be used and 5 becomes the divisor. When no number other than 1 can divide evenly into two or more of the amounts, the division is completed and the LCD is then obtained by multiplying the divisors and amounts in the bottom row.

$$2 \times 2 \times 3 \times 5 \times 1 \times 3 \times 1 \times 2 = 360$$

360 is the LCD of $\frac{5}{12} \frac{4}{18} \frac{7}{20}$ and $\frac{3}{40}$.

   (e) Now that we have determined the LCD, we can add the fractions.

$$\frac{5}{12} = \frac{150}{360}$$

$$\frac{4}{18} = \frac{80}{360}$$

$$\frac{7}{20} = \frac{126}{360}$$

$$\frac{3}{40} = \frac{27}{360}$$

$$\frac{383}{360} = 1\frac{23}{360}$$

Personal Health Practices—1986

	Percent
Sleeps six hours or less	22.0%
Never eats breakfast	24.3
Snacks every day	39.0
Current smoker	30.1
Overweight by over 30%	13.0

U.S. Bureau of the Census, *Statistical Abstract of the United States*: 1988 (108th edition) Washington, DC

2. Add $3\frac{1}{2}$ and $2\frac{5}{8}$.

LCD is 8.

(a)
$$\begin{array}{rl} 3 & \frac{1}{2} = \frac{4}{8} \\ 2 & \frac{5}{8} = \frac{5}{8} \\ \hline 5 & \frac{9}{8} = 1\frac{1}{8} \end{array}$$

$$5 + 1\frac{1}{8} = 6\frac{1}{8}$$

(b)
$$3\frac{1}{2} = \frac{7}{2} \qquad \frac{7}{2} = \frac{28}{8}$$
$$2\frac{5}{8} = \frac{21}{8} \qquad \frac{21}{8} = \frac{21}{8}$$
$$\frac{49}{8} = 6\frac{1}{8}$$

When mixed numbers are to be added, the whole numbers and fractions may be added separately as in *(a)* above, and then the totals added together. Another method is to change the mixed numbers to improper fractions and then add, as in *(b)* above. Either method may be used when the mixed numbers are small, but when the problem contains large mixed numbers it is generally best not to change them to improper fractions but rather to add the whole numbers and fractions separately and then add the totals.

Subtraction of Fractions

The method of subtracting fractions resembles that of addition. The lowest common denominator is determined and the fractions are expressed with common denominators. Instead of adding the numerators, we subtract.

1. Subtract $\frac{5}{8}$ from $\frac{7}{8}$.

$$\begin{array}{r} \frac{7}{8} \\ -\frac{5}{8} \\ \hline \frac{2}{8} = \frac{1}{4} \end{array}$$

Since the fractions already have a common denominator, we merely subtract 5 from 7. The answer, 2, is placed over the common denominator 8, and the fraction is reduced to lowest terms.

2. Take $\frac{3}{5}$ from $\frac{5}{6}$.

$$\begin{array}{r} \frac{5}{6} = \frac{25}{30} \\ -\frac{3}{5} = \frac{18}{30} \\ \hline \frac{7}{30} \end{array}$$

The LCD is 30, and the result of the subtraction, $\frac{7}{30}$, is already expressed in lowest terms.

3. Subtract $\frac{2}{5}$ from $\frac{11}{7}$.

$$\begin{array}{r} \frac{11}{7} = \frac{55}{35} \\ -\frac{2}{5} = \frac{14}{35} \\ \hline \frac{41}{35} = 1\frac{6}{35} \end{array}$$

In the above example, a proper fraction is subtracted from an improper fraction. The result is an improper fraction and is correctly changed to a mixed number.

4. Take $\frac{2}{3}$ from 8.

$$\begin{array}{rr} 8 & 7\frac{3}{3} \\ -\frac{2}{3} & -\frac{2}{3} \\ \hline & 7\frac{1}{3} \end{array}$$

In order to subtract $\frac{2}{3}$ from the whole number 8, we borrow 1 from the 8 and express it as thirds. We bring down the 7 and then subtract $\frac{2}{3}$ from $\frac{3}{3}$.

5. Subtract $3\frac{1}{2}$ from $12\frac{3}{5}$.

$$\begin{array}{lrr} \text{minuend} & 12\frac{3}{5} = & \frac{6}{10} \\ \text{subtrahend} & -3\frac{1}{2} = & \frac{5}{10} \\ \hline \text{remainder} & 9 & \frac{1}{10} = 9\frac{1}{10} \end{array}$$

In some problems, the fraction in the subtrahend may be larger than the fraction in the minuend. When this occurs, it is necessary to borrow 1 from the whole number in the minuend and add the fractional equivalent of the borrowed 1 to the existing fraction in the minuend, so that subtraction will be possible.

6. Subtract $7\frac{3}{4}$ from $82\frac{1}{4}$.

$$\begin{array}{r} 82\frac{1}{4} = 81\frac{5}{4} \\ -7\frac{3}{4} = 7\frac{3}{4} \\ \hline 74\frac{2}{4} = 74\frac{1}{2} \end{array}$$

7. Subtract $8\frac{3}{4}$ from $57\frac{1}{3}$.

$$\begin{array}{r} 57\frac{1}{3} = 57\frac{4}{12} = 56\frac{16}{12} \\ -8\frac{3}{4} = 8\frac{9}{12} = 8\frac{9}{12} \\ \hline 48\frac{7}{12} \end{array}$$

Quik-Quiz

Add the following.

1. $\frac{3}{8} + \frac{5}{6}$

2. $\frac{11}{12} + \frac{9}{10}$

3. $3\frac{5}{8}$ $+5\frac{9}{10}$

4. $7\frac{1}{2} + \frac{11}{8}$

5. $\frac{3}{5}$ $\frac{2}{7}$ $\frac{5}{8}$

6. $\frac{3}{10}$ $\frac{2}{5}$ $2\frac{1}{2}$

7. $25\frac{3}{4}$ $8\frac{1}{2}$ 12

8. $52\frac{1}{2}$ $\frac{8}{5}$ $35\frac{1}{4}$

Subtract the following:

9. $63\frac{1}{2}$ $-5\frac{1}{8}$

10. $49\frac{1}{5}$ $-28\frac{3}{4}$

11. $\frac{72}{2}$ $-\frac{81}{3}$

12. 315 $-84\frac{2}{3}$

1. $1\frac{5}{24}$; **2.** $1\frac{49}{60}$; **3.** $9\frac{21}{40}$; **4.** $8\frac{7}{8}$; **5.** $1\frac{143}{280}$; **6.** $3\frac{1}{5}$; **7.** $46\frac{1}{4}$; **8.** $89\frac{7}{20}$; **9.** $58\frac{3}{8}$; **10.** $20\frac{9}{20}$; **11.** 9; **12.** $230\frac{1}{3}$.

Assignment 7–1

Addition of Fractions

Name ____________________

Date ____________________

Find the *LCD* of the following fractions:

1. $\frac{3}{9} + \frac{7}{8}$

2. $\frac{11}{12} + \frac{15}{16}$

3. $\frac{7}{12} + \frac{9}{10}$

4. $\frac{1}{2} + \frac{3}{4} + \frac{5}{8} + \frac{2}{7}$

5. $\frac{21}{32} + \frac{7}{8} + \frac{5}{18}$

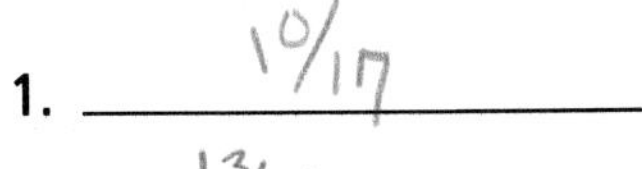

1. ____________________
2. ____________________
3. ____________________
4. ____________________
5. ____________________

Add the following and express the answer in lowest terms as a common fraction or mixed number:

6. $\frac{3}{5}$, $\frac{1}{3}$, $\frac{5}{6}$, $\frac{3}{4}$

7. $5\frac{3}{5}$, $12\frac{1}{2}$, $15\frac{3}{4}$

8. $12\frac{1}{4}$, $17\frac{3}{8}$, $11\frac{2}{3}$

9. $23\frac{11}{12}$, $120\frac{2}{3}$, $225\frac{6}{7}$

10. $2\frac{1}{2}$, $\frac{11}{8}$, $16\frac{1}{4}$, 83

Subtract:

11. $\frac{7}{9} - \frac{3}{5}$

12. $\frac{25}{4} - \frac{5}{6}$

13. $\frac{9}{14} - \frac{3}{10}$

14. $\frac{41}{6} - \frac{17}{20}$

15. $\frac{19}{3} - \frac{7}{6}$

16. $7\frac{3}{4} - 2\frac{7}{8}$

17. $93 - 57\frac{13}{16}$

18. $80\frac{9}{10} - 79\frac{3}{5}$

19. $\frac{75}{5} - 8\frac{1}{4}$

20. $\frac{328}{3} - \frac{132}{2}$

Assignment 7–2

Name ______________________

Date ______________________

Addition and Subtraction of Fractions

1. Tillie McCullough purchased three pieces of cotton print fabric at a remnant sale. If they were $2\frac{1}{2}$, $3\frac{5}{8}$, and $4\frac{1}{4}$ yards, respectively, what was the total amount of yardage purchased?

____

2. From a 90-foot length of wire, two pieces, $37\frac{1}{2}$ feet each, were cut. What was the length of the remaining piece?

____

3. The Jenkins Company must ship an order in three separate cartons weighing $22\frac{1}{2}$, $17\frac{3}{4}$, and 50 pounds respectively. What will be the total weight of the shipment?

____

4. A gas tank which holds $18\frac{1}{2}$ gallons of gas when full, presently contains $4\frac{1}{4}$ gallons. How much gas is needed to fill the tank?

____

5. Harry Buttimer owns three adjoining parcels of land that measure $52\frac{1}{2}$, $70\frac{1}{4}$, and $29\frac{7}{12}$ feet wide. If he wants to erect a wirescreen fence across the front of his land, how many feet of fencing must he purchase?

____

6. A metal press manufactured by Company A weighs $27\frac{5}{8}$ pounds while the same size press manufactured by Company B weighs $31\frac{3}{4}$ pounds. How much lighter is Company A's product?

____

7. During a busy week, cab owner Williams made gasoline purchases of $12\frac{1}{2}$, $16\frac{7}{10}$, $16\frac{1}{4}$, and $15\frac{3}{10}$ gallons. What was the total amount of gasoline purchased?

____

8. How many feet of rope will remain if three pieces $6\frac{1}{2}$, 23, and $56\frac{3}{4}$ feet are cut from a 100-foot roll?

____

9. What is the total weight of a can of paint if the can weighs $\frac{5}{8}$ ounces and the contents $15\frac{1}{2}$ ounces?

____

10. How much must be cut from the edge of a piece of glass $16\frac{3}{8}$ inches wide, in order for it to fit into an opening $15\frac{1}{4}$ inches wide?

____

11. Tires produced by the ABC Company contain a $\frac{1}{2}$ inch tread, while the tires produced by XYZ Company contain a $\frac{9}{16}$ inch tread. How much additional tread do the XYZ tires contain?

____

12. If Arthur combines $3\frac{1}{2}$, 5, and $12\frac{1}{4}$ ounces of liquid in a 32-ounce jar, how many more ounces can the jar hold?

____

Chapter 8

Multiplication and Division of Fractions

My situation is so bad that now even my plumber no longer makes house calls.

Learning Goals

Upon completion of this chapter, you should be able to:

1. Multiply and divide fractional amounts, using cancellation if necessary.
2. Multiply a series of fractions, using cancellation.

Multiplication of Fractions

Fractions to be multiplied do not have to be changed to fractions with a common denominator. Merely multiply the numerators to obtain the new numerator, and multiply the denominators to obtain the new denominator. The answer should be shown reduced to lowest terms.

1. Multiply $\frac{3}{8}$ times $\frac{5}{7}$. $\quad \frac{3}{8} \times \frac{5}{7} = \frac{3 \times 5}{8 \times 7} = \frac{15}{56}$
2. Multiply 7 times $\frac{2}{3}$. $\quad \frac{7}{1} \times \frac{2}{3} = \frac{7 \times 2}{1 \times 3} = \frac{14}{3} = 4\frac{2}{3}$
3. Multiply $\frac{3}{4} \times 12$. $\quad \frac{3}{4} \times \frac{12}{1} = \frac{3 \times 12}{4 \times 1} = \frac{36}{4} = 9$

Cancellation

Problems can often be simplified by the use of cancellation since the value of a fraction does not change if the numerator and denominator are divided by the same number. Before multiplying, try to find a common factor that will divide into any one of the numerators and any one of the denominators regardless of their position in the problem.

1. $\frac{7}{12} \times \frac{3}{5}$ $\qquad \frac{7}{\underset{4}{\cancel{12}}} \times \frac{\overset{1}{\cancel{3}}}{5} = \frac{7}{20}$ The 3 and 12 are divisible by 3.

2. $\frac{5}{7} \times \frac{10}{12}$ $\qquad \frac{5}{7} \times \frac{\overset{5}{\cancel{10}}}{\underset{6}{\cancel{12}}} = \frac{25}{42}$ The 10 and 12 are divisible by 2.

3. $\frac{3}{4} \times \frac{2}{3}$ $\qquad \frac{\overset{1}{\cancel{3}}}{\underset{2}{\cancel{4}}} \times \frac{\overset{1}{\cancel{2}}}{\underset{1}{\cancel{3}}} = \frac{1}{2}$ 2 and 4 are divisible by 2; and 3 goes into both of the 3s.

Mixed numbers can be multiplied by changing them to improper fractions before multiplication. If possible, cancellation may then be used to simplify the problem.

1. $5\frac{1}{2} \times 7\frac{3}{4}$ $\qquad \frac{11}{2} \times \frac{31}{4} = \frac{341}{8} = 42\frac{5}{8}$

2. $3\frac{3}{5} \times 6\frac{2}{3}$

without cancellation

$$\frac{18}{5} \times \frac{20}{3} = \frac{360}{15} = 24$$

with cancellation

$$\frac{\overset{6}{\cancel{18}}}{\underset{1}{\cancel{5}}} \times \frac{\overset{4}{\cancel{20}}}{\underset{1}{\cancel{3}}} = \frac{24}{1} = 24$$

Although mixed numbers can always be multiplied by changing to improper fractions, another method, called the partial-products method, is available. It is generally used when large mixed numbers are involved.

1. Multiply $92\frac{2}{3}$ times $81\frac{1}{2}$.

   Using the improper fractions method results in larger numbers having to be multiplied together:

$$\frac{\overset{139}{\cancel{278}}}{3} \times \frac{163}{\underset{1}{\cancel{2}}} = \frac{22,657}{3} = 7,552\frac{1}{3}$$

Using the partial-products method:

$$
\begin{array}{rcl}
 & & 81\frac{1}{2} \quad \text{multiplicand} \\
 & & \times\, 92\frac{2}{3} \quad \text{multiplier} \\
\hline
\frac{2}{3} \times \frac{1}{2} & = & \frac{1}{3} \\
\frac{2}{3} \times \frac{81}{1} & = & 54 \\
\frac{92}{1} \times \frac{1}{2} & = & 46 \\
92 \times 81 & = & 7{,}452 \\
\hline
 & & 7{,}552\frac{1}{3}
\end{array}
$$

In the partial-products methods, the whole number and fraction in the multiplicand are each multiplied by the fraction in the multiplier and then by the whole number in the multiplier. The partial products are then totaled together to arrive at the answer, $7{,}552\frac{1}{3}$.

Multiplication of a Series of Fractions

1. $\frac{3}{8} \times 9 \times \frac{4}{7} \times \frac{10}{9} \qquad \frac{3 \times \overset{1}{\cancel{9}} \times \overset{1}{\cancel{4}} \times \overset{5}{\cancel{10}}}{\underset{\underset{1}{\cancel{2}}}{\cancel{8}} \times 1 \times 7 \times \underset{1}{\cancel{9}}} = \frac{15}{7} = 2\frac{1}{7}$

Division of Fractions

To divide fractions *(a),* the fraction representing the divisor is first inverted, and the two fractions are then multiplied. Therefore, division is the same as multiplication except that the divisor must first be inverted. When a fraction is inverted, the numerator becomes the new denominator, and the denominator becomes the new numerator. $\frac{5}{8}$ inverted becomes $\frac{8}{5}$, and $\frac{12}{11}$ becomes $\frac{11}{12}$. When a mixed number is involved *(b),* it must first be changed to an improper fraction. If a whole number is involved *(c),* it is first changed to a fraction.

a. Divide $\frac{3}{8}$ by $\frac{1}{3}$. $\quad \frac{3}{8} \div \frac{1}{3} = \frac{3}{8} \times \frac{3}{1} = \frac{9}{8} = 1\frac{1}{8}$

b. $\dfrac{5\frac{2}{3}}{2\frac{1}{8}} \quad 5\frac{2}{3} \div 2\frac{1}{8} = \frac{17}{3} \div \frac{17}{8} = \frac{\overset{1}{\cancel{17}}}{3} \times \frac{8}{\underset{1}{\cancel{17}}} = \frac{8}{3} = 2\frac{2}{3}$

c. Divide 12 by $\frac{2}{3}$. $\quad \frac{12}{1} \div \frac{2}{3} = \frac{\overset{6}{\cancel{12}}}{1} \times \frac{3}{\underset{1}{\cancel{2}}} = \frac{18}{1} = 18$

Quik-Quiz

Multiply:

1. $\frac{3}{8} \times \frac{2}{7}$
2. $\frac{5}{6} \times \frac{11}{12}$
3. $3\frac{1}{2} \times 9\frac{1}{4}$
4. $\frac{21}{3} \times 9$

______ ______ ______ ______

5. $\frac{93}{3} \times \frac{5}{6}$
6. $\frac{2}{3} \times \frac{5}{6} \times \frac{3}{4}$
7. $7\frac{1}{2} \times 8 \times 2\frac{1}{4}$
8. $526\frac{3}{4} \times 80\frac{5}{8}$

______ ______ ______ ______

Divide:

9. $\frac{5}{8} \div \frac{3}{4}$
10. $\dfrac{6\frac{1}{2}}{2\frac{1}{4}}$
11. $500 \div 7\frac{1}{2}$
12. $\dfrac{12\frac{7}{8}}{10\frac{3}{4}}$

______ ______ ______ ______

1. $\frac{3}{28}$; **2.** $\frac{55}{72}$; **3.** $32\frac{3}{8}$; **4.** 63; **5.** $25\frac{5}{6}$; **6.** $\frac{5}{12}$; **7.** 135; **8.** $42{,}469\frac{7}{32}$; **9.** $\frac{5}{6}$; **10.** $2\frac{8}{9}$; **11.** $66\frac{2}{3}$; **12.** $1\frac{17}{86}$.

Assignment 8–1

Multiplication and Division of Fractions

Name ______________________

Date ______________________

Multiply:

1. $\frac{11}{25} \times \frac{3}{7} =$

2. $2\frac{1}{2} \times 5\frac{3}{4} =$

3. $23\frac{1}{7} \times 16\frac{1}{3} =$

4. $\frac{4}{7} \times 20\frac{3}{4} =$

5. $3\frac{5}{6} \times 39 =$

6. $\frac{11}{12} \times \frac{21}{23} \times \frac{8}{33} =$

7. $62\frac{2}{5} \times 85\frac{7}{8} =$

8. $123\frac{3}{10} \times 306\frac{2}{3} =$

9. $\frac{3}{8} \times 3\frac{5}{6} \times 12 =$

10. $3\frac{1}{2} \times 5\frac{2}{5} \times 6\frac{1}{3} =$

Divide:

11. $\frac{3}{4} \div \frac{1}{16} =$

12. $\frac{11}{15} \div \frac{7}{8} =$

13. $\frac{8\frac{1}{2}}{\frac{5}{6}} =$

14. $3\frac{1}{2} \div \frac{7}{12} \div \frac{1}{3} =$

15. $273 \div \frac{9}{4} =$

16. $23\frac{2}{9} \div 12\frac{2}{3} =$

17. $\frac{21}{35} \div \frac{8}{15} =$

18. $83\frac{1}{2} \div 12\frac{7}{8} =$

19. $\frac{\frac{13}{16}}{3\frac{5}{7}} =$

20. $300 \div 7\frac{1}{2} =$

Assignment 8–2

Multiplication and Division of Fractions

Name ______________________

Date ______________________

1. If Milton is paid \$360 per week, how much does Smith receive if his salary is $\frac{5}{8}$ as much?

____

2. How many $2\frac{1}{2}$ gallon cans of oil can be filled from a tank car holding 500 gallons?

____

3. If the speed of a race car averaged $82\frac{7}{10}$ miles per hour for $2\frac{1}{2}$ hours, how many total miles did it travel?

____

4. If 8 sheets of $\frac{3}{16}$ inch thick wood are pressed together, what will be the thickness of the finished sheet of plywood?

____

5. How many pieces of rubber tubing $6\frac{1}{4}$ feet long can be cut from a 200-foot roll?

____

6. If the Ace Manufacturing Company began in business with 96 employees and now has $7\frac{3}{8}$ times as many, what is the total number of employees at present?

____

7. If a warehouse area contains 2,800 square feet of floor space, how many containers can be stored here if each container requires $12\frac{1}{2}$ square feet of space?

____

8. If Don Snepp purchased 25 shares of stock at $\$18\frac{2}{5}$ per share and 16 shares at $\$21\frac{1}{4}$ per share, what was the total dollar amount of his purchase?

____

9. If $\frac{1}{200}$ of the original contents of a 3,500 gallon tank of liquid evaporates each day, how many gallons will be lost after seven days?

122.5

10. Hatcher borrowed \$8,400, and has paid back $\frac{11}{12}$ of the original loan. How much money does he still owe the bank?

____

11. If the weight of a 5,300-pound freight car increases $3\frac{1}{8}$ times when fully loaded, what will be its weight with a full load?

____

12. How many $2\frac{1}{4}$-ounce containers can a pharmacist fill from a 38-ounce supply?

____

Chapter 9

Fraction–Decimal Conversion

If it is illegal to send obscene materials through the mails, how come my electric bill gets through.

Learning Goals

Upon completion of this chapter, you should be able to:

1. Convert a fraction to a decimal.
2. Convert a decimal to a fraction.
3. Simplify conversion, using a table of equivalents.

Since fractions and decimals represent parts of a whole unit, a fraction can be changed and shown as a decimal and a decimal can be changed and shown as a fraction. In many cases, such conversion may simplify the mechanical process of working out a particular problem. For instance, if we wish to multiply $25\frac{1}{2}$ times 358, we can change the $25\frac{1}{2}$ to the improper fraction $\frac{51}{2}$ and then multiply $\frac{51}{2} \times 358$. Another way, however, is to express $25\frac{1}{2}$ as its decimal equivalent of 25.5 and then multiply 25.5×358.

Changing a Fraction to a Decimal

To convert a fraction to a decimal, divide the numerator by the denominator.

Example 1. Express $\frac{3}{4}$ as a decimal.

$$\begin{array}{r} .75 \\ 4\overline{)3.00} \\ \underline{2\,8} \\ 20 \\ \underline{20} \end{array} \qquad \frac{3}{4} \text{ equals } .75$$

Households Touched by Crime—1986

	Percent
Violent crime	4.7%
Theft	17.3
Burglary	5.3
Motor vehicle theft	1.4

U.S. Bureau of the Census, *Statistical Abstract of the United States*: 1988 (108th edition) Washington, DC.

Example 2. Express $8\frac{1}{2}$ as a decimal.

$$8\frac{1}{2} = \frac{17}{2} \qquad \begin{array}{r} 8.5 \\ 2\overline{)17.0} \\ \underline{16} \\ 1\,0 \\ \underline{1\,0} \end{array} \qquad 8\frac{1}{2} = 8.5$$

Example 3. Express $\frac{62}{10}$ as a decimal.

$$\begin{array}{r} 6.2 \\ 10\overline{)62.0} \\ \underline{60} \\ 2\,0 \\ \underline{2\,0} \end{array} \qquad \frac{62}{10} = 6.2$$

Example 4. Express $\frac{2}{7}$ as a decimal rounded off to nearest hundredths.

$$\begin{array}{r} .285 \\ 7\overline{)2.000} \\ \underline{1\,4} \\ 60 \\ \underline{56} \\ 40 \\ \underline{35} \\ 5 \end{array} \qquad .285 \text{ equals } .29$$

Changing a Decimal to a Fraction

To convert a decimal to a fraction, write the decimal as the numerator with the decimal point removed. For the denominator, enter the number one, followed by as many zeros as there were digits after the decimal point in the original decimal. Reduce the fraction to lowest terms.

Example 1. Express .25 as a fraction.

$$.25 = \frac{25}{100} = \frac{1}{4}$$

Example 2. Express .235 as a fraction.

$$.235 = \frac{235}{1{,}000} = \frac{47}{200}$$

Example 3. Express 9.12 as a fraction.

$$9.12 = 9\frac{12}{100} = 9\frac{3}{25}$$

The following table shows the equivalent decimal and percentage figures for fractions from $\frac{1}{2}$ to $\frac{15}{16}$. Conversion of fractions and decimals to percentage and of percentage to decimals and fractions, will be discussed in the unit dealing with percentage.

Fraction, Decimal, and Percentage Equivalents

Denom-inator	Numerators														
1.00 or 100%	1	2	3	4	5	6	7	8	9	10	11	12	13	14	15
2	.50 50%														
3	.333 $33\frac{1}{3}\%$	.666 $66\frac{2}{3}\%$													
4	.25 25%	.50 50%	.75 75%												
5	.20 20%	.40 40%	.60 60%	.80 80%											
6	.166 $16\frac{2}{3}\%$	.333 $33\frac{1}{3}\%$	.50 50%	.666 $66\frac{2}{3}\%$	.833 $83\frac{1}{3}\%$										
7	.142 $14\frac{2}{7}\%$	.285 $28\frac{4}{7}\%$	.428 $42\frac{6}{7}\%$	.571 $57\frac{1}{7}\%$	.714 $71\frac{3}{7}\%$	.857 $85\frac{5}{7}\%$									
8	.125 $12\frac{1}{2}\%$	.25 25%	.375 $37\frac{1}{2}\%$	.50 50%	.625 $62\frac{1}{2}\%$	.75 75%	.875 $87\frac{1}{2}\%$								
9	.111 $11\frac{1}{9}\%$	.222 $22\frac{2}{9}\%$	.333 $33\frac{1}{3}\%$	.444 $44\frac{4}{9}\%$	.555 $55\frac{5}{9}\%$	.666 $66\frac{2}{3}\%$	.777 $77\frac{7}{9}\%$	.888 $88\frac{8}{9}\%$							
10	.10 10%	.20 20%	.30 30%	.40 40%	.50 50%	.60 60%	.70 70%	.80 80%	.90 90%						
11	.090 $9\frac{1}{11}\%$	.181 $18\frac{2}{11}\%$	.272 $27\frac{3}{11}\%$	.363 $36\frac{4}{11}\%$	.454 $45\frac{5}{11}\%$	.545 $54\frac{6}{11}\%$	.636 $63\frac{7}{11}\%$	.727 $72\frac{8}{11}\%$	.818 $81\frac{9}{11}\%$	.909 $90\frac{10}{11}\%$					
12	.083 $8\frac{1}{3}\%$	.166 $16\frac{2}{3}\%$	.25 25%	.333 $33\frac{1}{3}\%$	.416 $41\frac{2}{3}\%$	.50 50%	.583 $58\frac{1}{3}\%$	.666 $66\frac{2}{3}\%$	.75 75%	.813 $83\frac{1}{3}\%$	.916 $91\frac{2}{3}\%$				
13	.077 $7\frac{9}{13}\%$	.153 $15\frac{5}{13}\%$	.230 $23\frac{1}{13}\%$	.307 $30\frac{10}{13}\%$	.385 $38\frac{6}{13}\%$	.462 $46\frac{2}{13}\%$	.538 $53\frac{11}{13}\%$	.615 $61\frac{7}{13}\%$	.692 $69\frac{3}{13}\%$	.769 $76\frac{12}{13}\%$	.846 $84\frac{8}{13}\%$	.923 $92\frac{4}{13}\%$			
14	.071 $7\frac{1}{7}\%$	.142 $14\frac{2}{7}\%$	.214 $21\frac{3}{8}\%$	.285 $28\frac{4}{7}\%$	.357 $35\frac{5}{7}\%$	.428 $42\frac{6}{7}\%$	.50 50%	.571 $57\frac{1}{7}\%$	.642 $64\frac{2}{7}\%$	.714 $71\frac{3}{7}\%$	.786 $78\frac{4}{7}\%$	.857 $85\frac{5}{7}\%$	.929 $92\frac{6}{7}\%$		
15	.066 $6\frac{2}{3}\%$	.133 $13\frac{1}{3}\%$	.20 20%	.266 $26\frac{2}{3}\%$	.333 $33\frac{1}{3}\%$	.40 40%	.466 $46\frac{2}{3}\%$	.533 $53\frac{1}{3}\%$	.60 60%	.666 $66\frac{2}{3}\%$	.733 $73\frac{1}{3}\%$	.80 80%	.866 $86\frac{2}{3}\%$	.933 $93\frac{1}{3}\%$	
16	.062 $6\frac{1}{4}\%$	.125 $12\frac{1}{2}\%$	.1875 $18\frac{3}{4}\%$	.25 25%	.3125 $31\frac{1}{4}\%$	.375 $37\frac{1}{2}\%$	.4375 $43\frac{3}{4}\%$	.50 50%	.5625 $56\frac{1}{4}\%$	.625 $62\frac{1}{2}\%$	.6875 $68\frac{3}{4}\%$	.75 75%	.8125 $81\frac{1}{4}\%$	.875 $87\frac{1}{2}\%$	.9375 $93\frac{3}{4}\%$

Quik-Quiz

Convert to decimals:

1. $\frac{7}{10}$ **2.** $\frac{62}{100}$ **3.** $\frac{26}{32}$ **4.** $\frac{55}{250}$ **5.** $\frac{72}{900}$

Convert to decimals rounded off to nearest hundredths:

6. $\frac{11}{16}$ **7.** $8\frac{3}{4}$ **8.** $27\frac{5}{8}$ **9.** $\frac{12}{360}$ **10.** $\frac{7}{9}$

Convert to fractions or mixed numbers and reduce to lowest terms:

11. .65 **12.** .672 **13.** 9.125 **14.** 32.9 **15.** 92.735

1. .7; **2.** .62; **3.** .8125; **4.** .22; **5.** .08; **6.** .69; **7.** 8.75; **8.** 27.63; **9.** .03; **10.** .78; **11.** $\frac{13}{20}$; **12.** $\frac{84}{125}$; **13.** $9\frac{1}{8}$; **14.** $32\frac{9}{10}$; **15.** $92\frac{147}{200}$.

Assignment 9–1

Fraction-Decimal Conversion

Name ____________________

Date ____________________

Convert the following fractions to their decimal equivalents:

1. $\frac{3}{4}$ 2. $\frac{6}{24}$ 3. $\frac{1}{8}$ 4. $\frac{3}{25}$ 5. $\frac{7}{5}$

6. $\frac{3}{8}$ 7. $\frac{23}{25}$ 8. $\frac{8}{50}$ 9. $\frac{72}{150}$ 10. $\frac{14}{200}$

11. $\frac{13}{16}$ 12. $\frac{27}{48}$ 13. $\frac{65}{250}$ 14. $\frac{36}{300}$ 15. $\frac{125}{500}$

Convert the following fractions to decimals rounded off to nearest hundredths:

16. $\frac{2}{7}$ 17. $\frac{11}{12}$ 18. $\frac{9}{16}$ 19. $\frac{57}{80}$ 20. $\frac{121}{360}$

21. $\frac{11}{16}$ 22. $\frac{7}{8}$ 23. $\frac{5}{7}$ 24. $\frac{81}{360}$ 25. $\frac{63}{200}$

Convert the following decimals to fractions or mixed numbers and reduce to lowest terms when possible:

26. .87

27. 8.12

28. 827.86

29. 50.335

30. .1875

31. .3338

32. 189.62

33. .199

34. 824.363

35. 67.702

Section 3

Percent

Chapter 10

Introduction to Percentage; Conversion to Decimals and Fractions

I finally found a house I can afford. Now to get it out of the tree.

Learning Goals

Upon completion of this chapter, you should be able to:

1. Define a percent.
2. Convert a percent to a decimal and a decimal to a percent.
3. Convert a percent to a fraction and a fraction to a percent.

Percent is a method of expressing hundredths. The fraction $\frac{29}{100}$ means 29 equal parts out of 100 equal parts, and is read "twenty-nine hundredths." The decimal .29 likewise represents twenty-nine hundredths. Using percent, twenty-nine hundredths is shown as 29%. The symbol % is used to denote percent, and 100% of something is the entire amount. In order to multiply or divide by a percent, it must first be changed to either a decimal or fraction.

Converting Percents to Decimals

To change a percent to a decimal, drop the percent sign and move the decimal point two places to the left.

Examples:

1. 38% = .38
2. 12% = .12
3. 89% = .89
4. 7% = .07
5. 153% = 1.53
6. 70% = .70 = .7
7. 250% = 2.50 = 2.5
8. $3\frac{1}{2}\% = .03\frac{1}{2} = .035$

9. 7.5% = .075

10. 300% = 3.00 = 3

11. .2% = .002

12. $\frac{1}{4}\% = .00\frac{1}{4} = .0025$

Converting Decimals to Percents

To change a decimal to a percent, move the decimal point two places to the right and add a percent sign. A whole number is converted to a percent by moving the decimal two places to the right and adding the percent sign.

Examples:

1. .09 = 9%
2. .17 = 17%
3. .362 = 36.2%
4. 1.37 = 137%
5. .2 = 20%
6. 9 = 900%
7. $.03\frac{1}{4} = 3\frac{1}{4}\%$
8. 1.89 = 189%
9. 27 = 2700%
10. $.2\frac{1}{2} = .25 = 25\%$
11. 23.2 = 2320%
12. $.3\frac{1}{4} = .325 = 32.5\%$

Changing Percents to Fractions

A percent is converted to a fraction by dropping the percent sign and writing the number over 100. Reduce to lowest terms when possible.

Examples:

1. $7\% = \frac{7}{100}$
2. $25\% = \frac{25}{100} = \frac{1}{4}$
3. $37\% = \frac{37}{100}$
4. $109\% = \frac{109}{100} = 1\frac{9}{100}$
5. $50\% = \frac{50}{100} = \frac{1}{2}$
6. $89\% = \frac{89}{100}$
7. $18\% = \frac{18}{100} = \frac{9}{50}$
8. $3\% = \frac{3}{100}$
9. $140\% = \frac{140}{100} = 1\frac{40}{100} = 1\frac{2}{5}$
10. $33\% = \frac{33}{100}$
11. $5\% = \frac{5}{100} = \frac{1}{20}$
12. $900\% = \frac{900}{100} = 9$

When the percentage amount contains a decimal, move the decimal point two places to the left and drop the percent sign. Write the number over the appropriate multiple of ten and reduce to lowest terms when possible.

Examples

1. $38.2\% = .382 \quad \frac{382}{1{,}000} = \frac{191}{500}$
2. $37.25\% = .3725 \quad \frac{3{,}725}{10{,}000} = \frac{149}{400}$

If the percentage contains a fractional ending, drop the percent sign and write the number over 100. Change to a proper fraction and reduce to lowest terms.

Examples:

1. $6\frac{1}{3}\% = \frac{6\frac{1}{3}}{100} \quad \frac{\frac{19}{3} \times 3}{100 \times 3} = \frac{19}{300}$

2. $2\frac{2}{7}\% = \frac{2\frac{2}{7}}{100} = \frac{\frac{16}{7}}{\frac{100}{1}} = \frac{16}{7} \times \frac{1}{100} = \frac{16}{700} = \frac{4}{175}$

Changing Fractions to Percents

To change a fraction to a percent, reduce the fraction to lowest terms when possible and then divide the numerator by the denominator, showing the answer to two decimal places. Convert the decimal to a percent by moving the decimal point two places to the right and adding the percent sign.

Working Mothers—Place of Care for Children Under Five

In own home	31%
Organized child-care	23
Nonrelatives' homes	22
Grandparents' home	10
Mother's place of work	8
Other relatives' homes	5
Kindergarten	1

The Wall Street Journal, 6/3/88
U.S. Census Bureau

Examples:

1. $\frac{3}{4}$ $\quad 4\overline{)3.00}$ = .75 (28, 20, 20) $\quad .75 = 75\%$

2. $\frac{2}{60} \quad \frac{2}{60} = \frac{1}{30} \quad 30\overline{)1.00}$ = .03 (90, 10) $= .03\frac{1}{3} = 3\frac{1}{3}\%$

3. $\frac{11}{7} \quad 7\overline{)11.00}$ = $1.57\frac{1}{7}$ (7, 40, 35, 50, 49, 1) $= 1.57\frac{1}{7} = 157\frac{1}{7}\%$

4. $18\frac{1}{2} \quad \frac{1}{2} = .50 \quad$ thus $18\frac{1}{2} = 18.50 = 1{,}850\%$

Quik-Quiz

Convert to decimals:

1. 28% ______
2. 189% ______
3. 20% ______
4. $7\frac{1}{2}\%$ ______
5. $8\frac{1}{4}\%$ ______

Convert to percents:

6. 83 ______
7. 3.02 ______
8. 17.2 ______
9. $.02\frac{1}{2}$ ______
10. $.6\frac{1}{4}$ ______

Convert to fractions:

11. 17% ______
12. 58% ______
13. 2,500% ______
14. 11.8% ______
15. 6.75% ______

Convert to percents:

16. $\frac{4}{5}$ ______
17. $\frac{17}{50}$ ______
18. $\frac{10}{7}$ ______
19. $67\frac{1}{2}$ ______
20. $\frac{3}{90}$ ______

1. .28; **2.** 1.89; **3.** .2; **4.** .075; **5.** .0825: **6.** 8300%; **7.** 302%; **8.** 1,720%; **9.** 2.5%; **10.** 62.5%; **11.** $\frac{17}{100}$; **12.** $\frac{29}{50}$; **13.** 25; **14.** $\frac{59}{500}$; **15.** $\frac{27}{400}$; **16.** 80%; **17.** 34%; **18.** $142\frac{6}{7}\%$; **19.** 6,750%; **20.** $3\frac{1}{3}\%$.

Assignment 10–1

Introduction to Percentage; Conversion to Decimals and Fractions

Name ____________________

Date ____________________

Change the following percents to decimals:

1. 9%

2. 62%

3. 116%

4. 952%

5. 380%

6. $8\frac{1}{2}\%$

7. 3.7%

8. 2.25%

9. $\frac{3}{4}\%$

10. 360%

Change the following decimals to percents:

11. .03

12. 2.99

13. .39

14. 6.5

15. .128

16. .007

17. 16.2

18. $.7\frac{1}{2}$

19. 2.01

20. $.08\frac{1}{2}$

Change the following percents to fractions:

21. 9% 

22. 26% 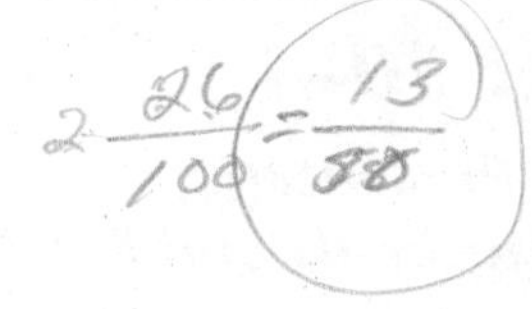

23. 720%

24. 828% 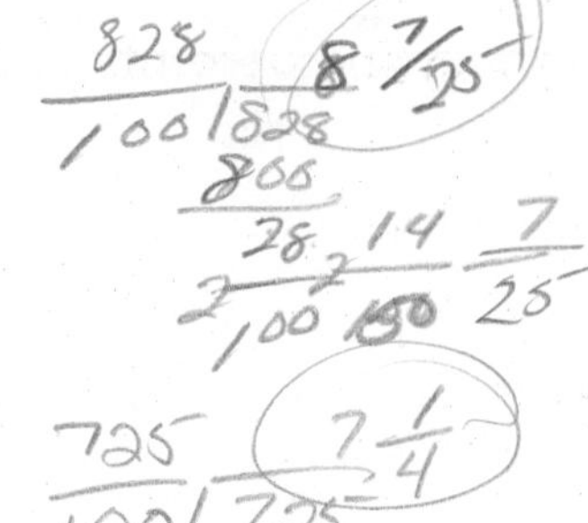

25. 18.6%

26. 7.25%

27. $8\frac{1}{9}\%$

28. $12\frac{2}{3}\%$ 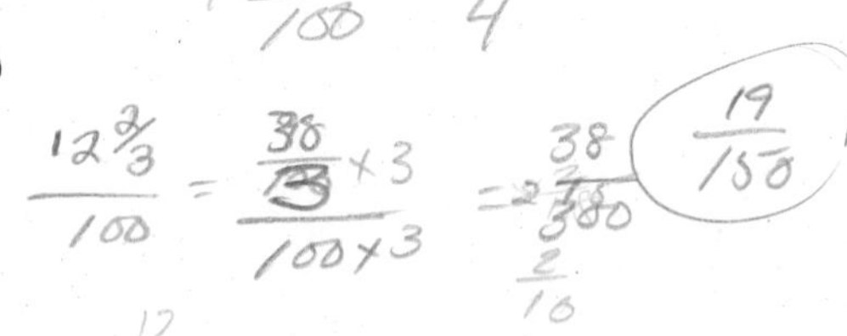

Change the following fractions to percents:

29. $\frac{1}{5}$

30. $\frac{9}{18}$

31. $\frac{7}{21}$ 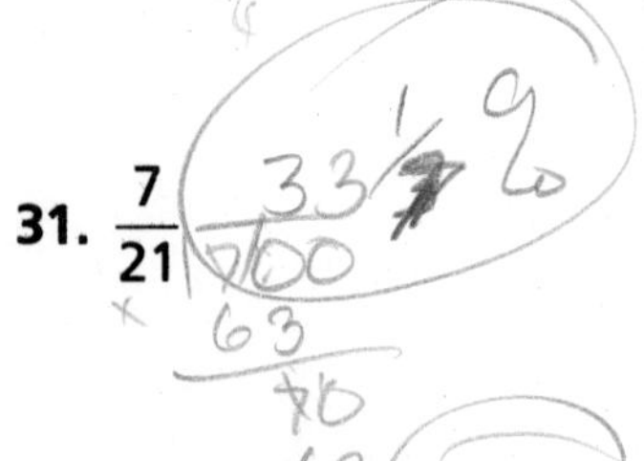

32. $\frac{9}{10}$

33. $\frac{9}{25}$

34. $\frac{3}{100}$

35. $\frac{27}{300}$

Assignment 10–2

Introduction to Percentage; Conversion to Decimals and Fractions

Name ______________________

Date ______________________

Fill in the missing amounts, reducing fractions to lowest terms when possible:

Fraction	Decimal	Percent
1. ________	.25	2. ________
3. ________	4. ________	12%
$\frac{3}{5}$	5. ________	6. ________
7. ________	8. ________	160%
9. ________	.835	10. ________

$\frac{17}{100}$ ______ 11. ______ 12. ______

13. ______ .15 ______ 14. ______

15. ______ 16. ______ $87\frac{1}{2}\%$ ______

$12\frac{1}{2}$ ______ 17. ______ 18. ______

19. ______ .003 ______ 20. ______

Chapter 11

Base, Rate, and Percentage

Look at it this way. You're in excellent shape for someone who is 60. Forget the fact that you're only 45.

Learning Goals

Upon completion of this chapter, you should be able to:

1. Correctly use percent.
2. Use the proper formulas to find base, rate, and percent.
3. Determine rate or amount of increase or decrease as necessary.

There are generally three elements to be considered in percentage problems. These are *base, rate,* and *percentage.*

The base is the principal amount and represents 100 percent. The rate is the relationship between the base and a part of the base, and is expressed as a percent. The percentage is the amount received by applying the rate to the base and, depending on the rate used, may be more or less than the base. The symbol for percent is % and is called a percent sign.

For instance, 9% of $100 is $9. The base is $100, the rate is 9%, and the percentage is $9. If any two parts are known, the third can be found. The following are the formulas used:

Five Largest Credit Card Lenders

	Percent
Citicorp	17%
Chase Manhattan	6
BankAmerica	5
First Chicago	5
Sears Discover	4

The Wall Street Journal, 10/4/88

Percentage = Rate × Base ($P = R \times B$)

Rate = Percentage ÷ Base $\left(R = \frac{P}{B}\right)$

Base = Percentage ÷ Rate $\left(B = \frac{P}{R}\right)$

To Find a Percent of a Number

A common problem in percentage involves finding a given percent of a certain amount. The formula used is $P = R \times B$.

Example 1. What is 12% of 300?

$$P = R \times B$$
$$P = .12 \times 300$$
$$P = 36$$

Since 12% can also be converted to the fraction $\frac{12}{100}$, which can be reduced to $\frac{3}{25}$, the problem can also be solved by multiplying 300 by $\frac{3}{25}$.

$$\frac{3}{25} \times 300 = \frac{900}{25} = 36$$

Example 2. A pension plan deduction of $2\frac{1}{2}$% is made from the monthly paycheck of Jules Fraden. If he made \$860 last month, what was the amount deducted for the pension plan?

$$P = R \times B$$
$$P = .025 \times \$860$$

$$\begin{array}{r} 860 \\ \times .025 \\ \hline 4300 \\ 1720 \\ \hline 21.500 \end{array} = \$21.50$$

Example 3. Find 118% of \$62.50.

$$P = R \times B$$
$$P = 1.18 \times \$62.50$$

$$\begin{array}{r} 62.50 \\ 1.18 \\ \hline 500\ 00 \\ 625\ 0 \\ 6250 \\ \hline 73.7500 \end{array} = \$73.75$$

To Find What Percent One Number Is of Another

Certain problems involve finding the rate. $R = \frac{P}{B}$ *is the formula used to find what percent one amount is of another amount.*

Example 1. 74 is what percent of 200?

$$R = \frac{P}{B}$$

$$R = \frac{74}{200} = \frac{37}{100}$$

$$100\overline{)37.00} = .37 = 37\%$$

```
       .37 = 37%
100)37.00
    30 0
     7 00
     7 00
```

Example 2. 50 students in a history class took a test and 39 received a passing grade. What percent of the class passed the test? The problem is solved by determining what percent 39 is of 50.

$$R = \frac{P}{B}$$

$$R = \frac{39}{50}$$

```
     .78 = 78%
50)39.00
   35 0
    4 00
    4 00
```

Example 3. What percent of 18 is 7?

$$R = \frac{P}{B}$$

$$R = \frac{7}{18}$$

$$.38 = .38\frac{16}{18} = .38\frac{8}{9} = 38\frac{8}{9}\%$$

```
    .38
18)7.00
   5 4
   1 60
   1 44
     16
```

U.S. Living Arrangements of 185 Million People 15 Years and Older—1987

	Percent
Living alone	11.5%
With spouse	55.9
With other relative	26.7
With nonrelatives	5.9

U.S. Bureau of the Census, *Statistical Abstract of the United States*: 1988 (108th edition) Washington, DC.

Finding a Number When a Percent of It Is Known

Other problems involve finding the base. $B = \frac{P}{R}$ *is the formula used to find the whole amount when given a part of the whole amount and the percent of the whole that the part represents.*

Example 1. $34.20 is 9% of what amount?

$$B = \frac{P}{R}$$

$$B = \frac{34.20}{.09}$$

```
    380. = $380
 9)3420.
   27
    72
    72
```

Example 2. How much does Jacobsen have in his savings account if the bank paid him a $9\frac{1}{2}$% interest payment of $159.03?

$$B = \frac{P}{R}$$

$$B = \frac{159.03}{.095}$$

```
      1674. = $1,674
 95)159030.
    95
    640
    570
     703
     665
      380
      380
```

Example 3. $7\frac{1}{4}$% of what number is 58?

$$B = \frac{P}{R}$$

$$B = \frac{58}{.0725}$$

```
       800. = 800
 725)580000.
     5800
```

In addition to the formulas already presented for finding percentage, rate, and base, a circle chart that illustrates all three formulas is another aid in determining what to do.

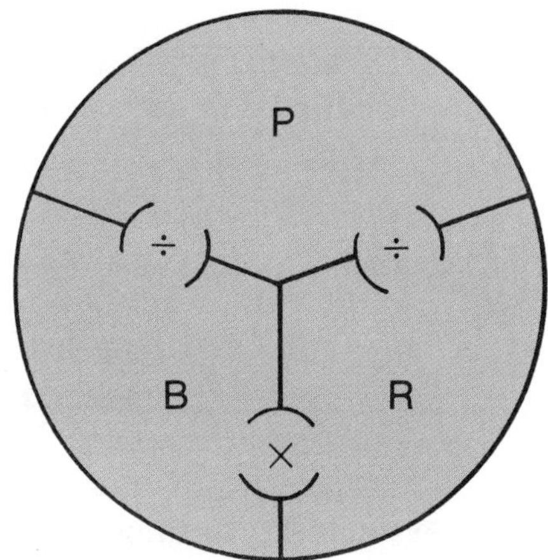

To Find Percentage	$P = B \times R$
To Find Base	$B = P \div R$
To Find Rate	$R = P \div B$

Percent of Increase and Decrease

Two types of percent problems that frequently occur deal with either an increase or a decrease. Every day your local newspaper or TV news programs feature stories and items dealing with increases or decreases in retail and wholesale prices, costs, employment statistics, stock prices, and various investments. Generally these increases and decreases are stated in terms of rate of increase or decrease, or percent of increase or decrease.

Amount or Rate of Increase

Example 1. Superior Motor Car Company announces an 8% price increase, effective next year, for all its cars. If you wait until next year, what will you have to pay for a certain model car that presently sells for $12,500?

$12,500 × .08 = $1,000 increase
$12,500 + $1,000 = $13,500 new price

The current or original price represents the base value or 100%. An increase of 8% added to the current price (100% + 8%) equals 108%, which means that our new price will represent 108% of the old price.

$12,500 × 1.08 = $13,500 new price

Principal Professional Degrees, 1985–1986

Law	48%
Medicine	21
Theology	10
Dentistry	7

The Wall Street Journal, 1/28/88
U.S. Education Department

Example 2. Superior Motor Car Company has recently announced that its popular Model 870XZ, currently priced at $12,500, will continue to be produced next year. It will come with an increased number of options, a wider variety of color combinations, and a suggested price of $13,500. Comparing the current price and next year's price, what is the rate of increase proposed?

To find the rate of increase, determine the amount of increase and what percent the amount of increase is of the original price.

$13,500 − $12,500 = $1,000 amount of increase

Divide, to find what percent $1,000 is of $12,500.

$$\frac{\$1,000}{\$12,500} = .08 = 8\% \text{ rate of increase}$$

Example 3. Superior Motor Car Company has announced a $13,500 price for its popular Model 870XZ, which represents an increase of 108% over last year. What was last year's price for the car?

Since $13,500 represents 108% of last year's price, the answer is found as follows:

$$\frac{\$13,500}{1.08} = \$12,500 \text{ old price}$$

Amount or Rate of Decrease

Example 1. Smith purchases a refrigerator, regularly priced at $850, during a sale at which prices are reduced by 20%. What is the sale price of the refrigerator?

$850 × .20 = $170 reduction
$850 − $170 = $680 sale price

If the regular price (100%) is reduced by 20%, the sale price represents 80% of the regular price and can be found as follows:

.80 × $850 = $680 sale price

Example 2. Smith purchases a refrigerator for $680 that was regularly priced at $850. Find the percent of reduction in price of the refrigerator.

To find the rate or percent of reduction, find the dollar amount of the reduction and what percent this dollar amount is of the original price.

$850 − $680 = $170 amount of reduction

$$\frac{\$170}{\$850} = .20 = 20\% \text{ reduction}$$

Example 3. After a discount of 20%, Smith pays $680 for a refrigerator. What was the regular retail price of the refrigerator?

After deducting 20%, the price Smith paid represents 80% of the original price (100% − 20% = 80%).

$$\$680 = 80\%$$

$$\frac{\$680}{.80} = \$850 \text{ original price}$$

"If not for anything else, you should try to make your marriage work for the sake of your 7% mortgage."

From *The Wall Street Journal,* with permission of Cartoon Features Syndicate.

Quik-Quiz

1. Find 16% of 500
   ($P = R \times B$)

   ____

2. Find $7\frac{1}{2}$% of \$800
   ($P = R \times B$)

   ____

3. Find 225% of 480
   ($P = R \times B$)

   ____

4. What percent of 264 is 198?
   ($R = \frac{P}{B}$)

   ____

5. What percent of \$3,200 is \$522?
   ($R = \frac{P}{B}$)

   ____

6. $15\frac{1}{2}$% of what number is 186?
   ($B = \frac{P}{R}$)

   ____

7. \$2,846.25 is $17\frac{1}{4}$% of what amount?
   ($B = \frac{P}{R}$)

   ____

8. What is $\frac{1}{2}$% of 60?
   ($P = R \times B$)

   ____

9. Find 20% of 475
   ($P = R \times B$)

   ____

10. What percent of 33 is 22?
    ($R = \frac{P}{B}$)

    ____

1. 80; **2.** \$60; **3.** 1,080; **4.** 75%; **5.** $16\frac{5}{16}$%; **6.** 1,200; **7.** \$16,500; **8.** .3; **9.** 95; **10.** $66\frac{2}{3}$%.

Assignment 11–1

Finding Percentage P = R × B

Name ______________________

Date ______________________

1. The price of an automobile is $9,890. If it is increased by 10 percent, what is the new price?

   98900

2. The enrollment last semester at Washington High School was 850 students. If there has been an 8 percent increase, how many students are now attending the school?

   .68%

3. Salesman Szukalski is paid a commission of 8 percent of the total amount of his sales. If he sold $3,880 worth of merchandise last week, how much was Szukalski paid?

   $ 310.40

4. What amount of sales tax must be added to a purchase of $70 if the tax rate is $5\frac{1}{2}$ percent?

   3.85 %

5. If 8.2 percent of the liquid in a 1,000 gallon storage tank has evaporated due to excessive heat, how many gallons now remain in the tank?

   ____

6. Tille McCullough wants to purchase a property priced at $235,000. If a 20 percent down payment is required, how much will she need in order to purchase the property?

____

7. The Lindsey Furniture store advertises a sale of sofas at a reduction of 18 percent off the regular price. What is the sale price of a sofa which regularly sells for $699?

____

8. Kerr recently sold some common stock for which he originally paid $370. If it had increased in value by 116 percent, how much did he receive for the stock?

____

9. Printer McConnell wants to purchase a new printing press costing $2,500. If he can borrow 65 percent of the purchase price from the bank, how much cash will he need in order to buy the press?

____

10. Broker Ziegler sold a building for $152,950. How much did he make if his commission is $5\frac{1}{2}$ percent of the sale price of the property?

____

Assignment 11–2

Finding Rate $R = \frac{P}{B}$

Name ______________________________

Date ______________________________

1. There are 28,300 registered voters in the city of Newport. What percent of them voted in the election for city council if 23,206 votes were cast?

____

2. If 56 students in a class of 70 passed an examination, what percent of the class passed the test?

____

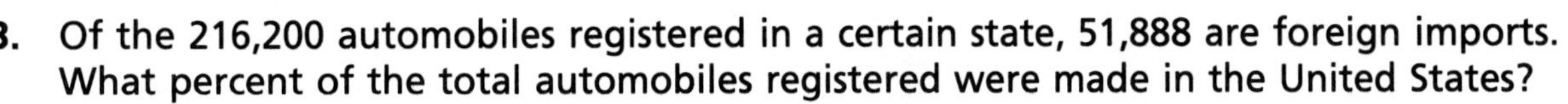

3. Of the 216,200 automobiles registered in a certain state, 51,888 are foreign imports. What percent of the total automobiles registered were made in the United States?

____

4. During a recent three-day sale, Central City Radio and TV sold 180 color sets out of their total inventory of 250. What percent of the original inventory was sold?

____

5. A luxury sedan is advertised to sell at \$21,350. If \$3,416 is the profit to the dealer, what percent of the selling price is the dealer's profit?

____

6. If Sam Jordan borrows $7,500 from the Merchants Bank and is charged $900 interest, what rate of interest did the Merchants Bank charge for the loan?

____

7. A shipment of sets of dishes and glassware valued at $136,000 is delivered to a retailer. What is the rate of breakage if $4,760 worth of glassware is broken?

____

8. The cost of a power mower usually priced at $175 is reduced to $145.25 for a special sale. What is the percent of reduction?

____

9. Susan Cowan purchases seven $10,000 municipal bonds and receives yearly interest of $8,225. What is the annual rate of return on Susan's investment?

____

10. Tim Clary is currently renting a condominium, as a monthly tenant, for $750 per month. The owner has offered Tim a two-year lease at a monthly rental of $810. This will represent a rent increase of what percent?

____

Assignment 11–3

Finding Base $B = \frac{P}{R}$

Name ____________________

Date ____________________

1. Pasqual purchased a car with a 12 percent down payment of $1,872. What was the full price of the car?

   ____

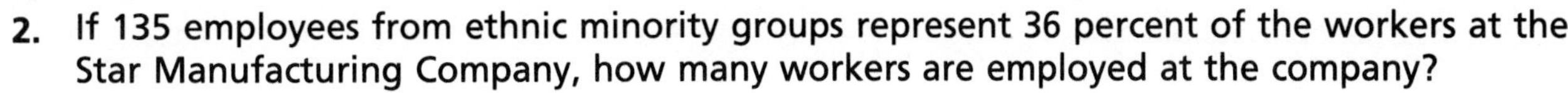

2. If 135 employees from ethnic minority groups represent 36 percent of the workers at the Star Manufacturing Company, how many workers are employed at the company?

   ____

3. Nesbitt paid a real property tax bill of $479.60 for the current year. If this bill was 10 percent higher than last year's bill, what did Nesbitt pay last year?

   ____

4. How much money will Hawkins have to invest at a $12\frac{1}{2}$ percent return in order to make $3,125?

   ____

5. Jacobsen is paid a commission of 8 percent based on the total amount of his sales. If he earns $2,320 this month, what was the amount of his sales?

   ____

6. If Frustuck paid a combined state and federal income tax of $4,572, which represented 18 percent of his total income, how much did Frustuck earn?

____

7. A dealer offers a 20 percent discount, amounting to $139.80 on a 19-inch color TV set. What is *(a)* the regular price, and *(b)* the discount price of the set?

(a) ________________

(b) ________________

8. Ann Taylor, a real estate agent, charges the owner a commission of $6\frac{1}{2}$ percent of the selling price of a property. If Ann earned a commission of $17,875, what was the sales price of the property?

____

9. If a certain type of ore contains 18 percent copper, what number of tons of ore must be mined in order to obtain 63 tons of copper?

____

10. How much will Smith have to invest in corporate bonds paying $10\frac{3}{4}$ percent annually in order to earn an income of $15,000 per year? Round answer to nearest dollar.

____

Assignment 11–4

Base, Rate, and Percentage

Name ______________________

Date ______________________

1. 21 is what percent of 28? ______

2. What percent of 900 is 18? ______

3. What percent of $820 is $172.20? ______

4. $6.51 is what percent of $93? ______

5. 95.625 is what percent of 76.5? ______

6. $6\frac{1}{2}$% of what amount is $1.82? ______

7. $18\frac{1}{2}$% of what number is 333? ______

8. $187.50 is $7\frac{1}{2}$% of what amount? ______

9. 118% of what number is 236? ______

10. 28 is 350% of what number? ______

11. What percent of 82 is 4.1? ____

12. What percent of 1,678 is 352.38? ____

13. What is 17% of 200? ____

14. What is 2.5% of 720? ____

15. What is 9% of 1,250? ____

16. What is $18\frac{1}{2}$% of $1,926? ____

17. What is 39% of $7,500? ____

18. What is .7% of $180? 126.00

19. What is $33\frac{1}{3}$% of $780? ____

20. What is $66\frac{2}{3}$% of $334.80? $223.17

R B P

Assignment 11–5

Base, Rate, and Percentage

Name ______________________

Date ______________________

1. Harry Frustuck paid a current state income tax of $2,150, which was 12 percent more than last year's tax. To the nearest dollar, what was the amount of last year's tax?

____

2. The legal speed limit in Lincoln County was recently decreased from 65 MPH to 55 MPH. What was the percent of decrease to the nearest percent?

____

3. The population of San Francisco is expected to reach 825,000 in 1995. If the present population is 693,000, what is the expected percent of increase to the nearest percent?

____

4. If the cost of a $63,000 printing press is increased by 9½ percent, and a 5 percent sales tax is added to the price, what is the selling price of a new press?

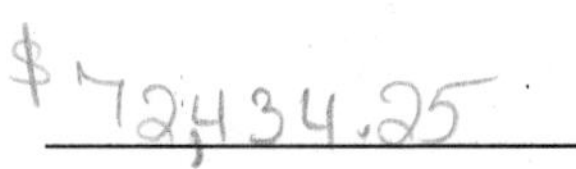

____

5. The Amy-Lou Distribution Company reported current sales of $16,000,000, which represented 125 percent of last year's sales. What was the amount of last year's sales?

____

6. If Pitts Auto parts advertises a $15. reduction on its regular $59.95 car battery, what is the percent of savings?

New selling price $44.95 (75%)

____

7. Titan Tire Company advertises that its Model F 810 fiberglass radial tire will give 25,000 miles of carefree road wear. Its slightly higher-priced fiberglass and steel radial is warranted to provide approximately 18 percent more wear than its Model F 810. How many miles of wear can an owner expect from a fiberglass and steel radial?

29500.00

8. Atlantic Distributors reports that profits for the year declined by 7.2 percent to $326,520. To the nearest dollar, what was last year's profit?

$351,853.00

9. The average daily wage for U.S. industrial workers is reported at $116.00 which is up $8.50 from last year. What is the percent of increase, to the nearest tenth of a percent?

7.9%

10. If a state legislature votes a 25 percent increase of a current 6 percent sales tax rate, what will Taylor have to pay for a TV set priced at $900?

$967.50

Section 4

Cash and Payrolls

Chapter 12

Banking Records

The only time I'll pick up a check is when it is made out to me.

Learning Goals

Upon completion of this chapter, you should be able to:

1. Discuss the meaning of cash.
2. Define internal control.
3. Explain sound internal control procedures for cash.
4. Indicate the reason for having a bank signature card.
5. Indicate what goes into a bank deposit ticket.
6. Define a check.
7. Complete the writing of a check.
8. Explain the reason for a check stub.
9. Discuss the reasons for a bank statement.
10. Explain the purpose of a bank reconciliation.
11. Prepare a bank reconciliation.

Cash is any medium of exchange which a bank will accept for deposit and immediately credit to a depositor's account. Cash has worldwide usefulness, high value for its size, and no convenient way in which ownership can be established. With its easy transferability, cash is the most likely business asset to be diverted or misappropriated by employees.

Internal Control

A good business internal control procedure for cash is to assign responsibilities so that the work of one employee must agree with, but not duplicate, the work of another. To protect cash from improper use or withdrawal, there are several steps that should be established, including the following:

1. The person handling cash receipts should have nothing to do with cash payments.
2. The person responsible for record-keeping should have no access to cash.
3. Each day's cash receipts should be deposited in the bank intact. This way, the book and bank receipt records will always agree.
4. Each cash sale should be rung up on a cash register located in plain sight of the customer. This way the customer can see that the proper billing has been entered on the register.
5. All cash disbursements should be made by check.
6. All checks should be prenumbered at the printer's and voided checks should not be discarded.
7. Checks should only be signed if supported by approved invoices.
8. If possible, checks should be signed by one person and countersigned by another.
9. A check protector system, perforating the amount of a check into the check itself, makes it difficult to change the amount.
10. When a check is signed, all supporting documents should be stamped "paid" to prevent duplicate payments.

Average Salaries of Faculty Members in 4-Year Colleges and Universities—1987

	Public ($000)	*Private* ($000)
Professor	$45.3	$50.3
Associate professor	34.2	34.9
Assistant professor	28.5	28.3
Instructor	21.8	20.4

U.S. Bureau of the Census, *Statistical Abstract of the United States*: 1988 (108th edition) Washington, DC.

Signature Card

When opening a bank checking account, the customer is given an identifying number and a signature card that must be signed by each person authorized to sign checks on that account. The bank can only clear checks with approved signatures. However, more than two signatures should be on file in case an employee is ill or on vacation.

Bank of America **Authorized Signatures**

Quality Hardwood Floors — ACCOUNT NAME

0 6 3 7 5 — BRANCH NO. 3 3 5 4 6 — ACCOUNT NO.

PLEASE SIGN YOUR NAME EXACTLY AS YOU WILL SIGN YOUR CHECKS/DEBITS

1 Ron Seligman 2 Melvin Steiner

3 Sally Short 4 Sharon Santucci

(FOR BANK USE ONLY)

[X] NEW ACCOUNT [ ] ADD A NAME(S) [ ] UPDATED SIGNATURE(S)

[ ] NEW TEL-135 (ALL SIGNERS) [ ] DOCUMENTATION ATTACHED [ ] DELETION

TEL-135 7-87 Bank of America NT&SA • Member FDIC

Deposit Ticket

When making a bank deposit, list the details of the deposit on a printed form supplied by the bank. A summary type of deposit slip prepared by James Roe is illustrated below. It contains his bank and account number, name and address, date of deposit, and the amount of currency and coin, as well as the amount of each check being deposited by Mr. Roe into his account. The upper right corner of a check contains a two-part American Bankers Association number in fractional form (see check illustrations). The upper portion identifies location and name of the issuing bank and is entered on the deposit slip. The lower number indicates in which of 12 Federal reserve districts the bank is located.

72 | 1210-0062-793
BRANCH NO.

James Roe
NAME

890 Ninth Avenue
ADDRESS

San Francisco, California
CITY STATE

March 19 19--
DATE

Bank of America
National Trust and Savings Association

LIST CHECKS BY BANK NUMBER	DOLLARS	CENTS
CURRENCY	125	00
COIN		
CHECKS		
11-68	63	50
11-27	39	50
TOTAL DEPOSIT	228	00

IF MORE THAN 6 CHECKS, LIST ON REVERSE SIDE. ENTER TOTAL HERE.

Check and Check Stub

A check is a negotiable instrument signed by a depositor ordering the bank to pay an amount from funds on deposit to the order of a designated party. There are three parties to a check: the *drawer,* the person signing the check; the *drawee,* the bank on which the check is drawn; and the *payee,* the one to whose order the check is drawn.

Checks come in many forms. The names and addresses of the depositor are often printed on each check. The checks should be printed in numerical sequence, and the bank's identification number and the depositor's account number usually are printed in the lower portion of the check with magnetic ink.

Checks are far superior to cash. A checking account gives a record of every payment and to whom the money is paid. If the canceled checks are returned by the bank, they can serve as receipts should it become necessary to show proof of payment. If a returned check is lost or misplaced, the bank can produce a copy, front and back, from microfilm that it keeps on all checks. Many banks, with the depositor's approval, do not mail canceled checks to customers, to reduce processing costs and postage. However, banks have set up the safekeeping program whereby a customer can request a microfilm copy of the check if needed.

In order for individuals to keep track of funds in their checking accounts, checkbooks are provided with either a section called a check register or check stubs attached to the checks. The following illustration shows two checks written by Mr. Roe and the check stubs that he will retain after detaching the checks. These check stubs contain a record of checks written, to whom made payable and for what purpose, date and amount,

Top Five Network TV Sports Advertisers—1986

	($ millions)
Anheuser-Busch	$96
General Motors	95
Philip Morris	89
Ford Motor	46
U.S. Armed Forces	44

The Wall Street Journal, 12/14/87
Sports, Inc.

any deposits made, and the account balance before and after writing the check.

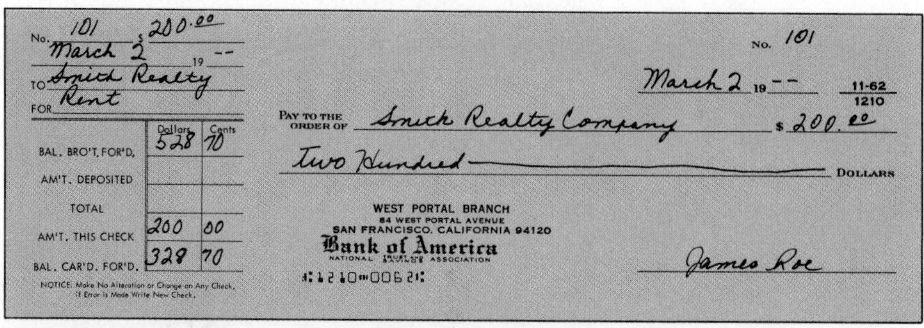

No. 101 $ 200.00
March 2 19 --
TO Smith Realty
FOR Rent

	Dollars	Cents
BAL. BRO'T. FOR'D.	528	70
AM'T. DEPOSITED		
TOTAL		
AM'T. THIS CHECK	200	00
BAL. CAR'D. FOR'D.	328	70

NOTICE: Make No Alteration or Change on Any Check. If Error is Made Write New Check.

No. 101

March 2 19 -- 11-62/1210

PAY TO THE ORDER OF Smith Realty Company $ 200.00

Two Hundred ——— DOLLARS

WEST PORTAL BRANCH
84 WEST PORTAL AVENUE
SAN FRANCISCO, CALIFORNIA 94120
Bank of America
NATIONAL TRUST AND SAVINGS ASSOCIATION

⑆1210⑈0062⑆

James Roe

No. 102 $ 15.80
March 5 19 --
TO Pacific Gas and
FOR Electric Company

	Dollars	Cents
BAL. BRO'T. FOR'D.	328	70
AM'T. DEPOSITED	12	17
TOTAL	340	87
AM'T. THIS CHECK	15	80
BAL. CAR'D. FOR'D.	325	07

NOTICE: Make No Alteration or Change on Any Check. If Error is Made Write New Check.

No. 102

March 5 19 -- 11-62/1210

PAY TO THE ORDER OF Pacific Gas and Electric Company $ 15.80

Fifteen and 80/100 ——— DOLLARS

WEST PORTAL BRANCH
84 WEST PORTAL AVENUE
SAN FRANCISCO, CALIFORNIA 94120
Bank of America
NATIONAL TRUST AND SAVINGS ASSOCIATION

⑆1210⑈0062⑆

James Roe

Checking Accounts

Most banks usually charge a fee, or require a minimum balance, for checking accounts. For people who write only a few checks, there is usually a fixed charge per check. Some accounts charge a fixed monthly fee with unlimited check writing. Other accounts have a variable monthly fee depending on the number of checks written and/or the minimum monthly balance. Also, checking accounts often earn interest based on minimum or average monthly balance.

Bank Statement

Once a month banks usually provide each commercial depositor with a bank statement along with the canceled checks. This statement shows the transactions in the checking account for the month with regard to checks that have cleared and deposits made, as well as certain charges that may be made by the bank for such items as a Christmas Club deduction, late charge, loan collection charge, customer's check returned due to insufficient funds (NSF), transfer of funds requested by the depositor, automatic teller machine (ATM) withdrawals, and stop payments.

The basic format of a bank statement shows the bank balance at the beginning of the month, deposits and other additions to the account, checks and other charges deducted from the account, and the end-of-the-month bank balance.

In a bank statement, each deposit and check, preferably in numerical sequence, should be listed separately, as well as any special charges and credits. In addition, a summary should be provided showing the number and amount of all checks cleared and all deposits made during the month.

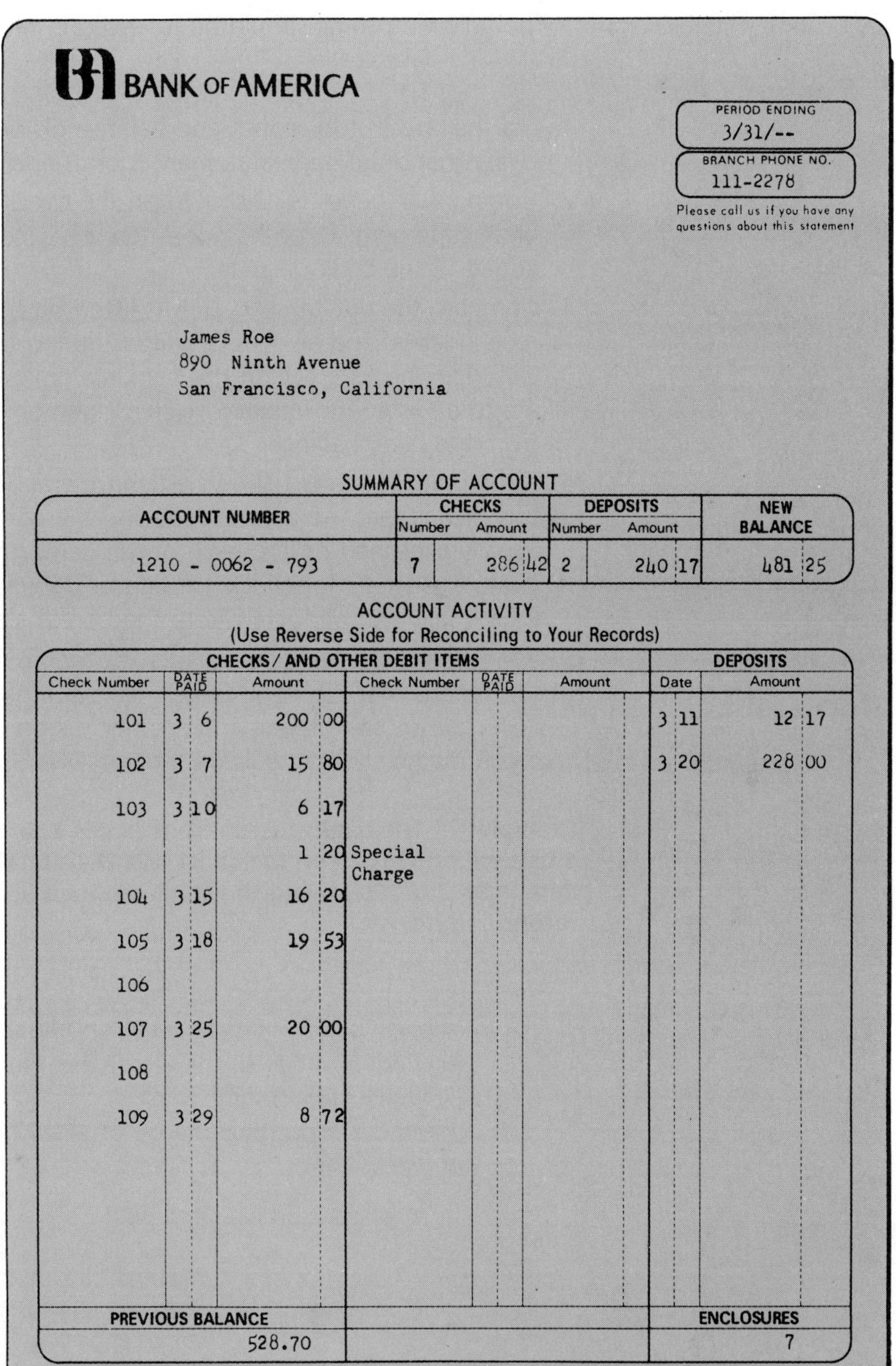

BANK OF AMERICA

PERIOD ENDING 3/31/--

BRANCH PHONE NO. 111-2278

Please call us if you have any questions about this statement

James Roe
890 Ninth Avenue
San Francisco, California

SUMMARY OF ACCOUNT

ACCOUNT NUMBER	CHECKS Number	CHECKS Amount	DEPOSITS Number	DEPOSITS Amount	NEW BALANCE
1210 - 0062 - 793	7	286 42	2	240 17	481 25

ACCOUNT ACTIVITY
(Use Reverse Side for Reconciling to Your Records)

Check Number	Date Paid	Amount	Check Number	Date Paid	Amount	Deposits Date	Deposits Amount
101	3 6	200 00				3 11	12 17
102	3 7	15 80				3 20	228 00
103	3 10	6 17					
		1 20	Special Charge				
104	3 15	16 20					
105	3 18	19 53					
106							
107	3 25	20 00					
108							
109	3 29	8 72					

PREVIOUS BALANCE 528.70

ENCLOSURES 7

Bank Reconciliation

The balance shown on the bank statement almost always will not agree with the balance indicated on the depositor's books, check register, or check stub. The reason for the differences in balances may be due to checks that have not yet cleared the bank, deposits made the last day or two of the month that have not yet been recorded on the bank statement, various charges or collections made by the bank that have not yet been recognized by the depositor and possibly errors in recording, adding, or subtracting deposits or checks.

The following steps should be followed in reconciling the bank and depositor's balances:

1. List the check stub month-end balance on one side of the bank reconciliation and the bank statement month-end balance on the other side.
2. Compare all deposits as shown on the check stubs with deposits on the bank statement. Deposits not entered on the bank statement are to be added to the bank balance.
3. Compare the outstanding checks listed on the prior month's bank reconciliation and all checks written during the current month with the canceled checks listed on the bank statement. Checks still outstanding are to be listed individually by check number and amount and deducted from the bank balance.
4. If the bank statement shows a debit memo (DM) next to an amount, this means that the bank is reducing the bank balance for a reason usually explained on the back of the bank statement. Debit memo charges, such as for check printing or NSF checks should be listed individually and deducted from the book balance.
5. If the bank statement shows a credit memo (CM) next to an amount, this means that the bank is increasing the bank balance, such as for the collection of the interest and/or principal on an outstanding note. Each credit memo should be listed separately and added to the book balance.

Example 1. The bank statement of James Roe, shown on page 131, shows a balance of $481.25 on March 31. His checkbook balance as of the same date is $493.67. Following the steps outlined above reveals these reconciling items:

1. **A deposit of $53.80 was made on March 31.**
2. **Old check number 98 for $10.38 and check number 110 for $32.20 are outstanding.**
3. **A bank check printing charge of $1.20 has not been recorded in the checkbook.**

The bank reconciliation is as follows:

James Roe
Bank Reconciliation
March 31, 19--

Balance per depositor's records	**$493.67**	**Balance per bank statement**		**$481.25**
		Add: Deposits in transit, 3/31		**53.80**
				$535.05
Deduct: Check printing charge	**1.20**	**Deduct: Outstanding checks:**		
		No. 98	**$10.38**	
		No. 110	**32.20**	**42.58**
Reconciled balance	**$492.47**	**Reconciled balance**		**$492.47**

Student Review

1. Complete the following check and check stub for Berkey Tractor Co., assuming a beginning checkbook balance of $1,243.64, a deposit of $305.98 on October 16, 1990, and check number 572, payable to Local Telephone, dated October 16, 1990, for $106.18, with the check signed by Rick Davis and Jan Rourke.

2. From the following, determine the adjusted ending checkbook balance:

Checkbook balance before adjustments	$6,230
NSF check	110
Outstanding checks	1,175
Note collected by bank	1,000
Bank service charge	8

$ 7112.00

3. From the following, determine the adjusted ending bank balance:

Bank balance before adjustments	$3,877
Deposit in transit	814
Check printing charge	7
Interest earned on checking account	15
Outstanding checks	972

$ 3719.00

4. The May 31 bank statement of Levin Photography shows an ending balance of $2,784.54. Two checks, number 811 for $307.16 and number 812 for $68.71, are outstanding. The bank statement shows a debit memo of $45 on an NSF check, a debit memo of $10 on a bank collection charge, and a credit memo of $500 on the collection of a note. A deposit of $409.77 on May 31 is not on the bank statement. Prepare a bank reconciliation. The checkbook balance is $2,373.44.

Solutions to Student Review

1.

NO. 572 $ 106 18/100
DATE Oct. 16 19 90
TO Local Telephone
FOR Phone Bill

	dollars	cents
Balance Forward	1,243	64
Deposited	305	98
Deposited		
TOTAL	1,549	62
This Check	106	18
Balance	1,443	44

Berkey Tractor Co.
2961 Wilma Dr.
Belmont, Ca. 94002

572

Oct 16, 19 90

11-35/1210

PAY TO THE ORDER OF Local Telephone $ 106 18/100

One hundred six and 18/100 DOLLARS

Bank of America NT & SA
NORIEGA-31ST BRANCH 296
P.O. BOX 37001 RINCON ANNEX
SAN FRANCISCO, CA 94137

MEMO Phone bill

Rick Davis
Jan Rourke

⑆121000358⑆

2.

Balance before adjustments		$6,230
Add note collected by bank		1,000
Total		$7,230
Deduct: NSF check	$110	
Bank service charge	8	118
Adjusted checkbook balance		$7,112

$ 7,112

3.

Balance before adjustments	$3,877
Add deposits in transit	814
Total	$4,691
Deduct outstanding checks	972
Adjusted bank balance	$3,719

$ 3,719

4.

Levin Photography
Bank Reconciliation
May 31, 19--

Balance per depositor's records		$2,373.44	Balance per bank statement		$2,784.54
Add collection on note		500.00	Add deposit in transit, 5/31		409.73
Total		$2,873.44	Total		$3,194.31
Deduct: NSF check	$45.00		Deduct: Outstanding checks:		
Bank coll. charge	10.00	55.00	No. 811	$307.16	
			No. 812	68.71	375.87
Reconciled balance		$2,818.44	Reconciled balance		$2,818.44

Assignment 12–1
Banking Records

Name ______________________

Date ______________________

A. Complete the totals and balances on the following check stubs proceeding in numerical order and carrying each balance to the succeeding check stub.

No. 201 $ 175.00
June 1 19__
TO Sims Realty
FOR Rent

	Dollars	Cents
BAL. BRO'T. FOR'D.	621.	10
AM'T. DEPOSITED		
TOTAL		
AM'T. THIS CHECK	175.	00
BAL. CAR'D. FOR'D.	446	10

NOTICE: Make No Alteration or Change on Any Check, if Error is Made Write New Check.

No. 202 $ 16.23
June 2 19__
TO Pacific Gas and
FOR Electric Company

	Dollars	Cents
BAL. BRO'T. FOR'D.	446	10
AM'T. DEPOSITED		
TOTAL		
AM'T. THIS CHECK	16.	23
BAL. CAR'D. FOR'D.	429	87

NOTICE: Make No Alteration or Change on Any Check, if Error is Made Write New Check.

No. 203 $ 6.19
June 7 19__
TO City Telephone
FOR Company

	Dollars	Cents
BAL. BRO'T. FOR'D.	429	87
AM'T. DEPOSITED		
TOTAL		
AM'T. THIS CHECK	6.	19
BAL. CAR'D. FOR'D.	423	68

NOTICE: Make No Alteration or Change on Any Check, if Error is Made Write New Check.

No. 204 $ 19.70
June 12 19__
TO Cabrillo
FOR Shoe Shop

	Dollars	Cents
BAL. BRO'T. FOR'D.	423	68
AM'T. DEPOSITED	478	00
TOTAL		
AM'T. THIS CHECK	19	70
BAL. CAR'D. FOR'D.	881	98

NOTICE: Make No Alteration or Change on Any Check, if Error is Made Write New Check.

No. 205 $ 52.16
June 19 19__
TO Lincoln Garage
FOR Motor tune-up

	Dollars	Cents
BAL. BRO'T. FOR'D.	881	98
AM'T. DEPOSITED		
TOTAL		
AM'T. THIS CHECK	52	16
BAL. CAR'D. FOR'D.	829	82

NOTICE: Make No Alteration or Change on Any Check, if Error is Made Write New Check.

No. 206 $ 36.10
June 22 19__
TO Superior Market
FOR On Account

	Dollars	Cents
BAL. BRO'T. FOR'D.	829	82
AM'T. DEPOSITED		
TOTAL		
AM'T. THIS CHECK	36	10
BAL. CAR'D. FOR'D.	793	72

NOTICE: Make No Alteration or Change on Any Check, if Error is Made Write New Check.

No. 207 $ 20.00
June 23 19__
TO United Crusade
FOR Contribution

	Dollars	Cents
BAL. BRO'T. FOR'D.	793	72
AM'T. DEPOSITED	26	18
TOTAL		
AM'T. THIS CHECK	20	00
BAL. CAR'D. FOR'D.	799	90

NOTICE: Make No Alteration or Change on Any Check, if Error is Made Write New Check.

No. 208 $ 8.92
June 25 19__
TO Stanley
FOR Record Shop

	Dollars	Cents
BAL. BRO'T. FOR'D.	799	90
AM'T. DEPOSITED		
TOTAL		
AM'T. THIS CHECK	8	92
BAL. CAR'D. FOR'D.	790	98

NOTICE: Make No Alteration or Change on Any Check, if Error is Made Write New Check.

No. 209 $ 35.00
June 29 19__
TO The Emporium
FOR On account

	Dollars	Cents
BAL. BRO'T. FOR'D.	790	98
AM'T. DEPOSITED	12	28
TOTAL		
AM'T. THIS CHECK	35	00
BAL. CAR'D. FOR'D.	768	26

NOTICE: Make No Alteration or Change on Any Check, if Error is Made Write New Check.

815.10

B. Based on the completed check stubs in A above, and the following additional information, prepare a bank reconciliation.

The bank statement shows a bank balance of $815.10 on June 30. Checks numbered 204, 208, and 209 have not cleared the bank. The deposit of June 29 is not on the current bank statement. The bank statement shows a debit memo of $4.50 for check printing charges.

C. Complete the following checks and check stubs for Douglas Hardware, assuming a beginning checkbook balance of $1,873.27, with all checks signed by Terence Douglas and Peter Mitcho.

1. Check number 325 to Area Electric Co., dated April 4, 1990, for $105.16.

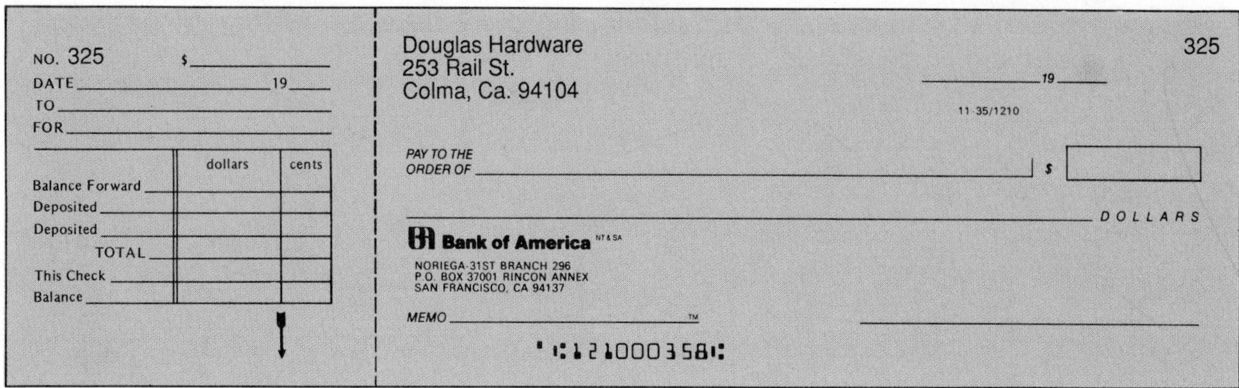

NO. 325 $____
DATE ____ 19__
TO ____
FOR ____

	dollars	cents
Balance Forward		
Deposited		
Deposited		
TOTAL		
This Check		
Balance		

Douglas Hardware
253 Rail St.
Colma, Ca. 94104

325

____ 19__

11-35/1210

PAY TO THE ORDER OF ____ $

____ DOLLARS

Bank of America NT&SA
NORIEGA-31ST BRANCH 296
P.O. BOX 37001 RINCON ANNEX
SAN FRANCISCO, CA 94137

MEMO ____

:121000358:

2. A deposit of $318.65 on April 7, 1990. Check number 326, dated April 7, to Broker Realty for April rent, $500.

NO. 326 $____
DATE ____ 19__
TO ____
FOR ____

	dollars	cents
Balance Forward		
Deposited		
Deposited		
TOTAL		
This Check		
Balance		

Douglas Hardware
253 Rail St.
Colma, Ca. 94104

326

____ 19__

11-35/1210

PAY TO THE ORDER OF ____ $

____ DOLLARS

Bank of America NT&SA
NORIEGA-31ST BRANCH 296
P.O. BOX 37001 RINCON ANNEX
SAN FRANCISCO, CA 94137

MEMO ____

:121000358:

3. Check number 327 to Grace Advertisers, dated April 8, for $105.

NO. 327 $____
DATE ____ 19__
TO ____
FOR ____

	dollars	cents
Balance Forward		
Deposited		
Deposited		
TOTAL		
This Check		
Balance		

Douglas Hardware
253 Rail St.
Colma, Ca. 94104

327

____ 19__

11-35/1210

PAY TO THE ORDER OF ____ $

____ DOLLARS

Bank of America NT&SA
NORIEGA-31ST BRANCH 296
P.O. BOX 37001 RINCON ANNEX
SAN FRANCISCO, CA 94137

MEMO ____

:121000358:

Assignment 12–2

Banking Records

Name ____________________

Date ____________________

1. From the following, determine the adjusted ending checkbook balance:

Checkbook balance before adjustments		$2,510
Note collected by bank	$525	
Interest collected by bank	30	555
Bank collection charge		10
NSF check		35

$ 3565.00
$ 3020.00

2. From the following, determine the adjusted ending checkbook balance:

Checkbook balance before adjustments	$12,960
Interest earned on checking account	52
Check printing charge	6
Deposit in transit	823
Stop payment check	4

$ 13,825.00

3. From the following, determine the adjusted ending bank balance:

Bank balance before adjustments	$11,687
Deposit in transit	816
NSF check	103
Check printing charge	5
Outstanding checks	739

$ 11,656.00
11,764.00

4. When Pratt Hydraulic received its bank statement, the ending balance was $3,116.90. Two checks, number 215 for $261.20 and number 218 for $81.70, had not cleared the bank. A deposit of $271.18, made on the last day of the month, was not included on the current bank statement. The bank statement shows a debit memo of $8 for a bank service charge. Prepare a bank reconciliation if the checkbook balance is $3,053.18.

5. Hector Fish & Poultry received its month-end bank statement, showing an ending balance of $4,615.87. The statement shows that the bank had collected and deposited a note for $1,500. The statement also shows a bank collection charge of $15, interest earned of $18.02, and an NSF check for $36.24. The last deposit of the month for $552.63 was not entered on the bank statement, while checks numbered 337, 338, and 340 for $62.18, $400, and $110.24, respectively, were oustanding. If the month-end checkbook balance is $3,129.30, prepare a bank reconciliation.

6. Bush Ice Cream Shoppe receives its monthly bank statements showing an ending bank balance of $1,847.53. There are two checks outstanding, number 171 for $185 and number 172 for $92.14. The last deposit of the month, for $509.45, is not on the bank statement. The account earned interest for the month of $5.61 and the bank statement shows a bank service charge of $7. *(a)* Determine the checkbook balance and *(b)* prepare a bank reconciliation.

(a) 2185.45

(b) IN NOTE BOOK.

 Multiple Sports with Amy Hengst, Accountant

You have just graduated from college with a B.A. degree in accounting. After going through several job interviews, you accept an accounting position with Multiple Sports. Your supervisor is the controller of the company, Amy Hengst.

After completing the necessary forms with personnel on February 1, 1990, Amy asks you to prepare and make the bank deposit, prepare the monthly bank reconciliation, and write any checks for payments due this day.

The first thing you do is remove the currency, coins, and customer checks from the overnight safe and prepare the deposit slip. The undeposited receipts from the previous day included $302 in currency, $18.74 in coins, and two checks, number 12-24 for $18.75 and number 18-96 for $46.32. You go to the bank and deposit the prior day's receipts. At that time, a bank representative gives you the following January bank statement, as well as the canceled checks.

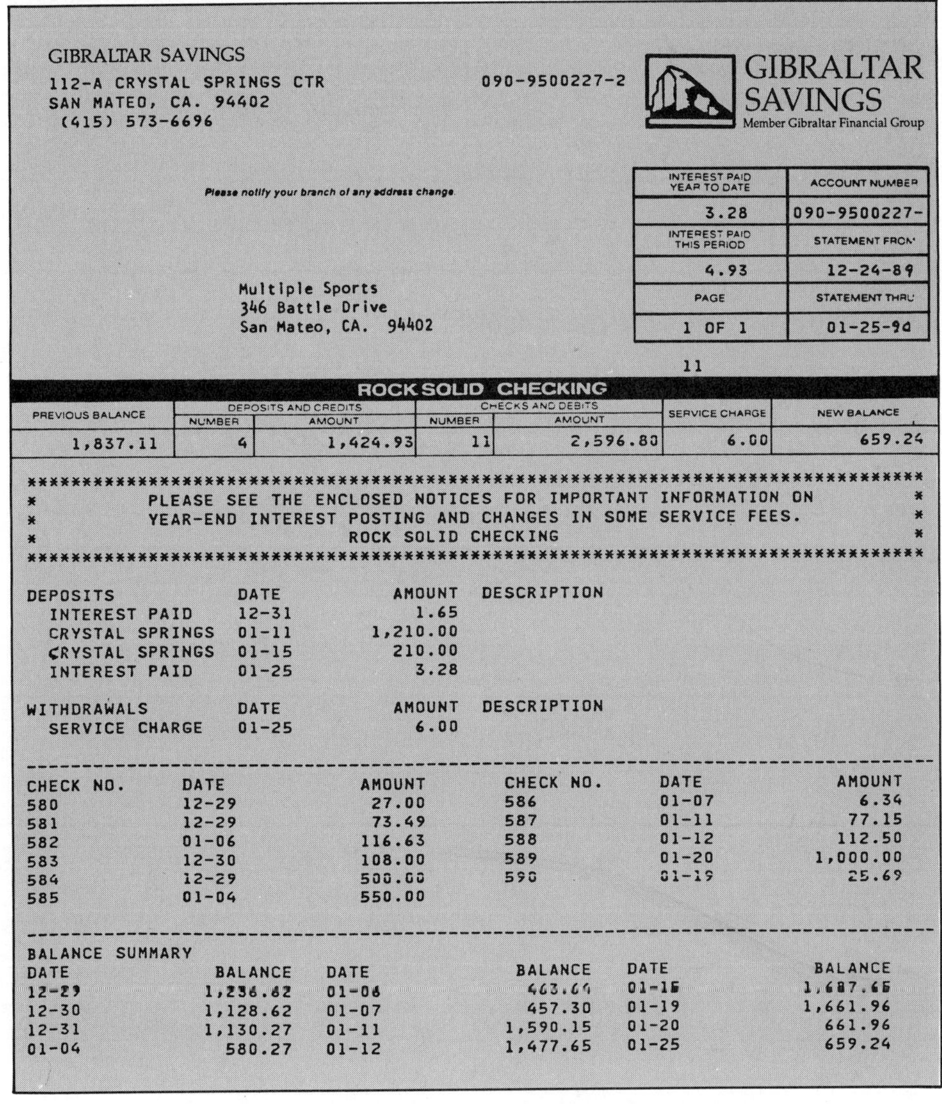

GIBRALTAR SAVINGS
112-A CRYSTAL SPRINGS CTR
SAN MATEO, CA. 94402
(415) 573-6696

090-9500227-2

GIBRALTAR SAVINGS
Member Gibraltar Financial Group

Please notify your branch of any address change.

Multiple Sports
346 Battle Drive
San Mateo, CA. 94402

INTEREST PAID YEAR TO DATE	ACCOUNT NUMBER
3.28	090-9500227-
INTEREST PAID THIS PERIOD	STATEMENT FROM
4.93	12-24-89
PAGE	STATEMENT THRU
1 OF 1	01-25-90

11

ROCK SOLID CHECKING

PREVIOUS BALANCE	DEPOSITS AND CREDITS NUMBER	DEPOSITS AND CREDITS AMOUNT	CHECKS AND DEBITS NUMBER	CHECKS AND DEBITS AMOUNT	SERVICE CHARGE	NEW BALANCE
1,837.11	4	1,424.93	11	2,596.80	6.00	659.24

PLEASE SEE THE ENCLOSED NOTICES FOR IMPORTANT INFORMATION ON YEAR-END INTEREST POSTING AND CHANGES IN SOME SERVICE FEES. ROCK SOLID CHECKING

DEPOSITS	DATE	AMOUNT	DESCRIPTION
INTEREST PAID	12-31	1.65	
CRYSTAL SPRINGS	01-11	1,210.00	
CRYSTAL SPRINGS	01-15	210.00	
INTEREST PAID	01-25	3.28	

WITHDRAWALS	DATE	AMOUNT	DESCRIPTION
SERVICE CHARGE	01-25	6.00	

CHECK NO.	DATE	AMOUNT	CHECK NO.	DATE	AMOUNT
580	12-29	27.00	586	01-07	6.34
581	12-29	73.49	587	01-11	77.15
582	01-06	116.63	588	01-12	112.50
583	12-30	108.00	589	01-20	1,000.00
584	12-29	500.00	590	01-19	25.69
585	01-04	550.00			

BALANCE SUMMARY

DATE	BALANCE	DATE	BALANCE	DATE	BALANCE
12-29	1,236.62	01-06	463.64	01-15	1,687.65
12-30	1,128.62	01-07	457.30	01-19	1,661.96
12-31	1,130.27	01-11	1,590.15	01-20	661.96
01-04	580.27	01-12	1,477.65	01-25	659.24

Upon returning to your office, after a get-acquainted coffee break, you prepare the bank reconciliation. In comparing the checks issued through January 25, 1990, with the returned canceled checks, you discover that check numbers 591 for $121.37 and 592 for $254.84 are outstanding. In addition, a deposit of $746.52 was made late in the day on January 25, 1990. Also, you note that the ending checkbook balance on January 25, 1990, is $1,032.62.

When the bank reconciliation is completed, you determine that only one bill is to be paid today. You note that the checkbook balance is $942.84, and you write check number 601 to Sports Suppliers, Inc., for $194.18. The check is to be cosigned by Amy Hengst and Michael Kelly.

1. Prepare the bank deposit slip.

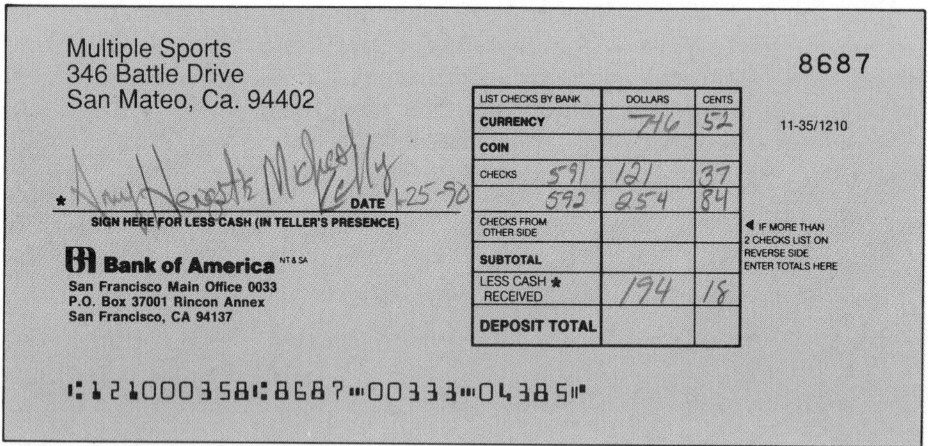

Multiple Sports
346 Battle Drive
San Mateo, Ca. 94402

8687

11-35/1210

* Amy Hengst & Michael Kelly DATE 1-25-90
SIGN HERE FOR LESS CASH (IN TELLER'S PRESENCE)

Bank of America NT&SA
San Francisco Main Office 0033
P.O. Box 37001 Rincon Annex
San Francisco, CA 94137

LIST CHECKS BY BANK	DOLLARS	CENTS
CURRENCY	746	52
COIN		
CHECKS 591	121	37
592	254	84
CHECKS FROM OTHER SIDE		
SUBTOTAL		
LESS CASH * RECEIVED	194	18
DEPOSIT TOTAL		

◀ IF MORE THAN 2 CHECKS LIST ON REVERSE SIDE ENTER TOTALS HERE

⑆121000358⑆8687⑈00333⑈04385⑈

2. Prepare the bank reconciliation.
3. Fill in the check stub and write check number 601.

Multiple Sports
Bank Reconciliation
January 25, 1990

NO. 601 $ 194.18
DATE Jan 25 19 90
TO Sports Suppliers Inc
FOR One

	dollars	cents
Balance Forward	942	84
Deposited	746	52
Deposited		
TOTAL		
This Check	194	18
Balance	1033	62

Multiple Sports
346 Battle Drive
San Mateo, Ca. 94402

601

Jan 25 19 90

11-35/1210

PAY TO THE ORDER OF Sports Suppliers Inc. $ 194.18

One Hundred Ninety-Four 18/100 DOLLARS

Bank of America NT&SA
NORIEGA-31ST BRANCH 296
P.O. BOX 37001 RINCON ANNEX
SAN FRANCISCO, CA 94137

MEMO ______ TM

Amy Hengst & Michael Kelly

⑆121000358⑆

Chapter 13

Gross Earnings

The problem is that my paycheck comes minus tax while my bills come plus tax.

Learning Goals

Upon completion of this chapter, you should be able to:

1. Calculate gross hourly wages or salaries.
2. Convert salaries when the pay period changes.
3. Determine overtime pay by the standard and premium methods.

Determining Gross Earnings

A necessary bookkeeping procedure for a business firm is the determination of the payroll. Accurate payroll records are essential for several reasons:

1. The employer would like to have knowledge and control of all operating costs.
2. The employee is entitled to be paid at the agreed rate for the time worked.
3. Various so-called voluntary and involuntary withholdings must be made on each employee's gross earnings to be paid to government and private institutions.
4. Certain withholdings stop each year after an employee has earned the required amount.

Gross Pay

The term *wages* generally refers to compensation for labor, while the term *salary* usually refers to payment for services.

An employee's wage, if there is no overtime, is the rate per hour times the hours worked.

W is wages

Rh is rate per hour

Hw is hours worked

THIS SIDE OUT

No. 45

NAME RONALD SELIGMAN

PAY ENDING NOV. 10, 19 90

MARITAL STATUS SINGLE

REG. TIME HRS. 44 RATE 8.50 AMT. $ 374.00

OVERTIME HRS. 4 RATE 4.25 AMT. $ 17.00

TOTAL EARNINGS $ 391.00

TOTAL DEDUCTIONS $ 110.86

NET WAGES $ 280.14

DEDUCTIONS		
FEDERAL WITHHOLDING TAX	50	00
STATE WITHHOLDING TAX	10	68
SOCIAL SECURITY TAX	29	91
STATE UNEMPLOYMENT INSURANCE	3	52
DUES	10	00
INSURANCE	6	75
OTHER		
TOTAL DEDUCTIONS	110	86

BACK—See Over

PAY ENDING NOV. 10, 19 90

No. 45

NAME RONALD SELIGMAN

	MORNING	LUNCH		NIGHT	EXTRA	
	IN	OUT	IN	OUT	IN	OUT
16						
1/17						
2/18						
3/19						
4/20						
5/21	8:14	12:14	12:59	5:00		
6/22	8:15	12:16	1:00	5:01		
7/23	8:15	12:15	1:02	5:01		
8/24	8:20	12:20	1:00	4:59		
9/25	8:13	12:15	1:01	5:01		
10/26	9:00	–	–	1:00		
11/27						
12/28						
13/29						
14/30						
15/31						

AIGNER FORM NO. 10-239 PRINTED IN USA

FRONT—See Over

Example 1. Bill Funke is paid $7.35 per hour and worked 40 hours this week. Determine his gross wages for the current week.

$$W = Rh \times Hw$$

$$W = \$7.35 \times 40 = \$294.00$$

An employee's salary is usually paid:

Weekly	**52 times per year**
Biweekly	**26 times per year—every 2 weeks**
Semimonthly	**24 times per year—twice a month**
Monthly	**12 times per year**

Sometimes salaried employees have their pay period changed, e.g., from semimonthly to biweekly, or two employees paid over different time periods would like to compare their gross earnings over a set period of time. To convert a monthly pay period, or fraction thereof, to a weekly pay period, or multiple thereof, a simple procedure would be to annualize the salary of the one method of pay by multiplication, and then divide by the number of pay periods annually in the other time period.

Example 2. Bob De Young earns $180 per week. He would like to know what his earnings would be *(a)* biweekly, *(b)* semimonthly, *(c)* monthly.

(a) $180 × 2 = $360

(b) $180 × 52 = $9,360 ÷ 24 = $390

(c) $180 × 52 = $9,360 ÷ 12 = $780

Example 3. George Stewart earns $650 per month. Find his earnings *(a)* semimonthly, *(b)* weekly, *(c)* biweekly.

(a) $650 ÷ 2 = $325

(b) $650 × 12 = $7,800 ÷ 52 = $150

(c) $650 × 12 = $7,800 ÷ 26 = $300

Overtime Pay

Employers engaged in interstate commerce are required by the Federal Fair Labor Standards Act to pay their employees a minimum rate of one and one-half times the regular pay rate for all hours worked in excess of 40 hours per week. In addition, union agreements and state legislation frequently require overtime pay for hours worked in excess of eight per day, for night shifts, and for work on Saturdays, Sundays, and holidays.

One of two methods is generally used to determine gross pay for employees who are entitled to overtime excess pay. One way is to compute standard pay for a standard work period and overtime pay for the excess hours worked. A second method frequently used is to compute an employee's pay at the regular rate for the total time worked and then add to it the excess premium pay.

Overtime Pay Method

Standard pay would be the rate per hour times the standard hours per pay period, while overtime pay would be the excess hours times the overtime rate.

Example 1. Joe Randall works in a grocery store. He is paid \$8 per hour for a standard workweek of 35 hours and time and a half for overtime. Find his *(a)* standard pay, *(b)* overtime pay, and *(c)* gross pay for a week when he worked 39 hours.

$W = Rh \times Hs + Ro \times Ho$

Ro = Overtime rate

Ho = Overtime hours

(a) $\$8 \times 35 \text{ hours} = \$280$

(b) $8 \times 1\frac{1}{2} \times 4 \text{ hours} = \$48$

(c) $\$280 + \$48 = \$328$

Note: In *(b)* above, the rate for overtime work ($1\frac{1}{2}$) may be multiplied by either the regular pay or the overtime hours, whichever is easier.

For example:

$$\$8 \times 1\frac{1}{2} = \$12 \times 4 = \$48$$

or

$$4 \times 1\frac{1}{2} = 6 \times \$8 = \$48$$

Excess Premium Pay Method

Regular pay would be the rate per hour times the hours worked, while premium pay would be the excess rate per hour times the overtime hours worked.

This method separates the regular pay for the actual hours worked from the bonus or premium amount paid for overtime work. Employers like this method because it often pinpoints carelessness in work planning, and the amount of expense that could be reduced with better management control. Also, occasionally dues and fringe benefits are payable as a percent of regular pay for total hours worked.

Physicians, by Principal Specialties—1985	(in thousands)
Internal medicine	78.8
General practice	65.1
General surgery	36.4
Pediatrics	31.8
Obstetrics	29.7
Psychiatry	28.9

U.S. Bureau of the Census, *Statistical Abstract of the United States*: 1988 (108th edition) Washington, DC.

Example 1. Assume the same facts as in the last example except that we want to find the employee's overtime premium pay.

$$W = Rh \times Hw + Re \times Ho$$

(a) $\$8 \times 39 \text{ hours} = \$312$

(b) $\$8 \times \frac{1}{2} \times 4 \text{ hours} = \$16$

(c) $\$312 + \$16 = \$328$

Note that in the premium method, it is ascertained that the employer had to pay an extra $16 because the employee worked overtime. It is misleading to say that the employer had to pay a penalty of $48 for overtime, as implied in the earlier overtime pay example, since the employer did get four additional hours of work from the employee.

"He gave me sort of a conditional raise . . . when hell freezes over."

Student Review

1. The following workers receive time and a half for all hours worked in excess of 7 per day or 35 per week. Complete the weekly payroll register to arrive at gross earnings.

Name	Daily Hours						Regular Hourly Rate	Earnings		
	M	Tu	W	Th	F	S		Standard	Overtime	Total
Alfonso, L.	7	7	5	5	9	3	$9.20	$ 312.80	$ 27.60	$ 340.40
Rowe, P.	8	9	7	7	3		8.50	$ 297.00	$ 38.27	$

1. 312.80 27.60 340.40 2. 297.00 38.25 335.25

2. Shirley Barger is a refrigerator maintenance worker. She receives $12.50 per hour for a standard 40-hour workweek and time and a half for hours worked in excess of 40. If Ms. Barger worked 43 hours during the current week, find her *(a)* standard pay, *(b)* overtime pay, *(c)* gross pay for the week.

(a) $______ *(b)* $______ *(c)* $______

3. The following workers receive time and a half for all hours worked in excess of 8 per day or 40 per week. Complete the weekly payroll register to arrive at gross earnings.

Name	Daily Hours						Regular Hourly Rate	Earnings		
	M	Tu	W	Th	F	S		Regular	Premium	Total
Bates, A	8	8	8	10	7		$12.60	$	$	$
Paz, J.	9	9	8	6	8	4	15.30	$	$	$

4. Jo Kennedy, a movie projectionist, is paid $11.80 per hour, with time and one-quarter for hours worked in excess of 35 hours per week. If Ms. Kennedy works 42 hours during the current week, find her *(a)* total regular earnings, *(b)* overtime premium earnings, and *(c)* gross pay for the week.

(a) $______ *(b)* $______ *(c)* $______

5. Donald Smith earns a biweekly salary of $975. If his company changes to a semimonthly pay period, determine his semimonthly salary.

$______

Solutions to Student Review

1. Alfonso, L.

Standard ($9.20 × 34 hours) = $312.80 — $ 312.80

Overtime $\left(\$9.20 \times 1\frac{1}{2} \times 2 \text{ hours}\right) = \$27.60$ — $ 27.60

Total ($312.80 + $27.60) = $340.40 — $ 340.40

Rowe, P.

Standard ($8.50 × 31 hours) = $263.50 — $ 263.50

Overtime $\left(\$8.50 \times 1\frac{1}{2} \times 3 \text{ hours}\right) = \$38.25$ — $ 38.25

Total (263.50 + $38.25) = $301.75 — $ 301.75

2. *(a)* $12.50 × 40 = $500.00 — *(a)* $ 500.00

(b) $\$12.50 \times 1\frac{1}{2} \times 3 = \$56.25$ — *(b)* $ 56.25

(c) $500.00 + $56.25 = $556.25 — *(c)* $ 556.25

3. Bates, A.

Regular ($12.60 × 41 hours) = $516.60 — $ 516.60

Premium $\left(\$12.60 \times 1\frac{1}{2} \times 2 \text{ hours}\right) = \$12.60$ — $ 12.60

Total ($516.60 + $12.60) = $529.20 — $ 529.20

Paz, J.

Regular ($15.30 × 44 hours) = $673.20 — $ 673.20

Premium $\left(\$15.30 \times \frac{1}{2} \times 4 \text{ hours}\right) = \$30.60$ — $ 30.60

Total ($673.20 + $30.60) = $703.80 — $ 703.80

4. *(a)* $11.80 × 42 = $495.60 — $ 495.60

(b) $\$11.80 \times \frac{1}{2} \times 7 = \$41.30$ — $ 41.30

(c) $495.60 + $41.30 = $536.90 — $ 536.90

5. $975 × 26 = $25,350

$25,350 ÷ 24 = $1,056.25 — $ 1,056.25

Assignment 13–1

Gross Earnings

Name ______________________

Date ______________________

A. The following workers receive time and a half for all hours worked in excess of 8 per day or 40 per week. Complete the weekly payroll register to arrive at gross earnings.

Name	Daily Hours M	Tu	W	Th	F	S	Regular Hourly Rate	Earnings Standard	Overtime	Total
Aaron, B.	8	8	8	8	8	—	$5.25	______	______	______
Johnson, B.	8	8	9	8	8	4	4.60	______	______	______
Travers, D.	8	8	9	8	8	—	6.80	______	______	______
Vernon, P.	7	7	8	8	8	4	7.70	______	______	______
Walters, R.	8	10	8	6	8	—	5.50	______	______	______
								______	______	______

B. Solve the following problems:

1. William Pressey, a salesclerk, receives $8.50 per hour for a standard workweek of 40 hours and time and a half for hours worked in excess of 40. If Mr. Pressey worked 45 hours during the current week, find his *(a)* standard pay, *(b)* overtime pay, and *(c)* gross pay for the week.

   (a) $ ______________

   (b) $ ______________

   (c) $ ______________

2. Bien Reyes, a machine operator, earns $6.75 per hour and is paid double time for hours worked in excess of $37\frac{1}{2}$ per week. If Mr. Reyes worked 43 hours during the current week, find his *(a)* standard pay, *(b)* overtime pay, and *(c)* gross pay for the week.

   (a) $ ______________

   (b) $ ______________

   (c) $ ______________

3. Mary Thompson, a freight loader, is paid $8.40 per hour and time and a half for hours worked in excess of 35 per week. During the current week, Ms. Thompson worked 40 hours. Find her *(a)* total standard earnings, *(b)* overtime earnings, and *(c)* gross pay for the week.

(a) $____________

(b) $____________

(c) $____________

4. Ideale Gambera, a telephone line repairer, is paid $9.18 per hour. He gets paid time and a half for hours worked in excess of 8 hours per day. If he worked 8 hours on Monday, 7 hours on Tuesday, 10 hours on Thursday, and 9 hours on Friday, determine his *(a)* total standard earnings, *(b)* overtime earnings, and *(c)* gross earnings for the week.

(a) $____________

(b) $____________

(c) $____________

5. Gordon Poon repairs typewriters. He earns $6.90 an hour and gets time and a half for hours in excess of 8 in one day. If he works 10 hours on Monday, 8 hours on Tuesday and on Wednesday, 6 hours on Thursday, and 9 hours on Friday, determine his *(a)* standard pay, *(b)* overtime pay, and *(c)* gross pay for the week.

(a) $____________

(b) $____________

(c) $____________

6. Paul Hewitt, a truck driver, is paid $6.10 per hour. However, he gets paid time and a half for hours worked in excess of 7 per day, and he gets paid double time for hours worked on Saturday. If he works 4 hours on Monday, 4 hours on Tuesday, 10 hours on Wednesday, 7 hours on Thursday and on Friday, and 4 hours on Saturday, determine his *(a)* standard pay, *(b)* overtime pay, and *(c)* gross pay for the week.

(a) $____________

(b) $____________

(c) $____________

7. Madeline Mueller is a butcher in a supermarket. She gets paid $11.23 per hour, time and a half for hours worked on Saturday, and double time for hours worked on Sunday. During the current week, she worked 45 hours, including 7 hours on Saturday and 4 hours on Sunday. Determine her *(a)* standard pay, *(b)* overtime pay, and *(c)* gross pay for the week.

(a) $____________

(b) $____________

(c) $____________

Assignment 13–2

Gross Earnings

Name ______________________

Date ______________________

A. The following workers receive time and a half for all hours worked in excess of 7 per day or 35 per week. Complete the weekly payroll register to arrive at gross earnings:

Name	*Daily Hours*						*Regular Hourly Rate*	*Earnings*		
	M	*Tu*	*W*	*Th*	*F*	*S*		*Regular*	*Premium*	*Total*
Bloomer, R.	7	7	7	7	7		$5.19	______	______	______
Everall, P.	7	7	—	7	8	4	4.92	______	______	______
Jabbar, A.	8	10	7	7	7	4	3.86	______	______	______
Riordan, M.	7	7	6	6	7	2	5.64	______	______	______
Settle, M.	7	7	10	—	7	7	4.80	______	______	______

B. Solve the following problems:

1. Eddie Wong, a computer operator, is paid $5.75 per hour and time and a half for hours worked in excess of 35 per week. During the current week, he worked 43 hours. Find his *(a)* total regular earnings, *(b)* overtime premium earnings, and *(c)* gross pay for the week.

(a) $______________

(b) $______________

(c) $______________

2. Maria Ramirez, an assembly line operator, is paid $7.10 per hour and time and one-quarter for hours worked in excess of 40 per week. If she works 44 hours during the current week, find her *(a)* total regular earnings, *(b)* overtime premium earnings, and *(c)* gross pay for the week.

(a) $______________

(b) $______________

(c) $______________

3. Barbara Thomas, a construction worker, is paid \$6.23 per hour for a standard 7-hour day and time and a half for overtime. For a day in which she worked $10\frac{1}{4}$ hours, determine her *(a)* regular pay, *(b)* overtime premium pay, and *(c)* gross pay for the day.

(a) \$__________

(b) \$__________

(c) \$__________

4. Joy Fudem, a lab technician, earns \$6.25 per hour, with time and a half for hours worked in excess of 40 hours per week. The employer withholds and pays Joy's union dues, which are 3 percent of total *regular* weekly earnings. If she worked 44 hours during a week, determine the amount of union dues withheld from her paycheck.

\$__________

5. Betty Underwood, a dispatcher, earns \$7.40 per hour, with time and one-quarter for hours worked in excess of 35 hours per week. Her employer contributes 4 percent to her retirement plan based on her total regular weekly earnings. If Ms. Underwood works 43 hours during the current week, determine her *(a)* regular pay, *(b)* premium pay, and *(c)* employer contribution to her retirement plan.

(a) \$__________

(b) \$__________

(c) \$__________

6. Jerry Gragg receives a weekly salary of \$460. His company is changing its pay period to semimonthly. If he is to receive the same total salary, determine his semimonthly gross salary.

\$__________

7. Arnold Jacobson is paid \$750 semimonthly. Determine how much he would receive if he were paid biweekly.

\$__________

8. The president of Alhambra Foods earns an annual gross salary of \$140,000. Determine the gross pay per period if she is paid *(a)* monthly, *(b)* biweekly.

(a) \$ 5384.62

(b) \$ \$11666.67

Multiple Sports with Amy Hengst, Accountant

On February 12, 1990, Amy asks you to determine the gross pay of those employees who are paid by the week on an hourly basis. From the time cards, you summarize the following information for the week ending February 9, 1990:

Name	Daily Hours						Regular Hourly Rate
	M	Tu	W	Th	F	S	
Barr, P.	8	8	8	9	11	—	$9.20
Ghnaim, W.	8	8	—	8	8	4	7.60
Ow, D.	8	8	8	6	8	3	8.45

For those employees paid on an hourly basis, the company pays time and a half for all hours worked in excess of 8 per day, 40 per week, or hours worked on Saturday.

In addition, for Gary Wong, who previously received a semimonthly salary of $962, the company has decided to change the pay period to weekly, beginning the week ending February 9.

1. Determine the *(a)* standard wages, *(b)* overtime wages, and *(c)* total gross wages of the three hourly employees.

	Barr	Ghnaim	Ow
(a)	$________	$________	$________
(b)	$________	$________	$________
(c)	$________	$________	$________

2. Determine the overtime premium earnings paid to each of the three hourly employees that could have been avoided by Multiple Sports if none of the hours worked was paid at overtime rates.

Barr ________

Ghnaim ________

Ow ________

3. Determine the gross salary earned by Gary Wong now that he is being paid by the week.

$________

Chapter **14**

Commission and Piece-Rate Wage Payments

I'm giving you a raise so that your last week here will be a happy one.

Learning Goals

Upon completion of this chapter, you should be able to:

1. Determine gross pay on a straight commission basis.
2. Calculate gross pay if paid a base salary plus a commission.
3. Arrive at gross pay with varying commission rates.
4. Establish the pay due a salesperson who incurs travel expenses and receives a travel advance.
5. Differentiate wage, commission, and piece-rate payment plans.
6. Calculate gross pay on a straight piece-rate basis.
7. Determine gross pay with varying piece-rates, based on different levels of production output.
8. Find the gross wage if paid by a combination of hourly wage and piece-rate bonus plans.

Commission Payments

If an employee's efforts can be measured in terms of units or dollars sold, he is often paid a commission. The commission can take many forms, but some of the more common methods include the following:

1. Salary plus commission.
2. Straight commission.

Salary Plus Commission

This payroll incentive plan is found typically in the retail sales field. An employee receives a minimum basic salary for being on the job. In addition, as a reward for a successful sales effort, the employee receives additional compensation, usually as a predetermined percent of dollar sales, though occasionally as a fixed amount per unit sold.

Example 1. Roger Loar is a shoe salesman in a department store. He receives a biweekly salary of $625 plus a commission of 5 percent of dollar sales. During the current pay period his total dollar sales amounted to $2,000. Find the gross salary earned by Mr. Loar.

Biweekly salary	**$625**
Commission, 5% of $2,000	**100**
Total salary earned	**$725**

Straight Commission

A salesperson working a straight commission receives no guaranteed pay. This individual is compensated either in relation to dollar sales or units sold. Very often this person is not an employee of a company, but rather an independent contractor who is a self-employed individual selling one or several of a company's products. There is a high element of risk involved since, if there is no sale, there is no pay. On the other hand, a successful salesperson can receive greater compensation.

Example 2. Joe Jaegar is a real estate salesman. He negotiated the sale of a personal residence that sold for $210,000. Determine Mr. Jaegar's commission if he is entitled to a brokerage fee of $1\frac{1}{2}$ percent of the selling price.

$210,000 × .015 = $3,150

Largest Foreign-Born U.S. Populations by Country of Birth—1980

	(in thousands)
1. Mexico	2,199.2
2. Germany	849.4
3. Canada	842.9
4. Italy	831.9
5. Cuba	607.8

U.S. Bureau of the Census, *Statistical Abstract of the United States*: 1988 (108th edition) Washington, DC.

Outside salespersons and independent contractors, selling door-to-door and out of town, often receive progressive commission rates with higher sales levels. To encourage traveling to out-of-the-way or distant locations, salespersons may receive a travel allowance, as well as a salary advance.

Example 3. Brian Merrill sells women's apparel to stores. He receives a commission of 8 percent on the first $20,000 of sales and 11 percent on the excess. For the current month, he drew a salary advance of $400, incurred travel expenses of $340 that will be reimbursed by his employer, and had total sales of $24,000. Determine the amount due to Mr. Merrill at the end of the month.

$20,000 × .08	**= $1,600**	
4,000 × .11	**= 440**	
Total commission	**$2,040**	
Plus travel expense	**340**	**$2,380**
Less salary advance		**400**
Amount due		**$1,980**

NUMBER OF CALLS	HOURS WORKED

CUSTOMER'S CALLED ON	COLLECTIONS
BENSON CARPETS	
DESERT FURNISHINGS	
TUCSON FLOOR DISPLAY	
CACTUS INTERIORS	

ENTERTAINMENT

PERSON ROBIN BEST
COMPANY BENSON CARPETS
PLACE BINO'S RESTAURANT
PURPOSE CARPET SALES

AMOUNT $ 71 –

PERSON
COMPANY
PLACE
PURPOSE

AMOUNT $

Recipients of Gifts — Item — Cost of Item

WEDNESDAY OCT. 3, 1990

CITY TUCSON, AZ.

MOTEL HOTEL ROADSIDE INN

ITEM	AMOUNT	
Hotel - Motel	63	–
Breakfast	3	75
Lunch	4	50
Dinner		
Plane - Rail - Bus Fare		
Local Taxi - Bus		
Auto Exp. - Repairs, Etc.		
Gas - Oil	11	25
Lubrication - Wash		
Garage - Parking		
Tolls		
Phone - Telegrams	2	60
Tips	15	00
Postage		
Entertainment	71	–
Miles 25 @ 24¢	6	–
TOTAL EXPENSE FOR DAY	177	10

Piece-Rate Payment

The concept of the piece-rate payment plan is to reward the worker based upon production output. It is similar to the straight commission plan for salespersons in that usually there is no guaranteed wage. The rate per piece of output is usually determined by a careful time and motion study of a particular job. The greater the productivity by the worker, the greater the pay. Following are some basic piece-rate plans.

Straight Piece-Rate Plan

The employee receives a fixed wage per unit of production.

Example 1. Leah Cooper assembles toy parts for a toy manufacturer. She receives 40 cents per unit assembled. This week she assembled 920 units. Find her gross pay for the week.

$$920 \times \$0.40 = \$368$$

Straight Piece-Rate Plus Bonus Plan

In order to give an employee an incentive for greater daily production, a company may offer its employees a basic minimum rate per unit, with a bonus for production beyond an established level.

Example 2. Robert Quigley loads cartons on freight cars. He is paid 12 cents for each carton loaded per day, with a bonus of 3 cents for cartons loaded in excess of 300. Find the wage paid to Mr. Quigley if he loaded 400 boxes on a given day.

400 × \$0.12 =	\$48.00
100 × \$0.03 =	3.00
Gross wage	\$51.00

Multi Piece-Rate Plan

To encourage maximum effort from each worker, a company might establish two or more piece-rate pay scales. A worker is paid at a lower piece-rate basis if output is below a preset level and is paid at a higher piece-rate basis if that level is exceeded. The idea is that *every* worker should exceed the minimum level of output, rewarding both the employee and the employer.

Example 3. Esther Selleck boxes candy items. She receives 40 cents per box if she boxes fewer than 150, and 50 cents per box if she boxes 150 or more. If she packages 148 boxes on Monday and 150 on Tuesday, determine her gross pay each day.

Monday	148 × \$0.40 = \$59.20
Tuesday	150 × \$0.50 = \$75.00

Combined Wage and Piece-Rate Payment Plan

Many wage payment plans have been developed that provide the employee with a basic wage for minimum daily levels of output, with a bonus per unit for production in excess of a preset standard.

Example 4. Willis Kirk, working in the packaging department, is paid an hourly wage of \$5.50 for an 8-hour day. For each package in excess of 120 in a day, he receives a bonus of 30 cents. Find Mr. Kirk's gross pay on a day he packaged 135 items.

8 × \$5.50 =	\$44.00
15 × \$0.30 =	4.50
Gross pay	\$48.50

Student Review

1. Abdul Jabbar is a carpet salesman. He receives a monthly salary of $900 plus a commission of 7 percent of dollar sales. For the current month his gross sales totaled $16,450. What is the gross salary earned by Mr. Jabbar?

$ ______________

2. Paul Tang is an outside salesman for a company. He receives a monthly commission of 6 percent on sales up to $15,000, and 8 percent on any excess dollar sales. The company covers his travel expenses and gives him a monthly salary advance of $325. If his sales for the current month totaled $19,100 and his travel expenses were $350, find the balance due Mr. Tang for the current month.

$ ______________

3. Judy Hubbell is paid on a piece-rate basis. She is paid 25 cents for each calculator cartridge loaded, with a bonus of 5 cents for each cartridge in excess of 250. Find her gross pay for the day if she loads 325 cartridges.

$ 85.00

4. Willie Thompson is paid on a differential piece-rate basis. For wrapping 90 pieces or less a day, he receives 70 cents per item wrapped. If he wraps in excess of 90 per day, he gets paid 80 cents for each item wrapped. Determine his gross pay if he wraps 85 pieces on Monday and 98 pieces on Tuesday.

Monday $ ______________

Tuesday $ 78.40

5. Carol Olivier works in the light-switch assembly department. She gets a minimum wage of $5.25 per hour. In addition, she receives 45 cents for each light switch assembled. Determine her gross pay for the 8 hour day in which she assembled 88 light switches.

$ ______________

Solutions to Student Review

1. Salary $ 900.00
Commission ($16,450 × .07) 1,151.50
Gross Salary $2,051.50

$ $2,051.50

2. Commission:
$15,000 × .06 = $900
4,100 × .08 = 328 $1,228
Travel expense + 350
$1,578
Travel advance − 325
Balance due $1,253

$ $1,253.00

3. Base pay (0.25 × 325) $81.25
Bonus ($0.05 × 75) 3.75
Gross pay $85.00

$ 85.00

4. Monday:
$0.70 × 85 = $59.50

Monday $ 59.50

Tuesday:
$0.80 × 98 = $78.40

Tuesday $ 78.40

5. $5.25 × 8 = $42.00
$0.45 × 88 = 39.60
Gross pay = $81.60

$ 81.60

Assignment 14–1

Commission and Piece-Rate Payments

Name ______________________

Date ______________________

1. Henry Hatcher is a department store salesman. He receives a monthly salary of $750 plus a commission of 8 percent of dollar sales. For the current month, his gross sales totaled $1,560. Find the gross salary earned by Mr. Hatcher.

$ 874.80

2. Juanita Pascual is a saleswoman, exclusively selling a particular type of luggage. She receives $6.80 per hour for a 40-hour week, plus a commission of $1.75 for each piece of luggage she sells. If she sells 15 pieces of luggage during the week, determine her gross pay.

$ 298.25

3. David Bingham is a door-to-door salesman for a company. He receives no salary but gets a commission of 20 percent of dollar sales. Find his commission for a month in which he had sales of $3,482.

$ 696.40

4. Burt Hirsch is a land development salesman. He receives a commission of 5 percent on the gross selling price of each lot. During the current period, he sold three lots for $9,000, $12,000, and $8,000, respectively. Find his total commission for the period.

$ ______________

5. Tom Lyon is a traveling salesman for a company. He receives a base salary of $550 per month. He also gets a commission of 3 percent of dollar sales up to $20,000, and 4 percent of dollar sales in excess of $20,000. During the current month his sales totaled $27,000. Determine his gross earnings for the current month.

$ 1430.00

6. Keith Kerr is an outside salesman for a company. He receives a monthly commission of 4 percent on sales up to $10,000, and 6 percent for any excess dollar sales. The company pays his travel expenses and gives him a salary advance of $300 to cover his costs while on the road. During the current month, his sales totaled $17,400 and his travel expenses were $260. Find the balance due Mr. Kerr at the end of the month.

$ ____________

7. Alex Schwarz is a traveling furniture salesman. He receives a monthly commission of $3\frac{1}{2}$ percent on sales up to $8,000, 5 percent on sales between $8,000 and $12,000, and $7\frac{1}{2}$ percent on sales in excess of $12,000. The company also reimburses him for travel expenses and provides him with a $325 travel advance. Determine the amount due Mr. Schwarz at the end of the month if his sales totaled $14,720 and his travel expenses were $405.

280 200 204.00

$ 764.00

8. Washington Realtors manages rental property for landlords, including collections of rents and payments of expenses. The landlord receives $750, the net rental after deducting $75 for repairs and a 4 percent commission on gross rents. Determine *(a)* the commission and *(b)* the gross rent.

(a) $ 2250.00

(b) $ ____________

9. The Reliable Auto Company employs three salespersons. They each get a base monthly salary of $300 and a monthly commission of 5 percent on their total sales. In addition, those salespersons whose sales exceed the average of the three receive a bonus of 6 percent on that person's sales in excess of the average. For the current month, the sales were as follows: *(a)* $10,320; *(b)* $14,655; *(c)* $12,810. Determine the gross earnings of each salesperson for the current month.

(a) $ 816.00

(b) $ 1156.35

(c) $ 953.40

Assignment 14–2

Commission and Piece-Rate Wage Payments

Name ______________________

Date ______________________

1. Ed Jordan is paid on a straight piece-rate plan per week. He receives $0.092 per piece wrapped. During the current week his production was as follows: Monday, 834; Tuesday, 861; Wednesday, 840; Thursday, 805; and Friday, 792. Find his gross pay for the week.

$ 380.14

2. Craig Kuhns packs cartons for shipment. He is paid 24 cents for each carton packed per day, with a bonus of 4 cents per carton in excess of 200. Find his gross pay for the week if his daily production was as follows: Monday, 220; Tuesday, 230; Wednesday, 180; Thursday, 200; and Friday, 175.

243.20

$ ______________________

3. The Bristol Manufacturing Company pays its workers in the assembly department on a differential piece-rate basis. For production of 150 pieces or less per day, a worker gets 28 cents per piece assembled. If he produces 151 pieces or more in a day, he gets 32 cents for all pieces assembled that day. If John Cook assembled 140 pieces on Monday and 175 pieces on Tuesday, find his pay for each of those two days.

Monday **$** 39.20

Tuesday **$** 56.00

4. The Tennis Stringer Company pays its workers on a differential piece-rate basis, with a base pay of $3.75 per hour. For stringing eight or fewer rackets a day, the employee gets $1.80 extra per racket strung. The employee who strings 9 through 12 rackets in a day gets $2.05 extra for each racket strung, while an employee who strings over 12 rackets in a day gets $2.35 extra per racket strung. Determine the gross earnings for an 8-hour day for employees A, B, and C, if they string 11 rackets, 7 rackets, and 15 rackets, respectively.

A. **$** ______________________

B. **$** ______________________

C. **$** ______________________

5. Jack O'Shaughnessy picks pears off trees. He works 50 hours a week and receives $3.75 an hour. In addition, he gets 9 cents for each carton of pears that he packs. Find his gross pay for a week in which he packed 480 cartons.

$ ___

6. Rob Mackey packs fruit for shipment. He gets a minimum pay of $4 per hour for an 8-hour day. However, if he packs in excess of 150 boxes in a day, he gets 120 percent of his regular hourly pay plus a bonus of 50 cents for each box he packs in excess of 150. Determine his gross wages for an 8-hour day if he packs *(a)* 140 boxes, *(b)* 165 boxes.

(a) $ ___

(b) $ ___

7. The employees of the assembly department of the Deluxe Auto Company receive a group bonus if the percent of total labor costs to sales for the current year is less than in the previous year. The bonus is 40 percent of the labor-cost savings in comparison to the prior year. Last year, labor costs in the department were $83,000 and total sales amounted to $415,000, while this year labor costs were $90,000 and sales were $520,000. Determine the total group bonus to the employees.

$ ___

8. Employees in the bottling department of the Purified Water Company receive a base pay of $4.80 per hour. In addition, the employees get a bonus of 75 percent of one hour's pay for each box of 25 bottles filled in excess of 200, while the employee's supervisor gets a bonus of 25 percent of the employee's hourly pay for each excess box. If employee A fills 190 bottles and employee B fills 250 bottles in an 8-hour day, determine *(a)* the gross pay earned by A, *(b)* the gross pay earned by B, and *(c)* the bonus earned by B's supervisor.

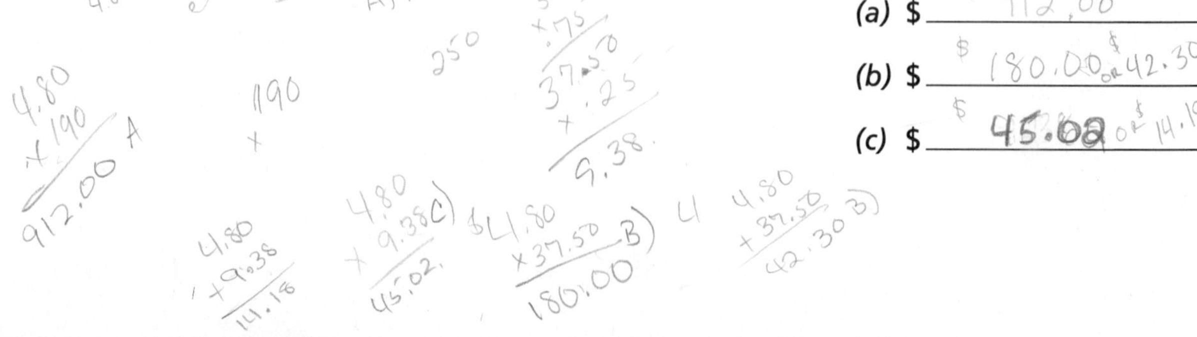

(a) $ ___

(b) $ ___

(c) $ ___

Multiple Sports with Amy Hengst, Accountant

Early in March 1991, Amy asks you to determine the gross wages for the previous month for those employees who are paid monthly. In addition to Amy's February monthly salary of $2,400, you review the February summary sheets of four other employees who are paid monthly.

Bernice Bedell and Anthony Dimauro are salespeople in the store. They each receive a salary of $1,200 per month plus a 6 percent commission on dollar sales. Bedell rang up sales of $15,210 in February; Dimauro had sales totaling $11,490.

Rene Perez sells sporting goods for Multiple Sports to various retail outlets in the surrounding region. He works strictly on a commission basis. He receives a monthly commission of 5 percent on sales up to $10,000, $7\frac{1}{2}$ percent on sales between $10,000 and $20,000, and 9 percent on sales in excess of $20,000. He also received a travel advance of $400 for February. Rene has February sales of $29,210 and incurs travel expenses of $424.

Victoria Powers strings tennis rackets. She receives a base salary of $500 for the month. In addition, she gets paid $3 for each racket strung with nylon and $5 for each racket strung with gut. During February she strung 315 rackets with gut and 198 rackets with nylon. For February, determine the gross pay earned by Bedell, Dimauro, and Powers, and the amount due Perez.

Bedell ____________

Dimauro ____________

Powers ____________

Perez ____________

% − × + $ ÷ +

Chapter 15

Payroll Deductions

I could live with my income—if Uncle Sam could live without it.

Learning Goals

Upon completion of this chapter, you should be able to:

1. Differentiate between gross and net pay.
2. Distinguish between voluntary and involuntary withholdings.
3. Calculate the FICA tax withheld on an employee's paycheck.
4. Note the changes in the FICA tax rates since enactment of the Social Security Act.
5. Determine if an employee has paid the maximum FICA tax for the year.
6. Understand that the employer matches the employee's FICA tax.
7. Solve for the amount of refund if an employee pays more than the maximum FICA tax for the year by working on two or more jobs.
8. Distinguish between FICA taxes on wages and self-employment tax on self-employed net income.
9. Figure the self-employment tax on self-employment net income.
10. Determine the amount owed on self-employment tax if wages and self-employment income combined exceed the maximum earnings subject to social security tax for the calendar year.

Deductions to Arrive at Net Pay

Most employees take home considerably less than their gross earnings. The main amounts deducted from most employees' earnings are for social security and federal, state, and local income taxes. A few states, California, New Jersey, New York, and Rhode Island, have disability insurance contributions paid by the employees. In addition, there are the so-called voluntary withholdings for such things as pension plans, union dues, charitable organizations, and insurance programs.

Social Security Tax

The Social Security Act allows qualified workers who retire after reaching a certain age to receive regular monthly payments and medical benefits. Funds to pay these benefits are obtained by tax levies as prescribed under the Federal Insurance Contributions Act, more commonly referred to as FICA.

This tax is paid for by a tax on an employee's earnings, with a matching contribution by the employer. If one is self-employed, the tax is assessed on the net earnings from that person's business, trade, or profession.

The employees' contributions are withheld from their wages each pay period. The employer must send the employees' contributions, and the employer's matching contribution, as well as the employees' federal income tax withheld, to the Internal Revenue Service by no later than the month following the end of each quarter. However, if at the end of any month the total undeposited taxes are $500 or more, but less than $3,000, the taxes must be deposited within 15 days after the end of the current month. If the undeposited taxes exceed $3,000 during designated times of a month, the deposits must be made at preset times during that month. A self-employed person's tax payment is payable yearly upon filing his or her federal income tax return.

Vital Statistics Recorded in 1986

	(in thousands)
Live births	3,731
Deaths	2,099
Marriages	2,400
Divorces	1,159

Life expectancy at birth:

Male	73.3 years
Female	78.3

U.S. Bureau of the Census, *Statistical Abstract of the United States*: 1988 (108th edition) Washington, DC.

A distinction should be made between employees and self-employed individuals, though occasionally the distinction is difficult to determine. A self-employed person, or independent contractor, is one who renders services to another individual or business for a fee but is not controlled or directed by the client. The fee paid to an independent contractor is not subject to payroll withholding taxes.

The table on page 170 shows the FICA rates that have been in effect since enactment of the Social Security Act. Since social security tax rates and maximum earnings subject to this tax are changed frequently by Congress, this text will use the tax rates and ceilings projected for 1990. Employees: 7.65 percent on the first $48,000, and self-employed: 15.3 percent on the first $48,000. Just before publication the ceiling was raised to $50,400.

An employee's Individual Earnings Record provides a running record each year of his or her hours worked, gross earnings, payroll deductions, and net pay. This record tells when an employee has earned $48,000 and is no longer subject to deductions for FICA taxes. It also supplies the information that must be given to each employee by no later than January 31 of the following year on a Form W-2, as illustrated in Chapter 16 on page 182.

Each employer must withhold, and match, at the going rate, the FICA tax until an employee has reached the maximum for a calendar year. The tax is on the amount paid in wages and is assessed in the year the wages are paid.

Example 1. John French earns $975 a week during the entire year. THe employer will withhold $74.59 a week for the first 49 weeks (7.65% of $975). Since Mr. French has earned $47,775 after 49 weeks, only $225 out of his $975 gross pay in the following week will be subject to social security withholding. If an employer withholds more than the maximum per year on an employee, the employer must return the excess withholding to the employee.

Example 2. In example 1, if December 31 should fall on a Friday, the employer would not withhold any additional social security tax if the employee was paid that day. However, if the employee is paid the following Monday, the employer would start withholding again at the rates applicable to the new year, even though Mr. French earned the money in the previous calendar year.

U.S. Population—1986

	(in millions)
Under age 5	18.2
5–17	45.1
18–24	27.7
25–34	42.8
35–44	33.1
45–64	45.0
65 and over	29.2

U.S. Bureau of the Census, *Statistical Abstract of the United States*: 1988 (108th edition) Washington, DC.

If an employee has more than one employer during a calendar year, each employer must withhold at the going rate until the employee reaches the maximum amount with that employer. This could result in an employee paying a total FICA tax in excess of the legal requirement. Any excess payments by the employee, as indicated by the combined figures on the Form W-2s submitted by the employers, can be applied by the employee as a credit on his or her federal income tax return. However, the employers cannot claim a refund for their combined excess contribution.

Example 3. Nena Alonzo worked for two employers during the current year. She earned $33,000 with the first employer and $20,000 with the second employer. The first employer withheld $2,524.50 for FICA ($33,000 × 7.65%), while the second employer withheld $1,530 ($20,000 × 7.65%). Each employer contributed a matching amount to the federal government. When filing her tax return in the early part of the following year, Mrs. Alonzo claimed a tax credit of $382.50 ($53,000 − $48,000 = $5,000 × 7.65%) for excess social security payments. The two employers will receive no tax refund or credit.

If an individual has earnings as an employee and as a self-employed person during the same calendar year, FICA tax on wages earned as an employee are withheld each paycheck. At the end of the year, any self-employed net earnings that will bring the total earnings up to the maximum of $48,000 will be subject to the self-employment tax. This is the case even if the self-employment earnings occurred first, because the employee taxes on earnings are the first paid.

Social Security Tax

Year	Wage Limitation	Employee: Tax Rate (Percent)	Employee: Maximum Amount of Tax	Self-Employed: Tax Rate (Percent)	Self-Employed: Maximum Amount of Tax
1937–49	$ 3,000	1.0 %	$ 30.00	*	*
1950	3,000	1.5	45.00	*	*
1951–53	3,600	1.5	54.00	2.25%	$ 81.00
1954	3,600	2.0	72.00	3.0	108.00
1955–56	4,200	2.0	84.00	3.0	126.00
1957–58	4,200	2.25	94.50	3.375	141.75
1959	4,800	2.5	120.00	3.75	180.00
1960–61	4,800	3.0	144.00	4.5	216.00
1962	4,800	3.125	150.00	4.7	225.60
1963–65	4,800	3.625	174.00	5.4	259.20
1966	6,600	4.2	277.20	6.15	405.90
1967	6,600	4.4	290.40	6.4	422.40
1968	7,800	4.4	343.20	6.4	499.20
1969–70	7,800	4.8	374.40	6.9	538.20
1971	7,800	5.2	405.60	7.5	585.00
1972	9,000	5.2	468.00	7.5	675.00
1973	10,800	5.85	631.80	8.0	864.00
1974	13,200	5.85	772.20	7.9	1,042.80
1975	14,100	5.85	824.85	7.9	1,113.90
1976	15,300	5.85	895.05	7.9	1,208.70
1977	16,500	5.85	965.25	7.9	1,303.50
1978	17,700	6.05	1,070.85	8.1	1,433.70
1979	22,900	6.13	1,403.77	8.1	1,854.90
1980	25,900	6.13	1,587.67	8.1	2,097.90
1981	29,700	6.65	1,975.05	9.3	2,762.10
1982	32,400	6.70	2,170.80	9.35	3,029.40
1983	35,700	6.70	2,391.90	9.35	3,337.95
1984	37,800	6.70†	2,532.60	11.3	4,271.40
1985	39,600	7.05	2,791.80	11.7	4,633.20
1986	42,000	7.15	3,003.00	12.3	5,166.00
1987	43,800	7.15	3,131.70	12.3	5,387.40
1988	45,000	7.51	3,379.50	13.02	5,859.00
1989	48,000	7.51	3,604.80	13.02	6,249.60
1990	50,400	7.65	3,855.60	15.3	7,711.20

* Self-employed persons were not covered until 1951.
† For 1984, the employer rate was 7%.

Example 4. Dick Szukalski had his own appliance repair shop for the first eight months of the year and had net earnings of $25,000. During the last four months of the year he worked as an employee and earned $25,950. Since social security tax of $1,985.18 on his earnings as an employee has already been withheld ($25,950 × 7.65%), Mr. Szukalski will have to pay a self-employment tax of $3,373.65 on his federal income tax return ($22,050 × 15.3%).

Disability Insurance

In some states, employees are required to contribute to a disability insurance (SDI) fund. This insurance tax provides weekly compensation to disabled employees and certain hospital benefits.

The disability deduction rates and maximum amounts subject to withholding vary in the four states requiring this insurance. In California, the present rate varies each year on the first $21,900 earned. As with the FICA tax, each employer must withhold from gross pay until earnings reach $21,900 during a given calendar year. If an employee has two or more employers and has paid more than the maximum in the calendar year, the excess payments can be applied by the employee as a credit on his or her state income tax return.

Example 1. Roy Avalos is an employee in California. He had two jobs during the current year. On the first job he had gross earnings of $15,000, while on the second job he earned $10,000. Find *(a)* the amount of disability insurance withheld by each employer, and *(b)* the amount of refund he can claim, assuming a rate of 1 percent.

(a) First job: $15,000 × .01 = $150.00
Second job: $10,000 × .01 = $100.00
Total withheld $250.00
(b) Refund of $31.00 ($25,000 − $21,900 = $3,100 × .01) = $31.00

"I'd like to give you a raise, but you know what they say about a fool and his money."

From *The Wall Street Journal*, with permission of Cartoon Features Syndicate.

Student Review

In the following problems assume an FICA tax rate of 7.65 percent for employees and 15.3 percent for self-employed individuals on the first $48,000, and an SDI rate of 1.2 percent on the first $21,900.

1. Daniel Hayes earns $410 a week. Determine the amount withheld from his weekly paycheck for FICA taxes.

$____________

2. Doris Lin earns $2,150 semimonthly. Determine the amount of FICA taxes withheld *(a)* each paycheck for the first 22 pay periods and *(b)* for the 23rd pay period of the year.

(a) $____________

(b) $____________

3. Norb Ludkey had two jobs during the current year. On the first job he earned $23,250 and on the second job he earned $27,710. Determine the amount of credit he can claim *(a)* on his federal return for excess FICA tax withheld, and *(b)* on his state return for excess SDI withheld.

(a) $____________

(b) $____________

4. Clare Thompson operates her own shoe store. She had net earnings of $37,315 for the year. Determine the self-employment tax she must include on her federal income tax return.

$____________

5. Ulf Wostner had his own computer software business early in the year and had net earnings of $19,550. He sold the business in June and was hired as a computer software salesman for the rest of the year. His salary and commissions totaled $30,800 on his Form W-2. Determine his FICA taxes *(a)* withheld as an employee and *(b)* to be paid as a self-employed person.

(a) $____________

(b) $____________

Solutions to Student Review

1. $410.00
× .0765
$ 31.37

$ 31.37

2. *(a)* $2,150.00
× .0765
$ 164.48

(b) $700.00
× .0765
$ 53.55

(a) $ 164.48

(b) $ 53.55

3. *(a)* $23,250 + 27,710 = $50,960; $50,960 − 48,000 = $ 2,960; $2,960.00 × .0765 = $ 226.44

$23,250	$50,960	$2,960.00
+ 27,710	− 48,000	× .0765
$50,960	$ 2,960	$ 226.44

(b) $21,900.00
× .012
$ 262.80

(a) $ 226.44

(b) $ 262.80

4. $37,315.00
× .153
$ 5,709.20

$ 5,709.20

5. *(a)* $30,800.00
× .0765
$ 2,356.20

(b)

$48,000	$17,200.00
− 30,800	× .153
$17,200	$ 2,631.60

(a) $ 2,356.20

(b) $ 2,631.60

Assignment 15–1

Payroll Deductions

Name ______________________

Date ______________________

In the following problems, assume a rate of 7.65 percent for employees on the first $48,000:

A. Solve the following problems:

1. Peter Taylor earns $350 a week. Determine the amount withheld weekly from his paycheck for FICA taxes.

   $ ______________

2. Maureen Kessler earns $450 every two weeks. Determine the amount withheld biweekly from her paycheck for FICA taxes.

   $ ______________

3. Bradley Hamilton earns $945 a week. Determine the amount of FICA taxes withheld *(a) each* week for the first 50 weeks, *(b)* for the 51st week, and *(c)* for the year.

   (a) $ ______________

   (b) $ ______________

   (c) $ ______________

4. Tom Kawakami earns $1,975 biweekly. Determine the amount of FICA taxes withheld *(a) each* paycheck for the first 24 pay periods, and *(b)* for the 25th pay period.

   (a) $ ______________

   (b) $ ______________

5. Jennifer Bowman had two jobs during the year. In the first job she earned $29,600, and in the second job she earned $20,900. Determine the amount of FICA tax withheld on *(a)* job 1, and *(b)* job 2, and the amount of credit *(c)* she can claim on her federal income tax return and *(d)* her employers can claim.

   (a) $ ______________

   (b) $ ______________

   (c) $ ______________

   (d) $ ______________

6. Melinda Owens earned $980 a week for the entire calendar year and is paid each Friday. *(a)* If December 31 falls on a Friday, determine the amount of FICA tax withheld by her employer. *(b)* If December 31 falls on a Tuesday, determine the amount her employer will withhold from her Friday paycheck for FICA taxes.

(a) $______________

(b) $______________

7. Mary Haworth earns $1,700 a month. Determine the amount deducted from her gross salary for FICA taxes for the month of October.

$______________

8. Barry Bloom earned $2,400 a month during the entire 1989 year. In 1990, with a 10 percent pay increase, he earned $2,640 each month for the entire year. If the company always pays on the first working day of the following month, determine the total amount of FICA withheld from Mr. Bloom's paycheck for 1990, as reported on his Form W-2.

$______________

B. For each of the following employees, determine the amount of FICA taxes withheld for the week:

Employee	*Weekly Wage*	*Prior Earnings*	*FICA Withheld*
Arden	$375	$18,325	______
Blake	$990	$49,400	______
Carter	$935	$47,685	______
Dome	$820	$11,735	______

Assignment 15–2

Payroll Deductions

Name ____________________

Date ____________________

A. In the following problems, assume an FICA rate of 7.65 percent for employees and 15.3 percent for self-employed persons on the first $48,000 and a state disability insurance (SDI) rate of 0.8 percent on the first $21,900:

1. Lisa Green has her own apparel shop. She had net earnings of $8,450 for the current year. Determine the self-employment tax she must include on her federal income tax return.

$ ____________

2. Terry Krim operates his own liquor store. He had net earnings of $49,600 for the year. Determine the self-employment tax he must include on his federal income tax return.

$ ____________

3. Karen Freed earned $10,100 as an employee during the first part of the year. Then she started her own business and earned $7,450 for the balance of the year. Determine her FICA taxes *(a)* as an employee and *(b)* as a self-employed person.

(a) $ ____________

(b) $ ____________

4. Bertha Douglas earned $34,145 as an employee during the first part of the year. Later, she went into business for herself and earned $14,560 for the balance of the year. Determine her FICA taxes *(a)* as an employee, and *(b)* as a self-employed individual.

(a) $ ____________

(b) $ ____________

5. Duke Clayton was self-employed during the first part of the year and had net earnings of $23,475. Beginning in May, he went to work for a company and earned $29,490 for the balance of the year. Determine his FICA taxes *(a)* as a self-employed person and *(b)* as an employee.

(a) $ ____________

(b) $ ____________

6. Robert Plotkowski is an employee in California. Going into the current week his gross earnings were $11,248. During the current week he earned $216. Determine the amount withheld this week from his paycheck for *(a)* FICA taxes and *(b)* state disability insurance.

(a) $____________

(b) $____________

7. Marc Benioff receives a biweekly paycheck. Up to the current pay period, he had earned $21,842. If his gross pay for the current biweekly pay period is $432, determine the amount withheld from his paycheck for *(a)* FICA taxes and *(b)* state disability insurance.

(a) $____________

(a) $____________

8. Irwin Phillips earns $525 a week as an emploee. Determine the amount of state disability insurance withheld during *(a)* each of the first 41 weeks and *(b)* the 42nd week.

(a) $____________

(b) $____________

9. Nadine Anohin is paid weekly. Assuming that her entire gross wage is subject to FICA withholding, determine her gross wage for the week if the amount of her FICA withholding is $13.23.

$____________

10. Steve Moorhouse worked $45\frac{1}{2}$ hours during the first week of the year. He earned $6.21 per hour, plus time and a half for hours worked in excess of 40 per week. Find the amount withheld for *(a)* FICA taxes and *(b)* state disability insurance.

(a) $____________

(b) $____________

Multiple Sports with Amy Hengst, Accountant

As a service to its employees, Multiple Sports provides information with regard to retirement and other fringe benefits offered by the company as well as payroll tax assistance. Amy designates you to answer employee questions with regard to the various voluntary and involuntary withholdings and their possible effects on the employees' personal income tax returns. You are to assume an FICA tax rate of 7.65 percent on the first $48,000 and a state disability insurance (SDI) rate of 0.9 percent on the first $21,900 for 1990 and 1991. In January and February 1991, you received the following inquiries, among others:

1. Sandra Sanchez earned $640 biweekly for the entire year in 1990. She wants to know *(a)* how much in FICA taxes should have been withheld each paycheck and, on her Form W–2, the total indicated amount withheld for *(b)* FICA and *(c)* SDI.

(a) $________________

(b) $________________

(c) $________________

2. Ann Kelly started working for Multiple Sports in August 1990. Her 1990 W–2 shows that her gross wage from Multiple Sports was $16,492. Previously in 1990, she was self-employed and earned $34,620. She wants to know if she must pay self-employment tax and, if so, how much.

$________________

3. Margaret Weiss also started working at Multiple Sports in August 1990. Her W–2 from her previous job shows that she had gross wages of $36,925 in 1990, while her 1990 W–2 from Multiple Sports shows gross wages of $13,710. She wants to know how much of a refund she can claim *(a)* on her federal income tax return for excess FICA tax withheld and *(b)* on her California income tax return for excess SDI withheld.

(a) $________________

(b) $________________

4. Kathleen Shanahan, the executive vice president of Multiple Sports, earns $2,100 semimonthly. She noted that her FICA withholdings decreased on her 23rd paycheck. She wants to know how much FICA tax should have been withheld *(a)* from *each* of the first 22 paychecks, *(b)* from her 23rd paycheck, *(c)* from her 24th paycheck if paid on December 31, 1990, and *(d)* from her 24th paycheck if paid on January 2, 1991.

(a) $__________

(b) $__________

(c) __________

(d) $__________

% − X + $ ÷ +

Chapter 16

Federal Income Tax Withholding

I asked the IRS if birth control pills were deductible—only if they don't work.

Learning Goals

Upon completion of this chapter, you should be able to:

1. Understand how to read a Form W-2.
2. Realize the significance of a Form W-4.
3. Recognize the effect of exemption allowances on federal income tax withheld.
4. Calculate the amount of federal income tax withheld from an employee's gross wage by using the wage-bracket tables.
5. Calculate the amount of federal income tax withheld by using the percentage-method withholding table.
6. Understand the similarities of the wage-bracket and percentage methods for federal income tax withholding.

Since many individual wage earners could not be expected to save enough money to pay their federal income tax each year, Congress passed a payroll withholding plan. The employer must withhold from each employee's wage a certain percent or amount which is to be deposited with a Federal Reserve bank or the district office of the Director of Internal Revenue and credited to the employee's account. The employer, in effect, acts as the tax collecting agent for the federal government.

On or before January 31 of the following year, or within 30 days after the last wages are paid when an employee's employment terminates, the employer must give each employee at least two copies of Form W-2. This form shows the total wages and other compensation, as well as income tax and social security tax withheld. Employees attach copy B to their personal federal income tax returns and keep the employee's copy for their own records.

The amount of federal income tax withheld depends on the amount of the earnings, the pay period, and the number of allowances claimed by the employee. Each employee must complete and sign a withholding allowance certificate, Form W-4. If the employee does not complete Form W-4, the employer must treat the employee as a single person, claiming no allowances.

Prior to the Tax Reform Act of 1969, each exemption claimed by taxpayers on their federal tax return reduced taxable income by $600. Effective July 1, 1970, each exemption allowed a deduction from taxable income of $650, with an additional increase to $675 provided in 1971. Beginning in 1972, each exemption was worth a reduction from taxable income of $750. Starting in 1979, each exemption reduced taxable income by $1,000. An inflation factor raised the 1985 exemption to $1040 and the 1986 exemption to $1,080. The exemption was increased to $1900 in 1987, $1,950 in 1988, and $2,000 in 1989.

Individuals are allowed an exemption for themselves, their spouse, and each person who qualifies as a dependent of the taxpayer. Generally speaking, a dependent is a person who meets the following tests:

States with the Most/Least Physicians per 100,000 Population—1985

Most	
1. Maryland	315
2. Massachusetts	311
3. New York	298
4. Connecticut	282
5. California	242
Least	
1. Mississippi	119
2. Idaho	120
3. Wyoming	130
4. Alaska	132
5. South Dakota	132

U.S. Bureau of the Census, *Statistical Abstract of the United States*: 1988 (108th edition) Washington, D.C.

1. Receives over one-half of his or her support from the taxpayer.
2. Is either closely related to the taxpayer or lives in the taxpayer's home, as a member of the family for the entire year.
3. Has gross income during the year of less than $2,000; unless he or she is a child of the taxpayer and is under 19 years of age; or, if 19 or older, is a full-time student of an accredited educational institution during all or part of at least five months of the year.

In addition, a taxpayer may claim an additional standard deduction if he or she is blind (noncorrectible vision of 20–200 or worse) or is 65 years of age or older.

The federal income tax is a progressive tax. This means that the tax rate increases for each additional increment of taxable income. The amounts to be withheld by an employer are determined on a graduated scale. If employees had no outside income, took the standard deduction, and

1 Control number

OMB No. 1545-0008

2 Employer's name, address, and ZIP code
Sandra L. Frankel, DDS
458 Victory Way
Madison, Wisconsin 53701

3 Employer's identification number 43-1976139
4 Employer's state I.D. number
5 Statutory employee ☐ Deceased ☐ Pension plan ☐ Legal rep. ☐ 942 emp. ☐ Subtotal ☐ Deferred compensation ☐ Void ☐
6 Allocated tips
7 Advance EIC payment

8 Employee's social security number 567-54-2696
9 Federal income tax withheld 3,248.71
10 Wages, tips, other compensation 27,186.00
11 Social security tax withheld 2,079.73

12 Employee's name, address, and ZIP code
Curtis Joe
821 Hyde Rd.
Madison, Wisconsin 53701

13 Social security wages 27,186
14 Social security tips
16
16a Fringe benefits incl. in Box 10
17 State income tax
18 State wages, tips, etc.
19 Name of state
20 Local income tax
21 Local wages, tips, etc.
22 Name of locality

Form **W-2 Wage and Tax Statement 1989**
This information is being furnished to the Internal Revenue Service.
Copy B To be filed with employee's FEDERAL tax return
Dept. of the Treasury—IRS

Form **W-4** Department of the Treasury Internal Revenue Service

Employee's Withholding Allowance Certificate

► For Privacy Act and Paperwork Reduction Act Notice, see reverse.

OMB No. 1545-0010 **1989**

1 Type or print your first name and middle initial — Last name: Georgia Morris
2 Your social security number: 107-63-8712

Home address (number and street or rural route): 355 Victory Blvd.

City or town, state, and ZIP code: Miami, Florida 33101

3 Marital Status: ☐ Single ☒ Married ☐ Married, but withhold at higher Single rate.
Note: *If married, but legally separated, or spouse is a nonresident alien, check the Single box.*

4 Total number of allowances you are claiming (from line G above or from the Worksheets on back if they apply) . . . 4 | 2

5 Additional amount, if any, you want deducted from each pay . . . 5 | $

6 I claim exemption from withholding and I certify that I meet ALL of the following conditions for exemption:

- Last year I had a right to a refund of **ALL** Federal income tax withheld because I had **NO** tax liability; **AND**
- This year I expect a refund of **ALL** Federal income tax withheld because I expect to have **NO** tax liability; **AND**
- This year if my income exceeds $500 and includes nonwage income, another person cannot claim me as a dependent.

If you meet all of the above conditions, enter the year effective and "EXEMPT" here . . . . . ► 6 | 19

7 Are you a full-time student? (**Note:** *Full-time students are not automatically exempt.*) . . . . . 7 ☐ Yes ☐ No

Under penalties of perjury, I certify that I am entitled to the number of withholding allowances claimed on this certificate or entitled to claim exempt status.

Employee's signature ► Georgia Morris Date ► November 2, 1989

claimed the same exemptions on their tax return and their Form W-4, then the amount of tax withheld should closely approximate their tax liability for the year. If the employee has substantial nonemployee income or substantial itemized deductions, then the Form W-4 should be modified.

Wages covered by income tax and social security withholding generally consist of all remuneration, whether in cash or other forms, paid to an employee for services performed. The term *wages* covers all types of employee remuneration, including salaries, vacation allowances, bonuses, and commissions. Wages paid in any form other than money are measured by the fair market value of the goods.

Income Tax Withholding— Wage-Bracket Method

Most employers find it convenient to determine income tax withholding from tables prepared by the Internal Revenue Service. The tables, which are subject to periodic changes as tax rates and exemptions are changed, are available for the following time periods: weekly, biweekly, semimonthly, monthly, and daily or miscellaneous. In addition, separate tables are required for single persons and for married persons.

For illustrative and classroom use, the weekly wage-bracket tables for single persons and the monthly wage-bracket tables for married persons are on the following pages.

States with Highest/Lowest Crime Rate per 100,000 Population—1986

Highest	
1. Florida	8,228
2. Texas	7,408
3. Arizona	7,321
4. Oregon	7,081
5. Colorado	7,032
Lowest	
1. West Virginia	2,317
2. North Dakota	2,605
3. South Dakota	2,716
4. Kentucky	3,092
5. Pennsylvania	3,102

U.S. Bureau of the Census, *Statistical Abstract of the United States*: 1988 (108th edition) Washington, DC.

Example 1. Robert Berman, an office manager, received a salary of $470 a week. A single person, he claimed two exemptions. Determine the federal income tax withheld from his weekly paycheck.

Answer: $59.00

Example 2. Bernard Schaffer, a printer, receives a monthly salary of $1,650. He is married and claims four exemptions. Determine the federal income tax withheld from his monthly paycheck.

Answer: $109.00

SINGLE Persons–**WEEKLY** Payroll Period

(For Wages Paid After December 1988)

And the wages are–		And the number of withholding allowances claimed is–										
At least	But less than	0	1	2	3	4	5	6	7	8	9	10
		The amount of income tax to be withheld shall be–										
$0	$25	$0	$0	$0	$0	$0	$0	$0	$0	$0	$0	$0
25	30	1	0	0	0	0	0	0	0	0	0	0
30	35	2	0	0	0	0	0	0	0	0	0	0
35	40	2	0	0	0	0	0	0	0	0	0	0
40	45	3	0	0	0	0	0	0	0	0	0	0
45	50	4	0	0	0	0	0	0	0	0	0	0
50	55	5	0	0	0	0	0	0	0	0	0	0
55	60	5	0	0	0	0	0	0	0	0	0	0
60	65	6	0	0	0	0	0	0	0	0	0	0
65	70	7	1	0	0	0	0	0	0	0	0	0
70	75	8	2	0	0	0	0	0	0	0	0	0
75	80	8	3	0	0	0	0	0	0	0	0	0
80	85	9	3	0	0	0	0	0	0	0	0	0
85	90	10	4	0	0	0	0	0	0	0	0	0
90	95	11	5	0	0	0	0	0	0	0	0	0
95	100	11	6	0	0	0	0	0	0	0	0	0
100	105	12	6	1	0	0	0	0	0	0	0	0
105	110	13	7	1	0	0	0	0	0	0	0	0
110	115	14	8	2	0	0	0	0	0	0	0	0
115	120	14	9	3	0	0	0	0	0	0	0	0
120	125	15	9	4	0	0	0	0	0	0	0	0
125	130	16	10	4	0	0	0	0	0	0	0	0
130	135	17	11	5	0	0	0	0	0	0	0	0
135	140	17	12	6	0	0	0	0	0	0	0	0
140	145	18	12	7	1	0	0	0	0	0	0	0
145	150	19	13	7	2	0	0	0	0	0	0	0
150	155	20	14	8	2	0	0	0	0	0	0	0
155	160	20	15	9	3	0	0	0	0	0	0	0
160	165	21	15	10	4	0	0	0	0	0	0	0
165	170	22	16	10	5	0	0	0	0	0	0	0
170	175	23	17	11	5	0	0	0	0	0	0	0
175	180	23	18	12	6	0	0	0	0	0	0	0
180	185	24	18	13	7	1	0	0	0	0	0	0
185	190	25	19	13	8	2	0	0	0	0	0	0
190	195	26	20	14	8	3	0	0	0	0	0	0
195	200	26	21	15	9	3	0	0	0	0	0	0
200	210	28	22	16	10	5	0	0	0	0	0	0
210	220	29	23	18	12	6	0	0	0	0	0	0
220	230	31	25	19	13	8	2	0	0	0	0	0
230	240	32	26	21	15	9	3	0	0	0	0	0
240	250	34	28	22	16	11	5	0	0	0	0	0
250	260	35	29	24	18	12	6	0	0	0	0	0
260	270	37	31	25	19	14	8	2	0	0	0	0
270	280	38	32	27	21	15	9	3	0	0	0	0
280	290	40	34	28	22	17	11	5	0	0	0	0
290	300	41	35	30	24	18	12	6	1	0	0	0
300	310	43	37	31	25	20	14	8	2	0	0	0
310	320	44	38	33	27	21	15	9	4	0	0	0
320	330	46	40	34	28	23	17	11	5	0	0	0
330	340	47	41	36	30	24	18	12	7	1	0	0
340	350	49	43	37	31	26	20	14	8	2	0	0
350	360	50	44	39	33	27	21	15	10	4	0	0
360	370	52	46	40	34	29	23	17	11	5	0	0
370	380	53	47	42	36	30	24	18	13	7	1	0
380	390	56	49	43	37	32	26	20	14	8	3	0
390	400	58	50	45	39	33	27	21	16	10	4	0
400	410	61	52	46	40	35	29	23	17	11	6	0
410	420	64	53	48	42	36	30	24	19	13	7	1
420	430	67	56	49	43	38	32	26	20	14	9	3
430	440	70	59	51	45	39	33	27	22	16	10	4
440	450	72	62	52	46	41	35	29	23	17	12	6
450	460	75	64	54	48	42	36	30	25	19	13	7
460	470	78	67	56	49	44	38	32	26	20	15	9
470	480	81	70	59	51	45	39	33	28	22	16	10
480	490	84	73	62	52	47	41	35	29	23	18	12
490	500	86	76	65	54	48	42	36	31	25	19	13
500	510	89	78	68	57	50	44	38	32	26	21	15
510	520	92	81	70	60	51	45	39	34	28	22	16
520	530	95	84	73	62	53	47	41	35	29	24	18
530	540	98	87	76	65	54	48	42	37	31	25	19

Page 24

(Continued on next page)

SINGLE Persons–**WEEKLY** Payroll Period

(For Wages Paid After December 1988)

And the wages are–		And the number of withholding allowances claimed is–										
At least	But less than	0	1	2	3	4	5	6	7	8	9	10
		The amount of income tax to be withheld shall be–										
$540	$550	$100	$90	$79	$68	$57	$50	$44	$38	$32	$27	$21
550	560	103	92	82	71	60	51	45	40	34	28	22
560	570	106	95	84	74	63	53	47	41	35	30	24
570	580	109	98	87	76	66	55	48	43	37	31	25
580	590	112	101	90	79	68	58	50	44	38	33	27
590	600	114	104	93	82	71	60	51	46	40	34	28
600	610	117	106	96	85	74	63	53	47	41	36	30
610	620	120	109	98	88	77	66	55	49	43	37	31
620	630	123	112	101	90	80	69	58	50	44	39	33
630	640	126	115	104	93	82	72	61	52	46	40	34
640	650	128	118	107	96	85	74	64	53	47	42	36
650	660	131	120	110	99	88	77	66	56	49	43	37
660	670	134	123	112	102	91	80	69	59	50	45	39
670	680	137	126	115	104	94	83	72	61	52	46	40
680	690	140	129	118	107	96	86	75	64	53	48	42
690	700	142	132	121	110	99	88	78	67	56	49	43
700	710	145	134	124	113	102	91	80	70	59	51	45
710	720	148	137	126	116	105	94	83	73	62	52	46
720	730	151	140	129	118	108	97	86	75	65	54	48
730	740	154	143	132	121	110	100	89	78	67	57	49
740	750	156	146	135	124	113	102	92	81	70	59	51
750	760	159	148	138	127	116	105	94	84	73	62	52
760	770	162	151	140	130	119	108	97	87	76	65	54
770	780	165	154	143	132	122	111	100	89	79	68	57
780	790	168	157	146	135	124	114	103	92	81	71	60
790	800	170	160	149	138	127	116	106	95	84	73	63
800	810	173	162	152	141	130	119	108	98	87	76	65
810	820	176	165	154	144	133	122	111	101	90	79	68
820	830	179	168	157	146	136	125	114	103	93	82	71
830	840	182	171	160	149	138	128	117	106	95	85	74
840	850	184	174	163	152	141	130	120	109	98	87	77
850	860	187	176	166	155	144	133	122	112	101	90	79
860	870	190	179	168	158	147	136	125	115	104	93	82
870	880	193	182	171	160	150	139	128	117	107	96	85
880	890	196	185	174	163	152	142	131	120	109	99	88
890	900	199	188	177	166	155	144	134	123	112	101	91
900	910	202	190	180	169	158	147	136	126	115	104	93
910	920	205	193	182	172	161	150	139	129	118	107	96
920	930	209	196	185	174	164	153	142	131	121	110	99
930	940	212	199	188	177	166	156	145	134	123	113	102
940	950	215	203	191	180	169	158	148	137	126	115	105
950	960	219	206	194	183	172	161	150	140	129	118	107
960	970	222	209	197	186	175	164	153	143	132	121	110
970	980	225	213	200	188	178	167	156	145	135	124	113
980	990	229	216	203	191	180	170	159	148	137	127	116
990	1,000	232	219	206	194	183	172	162	151	140	129	119
1,000	1,010	235	222	210	197	186	175	164	154	143	132	121
1,010	1,020	238	226	213	200	189	178	167	157	146	135	124
1,020	1,030	242	229	216	204	192	181	170	159	149	138	127
1,030	1,040	245	232	220	207	194	184	173	162	151	141	130
1,040	1,050	248	236	223	210	198	186	176	165	154	143	133
1,050	1,060	252	239	226	214	201	189	178	168	157	146	135
1,060	1,070	255	242	230	217	204	192	181	171	160	149	138
1,070	1,080	258	246	233	220	207	195	184	173	163	152	141
1,080	1,090	262	249	236	223	211	198	187	176	165	155	144
1,090	1,100	265	252	239	227	214	201	190	179	168	157	147
1,100	1,110	268	255	243	230	217	205	192	182	171	160	149
1,110	1,120	271	259	246	233	221	208	195	185	174	163	152
1,120	1,130	275	262	249	237	224	211	199	187	177	166	155
1,130	1,140	278	265	253	240	227	215	202	190	179	169	158
1,140	1,150	281	269	256	243	231	218	205	193	182	171	161
1,150	1,160	285	272	259	247	234	221	208	196	185	174	163
1,160	1,170	288	275	263	250	237	224	212	199	188	177	166
1,170	1,180	291	279	266	253	240	228	215	202	191	180	169
1,180	1,190	295	282	269	256	244	231	218	206	193	183	172
1,190	1,200	298	285	272	260	247	234	222	209	196	185	175

$1,200 and over — Use Table 1(a) for a **SINGLE person** on page 22. Also see the instructions on page 20.

MARRIED Persons–**MONTHLY** Payroll Period

(For Wages Paid After December 1988)

And the wages are–		And the number of withholding allowances claimed is–										
At least	But less than	0	1	2	3	4	5	6	7	8	9	10
		The amount of income tax to be withheld shall be–										
$0	$270	$0	$0	$0	$0	$0	$0	$0	$0	$0	$0	$0
270	280	1	0	0	0	0	0	0	0	0	0	0
280	290	3	0	0	0	0	0	0	0	0	0	0
290	300	4	0	0	0	0	0	0	0	0	0	0
300	320	7	0	0	0	0	0	0	0	0	0	0
320	340	10	0	0	0	0	0	0	0	0	0	0
340	360	13	0	0	0	0	0	0	0	0	0	0
360	380	16	0	0	0	0	0	0	0	0	0	0
380	400	19	0	0	0	0	0	0	0	0	0	0
400	420	22	0	0	0	0	0	0	0	0	0	0
420	440	25	0	0	0	0	0	0	0	0	0	0
440	460	28	3	0	0	0	0	0	0	0	0	0
460	480	31	6	0	0	0	0	0	0	0	0	0
480	500	34	9	0	0	0	0	0	0	0	0	0
500	520	37	12	0	0	0	0	0	0	0	0	0
520	540	40	15	0	0	0	0	0	0	0	0	0
540	560	43	18	0	0	0	0	0	0	0	0	0
560	580	46	21	0	0	0	0	0	0	0	0	0
580	600	49	24	0	0	0	0	0	0	0	0	0
600	640	53	28	3	0	0	0	0	0	0	0	0
640	680	59	34	9	0	0	0	0	0	0	0	0
680	720	65	40	15	0	0	0	0	0	0	0	0
720	760	71	46	21	0	0	0	0	0	0	0	0
760	800	77	52	27	2	0	0	0	0	0	0	0
800	840	83	58	33	8	0	0	0	0	0	0	0
840	880	89	64	39	14	0	0	0	0	0	0	0
880	920	95	70	45	20	0	0	0	0	0	0	0
920	960	101	76	51	26	1	0	0	0	0	0	0
960	1,000	107	82	57	32	7	0	0	0	0	0	0
1,000	1,040	113	88	63	38	13	0	0	0	0	0	0
1,040	1,080	119	94	69	44	19	0	0	0	0	0	0
1,080	1,120	125	100	75	50	25	0	0	0	0	0	0
1,120	1,160	131	106	81	56	31	6	0	0	0	0	0
1,160	1,200	137	112	87	62	37	12	0	0	0	0	0
1,200	1,240	143	118	93	68	43	18	0	0	0	0	0
1,240	1,280	149	124	99	74	49	24	0	0	0	0	0
1,280	1,320	155	130	105	80	55	30	5	0	0	0	0
1,320	1,360	161	136	111	86	61	36	11	0	0	0	0
1,360	1,400	167	142	117	92	67	42	17	0	0	0	0
1,400	1,440	173	148	123	98	73	48	23	0	0	0	0
1,440	1,480	179	154	129	104	79	54	29	4	0	0	0
1,480	1,520	185	160	135	110	85	60	35	10	0	0	0
1,520	1,560	191	166	141	116	91	66	41	16	0	0	0
1,560	1,600	197	172	147	122	97	72	47	22	0	0	0
1,600	1,640	203	178	153	128	103	78	53	28	3	0	0
1,640	1,680	209	184	159	134	109	84	59	34	9	0	0
1,680	1,720	215	190	165	140	115	90	65	40	15	0	0
1,720	1,760	221	196	171	146	121	96	71	46	21	0	0
1,760	1,800	227	202	177	152	127	102	77	52	27	2	0
1,800	1,840	233	208	183	158	133	108	83	58	33	8	0
1,840	1,880	239	214	189	164	139	114	89	64	39	14	0
1,880	1,920	245	220	195	170	145	120	95	70	45	20	0
1,920	1,960	251	226	201	176	151	126	101	76	51	26	1
1,960	2,000	257	232	207	182	157	132	107	82	57	32	7
2,000	2,040	263	238	213	188	163	138	113	88	63	38	13
2,040	2,080	269	244	219	194	169	144	119	94	69	44	19
2,080	2,120	275	250	225	200	175	150	125	100	75	50	25
2,120	2,160	281	256	231	206	181	156	131	106	81	56	31
2,160	2,200	287	262	237	212	187	162	137	112	87	62	37
2,200	2,240	293	268	243	218	193	168	143	118	93	68	43
2,240	2,280	299	274	249	224	199	174	149	124	99	74	49
2,280	2,320	305	280	255	230	205	180	155	130	105	80	55
2,320	2,360	311	286	261	236	211	186	161	136	111	86	61
2,360	2,400	317	292	267	242	217	192	167	142	117	92	67
2,400	2,440	323	298	273	248	223	198	173	148	123	98	73
2,440	2,480	329	304	279	254	229	204	179	154	129	104	79
2,480	2,520	335	310	285	260	235	210	185	160	135	110	85
2,520	2,560	341	316	291	266	241	216	191	166	141	116	91
2,560	2,600	347	322	297	272	247	222	197	172	147	122	97
2,600	2,640	353	328	303	278	253	228	203	178	153	128	103

Page 38

(Continued on next page)

MARRIED Persons–**MONTHLY** Payroll Period

(For Wages Paid After December 1988)

And the wages are–		And the number of withholding allowances claimed is–										
At least	But less than	0	1	2	3	4	5	6	7	8	9	10
		The amount of income tax to be withheld shall be–										
$2,640	$2,680	$359	$334	$309	$284	$259	$234	$209	$184	$159	$134	$109
2,680	2,720	365	340	315	290	265	240	215	190	165	140	115
2,720	2,760	371	346	321	296	271	246	221	196	171	146	121
2,760	2,800	377	352	327	302	277	252	227	202	177	152	127
2,800	2,840	383	358	333	308	283	258	233	208	183	158	133
2,840	2,880	391	364	339	314	289	264	239	214	189	164	139
2,880	2,920	402	370	345	320	295	270	245	220	195	170	145
2,920	2,960	413	376	351	326	301	276	251	226	201	176	151
2,960	3,000	424	382	357	332	307	282	257	232	207	182	157
3,000	3,040	436	389	363	338	313	288	263	238	213	188	163
3,040	3,080	447	400	369	344	319	294	269	244	219	194	169
3,080	3,120	458	411	375	350	325	300	275	250	225	200	175
3,120	3,160	469	423	381	356	331	306	281	256	231	206	181
3,160	3,200	480	434	387	362	337	312	287	262	237	212	187
3,200	3,240	492	445	398	368	343	318	293	268	243	218	193
3,240	3,280	503	456	410	374	349	324	299	274	249	224	199
3,280	3,320	514	467	421	380	355	330	305	280	255	230	205
3,320	3,360	525	479	432	386	361	336	311	286	261	236	211
3,360	3,400	536	490	443	396	367	342	317	292	267	242	217
3,400	3,440	548	501	454	408	373	348	323	298	273	248	223
3,440	3,480	559	512	466	419	379	354	329	304	279	254	229
3,480	3,520	570	523	477	430	385	360	335	310	285	260	235
3,520	3,560	581	535	488	441	395	366	341	316	291	266	241
3,560	3,600	592	546	499	452	406	372	347	322	297	272	247
3,600	3,640	604	557	510	464	417	378	353	328	303	278	253
3,640	3,680	615	568	522	475	428	384	359	334	309	284	259
3,680	3,720	626	579	533	486	439	393	365	340	315	290	265
3,720	3,760	637	591	544	497	451	404	371	346	321	296	271
3,760	3,800	648	602	555	508	462	415	377	352	327	302	277
3,800	3,840	660	613	566	520	473	426	383	358	333	308	283
3,840	3,880	671	624	578	531	484	438	391	364	339	314	289
3,880	3,920	682	635	589	542	495	449	402	370	345	320	295
3,920	3,960	693	647	600	553	507	460	413	376	351	326	301
3,960	4,000	704	658	611	564	518	471	424	382	357	332	307
4,000	4,040	716	669	622	576	529	482	436	389	363	338	313
4,040	4,080	727	680	634	587	540	494	447	400	369	344	319
4,080	4,120	738	691	645	598	551	505	458	411	375	350	325
4,120	4,160	749	703	656	609	563	516	469	423	381	356	331
4,160	4,200	760	714	667	620	574	527	480	434	387	362	337
4,200	4,240	772	725	678	632	585	538	492	445	398	368	343
4,240	4,280	783	736	690	643	596	550	503	456	410	374	349
4,280	4,320	794	747	701	654	607	561	514	467	421	380	355
4,320	4,360	805	759	712	665	619	572	525	479	432	386	361
4,360	4,400	816	770	723	676	630	583	536	490	443	396	367
4,400	4,440	828	781	734	688	641	594	548	501	454	408	373
4,440	4,480	839	792	746	699	652	606	559	512	466	419	379
4,480	4,520	850	803	757	710	663	617	570	523	477	430	385
4,520	4,560	861	815	768	721	675	628	581	535	488	441	395
4,560	4,600	872	826	779	732	686	639	592	546	499	452	406
4,600	4,640	884	837	790	744	697	650	604	557	510	464	417
4,640	4,680	895	848	802	755	708	662	615	568	522	475	428
4,680	4,720	906	859	813	766	719	673	626	579	533	486	439
4,720	4,760	917	871	824	777	731	684	637	591	544	497	451
4,760	4,800	928	882	835	788	742	695	648	602	555	508	462
4,800	4,840	940	893	846	800	753	706	660	613	566	520	473
4,840	4,880	951	904	858	811	764	718	671	624	578	531	484
4,880	4,920	962	915	869	822	775	729	682	635	589	542	495
4,920	4,960	973	927	880	833	787	740	693	647	600	553	507
4,960	5,000	984	938	891	844	798	751	704	658	611	564	518
5,000	5,040	996	949	902	856	809	762	716	669	622	576	529
5,040	5,080	1,007	960	914	867	820	774	727	680	634	587	540
5,080	5,120	1,018	971	925	878	831	785	738	691	645	598	551
5,120	5,160	1,029	983	936	889	843	796	749	703	656	609	563
5,160	5,200	1,040	994	947	900	854	807	760	714	667	620	574
5,200	5,240	1,052	1,005	958	912	865	818	772	725	678	632	585

$5,240 and over — Use Table 4(b) for a **MARRIED person** on page 22. Also see the instructions on page 20.

Income Tax Withholding—Percentage method

Some employers prefer not to use the wage-bracket tables in computing the amount of income tax to be deducted and withheld from a payment of wages to an employee. Instead they will make a percentage computation based on the following percentage-method withholding table and the appropriate rate table:

Percentage-Method Income Tax Withholding Table

Payroll Period	Amount of One Withholding Allowance
Weekly	$ 38.46
Biweekly	76.92
Semimonthly	83.33
Monthly	166.67
Quarterly	500.00
Semiannually	1,000.00
Annually	2,000.00
Daily or miscellaneous (per day of such period)	7.69

The steps in computing the income tax to be withheld under the percentage method are:

1. Multiply the amount of one withholding allowance (see table above) by the number of allowances claimed by the employee.
2. Subtract the amount from the employee's wages.
3. Determine amount to be withheld from appropriate rate tables on pages 190–91.

Five Largest Military Contractors—1987

	($ billions)
McDonnell Douglas	$7.7
General Dynamics	7.0
General Electric	5.8
Lockheed	5.6
General Motors—Hughes	4.1

The Wall Street Journal

Example 3. Assume in example 1 that the employer of Robert Berman used the percentage method. Compute the income tax to be withheld.

1. Total wage payment		**$470.00**
2. Amount of one exemption:	**$38.46**	
3. Number of exemptions claimed on Form W-4	**2**	
4. Line 2 multiplied by line 3		**76.92**
5. Amount subject to withholding (line 1 minus line 4)		**$393.08**
6. Tax to be withheld on $393.08 from Table 1—single person:		
Tax on first $378		**$53.55**
Tax on remainder $15.08 × 28%		**4.22**
Total to be withheld		**$ 57.77**

It should be noted that in this situation, the percentage method provided for a slightly lower amount to be withheld.

In determining the amount of income tax to be deducted and withheld using the percentage method, an employer may change the last digit of the cents column to zero or round off the cents to the nearest dollar. For example, if an employee earns a weekly wage of $280.59, the employer may eliminate the last digit and determine the income tax on the basis of a wage payment of $280.50, or the tax may be determined on the basis of a wage payment of $281.

WEEK ENDING → September 29, 1990

	NAME	Exemptions	HOURS							TOTAL HOURS	RATE	EARNINGS			TOTAL WAGES	DEDUCTIONS						NET PAY
			SUN.	MON.	TUES.	WED.	THURS.	FRI.	SAT.			REGULAR	OVERTIME Prem.	OTHER		SOC. SEC.	U.S. WITH. TAX	STATE WITH. TAX	Ret.		Total	
1	Jean Leonard	M4		8	8	8	8	8		40	9.10	364 00			364 00	27 85	22 00		21 84		71 69	292 31
2	Michael McQuade	S1		8	10	8	8	6		40	7.95	318 00	7 95		325 95	24 94	40 00		19 08		84 02	241 93
3	Joyce Pinney	S0		8	10	10	8	8	4	48	8.25	396 00	33 00		429 00	32 82	67 00		23 76		123 58	305 42
4	Yoko Uchida	M2		8	8	-	10	6	4	36	8.00	288 00	24 00		312 00	23 87	26 00		17 28		67 15	244 85
5																						
6	Totals											1,366 00	64 95		1,430 95	109 48	155 00		81 96		346 44	1,084 51

Tables for Percentage Method of Withholding

(For Wages Paid After December 1988)

TABLE 1—If the Payroll Period With Respect to an Employee Is Weekly

(a) SINGLE person—including head of household:

If the amount of wages (after subtracting withholding allowances) is: / *The amount of income tax to be withheld shall be:*

Not over $21 0

Over—	*But not over—*		*of excess over—*
$21	—$378	15%	—$21
$378	—$885	$53.55 plus 28%	—$378
$885	—$2,028	$195.51 plus 33%	—$885
$2,028		$572.70 plus 28%	—$2,028

(b) MARRIED person—

If the amount of wages (after subtracting withholding allowances) is: / *The amount of income tax to be withheld shall be:*

Not over $62 0

Over—	*But not over—*		*of excess over—*
$62	—$657	15%	—$62
$657	—$1,501	$89.25 plus 28%	—$657
$1,501	—$3,695	$325.57 plus 33%	—$1,501
$3,695		$1,049.59 plus 28%	—$3,695

TABLE 2—If the Payroll Period With Respect to an Employee Is Biweekly

(a) SINGLE person—including head of household:

If the amount of wages (after subtracting withholding allowances) is: / *The amount of income tax to be withheld shall be:*

Not over $42 0

Over—	*But not over—*		*of excess over—*
$42	—$756	15%	—$42
$756	—$1,769	$107.10 plus 28%	—$756
$1,769	—$4,055	$390.74 plus 33%	—$1,769
$4,055		$1,145.12 plus 28%	—$4,055

(b) MARRIED person—

If the amount of wages (after subtracting withholding allowances) is: / *The amount of income tax to be withheld shall be:*

Not over $123 0

Over—	*But not over—*		*of excess over—*
$123	—$1,313	15%	—$123
$1,313	—$3,002	$178.50 plus 28%	—$1,313
$3,002	—$7,389	$651.42 plus 33%	—$3,002
$7,389		$2,099.13 plus 28%	—$7,389

TABLE 3—If the Payroll Period With Respect to an Employee Is Semimonthly

(a) SINGLE person—including head of household:

If the amount of wages (after subtracting withholding allowances) is: / *The amount of income tax to be withheld shall be:*

Not over $46 0

Over—	*But not over—*		*of excess over—*
$46	—$819	15%	—$46
$819	—$1,917	$115.95 plus 28%	—$819
$1,917	—$4,393	$423.39 plus 33%	—$1,917
$4,393		$1,240.47 plus 28%	—$4,393

(b) MARRIED person—

If the amount of wages (after subtracting withholding allowances) is: / *The amount of income tax to be withheld shall be:*

Not over $133 0

Over—	*But not over—*		*of excess over—*
$133	—$1,423	15%	—$133
$1,423	—$3,252	$193.50 plus 28%	—$1,423
$3,252	—$8,005	$705.62 plus 33%	—$3,252
$8,005		$2,274.11 plus 28%	—$8,005

TABLE 4—If the Payroll Period With Respect to an Employee Is Monthly

(a) SINGLE person—including head of household:

If the amount of wages (after subtracting withholding allowances) is: / *The amount of income tax to be withheld shall be:*

Not over $92 0

Over—	*But not over—*		*of excess over—*
$92	—$1,638	15%	—$92
$1,638	—$3,833	$231.90 plus 28%	—$1,638
$3,833	—$8,786	$846.50 plus 33%	—$3,833
$8,786		$2,480.99 plus 28%	—$8,786

(b) MARRIED person—

If the amount of wages (after subtracting withholding allowances) is: / *The amount of income tax to be withheld shall be:*

Not over $267 0

Over—	*But not over—*		*of excess over—*
$267	—$2,846	15%	—$267
$2,846	—$6,504	$386.85 plus 28%	—$2,846
$6,504	—$16,010	$1,411.09 plus 33%	—$6,504
$16,010		$4,548.07 plus 28%	—$16,010

Page 22

TABLE 5—If the Payroll Period With Respect to an Employee Is Quarterly

(a) SINGLE person—including head of household:

If the amount of wages (after subtracting withholding allowances) is:		*The amount of income tax to be withheld shall be:*	
Not over $275		0	
Over—	*But not over—*		*of excess over—*
$275	—$4,913	15%	—$275
$4,913	—$11,500	$695.70 plus 28%	—$4,913
$11,500	—$26,358	$2,540.06 plus 33%	—$11,500
$26,358		$7,443.20 plus 28%	—$26,358

(b) MARRIED person—

If the amount of wages (after subtracting withholding allowances) is:		*The amount of income tax to be withheld shall be:*	
Not over $800		0	
Over—	*But not over—*		*of excess over—*
$800	—$8,538	15%	—$800
$8,538	—$19,513	$1,160.70 plus 28%	—$8,538
$19,513	—$48,030	$4,233.70 plus 33%	—$19,513
$48,030		$13,644.31 plus 28%	—$48,030

TABLE 6—If the Payroll Period With Respect to an Employee Is Semiannual

(a) SINGLE person—including head of household:

If the amount of wages (after subtracting withholding allowances) is:		*The amount of income tax to be withheld shall be:*	
Not over $550		0	
Over—	*But not over—*		*of excess over—*
$550	—$9,825	15%	—$550
$9,825	—$23,000	$1,391.25 plus 28%	—$9,825
$23,000	—$52,715	$5,080.25 plus 33%	—$23,000
$52,715		$14,886.20 plus 28%	—$52,715

(b) MARRIED person—

If the amount of wages (after subtracting withholding allowances) is:		*The amount of income tax to be withheld shall be:*	
Not over $1,600		0	
Over—	*But not over—*		*of excess over—*
$1,600	—$17,075	15%	—$1,600
$17,075	—$39,025	$2,321.25 plus 28%	—$17,075
$39,025	—$96,060	$8,467.25 plus 33%	—$39,025
$96,060		$27,288.80 plus 28%	—$96,060

TABLE 7—If the Payroll Period With Respect to an Employee Is Annual

(a) SINGLE person—including head of household:

If the amount of wages (after subtracting withholding allowances) is:		*The amount of income tax to be withheld shall be:*	
Not over $1,100		0	
Over—	*But not over—*		*of excess over—*
$1,100	—$19,650	15%	—$1,100
$19,650	—$46,000	$2,782.50 plus 28%	—$19,650
$46,000	—$105,430	$10,160.50 plus 33%	—$46,000
$105,430		$29,772.40 plus 28%	—$105,430

(b) MARRIED person—

If the amount of wages (after subtracting withholding allowances) is:		*The amount of income tax to be withheld shall be:*	
Not over $3,200		0	
Over—	*But not over—*		*of excess over—*
$3,200	—$34,150	15%	—$3,200
$34,150	—$78,050	$4,642.50 plus 28%	—$34,150
$78,050	—$192,120	$16,934.50 plus 33%	—$78,050
$192,120		$54,577.60 plus 28%	—$192,120

TABLE 8—If the Payroll Period With Respect to an Employee Is a Daily Payroll Period or a Miscellaneous Payroll Period

(a) SINGLE person—including head of household:

If the amount of wages (after subtracting withholding allowances) divided by the number of days in the payroll period is:		*The amount of income tax to be withheld per day shall be:*	
Not over $4.20		0	
Over—	*But not over—*		*of excess over—*
$4.20	—$75.60	15%	—$4.20
$75.60	—$176.90	$10.71 plus 28%	—$75.60
$176.90	—$405.50	$39.07 plus 33%	—$176.90
$405.50		$114.51 plus 28%	—$405.50

(b) MARRIED person—

If the amount of wages (after subtracting withholding allowances) divided by the number of days in the payroll period is:		*The amount of income tax to be withheld per day shall be:*	
Not over $12.30		0	
Over—	*But not over—*		*of excess over—*
$12.30	—$131.30	15%	—$12.30
$131.30	—$300.20	$17.85 plus 28%	—$131.30
$300.20	—$738.90	$65.14 plus 33%	—$300.20
$738.90		$209.91 plus 28%	—$738.90

Student Review

1. James Mitchell earns a gross salary of $2,720 a month. He is married and claims two exemptions. Using the wage-bracket tables, find the amount of federal income tax withheld from his monthly paycheck.

$ ________________

2. Kathryn Ott is single and earns $1,250 per week. She claims one exemption. Determine the federal income tax withheld from her weekly paycheck, using the wage-bracket tables.

$ ________________

3. Walter Cribbs earns a semimonthly salary of $1,120. He is single and claims two exemptions. Using the percentage method, determine the federal income tax withheld from his semimonthly paycheck.

$ ________________

4. Martha Sosa receives an hourly wage of $7.10, with time and a half for hours worked in excess of 35 hours per week. If she works 39 hours during the current week, is single, and claims one exemption at work, determine the amount withheld by *(a)* the wage-bracket tables, and *(b)* the percentage method.

(a) $ ________________

(b) $ ________________

5. Edward Diaz earns $9.41 per hour as a pharmacy clerk. He is married and claims three exemptions. Determine the Federal income tax withheld from his biweekly paycheck if the employer uses the percentage method and rounds off the cents. Diaz works 40 hours per week.

$ ________________

Solutions to Student Review

1. $321

2.

Salary	$1,250.00	Tax on $885	$195.51
1 exemption	− 38.46	Tax on excess:	
Net	$1,211.54	($1,211.54 − $885) × .33	+ 107.76
		Total tax withheld	$303.27

$303.27

3.

Salary	$1,120.00	Tax on $819	$115.95
2 exemptions	− 166.66	Tax on excess:	
Net	$ 953.34	($953.34 − $819) × .28	+ 37.62
		Total tax withheld	$153.57

$153.57

4.

$7.10 × 39 =	$276.90
$7.10 × $\frac{1}{2}$ × 4 =	+ 14.20
Gross wage =	$291.10

(a) $35

(b) Gross wage	$291.10	Tax on $21	$ 0
1 exemption	− 38.46	Tax on excess:	
Net	$252.64	($252.64 − $21) × .15	+ 34.75
		Total tax withheld	$34.75

(b) $34.75

5.

$9.41 × 80 =	$752.80		
Gross wage	$753.00	Tax on $123	$ 0
3 exemptions	230.76	Tax on excess:	
Net	$522.24	($522.24 − $123) × .15	+ 59.89
		Total tax withheld	$59.89

$59.89

Assignment 16-1

Federal Income Tax Withholding

Name ____________________

Date ____________________

A. Solve the following:

1. Erv Delman earns a gross salary of $925 a month. He is married and claims three exemptions. Using the wage-bracket tables, find the amount of federal income tax withheld from his monthly paycheck.

____

2. Ben Pilzner, a plant foreman, earns a weekly salary of $205. A single person, he claims one exemption. From the wage-bracket tables, find the amount of federal income tax withheld from his weekly paycheck.

____

3. Al Orler receives a weekly salary of $1,125. He is single and claims two exemptions. Using the wage-bracket tables, determine the federal income tax withheld from his weekly paycheck.

____

4. Robert Quigley is paid a monthly gross salary of $950. He is married and claims four exemptions. Find the federal income tax withheld each month by use of the wage bracket tables.

____

B. Complete the following weekly payroll register (assume that the FICA tax rate is 7.65 percent on the first $48,000, federal income taxes are withheld by use of the wage-bracket tables, and all employees listed are single):

				Deductions		
Name	*Exemptions*	*Total Wages*	*Prior Earnings*	*FICA*	*Federal Income Tax*	*Net Pay*
Bartlett, James	0	$ 290.36	$13,686.36	$______	$______	$______
Kroner, Peter	3	649.24	32,304.25	______	______	______
Murphy, Robert	1	1,022.36	47,073.28	______	______	______
Stollings, Janet	1	974.12	47,731.88	______	______	______
Wayne, Darlene	2	183.64	2,725.10	______	______	______

C.

1. The University of Higher Learning pays its faculty on a monthly basis. Complete the following payroll register, assuming that the FICA tax rate is 7.65 percent, federal income taxes are withheld by use of the wage-bracket tables, and all faculty members are married. No faculty member has accumulated $48,000 by the end of the current month.

			Deductions		
Name	*Exemptions*	*Salary*	*FICA*	*Federal Income Tax*	*Net Pay*
Cunningham, D.	2	$1,210	______	______	______
Gardner, P.	7	1,150	______	______	______
Lawson, L.	5	1,425	______	______	______
Riordan, M.	1	1,340	______	______	______
Tarnopol, L.	3	1,550	______	______	______
Ward, V.	4	1,340	______	______	______
Ziegler, S.	0	1,550	______	______	______
Totals		$9,565	______	______	______

2. Levinson Supermarket pays its employees on a weekly basis. Complete the following payroll register, assuming that the FICA tax rate is 7.65 percent, federal income taxes are withheld by using the wage-bracket tables, and all employees are single. No employee has earned $48,000 by the end of the current week.

			Deductions			
Name	*Exemptions*	*Salary*	*FICA*	*Federal Income Tax*	*Other*	*Net Pay*
Aaron, W.	3	$ 240	______	______	$ 25	______
Lee, R.	2	190	______	______	35	______
Stoupe, Y.	1	250	______	______	40	______
Vasquez, L.	7	230	______	______	30	______
Wong, L.	2	175	______	______	25	______
Totals		$1,085	______	______	______	______

Assignment 16-2
Federal Income Tax Withholding

Name ______________________________

Date ______________________________

A. Solve the following:

1. Judy Miner, a production supervisor, earns a biweekly salary of $1,050. She is married and claims one exemption. Using the percentage method, determine the federal income tax withheld from her biweekly paycheck.

   $ ______________

2. William Yee, a branch office manager, earns a semimonthly salary of $1,095. He is married and claims three exemptions. Using the percentage method, determine the federal income tax withheld from his semimonthly paycheck.

   $ ______________

3. Gretchan Green, an attorney working for a large law firm, is paid a monthly salary of $2,925. She is single and claims zero exemptions. Using the percentage method, determine the federal income tax withheld from her monthly paycheck.

   $ ______________

4. Randolph Williamson, a factory production worker, earns $10.50 per hour, with time and a half for hours worked in excess of $37\frac{1}{2}$ hours per week. If he works 42 hours during the current week, and gets paid weekly, determine by the percentage method the federal income tax withheld, assuming that he is single and claims two exemptions.

   $ ______________

5. Yvonne Holm, married and claiming four exemptions, works in the assembly department. She gets paid 25 cents per piece for the first 1,200 pieces assembled and 30 cents per piece for the excess during each two-week period. If she assembled 1,935 pieces during the current two-week period, determine the federal income tax withheld by the percentage method.

   $ ______________

6. Arthur Elston earns a weekly salary of $624.47. He is single and claims one exemption. Find the amount of federal income tax withheld from his weekly paycheck if his employer uses the percentage method and rounds off the cents.

$ ____________

7. Cynthia Peden sells in a department store and earns a commission of 8 percent of dollar sales per week. Her sales for the current week are $9,231. If she is single and claims one exemption, determine the federal income tax withheld by her employer if the last digit of the cents is eliminated and the employer uses *(a)* the wage-bracket tables, or *(b)* the percentage method.

(a) $ ____________

(b) $ ____________

8. Martha Scott, a substitute school teacher, substituted for one day at Lincoln Intermediate School. Her gross earnings for the day were $63.40. She is single and claims two exemptions. Find the amount of federal income tax withheld by use of the daily or miscellaneous percentage withholding tables.

$ ____________

B. The following is a summary payroll register for the Duggan Company for the year. Assume that each employee worked the entire year for the company at the same rate of pay. Determine the annual deductions and net pay if the FICA rate is 7.65 percent on the first $48,000 and the federal income tax is withheld by use of the percentage method. Hint—divide the annual salary by the number of pay periods in the year.

					Deductions		
Name	*Exemptions*	*Marital Status*	*Pay Period*	*Annual Salary*	*FICA*	*Federal Income Tax*	*Net Pay*
Billwiller, J.	2	M	monthly	$ 50,000	$	$	$
Fraden, J.	4	M	semimonthly	32,640			
Kirk, W.	3	M	weekly	23,790			
Ohman, A.	1	S	biweekly	18,434			
Swanson, S.	0	M	quarterly	16,760			
Wells, W.	2	S	biweekly	48,950			
Totals				$190,574			

Multiple Sports with Amy Hengst, Accountant

The receiving department of Multiple Sports has four full-time employees, including supervisor Lorna Smart. In addition, Tina Ho is called in occasionally for the day when the volume of goods received causes a backup. Ms. Smart, who is married, earns $2,650 a month and claims three exemptions. Each of the three full-time employees is paid over a different period of time. May Chow is single, claims one exemption and earns $556 a week. Patricia Green, who is married, claims two exemptions and is paid $1,100 semimonthly. Tracy Won is single, claims one exemption and earns $1,135 every two weeks. When Tina Ho, who is single and claims two exemptions, is called to help on a busy day, she earns $78.88 for the day.

Amy asks you to review one pay period on the individual earnings record of each of the above employees to see if the correct income tax is being withheld. The company is using the percentage method. In addition, Amy asks you to determine the amount of income tax that would have been withheld for Smart and Chow if the wage-bracket tables were used. Based on your review, you come up with the following income tax withholding amounts:

Percentage method:

Smart ____________

Chow ____________

Green ____________

Won ____________

Ho ____________

Wage-bracket method:

Smart ____________

Chow ____________

% − X + $ ÷ +

Section 5

Accounting Problems

Chapter 17

Trade and Cash Discounts

This computer is so human that when it breaks down, it needs coffee instead of oil.

Learning Goals

Upon completion of this chapter, you should be able to:

1. Comprehend the reasons for trade discounts.
2. Distinguish between the list price and the net price.
3. Calculate the amount of trade discount and the net price with a single trade discount.
4. Determine the net price if there are chain discounts.
5. Arrive at the single trade discount rate or the single net price rate equivalents of a given chain discount.
6. Determine the list price if given a net price and a single trade discount or a chain discount.
7. Differentiate between cash and trade discounts.
8. Understand the payment date to get a cash discount under ordinary dating, end-of-month dating, or receipt-of-goods dating.
9. Know the difference between cash discount and simple interest.
10. Calculate the amount credited and the balance still due if making a partial payment within the cash discount period.

Trade Discounts

Many manufacturers and wholesalers who sell merchandise to retailers issue catalogs that contain pictures and descriptions of the items and a listed catalog price. The *list price* is in the nature of a suggested retail price to be charged the customer and is not what the retailer pays for the item.

A discount sheet is generally provided for the various items in the catalog and the retailer deducts the appropriate discount from the list price in order to arrive at the *net price* the retailer will be charged for the item.

Also, some suppliers have a set price per unit for small purchases, with reductions in price for units purchased in excess of a certain quantity. For example, the cost of one chair might be listed at $80, but if the purchaser places an order to buy 50 or more chairs, a discount of 15 percent per chair can be taken.

In addition, if catalogs or price lists are published, the seller may prefer to alter prices periodically without the inconvenience and expense of a new publication. In all the above situations, the *list price* is the quoted selling price of an item, while the *trade discount* represents the current reduction in price to the buyer, with the difference representing the *net price.*

National CPA 4-Part Exam, Results for California, May 1987

Passed in one sitting	3%
Completed passing remaining parts	16
Conditionally passed 2–3 parts	31
Failed	50

Example 1. What is the net price of a sofa listed at $300 less a trade discount of 40 percent?

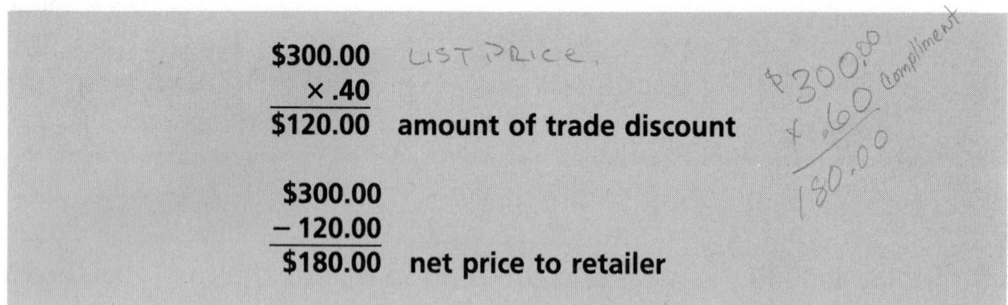

$300.00
× .40
$120.00 amount of trade discount

$300.00
− 120.00
$180.00 net price to retailer

Some firms allow additional discounts and these are known as series or chain discounts. Thus, an item may list for a certain price with discounts of 20 percent and 5 percent. Chain discounts are generally shown in order from the highest to lowest amount. The easiest method is to take the discounts in the order that they are shown; the first discount from the list price and each successive discount applied to the balance that was obtained in the previous calculation.

Example 2. What is the net price of a shipment of pottery listed at $3,000, with discounts of 20, 10, and 5 percents?

$3,000 × .20 = $600 first discount
$3,000 − $600 = $2,400

$2,400 × .10 = $240 second discount
$2,400 − $240 = $2,160

$2,160 × .05 = $108 third discount
$2,160 − $108 = $2,052

$2,052.00 net price

Another method of calculating the net price in the preceding problem is to multiply by the decimal complement of each rate of discount. The complement is the difference between the rate of discount and 100 percent, shown as a decimal.

List price \$3,000 subject to discounts of 20, 10, and 5 percents.

Complement of 20% is 80% = .80
10% is 90% = .90
5% is 95% = .95

\$3,000 × .80 = 2,400
2,400 × .90 = 2,160
2,160 × .95 = 2,052 = \$2,052.00 net price

It should also be remembered that a percentage amount may be shown as a fraction as well as being shown decimally. While 25 percent of an amount may be obtained by multiplying the amount by .25, the fractional equivalent of $\frac{1}{4}$ may also be used as the multiplier. If $33\frac{1}{3}$ percent is contained in a series of discounts, it may be easier to use $\frac{1}{3}$ as the multiplier.

Single Trade Discount Equivalent

The advantage of finding the single trade discount rate occurs when one buys regularly from the same vendor and receives the same chain discounts. It is easier to multiply once for each purchase to arrive at the net price than to multiply two or more times. However, it should be noted that a customer usually is more interested in the single net price rate rather than the single trade discount rate since the important consideration is determination of the net cost and not the amount of discount.

Example 3. Finding the single trade discount equivalent of chain discounts of 35, 20, and 10 percents.

100% equals the list price	**100%**
35% × 100 = 35	**− 35**
	65%
20% × 65 = 13	**− 13**
	52.0%
10% × 52 = 5.2	**− 5.2**
	46.8% net price rate

100% − 46.8% = 53.2% single trade discount equivalent

Example 4. Another method that may be used is multiplication of the decimal complements of the discounts to arrive at a single net price rate, and then subtraction of this rate from 100%.

> **1.00 − .35 = .65**
> **1.00 − .20 = .80**
> **1.00 − .10 = .90**
> **.65 × .80 × .90 = .468 = 46.8% net price rate**
> **100% − 46.8% = 53.2% single trade discount equivalent**

It should be observed that the single discount equivalent of a chain discount is always less than the sum of the individual discounts. In the above examples, the sum of the discounts is 65 percent, while the single discount equivalent is 53.2 percent.

Example 5. A customer made three separate purchases during the same month from the same vendor, with list prices of $500, $220, and $75. If all three purchases have chain discounts of 35, 20, and 10 percent, the customer would find it easier to determine each net price by multiplying once by 46.8 percent rather than by multiplying three times by 65, 80, and 90 percent.

Cash Discounts

Many firms allow a buyer a cash discount if a bill is paid within a certain number of days. The terms of payment are shown on the invoice that is sent to the buyer and shows the various items of merchandise purchased and the amount due.

Ordinary Dating

A typical invoice may show terms of 2/10, n/30. This means that a 2 percent discount may be deducted from the amount due if the bill is paid within 10 days from the date of invoice. The term *n*/30 indicates that the net amount is due in 30 days. Thus, if the buyer does not wish to take advantage of the cash discount, the bill must be paid in full within 30 days of the invoice date.

If freight or shipping charges have been added to the invoice by the seller, or if the buyer has returned a portion of the merchandise before making payment, such items must be deducted from the total amount of the invoice before calculating the discount deduction.

Five Largest Catalog Retailers—1986

	($ millions)
Sears	$3,711
J.C. Penney	2,332
Spiegel	882
Brylane (Limited)	475
L.L. Bean	368

The Wall Street Journal, 11/24/87
Blunt, Ellis & Loewi, Inc.

Example 1. Williams receives an invoice totaling $298 with terms of 2/10, n/30, and pays it within ten days of receipt. What is the amount of his remittance?

$298.00	**amount of invoice**
× .02	**cash discount rate of 2%**
5.9600	**= $5.96 amount of discount**
$298.00	
− 5.96	
$292.04	**amount paid**

Example 2. **The Kent Plumbing Company receives an invoice for copper pipe totaling $326.50 with terms of 3/10, n/60. The invoice total includes a shipping charge of $20.50. If the discount is taken, what is the amount to be paid?**

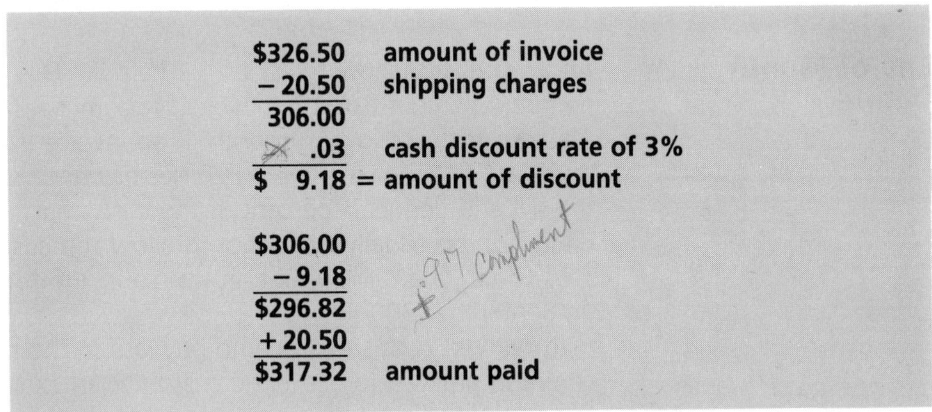

$326.50	amount of invoice
− 20.50	shipping charges
306.00	
× .03	cash discount rate of 3%
$ 9.18 =	amount of discount
$306.00	
− 9.18	
$296.82	
+ 20.50	
$317.32	amount paid

Example 3. **The Fineman Sporting Goods Company receives an invoice of $952.80 with terms of 2/15, n/60, which includes shipping charges of $38.20. If Fineman returns $82.60 worth of goods to the seller and remits payment 11 days from the invoice date, how much must she pay?**

$952.80	amount of invoice
− 38.20	shipping charges
$914.60	
− 82.60	cost of goods returned
$832.00	
× .02	cash discount rate of 2%
$ 16.64 =	amount of discount
$832.00	
− 16.64	
$815.36	
+ 38.20	
$853.56	amount paid

Cash Discount versus Simple Interest

A cash discount results in a direct percent decrease of the net price, regardless of how far in advance of the final due date the payment is made. Simple interest, on the other hand, is always expressed at an annual rate and must be adjusted for the length of the loan.

For example, if merchandise was purchased on March 15 at a net price of $1,000, with terms of 3/10, n/30, the buyer would save $30 by paying on, or before, March 25. However, even if the buyer had to borrow the $970 at 18 percent on March 25, the loan would be worthwhile since interest is expressed at an annual rate. Because the loan is only for 20 days, which is approximately one 18th of a year, 18 percent interest is the equivalent of 1 percent discount (18% × 1/18 of a year). Therefore, a $30 cash discount savings would only cost $9.70 in interest, which is 1 percent of $970.

End-of-Month Dating

An invoice may show terms of 4/10 e.o.m. This means that a customer can deduct 4 percent from the invoice if payment is made within the first 10 days of the following month. If an invoice is dated August 5, and the terms are 4/10 e.o.m., the purchaser has until September 10 to pay the bill and deduct 4 percent. If the customer elects not to take the cash discount, it is usually the policy to allow the customer an additional 20 days to pay the full amount. In this case, the full payment would be due on September 30.

In fairness to customers who buy late in the month, it has become common practice to allow the customer an extra month to pay and still get the cash discount if the invoice is dated on the 26th of the month or later. Therefore, if a purchase invoice is dated March 28, and the terms are 2/15 e.o.m., the customer can still get the 2 percent cash discount if payment is made by May 15.

The advantage of e.o.m. terms is that the seller will receive most payments at approximately the same time of the month.

Receipt-of-Goods Dating

An invoice may show terms of 3/15 r.o.g. This means that the customer has 15 days from the day the goods are received to pay the invoice and get a 3 percent cash discount. An additional 20 days is granted if the customer elects to pay in full.

This method is used when the time of arrival of goods is uncertain, such as in long-distance shipments. This allows the customer reasonable time to unload and inspect the goods and still pay within the discount period.

Partial Payments

A purchaser may often wish to make only a partial payment on the amount due. If the seller allows a discount on partial payments and the purchaser makes such a payment during the discount period allowed on the invoice, the purchaser is entitled to a discount on that part of the amount covered by the payment. Since a partial payment within the cash discount period represents payment after deducting the cash discount, the amount deducted from the invoice can be determined by dividing the amount paid by the complement of the cash discount rate.

Example 4. If Jenkins makes a partial payment of $250 within the discount period on an invoice totaling $529 with terms of 2/10, n/90, what amount is credited toward payment of the bill and what amount is still owed?

A discount rate of 2 percent means that Jenkins saves 2 cents on each dollar paid; thus $.98 paid cancels $1.00 of the bill. Dividing the partial payment by .98 will give the amount to be credited against the bill.

$250.00 ÷ .98 = 255.102 = $255.10 amount credited to bill

$529.00	amount of invoice
− 255.10	
$273.90	amount still due

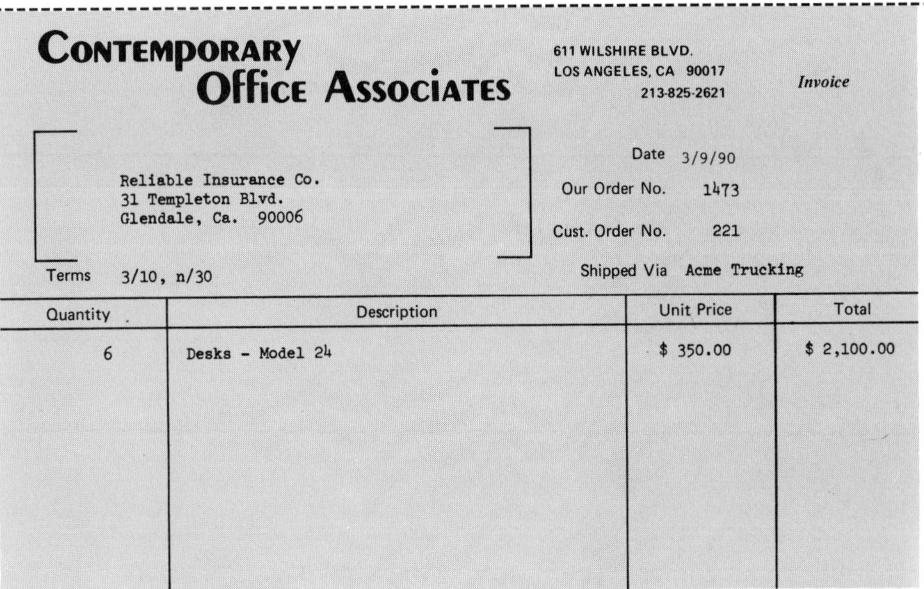

Contemporary Office Associates

611 WILSHIRE BLVD.
LOS ANGELES, CA 90017
213-825-2621

Invoice

Reliable Insurance Co.
31 Templeton Blvd.
Glendale, Ca. 90006

Date 3/9/90
Our Order No. 1473
Cust. Order No. 221

Terms 3/10, n/30

Shipped Via Acme Trucking

Quantity	Description	Unit Price	Total
6	Desks - Model 24	$ 350.00	$ 2,100.00

Example 5. In the Contemporary Office Associates invoice, the Reliable Insurance Company is entitled to a 3 percent cash discount if payment is made on or before March 19, 1990. Otherwise, the net price of $2,100 must be remitted by no later than April 8, 1990.

Student Review

1. Torres Corp. ordered four electric fans that list at $250 each, less trade discounts of 15 percent and 10 percent. If there is a $45 shipping charge, determine the total purchase price.

$____________

2. Bronson Paint Co. purchased several cases of paint on May 20 at a total cost of $750. If terms are 2/15, n/45 and full payment is made on June 4, determine the amount of the payment.

$____________

3. Sturgis Appliance Co. ordered several refrigerators on March 16 at a total cost of $2,100, with terms of 3/10, e.o.m. If $600 is paid on April 10, determine the balance due by April 30.

$____________

4. What is the single trade discount equivalent of a chain discount of 25 percent and 15 percent?

____

5. Hagachi Grocers orders a shipment of Japanese food supplies from Japan on May 3. The goods are shipped on May 15. An invoice for $1,750 is received on June 2, with terms of 3/10, r.o.g. The goods are received on July 28. Determine *(a)* the final date to take the cash discount and *(b)* the full amount paid within the cash discount period.

(a) ____________

(b) $____________

Solutions to Student Review

1. $ 250 × 4 = $1,000
$1,000 × .85 = $ 850
$ 850 × .90 = $ 765
$ 765 + $45 = $ 810

$ 810

2. $750 × .02 = $ 15
$750 − $15 = $735

$ 735

3. $600 ÷ .97 = $ 618.56
$2,100 − $618.56 = $1,481.44

$ 1,481.44

4. .75 × .85 = .6375

100.00%
− 63.75
36.25%

36.25%

5. *(a)* July 28–August 7 = 10 days

(b) $1,750 × .03 = $52.50
$1,750 − $52.50 = $1,697.50

(a) August 7

(b) $ 1,697.50

Assignment 17–1

Trade and Cash Discounts

Name ____________________

Date ____________________

A. Solve the following problems in trade discounts:

1. What is the net price of a shipment of lighting fixtures with a list price of $918.90 and trade discounts of $33\frac{1}{3}$ percent and 10 percent?

____

2. Jennings orders 3 electric motors that list at $83 each less trade discounts of 20 percent and 10 percent. If a $12 shipping charge is added to the total net cost, what is the amount of the remittance?

____

3. The Travers Paint Company lists exterior metal primer at $18.98 per gallon less 25 percent discount if purchased in cases of four gallons per case. What is the cost of eight cases?

____

4. What is the net price of a shipment of dinnerware listed at $2,350 with chain discounts of 20 percent, 15 percent, and 3 percent?

____

5. What is the single trade discount equivalent of chain discounts of 40 percent, 10 percent, and 5 percent?

____

B. Fill in the blanks in each of the following:

	Invoice Amount	*Invoice Date*	*Cash Discount Terms*	*Final Date of Discount*	*Amount of Cash Discount*	*Final Payment Date*
1.	$400	January 4	2/15, n/45	1-19	8.00	2-18
2.	$85.60	September 20	6/10 e.o.m.	9-30	5.14	
3.	$2,485	April 18	4/5 r.o.g. rec'd. July 5	July 10	99.40	July 30
4.	$123.17	March 27	5/20 e.o.m.			
5.	$1,122	May 30	3/20, n/60	June 19	33.66	July 29
6.	$543.15	February 4	2/6, e.o.m.			
7.	$32,495	June 1	2/10 r.o.g. rec'd. July 30	Aug 9	649.90	Aug 29
8.	$627	January 29	2/25, n/40			
9.	$462.83	April 30	1/15 r.o.g. rec'd. June 29	July 14	4.63	Aug. 3
10.	$14,403	July 31	3/12 e.o.m.			

Assignment 17–2

Trade and Cash Discounts

Name

Date

Solve the following problems in cash discounts:

1. The Kerr Company receives an invoice totaling $82.50 including a freight charge of $7.50. Terms are 3/10, n/60. If the discount is taken, what is the amount to be paid?

   $80.25

2. Espinosa receives an invoice totaling $69.70 with terms of 2/10, n/30. If he pays within two days of receipt, what is the amount of his payment?

   68.306

3. Alice Richardson purchases ceramic materials on May 10 at a net cost of $90, with terms of 4/15, n/60. If she makes payment in full on May 24, how much does she remit?

   86.40

4. Mulvaney receives an invoice of $688 for the purchase of a printing press. Terms are $7\frac{1}{4}$/10, n/120. If he takes advantage of the discount, how much will he save?

   189.20

5. The Alexander Variety Store receives a shipment of merchandise totaling $1,732 and returns $123.80 worth of paper goods and $37.20 of kitchen utensils. If terms are $2\frac{1}{2}$/10, n/120 and the discount is taken, what is the amount of the payment?

   $1531.72

6. Hearn purchases merchandise on August 12 for $450. If payment is made on September 8 and terms are 4/10 e.o.m., what is the amount of payment?

   $18.75

7. Plachy receives merchandise on March 29. If the invoice is dated March 26, determine when payment must be made to get the cash discount if the terms are *(a)* 3/15, n/30; *(b)* 3/15 e.o.m.; *(c)* 3/15 r.o.g.

(a) April 10 *(b)* May 15 *(c)* April 13.

8. Holm places an order on May 15 for $800 of skiing equipment. The invoice is received on June 1, with terms of 5/20 r.o.g. The goods must be shipped, and are received by Holm on July 28. Determine *(a)* the final date of payment to get the cash discount and *(b)* the full amount to be paid within the discount period.

(a) September 14

(b) $760.00

9. Weidman orders $2,500 of office equipment on July 15. The invoice, dated July 22, arrives with the merchandise on July 28. Invoice terms are 3/15 e.o.m. Determine *(a)* the final date to pay and get the discount, *(b)* the full amount to be paid within the discount period, and *(c)* the final date to pay the net price.

(a) August 15

(b) 2425.00

(c) Sept 4

10. Drake School orders school supplies on September 5. The invoice, dated September 20, is received with the goods on September 26. The invoice amount is $1,450, including a $35 shipping charge. If the terms are 3/10 e.o.m., determine *(a)* the final date to pay and get the discount, and *(b)* the amount necessary to pay in full if the cash discount is earned.

(a) Oct 10th

(b) 1407.55

11. Carpet Deluxe Company purchased an order of carpets on June 5 at a net cost of $5,250 including shipping charges of $325. If the cash terms are 1/15, n/30, what is the amount of full payment due on June 19?

5200.75

12. Anderson Variety Store makes a purchase on March 24 at a list price of $225, with a trade discount of 20 percent. If the cash terms are 3/10, n/30, determine the full balance paid on April 3.

173.25

Assignment 17–3

Trade and Cash Discounts

Name ____________________

Date ____________________

Solve the following:

1. The Johnson Company purchases five electronic calculators at $105 each less trade discounts of 20 percent and 30 percent. What is the net cost?

   $294.00

2. Jim Carson buys a desk for his office at a list price of $450 less trade discounts of 15 percent, 5 percent, and 10 percent. If there is a shipping charge of $20, what is the amount due?

   $307.04

3. Graber purchases a filing cabinet at a list price of $90, a typewriter at a list price of $110, and an office safe at a list price of $220. If each of these items has trade discounts of 20 percent and 25 percent, what is the net cost of each?

   filing cabinet $54.00

   typewriter $66.00

   office safe $132.00

4. What is the single discount equivalent of a chain discount of 20 percent, 10 percent, and $33\frac{1}{3}$ percent?

   52%

5. What is the list price of an electric saw that has a net price of $128.40, with trade discounts of 15 percent and 10 percent?

   $167.84

6. Saunders makes a partial payment of $180 on a bill totaling $351.20 with terms of 2/10, n/30. If payment is made within the discount period, what amount is credited to the account?

   $183.67

7. Joe's Furniture Store acquires furniture on September 21 at a cost of $450, with cash discount terms of 2/10, 1/30, n/60. If $200 is remitted on October 1, how much must be paid on October 21 in order to pay the balance due?

$ 243.46

8. Scott Lumber orders a shipment of plywood from a distant city. The invoice, dated October 24, shows a billing of $1,942, with terms of 1/15 r.o.g. If the plywood is received on January 14, and a payment of $1,500 is made on January 29, determine the *(a)* last day to pay the balance due, and *(b)* amount owed.

(a) ________

(b) ________

9. Merkadeau Paints orders $2,100 of exterior latex paint on February 15. The invoice, dated February 27, shows terms of 3/15 e.o.m. If $1,800 is paid on March 9, how much must be paid if the remaining balance is paid on March 30?

$234.00

10. Spice Roofing Company acquires materials on November 15 at a list price of $575, with a trade discount of 5 percent and a freight charge of $40. If the cash discount terms are 2/10, n/45 and $300 is remitted on November 25, how much is due on December 30?

____

11. Benson Office Equipment purchased file cabinets on July 20 at a list price of $2,850 and trade discounts of 15 percent and 10 percent. If the cash terms are 3/10 e.o.m. and $2,000 is remitted on August 10, what is the balance due on August 30?

$118.39

12. An order for coffee beans is sent to Colombia on January 20. An invoice accepting the order is received on March 2. The invoice, dated February 25, shows a net price of $18,750, with cash terms of 3/10 r.o.g. The coffee beans are received on May 4. If $15,000 is paid on May 14, determine the *(a)* final date of payment within the credit period, and *(b)* final amount due.

(a) ________

(b) ________

Multiple Sports with Amy Hengst, Accountant

On June 10, Multiple Sports received four invoices from suppliers for merchandise purchased.

Invoice A, dated June 9, was for the purchase of 200 basketballs at a published price of $20 each, with trade discounts of 30 percent off the catalog price and 20 percent for purchasing in excess of 100 units, with terms of n/30.

Invoice B, dated June 10, was for the purchase of 50 swim fins at $18 each, with terms of 3/15, e.o.m.

Invoice C, dated May 18, was for the purchase of 150 ski boots at $120 each. The boots, with terms of 2/20, r.o.g. were received on July 24.

Invoice D, dated June 8, was for the purchase of 40 rain jackets at $35 each, with terms of 2/15, 1/30, n/60.

Amy asks you to determine the following:

Invoice A: 1. Amount paid in full on July 9.

1. ___________

2. The single trade discount equivalent.

2. ___________

Invoice B: 1. Last day to pay and get the discount. 1. ___________

2. Full amount paid within the discount period.

2. ___________

Invoice C: 1. Last day to pay and get the discount. 1. ___________

2. Full amount paid within the discount period.

2. ___________

Invoice D: 1. Amount credited to the account of Multiple Sports when $800 is paid on June 23.

1. ___________

2. Balance paid in full on July 8.

2. ___________

Chapter 18

Markup and Markdown

I don't think I really deserve an F.
I agree, but its the lowest grade I'm allowed to give.

Learning Goals

Upon completion of this chapter, you should be able to:

1. Discuss the meaning of the term *markup* in relation to cost and selling price.
2. Understand the meaning of the terms *base, rate,* and *percentage* in determining cost, markup, and selling price.
3. Determine the amount of markup if the markup rate is on the cost.
4. Determine the amount of markup if the markup rate is on the selling price.
5. Distinguish between markup and *markdown.*
6. Discuss the meaning and the reasons for having markdowns.
7. Determine the amount of markdown if the markdown rate is on the original selling price or on the current selling price.

A successful business is able to sell its product at a price that will include the cost of manufacturing or purchasing the item, expenses in connection with making the sale, and a satisfactory profit. The difference between the cost and the retail, or selling, price represents the profit made and is called *markup.*

Some businesses use cost as the basis on which the markup percentage is calculated while others use selling, or retail, price as the base. The basic equation used in connection with markup problems is as follows:

Cost	+ Markup	= Selling price
\$20.00	+ \$5.00	= *S*
C	+ \$5.00	= \$25.00
\$20.00	+ *M*	= \$25.00

In Chapter 11, the meaning of the terms *base, rate,* and *percentage* was discussed. As a brief review, the **base** is the amount equal to 100 percent. It is also the amount to which we are making a comparison. For example, if we compare the population of city A to that of city B, city B's population would be the base. The base does not have to be the largest amount.

The **rate** is a fraction of the base, expressed as a percent. The rate can be more or less than 100 percent. The **percentage** is an amount equal to a rate. In a given problem, there may be several rates, each with its own percentage. For example, if a basketball player attempted 80 free throws and made 60 percent, or 48 free throws, the rate of success would be 60 percent, and the percentage of success would be 48. On the other hand, the rate of failure would be 40 percent, and the percentage of failure would be 32.

Since any percent problem deals with base, rate, and percentage, if two of the three are known, the third can be readily determined, using the basic formula:

Percentage *(P)* = Base *(B)* × Rate *(R)*

Since markup problems are concerned with percent, they can be solved by setting up the basic markup formula, as follows:

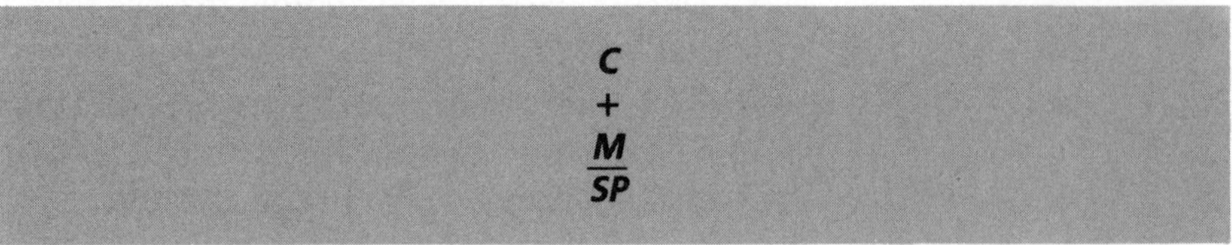

Then, based on the information given in a particular problem, indicate the given dollar amounts to the right of each of the three elements, and the given rates to the left, leaving blank the unknowns.

When Cost Is Used as the Base

Example 1. Assume an item that cost $40 is marked up 20 percent on the cost. Set the formula as follows:

$$\begin{array}{rcl} 100\% & C & \$40 \\ & + & \\ 20\% & \underline{M} & \\ & SP & \end{array}$$

In this problem, since we are comparing the markup rate to the cost, the cost must be the base, the amount equal to 100 percent. Once you know two amounts or two rates, you find the third by addition or subtraction. In this case, we now know that the selling price is 120 percent of the cost. Now we can find the amount of markup by multiplying $40 × 20% (base × rate) and we can find the amount of the selling price by multiplying $40 × 120%. The final solution will appear as follows:

$$\begin{array}{rcl} 100\% & C & \$40 \\ & + & \\ \underline{20\%} & \underline{M} & \underline{8} \\ 120\% & SP & \$48 \end{array}$$

Top Five Pizza Chains—1987

	($ millions)
Pizza Hut	$2,500
Domino's	1,800
Little Caesars	770
Pizza Inn	270
Godfather's	261

The Wall Street Journal, 1/12/88

Example 2. Assume an item that sells for $50 is marked up 25 percent on the cost. Set the formula as follows:

$$\begin{array}{rcl} 100\% & C & \\ & + & \\ 25\% & \underline{M} & \\ & SP & \$50 \end{array}$$

Since the markup is on the cost, the cost must be the base. If the cost plus the markup equals the selling price, then the selling price is 125 percent of the cost. Since the percentage is an amount equal to a given rate, when you have a rate and an amount referring to the same item, the amount has to be the percentage of that rate. When you know the percentage and its rate, you can find the base by dividing the percentage by its rate. In this problem, the cost base is $40, determined as follows:

$$B = \frac{P}{R} = \frac{\$50}{1.25} = \$40$$

Once we know the base, we can find the markup amount by multiplying its rate times the base. The final solution will appear as follows:

$$\begin{array}{rcl} 100\% & C & \$40 \\ & + & \\ \underline{25\%} & \underline{M} & \underline{10} \\ 125\% & SP & \$50 \end{array}$$

When Selling Price Is Used as the Base

Example 3. Assume an item that sells for $200 is marked up 60 percent on the selling price. Start with the markup formula and the known factors, as follows:

	C	
	+	
60%	*M*	
100%	*SP*	$200

In this problem, since we are comparing the markup rate to the selling price, the selling price must be the base. Since we know two rates, we can determine the cost rate by subtraction. We can now find the amount of markup by multiplying $200 × 60%, base times rate, and we can find the amount of the cost by multiplying $200 × 40%. The final solution will appear as follows:

40%	*C*	80
	+	
60%	*M*	120
100%	*SP*	$200

Example 4. Assume an item that costs $100 is marked up 60 percent on the selling price. Set the formula as follows:

	C	$100
	+	
60%	*M*	
100%	*SP*	

Since the markup is on the selling price, the selling price must be the base. If the cost plus the markup equals the selling price, then the cost is 40 percent of the selling price. Once you have an amount and a rate, other than 100 percent, referring to the same item, you have a rate and its percentage. To find the base, you divide the amount by its rate. In this problem, the selling price base is $250, determined as follows:

$$B = \frac{P}{R} = \frac{\$100}{.40} = \$250$$

Once we know the base, we can find the markup amount by multiplying its rate times the base. The final solution will appear as follows:

40%	*C*	$100
	+	
60%	*M*	150
100%	SP	$250

In summary, in any percent problem, including markups, when you know the base and a rate, you can find the percentage amount equal to the rate by multiplying the base times the rate. For example,

100% *C* $600
+
75% *M*
SP

The amount of markup is $450, the base of $600 times the markup rate on cost of 75 percent.

When you know a rate and its percentage, you can find the base by dividing the percentage by its rate. For example,

***C* $50**
+
80% *M*
100% *SP*

In this case, the markup is 80 percent of the selling price. However, you can never divide a markup rate into a cost amount and come up with a meaningful answer. Since you must divide an amount by its rate, you would first have to determine that the cost rate is 20 percent of the selling price. Then, if you divide the cost amount of $50 by the cost rate of 20 percent, the result will be the selling price base of $250.

Markdown

For various reasons, a company may decide to reduce the original selling price of merchandise by a stated amount of money or a stated percent of the original or current selling price. Sometimes the store is having a clearance sale to eliminate seasonal or obsolete merchandise, or the store might want to attract customers by having a storewide or special items sale. Also, competitor prices or slow-moving merchandise may cause a price reduction. Whatever the reasons, this reduction is called a markdown.

Just as with markups, a basic equation can be used in connection with markdown problems, as follows:

Original Selling Price (OSP) − Markdown (MD) = Sales Price (SP)

or

OSP
−
MD
=
SP

Example 1. A toaster has an original selling price of $45.82. Due to a closeout of that item, the price was marked down by $7.24. Find the sales price.

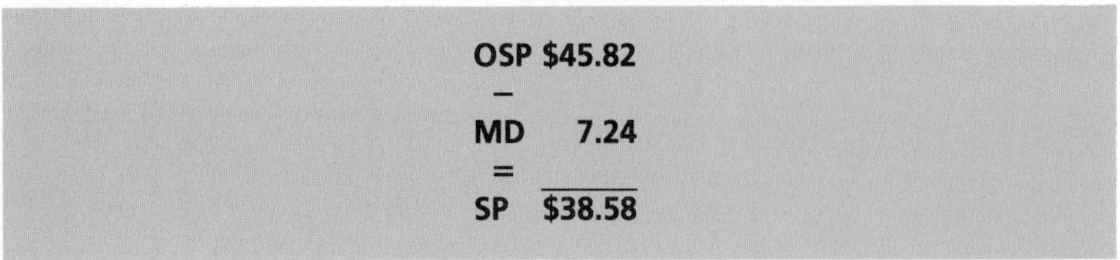

OSP $45.82
−
MD 7.24
=
SP $38.58

Example 2. A name-brand refrigerator had an original selling price of $420 at the time of purchase. During a special sales week, the refrigerator was marked down 28 percent on the original selling price. Determine the sales price.

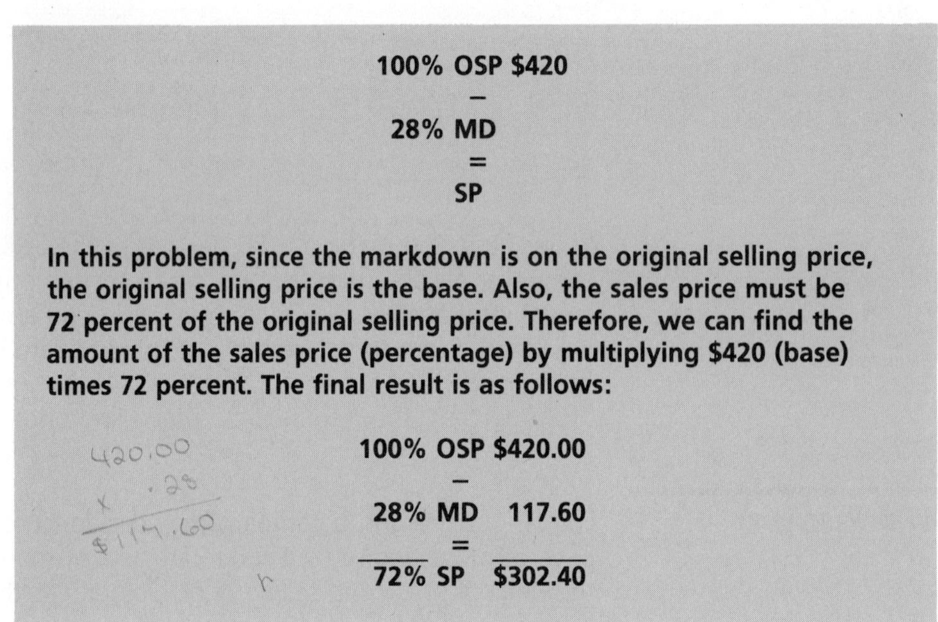

100% OSP $420
−
28% MD
=
SP

In this problem, since the markdown is on the original selling price, the original selling price is the base. Also, the sales price must be 72 percent of the original selling price. Therefore, we can find the amount of the sales price (percentage) by multiplying $420 (base) times 72 percent. The final result is as follows:

100% OSP $420.00
−
28% MD 117.60
=
72% SP $302.40

Example 3. A camera was marked down $52 from its original selling price. The new sales price is 75 percent of the original selling price. In determining the new sales price, the following facts are known:

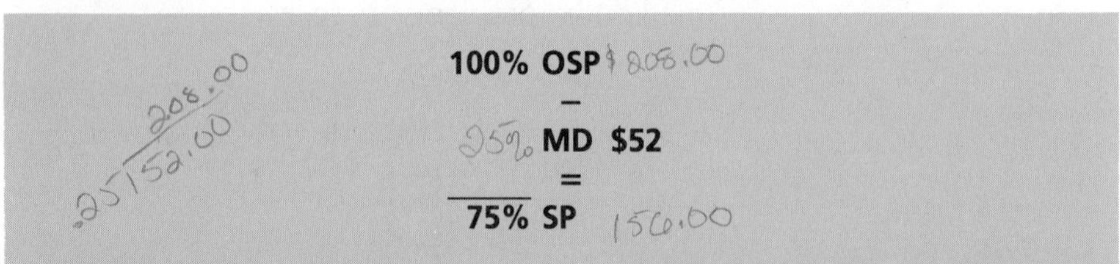

100% OSP
−
MD $52
=
75% SP

In this problem, the sales price is 75 percent of the original selling price. Therefore, the original selling price is the base. We also know by deduction that the markdown must be 25 percent of the original selling price. Therefore, we know a percentage, $52, and its rate, 25 percent. The base can be found by dividing the percentage by its rate. Once we know that the base is $208, the sales price can be determined by multiplying the base, $208, times the rate, 75 percent.

The final solution is as follows:

100%	OSP	$208
	−	
25%	MD	52
	=	
75%	SP	$156

Example 4. An overcoat was marked down 18 percent from its original selling price and now sells for $193.52. To find the amount of markdown, the following is given:

100%	OSP	
	−	
18%	MD	
	=	
	SP	$193.52

Once again, the original sales price is the base because the markdown rate is on the original sales price. Also, by deduction, we know that the sales price is 82 percent of the original selling price. In order to find the amount of markdown, we must first find the base by dividing the percentage, $193.52, by its rate, 82 percent. The markdown can now be found by multiplying the just-derived base, $236, by the markdown rate, 18 percent. The final solution is as follows:

100%	OSP	$236.00
	−	
18%	MD	42.48
	=	
82%	SP	193.52

Student Review

1. Kitchen installations, Inc., purchased several kitchen sinks at a cost of $500 each. If the markup is 40 percent on the cost, determine the installation price per sink.

$ 700.00

2. Darwin Janitorial Supplies sells a long-hosed vacuum cleaner for $180. If the markup is 35 percent on the selling price, determine the cost.

$ 243.00

3. Farm Machinery Corp. sells a tractor for $15,180, a markup of 38 percent on cost. The Tractor Co., a builder of tractors, sold the tractor to Farm Machinery Corp. at a 35 percent markup on cost. Determine the manufacturing cost to the Tractor Co.

$ ______

4. School Supplies Co. currently sells a binder for $3.68, which is a markdown of 20 percent on the original selling price. Determine the original selling price.

$ ______

5. Classic Books, Inc., purchased a set of books at a cost of $300. The books were originally listed for sale at a markup of 25 percent on selling price. Later the books were marked down 25 percent on the current sales price. Determine the current sales price.

$ ______

Solutions to Student Review

1.

100%	C	$500	SP = 140% of Cost
	+		
40%	M		SP = $500 × 1.4 = $700
	SP		

$ 700

2.

	C		C = 65% of SP
	+		
35%	M		C = $180 × .65 = $117
100%	SP	$180	

$ 117

3.

Farm Machinery Corp.

100%	C	
	+	
38%	M	
	SP	$15,180

SP = 138% of Cost
C = $15,180 ÷ 1.38 = $11,000

Tractor Co.

100%	C	
	+	
35%	M	
	SP	$11,000

SP = 135% of Cost
C = $11,000 ÷ 1.35 = $8,148.15

$ 8,148.15

4.

100%	OSP		SP = 80% of OSP
	−		
20%	MD		OSP = $3.68 ÷ .80 = $4.60
	SP	$3.68	

$ 4.60

5.

	C	$300	C = 75% of SP
	+		
25%	M		SP = $300 ÷ .75 = 400
100%	SP		

	OSP	$400
	−	
25%	MD	
100%	SP	

OSP = 125% of SP
SP = $400 ÷ 1.25 = $320

$ 320

Assignment 18–1
Markup

Name ______________________

Date ______________________

1. A hardware store puts a markup of $2.75 on paint that costs the store $11 per gallon. What is *(a)* the markup percent on cost, and *(b)* the selling price per gallon?

(a) 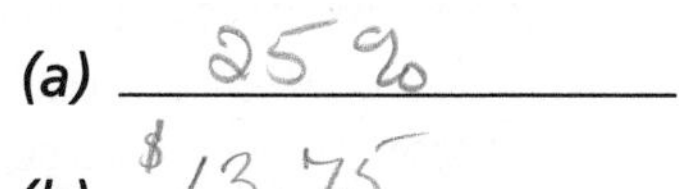

(b) $13.75

2. A furniture dealer places a markup of $18 on certain lamps. If the markup is 20 percent of the selling price, what is *(a)* the selling price, and *(b)* the dealer's cost?

(a) $40.50

(b) $22.50

3. The Smith Distributing Company sells a printing calculator costing $135.66 for $199.50. What is *(a)* the markup, and *(b)* the markup percent based on selling price?

(a) $64.84

(b) 32%

4. If an item has a $14.49 markup of 18 percent on cost, what is *(a)* the cost, and *(b)* the selling price?

(a) 2.61

(b) 17.10

5. Castlemont Furriers advertises a fur coat at $486. If this selling price represents 162 percent of cost, what is *(a)* the cost, and *(b)* the amount of profit?

(a) $300.00

(b) $186.00

6. The cost of a case of lubricating oil is \$7.74 and represents 75% of the selling price. What is *(a)* the selling price, and *(b)* the markup?

(a) \$ 9.68

(b) \$ 1.94

7. A shipment of metal tubing is sold by the Lacey Manufacturing Company for \$3,108.80. If the cost of manufacture is \$2,680.00 what is *(a)* the markup, and *(b)* the markup percent based on cost?

(a) ______

(b) ______

8. A wholesaler priced a 50-pound carton of nails at \$17.80. If the cost to the wholesaler is \$14.24, what is *(a)* the markup as a percent of the selling price, and *(b)* the cost as a percent of the selling price?

(a) ______

(b) ______

9. If an item cost Barington \$36, and a 27% markup on cost is expected, what should be *(a)* the amount of the selling price, and *(b)* the amount of markup?

(a) ______

(b) ______

10. A shipment of merchandise selling for \$398.00 has a markup of $18\frac{1}{2}$% of the selling price. What is the amount of *(a)* the markup, and *(b)* the cost?

(a) ______

(b) ______

Assignment 18–2
Markup

Name ______________________

Date ______________________

A. Fill in the missing blanks:

	Cost	*Markup*	*Selling Price*	*Markup Rate on Cost*	*Markup Rate on Selling Price*	*Cost Rate on Selling Price*	*Selling Price Rate on Cost*
1.	$800	$80	$880	10%			
2.	______	$120	______		15%		
3.	$500	______	______		20%		
4.	$20	______	______	30%			
5.	______	______	$410		40%		
6.	______	______	$60	50%			
7.	$120	______	______			25%	
8.	$2.80	______	______				130%
9.	______	______	$1.75	______			125%
10.	______	______	$24			60%	
11.	______	$10	______			80%	
12.	______	$0.80	______				140%

B. Solve the following:

1. A calculator cost $80 and is marked up 80% on selling price. What is the amount of markup?

____

2. A television set sells for $450. The markup is 25% on the cost. What is the amount of markup?

____

3. Dunkin Donuts Company sells donuts for $2.50 a dozen. If the markup is 40 percent of the cost, determine the markup.

____

4. Ace Tennis Shop sells a particular tennis racket for $65. If the cost is 45 percent of the selling price, determine the markup.

____

5. Short Clothes Company sells a suit at a markup of 110 percent on the cost. If the selling price is $220, determine *(a)* the markup, and *(b)* the cost.

(a) ______________

(b) ______________

6. Clifton Water Ways sells river rafts for $84. If the selling price is 175 percent of the cost, determine the cost.

____

7. Computer Distributing sells a home computer for $2,590. This represents a 40 percent markup on cost. Peach Computer, the manufacturer, sold the computer to Computer Distributing at a 60 percent markup on cost. Determine the manufacturing cost to Peach Computer.

____

8. Squier Auto Showroom sells a compact auto at a markup of $2,394, which is 42 percent of the selling price. If Mammoth Motors, the manufacturer, had sold the car to Squier at a markup of 35 percent on cost, determine the cost to manufacture the car.

____

Assignment 18–3

Markdown

Name ______________________

Date ______________________

A. Fill in the missing blanks:

	Original Selling Price	Amount of Markdown	Sales Price	Markdown Rate on Original Sales Price	Sales Price Rate on Original Sales Price
1.	$380	$79.80	$300.20	100 %	______
2.	$75.20	______	$63.92	______	______
3.	$35	______	______	14%	______
4.	______	______	$577.60	24%	______
5.	______	______	$190.08	______	48%
6.	______	$230.31	$622.69	______	______
7.	______	$741.15	______	______	19%
8.	______	$0.27	______	5%	______
9.	$519	______	______	______	64%
10.	______	$0.50	______	______	92%

B. Solve the following:

1. A VCR has an original selling price of $520. The store reduces the selling price by 15 percent. Determine the new sales price.

$442.00

2. A pet store has a sale on frogs. The current sales price is $24 for each frog. If the markdown is 20 percent of the original selling price, determine the amount of the original selling price.

____

3. A grandfather clock has a current sales price of $750.08. If the markdown is 21 percent of the original selling price, determine the amount of the markdown.

____

4. A tropical plant was originally priced for sale at $75. To speed up the sale, the plant was marked down to a current sales price of $52.50. Determine the rate of markdown on *(a)* the original selling price, and *(b)* the current sales price. Round off answers to the nearest whole percent.

(a) ________________

(b) ________________

5. A woman's suit was originally priced to sell at $225. The store marked down the price of the suit by 20 percent on the *current* sales price. Determine the current sales price.

____

6. A set of golf clubs cost the golf shop $374 and was priced to sell at a markup of 32 percent on selling price. Later, the set of golf clubs was marked down 14 percent on the original selling price. Determine the amount of the markdown.

____

7. A videocassette movie, purchased for $55.50, was marked up 26 percent on the selling price. Later, as retail prices fell, this movie was marked down 20 percent on the *current* sales price. Find the current sales price.

____

Multiple Sports with Amy Hengst, Accountant

On October 14, Amy noted that three shipments of goods were received: *(a)* The first shipment consisted of 20 pairs of the Pike tennis shoes. Each pair cost $22 and is to be marked up 40 percent on cost. *(b)* The second order was for 15 basketballs that cost $23.40 each and are to be marked up 40 percent on the selling price. *(c)* The third order received consisted of 55 baseball bats that Amy marked up to sell for $40 each. The bats were marked up 35 percent on cost.

In addition, two items in stock were marked down as sales leader items: *(d)* 15 sets of golf clubs, which were originally priced to sell for $180 each, were marked down 30 percent on the current selling price. *(e)* 100 packages of one dozen golf balls were marked down 25 percent on the original selling price and now sell for $12 a package.

From the above information, *Amy* asks you to determine:

(a) The selling price of the Pike tennis shoes.

____

(b) The selling price of each basketball.

____

(c) The cost of each baseball bat.

____

(d) The current sales price for each set of golf clubs.

____

(e) The original selling price of each package of golf balls.

____

Chapter 19

Merchandise Inventory

I bought an atomic-powered clock that will keep perfect time for 3,000 years and has a 30-day guarantee.

Learning Goals

Upon completion of this chapter, you should be able to:

1. Discuss the meaning of the term *merchandise inventory*.
2. Compare and contrast merchandise inventory and cost of goods sold.
3. Understand the problem when unsold merchandise at year-end has been acquired at different costs.
4. Compute the cost assigned to the end-of-the-year merchandise inventory and the cost of goods sold during the year, using the specific-identification method.
5. Compute the cost assigned to the year-end merchandise inventory and the cost of goods sold during the year, using the first-in, first-out method.
6. Compute the cost assigned to the year-end merchandise inventory and the cost of goods sold during the year, using the last-in, first-out method.
7. Distinguish between a simple average and a weighted average.
8. Compute the cost assigned to the end-of-the-year merchandise inventory and the cost of goods sold during the year, using the weighted-average method.

Many businesses do not sell merchandise; they sell services. Firms of professionals such as lawyers, doctors, and accountants, as well as other service enterprises such as barber and beauty shops, laundromats, and theaters, sell their services for a fee, otherwise known as *revenue*. Service enterprises have no merchandise inventory and, therefore, have no cost of goods sold.

A merchandising concern, on the other hand, earns its revenue by selling goods, or merchandise. The term *merchandise inventory* designates goods held for sale in the *normal* course of business. For example, if a furniture store buys desks and chairs to be sold to customers, these items would be considered as merchandise inventory. However, if the desks and chairs are purchased for use by the office personnel, even if they will subsequently be sold or replaced, these items would not be merchandise inventory.

A merchandising enterprise must match the selling price of the merchandise sold with its related cost. When all goods purchased or manufactured are sold within the current period, determination of cost of goods sold is fairly simple. The total cost of goods purchased or manufactured is also the cost of goods sold. However, this situation is seldom found in practice. Usually some of the goods acquired during the period are still on hand at the end of the period. A cost value must be assigned to these goods. If the cost of an inventory item never changes, the cost of those units sold, as well as the cost of the inventory still on hand at the end of the period, would be relatively easy to determine.

The problem arises when the cost of an item changes from one acquisition date to the next. For example, assume that a new clock shop is established. The business makes three separate purchases of a particular type of watch. First it buys 10 watches at $50 each; a few weeks later, another 5 watches are acquired at $59 each; shortly thereafter, the company purchases 3 more watches at $65 each. At the end of the period, the company still has 12 of these watches on hand and knows that

Five Largest Mainframe Computer Manufacturers—1986

IBM	67.8%
Amdahl	8.4
Unisys	7.5
Honeywell—Bull	7.3
National Advanced Systems	4.4

The Wall Street Journal, 11/23/87
International Data Corp.

SABRE CONTROLS, INC.
3419 Grand Avenue
OAKLAND, CALIFORNIA 94610

(415) 287-6394

PURCHASE ORDER

09934

Show this Purchase Order Number on all correspondence, invoices, shipping papers and packages.

TO
Kitchen Supplies, Inc.
412 Rockwell Dr.
Hayward, Ca. 94623

DATE: 11/21/90 REQUISITION NO: 8764
SHIP TO
Sabre Controls, Inc.
3419 Grand Ave.
Oakland, Ca. 94610

REQUISITIONED BY	WHEN SHIP	SHIP VIA	F.O.B. POINT	TERMS
CD	11/26/90	Truck	Dest.	2/10, n/30

QTY. ORDERED	QTY. RECEIVED	STOCK NO. / DESCRIPTION	UNIT PRICE	TOTAL
12		Strato Electric Range-Model 508	196 00	2,352 00
20		Reliable Microwave-Model 271	127 00	2,540 00
5		Merrill Chest Freezer, 15.8 cu. ft.	260 00	1,300 00
		Total		6,192 00

1. Please send 2 copies of your invoice.
2. Order is to be entered in accordance with prices, delivery and specifications shown above.
3. Notify us immediately if you are unable to ship as specified.

C Merty
AUTHORIZED BY

ORIGINAL

it has sold 6 watches. The problem is to determine the cost of the six watches sold.

There are four generally accepted methods for determining the cost of the goods sold; (1) specific identification, (2) first-in, first-out (FIFO), (3) last-in, first-out (LIFO), and (4) weighted average.

Specific Identification

When it is possible to identify each item in the inventory with a specific purchase and purchase price, the actual cost of the good sold can be directly applied. In the previous example, if 3 watches were sold from the first purchase, 2 from the second, and 1 from the third, assign specific costs to the inventory and goods sold as follows:

Total cost of 18 watches available for sale		$990
Less ending inventory, using specific purchase invoices:		
7 watches from the first purchase at $50 each	$350	
3 watches from the second purchase at $59 each	$177	
2 watches from the third purchase at $65 each	$130	
12 watches in the ending inventory (balance sheet)		$657
Cost of watches sold (income statement)		$333

Although this procedure may be considered the desirable approach in matching costs with revenues, in practice it may be difficult to apply because cost-identification procedures often are slow, burdensome, and costly. Also, this method allows for possible profit manipulation through the selection of a specific unit to be delivered on a sale.

The other three methods do not trace the actual *physical* flow of goods other than by coincidence.

First-In, First-Out (FIFO)

This method assumes that merchandise is sold in the order of purchase, regardless of the actual physical delivery of the goods. Since many businesses try to sell their older purchases first, the FIFO method can usually be supported as logical and realistic when it is difficult to determine cost by specific identification. Using this method, the ending inventory on the balance sheet most closely represents the most recent purchase costs.

In our example, FIFO costs are assigned to the inventory and goods sold as follows:

Total cost of 18 watches available for sale		$990
Less ending inventory, using FIFO purchase invoices:		
3 watches from the third purchase at $65 each	$195	
5 watches from the second purchase at $59 each	$295	
4 watches from the first purchase at $50 each	$200	
12 watches in the ending inventory (balance sheet)		$690
Cost of watches sold (income statement)		$300

Last-In, First-Out (LIFO)

This method assumes that the most recent purchase of a specific item of merchandise is sold first, again regardless of the actual physical delivery of the goods. The principal argument for LIFO is that, on the income statement, the most recent costs are matched against the current selling price, thus allowing for a more reasonable gross profit in terms of markup and replacement of merchandise.

In our example, LIFO costs are assigned to the inventory and goods sold as follows:

Total cost of 18 watches available for sale		$990
Less ending inventory, using LIFO purchase invoices:		
10 watches from the first purchase at $50 each	$500	
2 watches from the second purchase at $59 each	$118	
12 watches in the ending inventory (balance sheet)		$618
Cost of watches sold (income statement)		$372

Weighted Average

This method is based on the assumption that merchandise sold should be charged at an average cost, with the average cost influenced by the *number* of units acquired at each price. A weighted average takes into account the number of units acquired at each purchase, while a simple average only recognizes the different purchase costs and ignores the number of units acquired with each purchase. In our example, the simple average cost per unit (watch) is $58, determined by adding the three different purchase costs and dividing by three.

First purchase cost/unit	$ 50
Second purchase cost/unit	$ 59
Third purchase cost/unit	$ 65
Total purchase cost/unit	$174 ÷ 3 = $58

The weakness with the simple average is that it ignores the quantity acquired with each purchase. To illustrate this, if 99 watches were purchased at a cost of $60 each and 1 watch was subsequently purchased at $70, it would not be fair to say that the average purchase cost was $65. The weighted-average approach weights the cost in the direction of the greater number of units acquired, causing an ending inventory to fall somewhere between FIFO and LIFO.

In our example, weighted costs are asigned to the inventory and goods sold as follows:

Total cost of 18 watches available for sale	$990
Weighted-average cost per watch ($990 ÷ 18) $55	
Ending inventory (balance sheet) 12 watches at $55	$660
Cost of goods sold (income statement)	$330

Student Review

1. The Wordy Dictionary Co. sells the easy-to-carry college dictionary. Its beginning inventory and units purchased during the year are as follows:

Beginning inventory	500 at $30 = $15,000
June 26	1,000 at $32 = $32,000
October 2	1,200 at $33 = $39,600

If the ending inventory consists of 200 dictionaries from the June purchase and 600 dictionaries from the October purchase, determine the ending inventory by the specific-identification method.

$____________

2. Pawlowski Sports sells table tennis boards. Its beginning inventory and units purchased in the current year are as follows:

Beginning inventory	20 at $65 = $1,300
April 18	40 at $67 = $2,680
August 3	50 at $66 = $3,300

If the company sold 80 boards during the year at $95 each, determine (a) ending inventory and (b) cost of goods sold by the FIFO method.

(a) $____________

(b) $____________

3. The Ace Safe Co. sells home safes. Its beginning inventory and units purchased during the current year are as follows:

Beginning inventory	15 at $220 = $3,300
May 14	40 at $226 = $9,040
November 10	35 at $227 = $7,945

If 21 home safes are unsold at year end, determine the ending inventory by the LIFO method.

$____________

4. In Shape Corp. sells the stationary bicycle. Its beginning inventory and units purchased are as follows:

Beginning inventory	25 at $310 = $ 7,750
February 26	75 at $315 = $23,625
July 3	90 at $320 = $28,800

If 173 bicycles were sold for $410 each, determine (a) ending inventory and (b) gross profit by the weighted average method.

(a) $____________

(b) $____________

Solutions to Student Review

1. $32 × 200 = $ 6,400
$33 × 600 = $19,800
$26,200

$ 26,200

2.

Cost of goods available for sale	$7,280	
Ending inventory, $95 × 30	$2,850 (a)	
Cost of goods sold	$4,430 (b)	

(a) $ 2,850

(b) $ 4,430

3. $220 × 15 = $3,300
$226 × 6 = 1,356
$4,656

$ 4,656

4. Weighted average cost per unit:

$7,750 + $23,625 + $28,800 = $60,175 ÷ 190 = $316.71

Sales ($410 × 173)		$70,930.00
Cost of goods sold:		
Goods available	$60,175.00	
Ending inventory ($316.71 × 17)	5,384.07 (a)	
Cost of goods sold		54,790.93
Gross profit		$16,139.07 (b)

(a) $ 5,384.07

(b) $ 16,139.07

Assignment 19–1

Merchandise Inventory

Name ______________________

Date ______________________

1. Reliable Motors, Inc., started selling its M car during the current year. Units purchased and costs are as follows:

June 10	20 cars at $5,800 = $116,000
August 21	15 cars at $6,100 = $ 91,500
September 3	10 cars at $6,300 = $ 63,000

If the year-end inventory of M cars consists of three cars from the August purchase and four cars from the September purchase, determine Reliable Motor's ending inventory by the specific-identification method.

$ ______________

2. Gratsky Appliances sells Hot-Pot ovens. Its beginning inventory and units purchased during the current year are as follows:

Beginning inventory	5 ovens at $320 = $1,600
May 10	4 ovens at $360 = $1,440
October 30	2 ovens at $390 = $ 780
December 7	6 ovens at $375 = $2,250

If the company sold four ovens from the beginning inventory, two ovens from the May purchase, and two from the December purchase, determine the cost of ovens sold by the specific-identification method.

$ ______________

3. Finest Quality Jewelers made the following purchases of a particular diamond brooch during the current year:

March 12	7 brooches at $ 850 = $5,950
July 30	10 brooches at $ 975 = $9,750
October 15	4 brooches at $1,020 = $4,080

If the company sold four brooches from the March purchase, eight brooches from the July purchase, and one brooch from the October purchase, determine by the specific-identification method *(a)* ending inventory cost and *(b)* cost of brooches sold.

(a) $ ______________

(b) $ ______________

4. Eraser Pen Company makes and sells the Eraser Pen. During the year, its beginning inventory and job-order productions were as follows:

Beginning inventory	2,800 pens at $41 = $114,800
February 24	7,100 pens at $43 = $305,300
July 6	3,700 pens at $44 = $162,800
October 2	1,550 pens at $46 = $ 71,300

If the company sold all its beginning inventory, 6,600 pens from the February production, 3,300 pens from the July production, and 75 pens from the October production, determine ending inventory by the FIFO method.

$ ____________

5. Winning Sports is the new local distributor of the Starter Pistol. During the current year, it made the following purchases:

May 21	325 pistols at $275
July 6	210 pistols at $292
August 30	105 pistols at $305

If the company sold 314 pistols during the current year, determine *(a)* ending inventory, and *(b)* cost of pistols sold by the FIFO method.

(a) $ ____________

(b) $ ____________

6. Precision Instruments sells the Dental Scaler to dental offices. During the current year, the company sold 9,500 scalers at $75 each. Its beginning inventory and units purchased during the year were as follows:

Beginning inventory	1,400 scalers at $45
March 31	2,500 scalers at $47
July 3	3,700 scalers at $46
November 12	2,950 scalers at $48

If the company uses the FIFO method, determine *(a)* ending inventory, and *(b)* gross profit.

(a) $ ____________

(b) $ ____________

Assignment 19–2

Merchandise Inventory

Name ______________________

Date ______________________

1. Office Protection Company sells burglar alarm systems. During the current year, its beginning inventory and units purchased were as follows:

Beginning inventory	300 at $2,300
January 11	500 at $2,550
October 6	600 at $2,625

If the company sold 842 alarm systems during the current year, determine the cost of goods sold by the LIFO method.

$ ______________

2. The Sun-Visor Corporation sells a standard-size aluminum door. Its beginning inventory and units purchased during the year were as follows:

Beginning inventory	250 doors at $110
April 6	510 doors at $125
June 17	420 doors at $130

On July 4 a fire broke out, destroying several doors. Immediately, a physical count was taken, showing that 490 doors were still in salable condition. Using the LIFO inventory method, determine the inventory-on-hand cost figure after the July 4 fire.

$ ______________

3. Quality Office Supplies sells a three-drawer, locked, file cabinet for $285. During the current year, 2,775 file cabinets were sold. The beginning inventory and units purchased during the year were as follows:

Beginning inventory	625 at $140
March 21	1,810 at $155
June 28	955 at $150
November 7	320 at $160

If the company uses the LIFO method, determine *(a)* ending inventory, and *(b)* gross profit for the year.

(a) $ ______________

(b) $ ______________

4. Aragona Roofing sells tar paper by the roll. Its beginning inventory and rolls purchased during the current year were as follows:

Beginning inventory	200 rolls at $15
April 13	500 rolls at $16
July 6	400 rolls at $17

If the company sold 830 rolls of tar paper during the current year, determine the ending inventory by the weighted-average method.

$ ________________

5. Competitive Sports Company opened for business during the current year. The company sells the Royal tennis racket. Various purchases of this racket were made during the year as follows:

May 17	50 rackets at $55
August 28	35 rackets at $57
November 6	60 rackets at $52

If the company sold 118 Royal tennis rackets during the current year, determine the cost of goods sold by the weighted-average method.

$ ________________

6. Klear Copiers, Inc., sells the K-Rex 220 copy machine. During the current year, its beginning inventory and units purchased were as follows:

Beginning inventory	110 machines at $1,250
April 7	180 machines at $1,325
July 16	135 machines at $1,360
October 11	80 machines at $1,410

If the company sold 425 machines during the year, determine the ending inventory using *(a)* FIFO, *(b)* LIFO, and *(c)* weighted-average.

(a) $ ________________ *(b)* $ ________________ *(c)* $ ________________

7. Ngo Household Wares sells a specially designed illuminated table lamp for $210. During the current year, its beginning inventory and purchases were as follows:

Beginning inventory	90 lamps at $105
March 30	110 lamps at $110
June 21	150 lamps at $120
November 4	50 lamps at $115

The company sold 80 lamps from the beginning inventory, 95 lamps from the March purchase, 75 lamps from the June purchase, and 5 lamps from the November purchase. Determine the cost of goods sold for the current year using *(a)* FIFO, *(b)* LIFO, *(c)* weighted-average, and *(d)* specific-identification.

(a) $ ________________ *(c)* $ ________________

(b) $ ________________ *(d)* $ ________________

Multiple Sports with Amy Hengst, Accountant

Multiple Sports took a complete physical inventory count of unsold merchandise on December 31, 1990. The number of units on hand of each type of merchandise, along with the necessary description, was entered on separate inventory tags.

In January, Amy summarized several inventory tags, which she entered on the following inventory sheet.

Merchandise Inventory (Dec. 31, 1990)

Tag Number	Description	Quantity
51	All-Pro tennis shirts	48
52	Easy-Wear tennis shorts	27
53	Victory warm-up suits	21
54	Stylish tennis dresses	36

The beginning inventory and units purchased of the above tagged inventory items are as follows:

Tag 51			Tag 52			Tag 53			Tag 54		
Date	Units Purch.	Unit Cost	Date	Units Purch.	Unit Cost	Date	Units Purch.	Unit Cost	Date	Units Purch.	Unit Cost
Beg. Inv.	42	$34	Beg. Inv.	30	$40	Beg. Inv.	18	$75	Beg. Inv.	12	$53
4/11	105	$35	5/26	80	$42	2/17	60	$73	6/5	41	$54
8/10	85	$37	9/21	25	$43	10/4	55	$74	9/27	47	$57

Multiple Sports always uses LIFO for tag no. 51 items, FIFO for tag no. 52 items, specific identification for tag no. 53 items, and weighted-average for tag no. 54 items. For tag no. 53, the ending inventory consists of 3 warm-up suits from the 2/27 purchase and 18 warm-up suits from the 10/4 purchase.

Based on the given information, Amy asks you to compute the total cost assigned to the ending inventory of the four items listed.

No. 51 ____________

No. 52 ____________

No. 53 ____________

No. 54 ____________

Chapter 20

Depreciation and MACRS

People make machines necessary and then machines make people unnecessary.

Learning Goals

Upon completion of this chapter, you should be able to:

1. Discuss the meaning of the term *depreciation.*
2. Explain how depreciation differs from other expenses of a business.
3. Understand the meaning of *estimated life* and *salvage value.*
4. Distinguish between *physical life* and *functional life.*
5. Define and determine the *book value* or *undepreciated cost.*
6. Distinguish between *property used in business and property used personally.*
7. Calculate depreciation if partially used in business.
8. Solve for depreciation in the year of acquisition if owned for less than one year.
9. Using the straight-line method, determine the depreciation each year.
10. Using the declining-balance method of depreciation, calculate depreciation each year.
11. Compute depreciation each year under the sum-of-the-years'-digits method of depreciation.
12. Compare and contrast the various depreciation methods.
13. Discuss and calculate the income tax methods of cost recovery for real and personal property, using the modified accelerated cost recovery system (MACRS).

Pre-1981 Depreciation

Certain costs incurred by a business, such as rent, salaries, utilities, advertising, and repairs, can be deducted as an expense against the current year's income. When property is acquired with a useful life to a business of more than one year, the cost cannot be expensed immediately but must be spread over this estimated useful life. This process is known as depreciation.

Depreciation can be defined as the allocation of the net cost of a tangible (physical) business property over its estimated useful life. The *cost* of this property includes the net invoice price, freight charges, and installation costs. The *net cost* is the acquisition cost less the estimated salvage or residual value. The *salvage value* is an estimate, made at the time the property is acquired, of the amount that will be realized on its sale or other disposition after it is no longer useful in the business. The *book value,* or *undepreciated cost,* is the cost of property, less total accumulated depreciation recognized from the time of acquisition to the present time.

Example 1. Company A buys a typewriter at a total cost of $325. In three years the company expects to sell the typewriter for $50. The net cost, out of pocket expense, to be depreciated is $275.

Top Five U.S. Cities Visited by Foreign Travelers

New York	27.7%
Los Angeles	21.9
San Francisco	15.7
Honolulu	13.5
Miami	10.1

San Francisco Chronicle, 3/21/88
Lodging Hospitality © 1988 Universal Press

The kind of business property subject to a depreciation deduction consists of physical property having a limited useful life in excess of one year. Since land does not have a limited life, its cost cannot be depreciated. Examples of physical properties that may be depreciated include buildings, machinery, equipment, and transportation vehicles.

The useful life of the depreciable property is an estimate, made at the time the property is acquired, of how long this property will be used in the business. It does not necessarily refer to the physical life of the property. To illustrate, the typewriter referred to in example 1 may have a total physical life of 15 years before it becomes useless. However, the company policy may be to replace the typewriter with an improved model after three years. Useful life can be estimated by considering *physical* factors such as wear and tear, deterioration, and decay, and *functional* factors, such as obsolescence and inadequacy due to growth of the company.

The depreciation deduction is allowed only for property used in a trade or business. Depreciation may not be taken on property held for personal use, such as a personal residence or automobile. If property is used for business and personal purposes, depreciation may be taken only on the cost relating to the business portion.

Example 2. Five-sevenths of the total mileage of a car is for business purposes. If the car cost $8,400, depreciation could be taken each year on the $6,000 cost ($\frac{5}{7}$ of $8,400) attributable to business use.

Since depreciable property is not usually acquired at the beginning of the tax year, the general practice is to prorate the depreciation for the first year on the basis of the nearest number of months held. For example, any purchase made up to the 15th of a month is normally treated as acquired on the 1st of that month. A purchase made on the 16th of the month or later is usually treated as acquired the 1st of the following month. Since the depreciation process is based on an estimated life and an estimated salvage life, all depreciation problems in this book should be rounded off to the nearest dollar in order to avoid implying an accuracy that does not exist.

Any reasonable method that is consistently applied may be used in computing depreciation. The three most common methods are:

1. Straight-line
2. Declining-balance
3. Sum-of-the-years'-digits

Straight-Line Method

The most common and simplest method of computing depreciation is the straight-line method. The cost or other basis of the property less the estimated salvage value, if any, is deducted in equal annual amounts over the estimated useful life of the property.

Example 3. A truck is acquired on August 20 at a total cost of $13,000. It has an estimated life of four years and a salvage value of $1,600. Find the depreciation deduction for the first and second year.

$$\textbf{Annual depreciation} = \$13{,}000 - \$1{,}600 = \frac{\$11{,}400}{4} = \$2{,}850$$

First year: August 20 is considered to be September 1 and four months' depreciation can be taken.

$$\$2{,}850 \times \frac{4}{12} = \$950$$

Second year: A full year's depreciation of $2,850 can be taken.

Declining-Balance Method

The straight-line method provides for a constant amount of annual depreciation. The declining-balance method produces a constant rate of depreciation, applied to the book value of the property at the beginning of each year without regard to salvage value. However, once book value equals the salvage value, no additional depreciation may be taken. Since the undepreciated cost remaining each year will decrease, the amount of depreciation under the declining-balance method must also decrease.

The maximum rate that may be used to compute depreciation each year under the declining-balance method cannot exceed twice the rate that would be used under the straight-line method. The declining-balance method can only be used if the property has a useful life of at least three years.

Example 4. Morena Company purchases a new industrial scale on April 5 for \$8,000. The scale is given a five-year life with an estimated salvage value of \$1,000. Determine the depreciation for each year of use by the declining-balance method. The straight-line is 20 percent ($\frac{1}{5}$) per year. Under the declining-balance method, the scale may be depreciated at 40 percent ($\frac{2}{5}$) per year.

Year 1 $\$8{,}000 \times \frac{2}{5} \times \frac{9}{12} = \$2{,}400$

Year 2

\$8,000	(previous undepreciated cost)
− 2,400	(depreciation in Year 1)
\$5,600	(declining balance)

$\$5{,}600 \times \frac{2}{5} = \$2{,}240$

Year 3

$\$5{,}600 - 2{,}240 = \$3{,}360 \times \frac{2}{5} = \$1{,}344$

Year 4

$\$3{,}360 - 1{,}344 = \$2{,}016 \times \frac{2}{5} = \$806$

Year 5

$\$2{,}016 - 806 = \$1{,}210 \times \frac{2}{5} = \$484$

In year 5, the formula allows for depreciation of \$484. However, since the salvage value is \$1,000, only depreciation of \$210 can be deducted in year 5, with no additional depreciation allowed in subsequent years.

Sum-of-the-Years'-Digits Method

The straight-line method provides for the same amount of depreciation for each full year of property use. The sum-of-the-years'-digits method is similar to the declining-balance method in that the amount of depreciation taken is largest in the first year and becomes progressively smaller each year of the asset life. However, the rate of annual decrease by sum-of-the-years'-digits is not as severe as under declining-balance.

Under sum-of-the-years'-digits, depreciation each year is determined by multiplying a decreasing fraction times the cost of the asset less the estimated salvage value. The denominator of the fraction, which remains constant, is the total of the digits representing the years of estimated useful life of the property. For example, if the estimated useful life is three years, the denominator is six, the sum of 3 + 2 + 1. The numerator of the fraction changes each year, based on the years of useful life remaining at the beginning of the year for which the computation is made. For the first year of a three-year estimated useful life, the numerator would be 3, for the second year 2, and for the third year 1.

The sum-of-the-years'-digits method may be used only on new property that meets the declining-balance requirements.

If the property has a long life, the denominator of the fraction can be found by the following formula, assuming n is equal to the number of years of estimated life

$$\frac{n(n+1)}{2}$$

Thus, for property having a three-year life, the denominator could be determined as follows:

$$\frac{3(3+1)}{2} = 6$$

Example 5. Morena Company purchases a new industrial scale on January 2 for $8,000. The scale has a five-year life with an estimated salvage value of $1,500. Determine the depreciation for all five years by the sum-of-the-years'-digits method.

Year 1	**$8,000**	**cost**
	− 1,500	**salvage value**
	$6,500	**net cost**
	$6,500 × $\frac{5}{15}$ = $2,167	
Year 2	**$6,500 × $\frac{4}{15}$ = $1,733**	
Year 3	**$6,500 × $\frac{3}{15}$ = $1,300**	
Year 4	**$6,500 × $\frac{2}{15}$ = $ 867**	
Year 5	**$6,500 × $\frac{1}{15}$ = $ 433**	
Total depreciation	**$6,500**	

It should be noted that the depreciation will decrease by the same amount each full year, in this case by $\frac{1}{15}$ of $6,500, or $433.

Example 6. Assume the same facts as in example 5, except that the scale was purchased on April 5, as in example 4. Since the scale was not used for a full year in year 1, the fraction $\frac{5}{15}$ can only be applied for the portion of the year in which the property was used. However, the remaining portion of the fraction $\frac{5}{15}$ must be completed in year 2 before the fraction $\frac{4}{15}$ can be applied.

Year 1	**$\$6,500 \times \frac{5}{15} \times \frac{9}{12} =$**		**$1,625**
Year 2	**$\$6,500 \times \frac{5}{15} \times \frac{3}{12} =$**	**$ 524**	
	$+\$6,500 \times \frac{4}{15} \times \frac{9}{12} =$	**1,300**	**1,842**
Year 3	**$\$6,500 \times \frac{4}{15} \times \frac{3}{12} =$**	**$ 433**	
	$+\$6,500 \times \frac{3}{15} \times \frac{9}{12} =$	**975**	**1,408**
Year 4	**$\$6,500 \times \frac{3}{15} \times \frac{3}{12} =$**	**$ 325**	
	$+\$6,500 \times \frac{2}{15} \times \frac{9}{12} =$	**650**	**975**
Year 5	**$\$6,500 \times \frac{2}{15} \times \frac{3}{12} =$**	**$ 217**	
	$+\$6,500 \times \frac{1}{15} \times \frac{9}{12} =$	**325**	**542**
Year 6	**$\$6,500 \times \frac{1}{15} \times \frac{3}{12} =$**		**108**
Total depreciation			**$6,500**

Once again, it should be noted that the depreciation decreases by the same amount each full year, $433.

Post-1980 ACRS

Under the Economic Recovery Act of 1981, Congress enacted a new depreciation procedure for federal income tax purposes, known as the Accelerated Cost Recovery System (ACRS).

As a general rule, the cost of eligible business *personal* property usually was to be recovered over a three- or five-year period, based on the use of 150 percent declining balance, switching to straight-line in year 2, when the straight-line method provided a greater cost recovery. Under ACRS, the *entire* cost is to be recovered, which means that the salvage value, if any, is to be ignored. Three-year property included transportation vehicles such as cars and light-duty trucks, and research and experimentation equipment, while five-year property included computers, copiers, and other machinery, equipment, and furniture.

Under ACRS, the cost of *real* property, exclusive of the land, that was placed in service after 1980 and before March 16, 1984, is fully recoverable over a period of 15 years. Real property placed in service after March 15, 1984, and before May 9, 1985, is fully recoverable over a period of 18 years, while real property placed in service after May 8, 1985, and before January 1, 1987, is fully recoverable over a period of 19 years.

The depreciation deduction for federal income tax purposes must be calculated using the ACRS rules for assets placed in service after 1980 and before 1987.

Post-1986 MACRS

Under the Tax Reform Act of 1986, Congress enacted a modified accelerated cost recovery system (MACRS) that applies to all tangible property placed in service after December 31, 1986. Each item of property depreciated under MACRS is assigned a recovery life ranging from 3 to $31\frac{1}{2}$ years.

Personal Property.[1] As a general rule, the cost of eligible business personal property is to be recovered over a five- or seven-year period, depending on the type of property. Table 20–1 shows the prescribed rates. These rates use the double (200 percent) declining method, switching to the straight-line method, in the fourth year for five-year property, and the fifth year for seven-year property, when straight-line provides a greater cost recovery.[2] Also, a half-year convention is to be used in most situations, which means that a half-year of depreciation is taken for the first year the property is placed in service and in the year of disposition, regardless of the specific date of purchase or sale. If the property is held for the entire recovery period, a half-year of depreciation is allowable for the year following the recovery period. Under MACRS, cost recovery based on the nearest number of months held is not to be used for personal property.

Table 20–1 Applicable Percents

	Recovery Period	
Recovery Year	**Five Years**	**Seven Years**
1	20.00%	14.29%
2	32.00	24.49
3	19.20	17.49
4	11.52	12.49
5	11.52	8.93
6	5.76	8.92
7		8.93
8		4.46

[1] Certain business properties are treated as 3-, 10-, 15-, or 20-year property but, since not found in most businesses, will not be discussed in this text.

[2] In this text, the half-year convention will be followed. We will ignore the mid-quarter convention, which occurs when over 40 percent of the cost of depreciable property is acquired during the last three months of the tax year.

Effective in 1988, though the maximum amount of depreciation taken on other personal property assets each year is not limited, the maximum depreciation deduction for each passenger automobile is $2,560 in the year of purchase, $4,100 in the second year, $2,450 in the third, and $1,475 in each succeeding year. Congress enacted this provision in order to prevent businesses from taking large annual write-offs of very expensive automobiles.

Five Years. Tangible personal property eligible for cost recovery in five years under MACRS includes transportation vehicles, such as cars, buses, and trucks; computers; office machinery, such as typewriters, calculators, and copiers; and any property used in connection with research and experimentation.

Example 1. On February 5, 1990, Ellen Vuong bought a car for $10,000 to be used exclusively in her business. Using Table 20–1, her cost recovery is as follows:

Year	Depreciation	
1990	$ 2,000	($10,000 × .2)
1991	3,200	($10,000 × .32)
1992	1,920	($10,000 × .192)
1993	1,152	($10,000 × .1152)
1994	1,152	($10,000 × .1152)
1995	576	($10,000 × .0576)
	$10,000	

Seven Years. Tangible personal property eligible for cost recovery in seven years under MACRS includes office furniture, fixtures, and equipment, such as desks, files, safes, and most manufacturing machinery and equipment.

Example 2. On October 5, 1990, Dunston Corp. acquired several desks at a total cost of $14,500. Using Table 20–1, its cost recovery is as follows:

Year	Depreciation	
1990	$ 2,072	($14,500 × .1429)
1991	3,551	($14,500 × .2449)
1992	2,536	($14,500 × .1749)
1993	1,811	($14,500 × .1249)
1994	1,295	($14,500 × .0893)
1995	1,293	($14,500 × .0892)
1996	1,295	($14,500 × .0893)
1997	647	($14,500 × .0446)
	$14,500	

Instead of using the declining-balance method under MACRS, one can elect to use the straight-line method over the recovery period, ignoring any salvage value and taking a half-year depreciation the first year. Problems using the MACRS straight-line method will not be covered in this text.

Expense Deduction. A business can elect to expense up to $10,000 of the cost of most tangible *personal* property acquired within the tax year instead of capitalizing and depreciating the cost. However, for each dollar of cost of this property acquired during the year in excess of $200,000, the $10,000 maximum is reduced by one dollar. Also, the maximum total deduction for passenger automobiles of $2,560 in the year of purchase, as mentioned previously, still applies.

Example 3. In example 2, Dunston Corp. could have expensed up to $10,000 of the cost of the desks in 1990 and recovered the remaining cost of $4,500 over an eight-year period beginning in 1990.

Exâmple 4. If in example 2, Dunston Corp. had purchasesd a total of $206,000 in tangible personal property, including the desks, only up to $4,000 could be expensed in 1990.

Example 5. If a company purchased office furniture for $8,500 and a computer for $12,000 in the same year, it can elect to expense the entire $8,500 for the furniture and $1,500 for he computer, or any other combination adding up to $10,000, with the remaining balance recoverable over 7 years on the furniture, or 5 years on the computer.

Residential Rental Property. This includes any real property that is a rental building for which 80 percent or more of the gross rental income for the tax year is rental income from dwelling units. This property is depreciated by the straight-line method and a mid-month convention over 27.5 years. The mid-month convention means that property acquired, or disposed of, during a month is depreciated for one-half of that month.

Example 6. Ivan Quinones purchased an apartment building on September 25, 1990, for $400,000, of which $100,000 is assigned to the land. The MACRS depreciation rate for a full year is 3.636 percent, which is determined by dividing 1 by 27.5. The depreciation for 1990 is $\frac{3.5}{12}$ of a full year's depreciation.

1990: $\$300{,}000 \times .03636 \times \frac{3.5}{12} = \$3{,}182$

1991: $\$300{,}000 \times .03636 = \$10{,}908$

Note that the depreciation expense is the same as 1991 for each year through 2017 unless the apartment building was sold beforehand. In the year 2018, the remaining $\frac{2.5}{12}$ of .03636, or .00758, of $300,000 would be depreciated.

Nonresidential Real Property. This includes any real property that is not residential rental property. This property is depreciated by the straight-line method using a mid-month convention over 31.5 years.

Example 7. The Fits-All Locksmith Co. purchased a building for its business use on March 2, 1991, at a cost of \$325,000, including \$125,000 assigned to the land. The MACRS depreciation rate for a full year is 3.175 percent, which is determined by dividing 1 by 31.5. The depreciation for 1991 is $\frac{9.5}{12}$ of a full year's depreciation.

1991: $\$200{,}000 \times .03175 \times \frac{9.5}{12} = \$5{,}027$

1992: $\$200{,}000 \times .03175 = \$6{,}350$

Note that the depreciation expense will remain the same as in 1992 for the succeeding 29 years. In the 32nd year, the remaining $\frac{8.5}{12}$ of .03175, or .02249, of \$200,000 would be depreciated.

The IRS does provide tables for both 27.5 year and 31.5 year property which tells what percent of the original cost to depreciate each year, depending on the month of purchase. However, except for the first and last year, the depreciation rate for 27.5 year property is 3.636 or 3.637 percent each year, while the depreciation rate each year for 31.5 year property, except for the first and last year, is either 3.175 or 3.174 percent.

"Opinions are getting stronger!"

From *The Wall Street Journal,* with permission of Cartoon Features Syndicate

Student Review

1. The Big-Rig Equipment Co. acquired a pallet truck on August 22 at a cost of $8,800. If the truck has an estimated life of 6 years and a salvage life of $1,300, find the straight-line depreciation for *(a)* the first year and *(b)* the second year.

(a) $____________

(b) $____________

2. The Innovative Research Co. acquired several new lab scales on April 8 at a total cost of $2,800. If the scales have an estimated life of 5 years and a total salvage value of $700, determine the depreciation for *(a)* the third year and *(b)* the fourth year by the declining-balance method.

(a) $____________

(b) $____________

3. Digital Programmers acquired a countertop for $4,000 on September 28. Based on an estimated life of 8 years and a salvage value of $1,120, determine the depreciation for *(a)* the first year and *(b)* the second year by the sum-of-the-years'-digits method.

(a) $____________

(b) $____________

4. Rhonda Ng purchased a commercial building for $310,000 on August 20, 1990. If the cost assigned to the land was $93,000, determine the cost recovery in 1990 and 1991, using MACRS.

1990 $____________

1991 $____________

5. Air-Land-Sea Travel purchased a computer terminal for $15,000. Using MACRS, determine the cost recovery in *(a)* the first year and *(b)* the second year.

(a) $____________

(b) $____________

Solutions to Student Review

1. ($8,800 − $1,300) ÷ 6 = $1,250 Annual Depreciation

(a) $\$1,250 \times \frac{4}{12} = \$417$ — *(a)* $ 417

(b) $1,250 — *(b)* $ 1,250

2. $\$2,800 \times \frac{2}{5} \times \frac{9}{12} = \$840$—1st Year

$(\$2,800 - \$840) \times \frac{2}{5} = \$784$—2nd Year

(a) $(\$1,960 - \$784) \times \frac{2}{5} = \$470$—3rd Year — *(a)* $ 470

(b) $(\$1,176 - \$470) \times \frac{2}{5} = \$282$; however, book value equals salvage value after $6 depreciation in the 4th year. — *(b)* $ 6

3. $\frac{8(8 + 1)}{2} = 36$ Sum-of-the-Years' Digits

$4,000 − $1,120 = $2,880 Depreciable Cost

(a) $\$2,880 \times \frac{8}{36} \times \frac{3}{12} = \$160$ — *(a)* $ 160

(b) $\$2,880 \times \frac{8}{36} \times \frac{9}{12} = \$480$

$+ \$2,880 \times \frac{7}{36} \times \frac{3}{12} = +\$140$

$620 — *(b)* $ 620

4. $310,000 − $93,000 = $217,000 (Building)

1990 $217,000 × .0119 = $2,582 — 1990 $ 2,582

1991 $217,000 × .03175 = $6,890 — 1991 $ 6,890

5. *(a)* $15,000 × .20 = $3,000 — *(a)* $ 3,000

(b) $15,000 × .32 = $4,800 — *(b)* $ 4,800

Assignment 20–1

Depreciation

Name ____________________

Date ____________________

A. For each of the following, find the annual depreciation by the straight-line method to the nearest dollar.

	Cost	Salvage Value	Estimated Useful Life	Annual Depreciation
1.	$ 720	0	4 years	$ ________
2.	$ 1,940	$ 140	8 years	$ ________
3.	$24,365	$2,500	7 years	$ ________
4.	$ 6,424	0	11 years	$ ________

B. For each of the following, determine the undepreciated cost after the indicated number of years of business use, using the straight-line method of depreciation.

	Cost	Salvage Value	Estimated Useful Life	Years Used to Date	Undepreciated Cost
1.	$ 7,240	$1,640	8 years	6	$ ________
2.	$ 320	0	4 years	$1\frac{1}{2}$	$ ________
3.	$ 4,516	$ 500	6 years	5	$ ________
4.	$18,792	$1,800	9 years	$2\frac{1}{4}$	$ ________

C. **1.** Find the depreciation by the straight-line method for *(a)* the first year and *(b)* the second year of a printing press purchased on January 5, at a cost of $6,000, if the estimated life is 8 years and the estimated salvage value is $200.

(a) $ ________

(b) $ ________

2. Doris Kelly purchased a desk to be used in her business at a cost of $600. If she estimates a useful life of 6 years and a salvage value of $60, using the straight-line method, determine *(a)* the annual depreciation and *(b)* the book value of the desk at the end of 4 years.

(a) $ ________

(b) $ ________

3. If a cement mixer is purchased on November 10 at a cost of $4,500, find the straight-line depreciation for *(a)* the first year and *(b)* the second year, if the estimated life is 8 years and the estimated salvage value is $300.

(a) $__________

(b) $__________

4. The Devoulin Company acquired 10 adding machines on May 10 at a cost of $185 each. The adding machines were given an estimated life of 8 years, with a salvage value of $35 per machine. Find the total depreciation by the straight-line method for *(a)* the first year and *(b)* the second year.

(a) $__________

(b) $__________

5. A used automobile is purchased on April 8 at a cost of $3,200. It is used 80 percent in the business, has an estimated salvage value of $600, and an estimated useful life of 4 years. Determine the depreciation by the straight-line method *(a)* the first year and *(b)* the second year.

(a) $__________

(b) $__________

6. Gary Schaffer purchased a three-flat building on September 25 for $90,000. The cost of the building was determined to be $60,000, with the residual assigned to the land. Mr. Schaffer lives in one of the flats and rents out the other two. If the building is estimated to have a 25-year life, determine the depreciation by the straight-line method for *(a)* the first year and *(b)* the second year.

(a) $__________

(b) $__________

Assignment 20–2

Depreciation

Name ______________________

Date ______________________

A. The Mendelson Company purchased several new items of office equipment. For each of the following purchases, determine the annual depreciation for the indicated year of use by the declining-balance method.

	Cost	*Salvage Value*	*Estimated Useful Life*	*Current Year of Use*	*Depreciation for Current Year*
1.	$ 7,000	$1,000	8 years	1	$ ______________
2.	$ 2,500	0	5 years	2	$ ______________
3.	$10,800	$2,800	6 years	4	$ ______________
4.	$ 5,600	$ 800	4 years	4	$ ______________

B. **1.** On January 8, the Engster Cookie Company acquired a new cookie-slicing machine for $7,500, with an estimated useful life of 6 years. Determine the depreciation for *(a)* the first year and *(b)* the second year by the declining-balance method.

(a) $ ______________

(b) $ ______________

2. Using the declining-balance method, find the depreciation for *(a)* the first year and *(b)* the second year of a truck-trailer purchased on January 4 for $6,000, which is used 75 percent in the business, and has an estimated life of 6 years and an estimated salvage value of $500.

(a) $ ______________

(b) $ ______________

3. Several new office machines are purchased for a total cost of $9,000 on August 25. They have an estimated life of 5 years and a salvage value of $1,000. Determine the depreciation deduction for *(a)* the first year and *(b)* the second year by the declining-balance method.

(a) $ ______________

(b) $ ______________

4. Kuhns and Kerr formed a partnership known as K&K Investment Advisory Service. They purchased 2 new stock-quotation machines on November 5 at a total cost of $15,000. If the quote machines are given an estimated life of 5 years, with no salvage value, determine the maximum depreciation for *(a)* the first year and *(b)* the second year by the declining-balance method.

(a) $________________

(b) $________________

5. Pacchetti Builders purchased a new cement mixer on March 1 for $5,800. If the estimated useful life is 5 years, and the estimated salvage value is $800, determine the depreciation by the declining-balance method for *(a)* the fourth year and *(b)* the fifth year.

(a) $________________

(b) $________________

6. Morris Tow Truck Service acquired a tow truck on January 5, 1990, for $7,200. The truck was given an estimated life of 4 years and a salvage value of $500. On January 4, 1993, the tow truck was sold for $1,000. Indicate whether *(a)* the selling price was greater or less than the book value at the time of the sale and *(b)* by how much, using the declining-balance method for accounting purposes.

(a) $________________

(b) $________________

Assignment 20–3

Depreciation

Name ______________________

Date ______________________

A. The Offshore Oil Company purchased several new pieces of drilling equipment. For each of the following purchases, determine the annual depreciation for the indicated year of use by the sum-of-the-years'-digits method.

	Cost	*Salvage Value*	*Estimated Useful Life*	*Current Year of Use*	*Depreciation for Current Year*
1.	$ 1,600	$250	4	1	$ ____________
2.	$ 2,800	$100	9	2	$ ____________
3.	$18,600	0	15	12	$ ____________
4.	$ 3,000	$300	3	3	$ ____________

B. 1. By the sum-of-the-years'-digits method, find the depreciation for *(a)* the first year and *(b)* the second year of a machine purchased on January 10 at a cost of $7,500, with an estimated life of 6 years and an estimated salvage value of $1,200.

(a) $ ____________

(b) $ ____________

2. The Chipper Clipper Barber Shop purchased new chairs on January 3 for $9,000. The estimated useful life of the chairs is 8 years. Assuming that there is no estimated salvage value, determine the depreciation for *(a)* the first year and *(b)* the second year by the sum-of-the-years'-digits method.

(a) $ ____________

(b) $ ____________

3. K & F Industries acquired a printing press on May 20 at a cost of $35,000. It was given an estimated life of 8 years and a salvage value of $2,600. By the sum-of-the-years'-digits method, determine the depreciation for *(a)* the first year and *(b)* the second year.

(a) $ ____________

(b) $ ____________

4. If a new residential building, exclusive of the land, is purchased at a cost of $46,000 on September 29, find the depreciation for *(a)* the first year and *(b)* the second year, if the estimated life is 45 years, using the sum-of-the-year's-digits method.

(a) $__________

(b) $__________

5. The Speedie Delivery Company acquired a new delivery van on May 10, 1990, for $8,400. The van was given an estimated life of 4 years and a salvage value of $900. On January 8, 1993, the van was sold for $2,000. If the sum-of-the-years'-digits method was used for accounting purposes, determine *(a)* the depreciation for 1992 and *(b)* whether the selling price was greater or less than the undepreciated cost at the time of the sale, and *(c)* by how much.

(a) $__________

(b) $__________

(c) $__________

6. The Stewart Company purchased three new machines on April 5 at a cost of $8,000 each. The company could not decide which depreciation method to use. Therefore, the company decided to take straight-line on Machine 1, sum-of-the-years'-digits on Machine 2, and declining balance on Machine 3. Determine the depreciation for each machine in the *second* year if each machine is given an estimated life of 4 years and a salvage value of $800.

Machine 1 $__________

Machine 2 $__________

Machine 3 $__________

Assignment 20–4

MACRS

Name ______________________

Date ______________________

A. Advanced Medical Research Company purchased several pieces of equipment and furniture and a transportation vehicle in 1990. For each of the following purchases, determine the cost recovery for the indicated year by use of MACRS.

	Cost	*Recovery Period*	*Current Year of Use*	*Cost Recovery*
1.	$18,300	5 years	1	$________
2.	$ 9,720	7 years	1	$________
3.	$12,684	7 years	3	$________
4.	$14,650	5 years	2	$________
5.	$ 7,125	5 years	4	$________
6.	$13,860	7 years	8	$________

B. Marc Benioff purchased four residential-rental properties in 1990. For each property, determine the cost recovery for the indicated year by use of MACRS. The indicated cost is exclusive of land.

	Cost	*Month of Purchase*	*Current Year of Use*	*Cost Recovery*
1.	$280,000	April	1	$________
2.	$150,000	November	8	$________
3.	$172,000	March	10	$________
4.	$371,000	July	14	$________

C. **1.** Rosner Ambulance Service purchased a new ambulance on October 10, 1990, for $15,620. Determine the cost recovery in 1990, 1991, and 1992, using MACRS.

1986 $________

1987 $________

1988 $________

2. Samuel Powers, a research chemist, purchased research equipment on May 5, 1991, for $13,500. Determine his cost recovery in 1994, using MACRS.

1994 $________

3. If, in problem 2, Powers elected to expense $10,000 in 1991, determine his cost recovery in 1995 and 1996.

1995 $__________ 1996 $__________

4. Price Company purchased an electronic microscope on October 28, 1990, for $11,625. Determine the cost recovery in 1991 and 1992, using MACRS, recoverable over 7 years.

1991 $__________ 1992 $__________

5. If, in problem 4, Price Company purchased the microscope as research equipment, determine the cost recovery for 1992 and 1993.

1992 $__________ 1993 $__________

6. Derek Jensen purchased a commercial building for $260,000 on March 3, 1991. The cost assigned to the land was $110,000. Determine the cost recovery in 1991 and 1992, using MACRS.

1991 $__________ 1992 $__________

7. If, in problem 6, Jensen had purchased an apartment building, determine his cost recovery in 1991 and 1992.

1991 $__________ 1992 $__________

8. Vickie Lum purchased a duplex for $230,000 on August 12, 1990. The cost assigned to the land was $50,000. She lives in one of the units. Determine her cost recovery for 1990 and 1991, using MACRS.

1990 $__________ 1991 $__________

9. In problem 8, if Lum lived in one unit and rented the other unit professionally to an acupuncturist, determine her cost recovery in 1990 and 1991.

1990 $__________ 1991 $__________

10. Tasty Confectioners purchased a candy processing machine on May 2, 1991, for $22,730. The company elected to expense $10,000 in 1991. Determine cost recovery in 1991 and 1992, recoverable over 7 years.

1991 $__________ 1992 $__________

Multiple Sports with Amy Hengst, Accountant

After you helped Amy complete the year-end inventory sheets, she asks you to calculate depreciation on some of the depreciable items owned by Multiple Sports at December 31, 1990. A partial subsidiary ledger listing of the building and equipment owned by Multiple Sports shows the following:

						Depreciation	
Description	Date Acquired	Est. Life	Method	Cost	Salvage Value	Prior	Current
Computer	4/10/89	5 years	SYD	$ 9,240	$1,740	$ 1,875	______
Cash register	7/30/88	6	DDB	1,872	250	797	______
Office couch	4/28/90	5	SL	490	70	—	______
Building	11/4/87	25	SL	120,000	—	10,400	______

Amy always likes to recalculate the prior depreciation before determining the current year's depreciation. Amy asks you to help her recalculate the accuracy of the prior depreciation and then determine the current year's depreciation for the company accounting statements.

After completing the above calculations, Amy wants you to assist her in determining the depreciation for the calendar year 1990 for federal income tax purposes, using MACRS.

MACRS:

Computer ______________

Cash Register ______________

Office Couch ______________

Building ______________

Section 6

Simple Interest

Chapter 21

Introduction to Simple Interest

Use our easy credit plan—100 percent down.

Learning Goals

Upon completion of this chapter, you should be able to:

1. Define the meaning of the term *interest.*
2. Discuss the features of a *promissory note.*
3. Define the terms *principal*, *interest rate*, *time*, and *maturity value.*
4. Compute the number of days of a loan by 30-day-month time and by exact time.
5. Find the due date of a loan.
6. Define the terms *ordinary interest* and *accurate interest.*
7. Find simple interest by the cancellation method, using the formula $I = Prt$.
8. Determine the maturity value of a loan.

Simple Interest

When a man rents a house or a car, he must pay for the use of the property borrowed. This periodic payment is called rent. If he borrows money, he must usually pay rent for the use of that money. The rent charge for the use of the money is called *interest.*

Promissory Notes

A loan that includes payments of interest on the principal balance is usually evidenced by a negotiable instrument known as a promissory note. A promissory note is sometimes referred to as a two-party paper, because only two parties are involved initially.

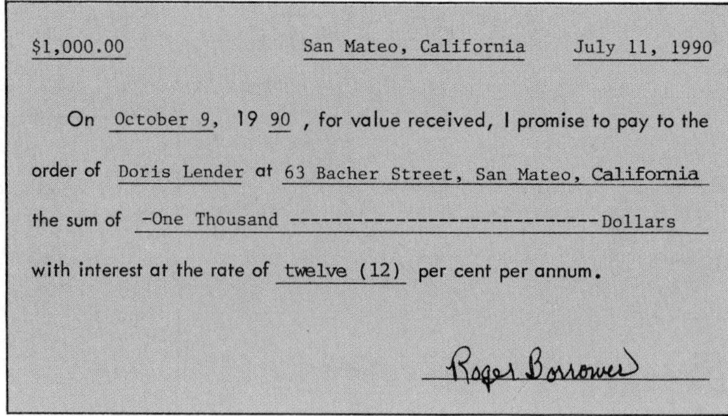

$1,000.00 San Mateo, California July 11, 1990

On October 9, 19 90 , for value received, I promise to pay to the order of Doris Lender at 63 Bacher Street, San Mateo, California the sum of -One Thousand ---------------------------- Dollars with interest at the rate of twelve (12) per cent per annum.

Roger Borrower

A note contains the promise of a party called the *maker*, or borrower, to pay another party, usually called the *payee*, or lender, a sum of money on a fixed or determinable date, or on demand.

Simple Interest Formula

When an individual or business borrows money, the amount borrowed is called the *principal*. When one borrows money, it is borrowed for a period of *time*, either in years or fraction of a year. The *rate* of interest represents the annual percent charged for the use of money. Interest rates are always expressed on an annual basis. The maturity value of a note is the sum of the amount borrowed and the amount of interest charged on the loan.

The amount of interest is the product of the principal, time, and rate. The formula may be expressed as follows:

$I = Prt$
I is the amount of interest
P is the principal, or amount borrowed
r is the rate of interest
t is the time of the loan, in years

Example 1. Determine interest on $300 at 9 percent for 2 years.

$$I = \$300 \times \frac{9}{100} \times 2$$
$$I = \$54$$

Note that the interest rate was presented in common fractional form ($\frac{9}{100}$). The interest rate in the formula could be presented in decimal fractional form (.09), but we would lose the advantage in many situations of canceling before, or sometimes instead of, multiplying.

Calendar

The amount borrowed and the interest rate on a loan are given. The number of days on a loan may be given, though in many cases it must be determined. If the days are not given, but are determinable, it is essential, in counting the days of a loan to know the exact number of days in each month. Except for February, the number of days in each month never changes. Since it takes the earth approximately $365\frac{1}{4}$ days to make a complete revolution around the sun, it becomes necessary to add an extra day to our calendar year every fourth year. February, which normally has 28 days, has a 29th day every fourth year, otherwise known as leap year. To determine if a particular year is a leap year, divide the last two digits of the calendar year by 4. If there is no remainder, that year is a leap year.

Example 2. 19*92* is a leap year becuse 92 is divisible by 4 without a remainder.

19*90* is not a leap year because 90 is not divisible by 4 without a remainder.

The table below lists the months and the number of days in each:

Month Name	Number of Days
January	31
February	28 (or 29 in leap year)
March	31
April	30
May	31
June	30
July	31
August	31
September	30
October	31
November	30
December	31

Computing Time

The two most common methods of computing the number of days of a loan are (1) 30-day-month time and (2) exact time.

Thirty-Day-Month Time

In many business transactions, for computational purposes, a year is considered to have 360 days, divided into 12 months of 30 days each. This is done in order to simplify the mathematics of interest calculations, with only an insignificant difference in the amount of interest charged.

Thirty-day-month time is usually found in long-term loans, such as on the purchase of a house or an automobile, with payments to be made over a period of years.

Average National Football League Salaries—1986

Quarterbacks	$333,600
Running backs	230,000
Defensive linemen	225,500
Linebackers	198,000
Receivers	197,000
Offensive linemen	194,700
Defensive back	178,000
Tight ends	164,600
Punters	107,000
Overall average	203,565

San Francisco Chronicle, 11/27/87
1987 Universal Press
Sports Industry News

If the period of the loan is less than one year, the number of days that the loan is outstanding, using 30-day-month time, can be determined as follows:

1. If the due date in the month the loan matures falls later than the day when the loan was made, count the number of months from the month of origin of the loan to the month of maturity and multiply by 30. Add to this product the difference between the day of maturity and the day of origin.

Example 3. Find the number of days from June 8 to November 12.

Months from June 8 to November 8 =	**5**
	× 30 days per month
	150 days
Days from Nov. 8 to Nov. 12	**+ 4 days**
Total number of days of loan, 30-day-month time	**154 days**

2. If the due date in the month the loan matures comes before the day when the loan was made, count the number of months from the month of origin of the loan to the month of maturity and multiply by 30. Deduct from this product the difference between the day of origin and the day of maturity.

Example 4. Find the number of days from May 20 to September 9.

Months from May 20 to Sept. 20 =	**4**
	× 30 days per month
	120 days
Days from Sept. 20 to Sept. 9	**− 11 days**
Total number of days of loan, 30-day-month time	**109 days**

If the length of time of a loan exceeds one year, it is preferable to use a compound-time method of computing 30-day-month time. Using this method, list on the top line the year, month, and day of maturity. Directly below, list the year, month, and day of origin. The maturity figures minus the origin figures will provide the years, months, and days that the note is outstanding.

Example 5. Find the number of days from July 30, 1990 to April 4, 1994.

Year	***Month***	***Day***
	15	
93	~~3~~	34
19~~94~~	**~~4~~**	**~~4~~**
− 1990	**7**	**30**
3 years	**8 months**	**4 days**

(1,080 days) + (240 days) + (4 days) = 1,324 days

If the number in the minuend is smaller than the number in the subtrahend, you must borrow. In this example, it was necessary to borrow one month, or 30 days, and one year, or 12 months.

When using 30-day-month time, if the day of origin is 31, and the month of maturity has 30 days, change the day of origin to 30. If February is the month of maturity, change the day of origin to 28 (29 if a leap year).

If in example 5, the note originated on July 31, 1990, the number of days of the loan would still be 1,324.

Exact Time

Most interest calculations use exact time. This method requires counting the actual number of days from the date of origin to the date of maturity.

Example 6. Find the number of days from March 20 to July 8.

March 20 to March 31	**=**	**11 days**
April	**=**	**30 days**
May	**=**	**31 days**
June	**=**	**30 days**
July	**=**	**8 days**
Total days—exact time		**110 days**

In all subsequent interest problems, if interest is to be calculated by exact time and the year is not mentioned, assume that February has 28 days.

Find the Due Date

The due date is the date when the note matures and is payable. If the time period of a loan is expressed in days, the due date can be found by counting the actual number of calendar days from the date of the loan. If the due date falls on a holiday or other nonbusiness day, the due date is advanced to the first business day that follows, with interest chargeable for the additional days. In this book, assume that the only nonbusiness days are January 1, July 4, and December 25.

Example 7. Find the due date of a 60-day loan dated April 15.

April 15—April 30	**= 15 days**
May	**= 31 days**
June 1—June 14	**= 14 days**
Total	**= 60 days**

The date due of the loan is June 14.

If the preceding loan were for 80 days, the due date is July 4. Since July 4 is a legal holiday, the due date is considered to be July 5, if this is a business day, and interest would be charged for 81 days.

If the time period of a loan is expressed in months, the due date will be the same day in the month of maturity as in the month of origin. If the month of maturity does not have the required day as the date of origin, the maturity date will be the last day of the month of maturity.

Example 8. Find the due date of a five-month note dated July 12. The maturity date will be December 12.

Example 9. Find the due date of a three-month note dated March 31. Since June has only 30 days, the maturity date is June 30.

In both of the preceding examples, the number of days of the note will depend on whether 30-day-month time or exact time is to be used. In example 8, using 30-day-month time, the note will be outstanding for 150 days, while using exact time, the life of the note will be 153 days.

Ordinary Interest

It is conventional business practice to use a 360-day business year. This makes it easier in most cases to compute the amount of interest to be charged, though it does allow a minor interest advantage to the lender. If the loan specified ordinary interest, the number of days in the year is assumed to be 360. Both 30-day-month time and exact time may be used with ordinary interest.

Example 10. Find "*t*" in the simple interest formula at ordinary interest at exact time on a a two-month note dated March 10.

$$t = \frac{61 \text{ days}}{360 \text{ days}}$$

If the preceding loan is at ordinary interest at 30-day-month time, then:

$$t = \frac{60 \text{ days}}{360 \text{ days}}$$

Accurate Interest

Accurate interest uses exact time and a 365-day year. This situation is typically found in government loans, though with the introduction of calculators and computers, many lending institutions are switching to a 365-day year.

Example 11. Find "*t*" in the simple interest formula at accurate interest at exact time on a three-month note dated November 4.

$$t = \frac{92 \text{ days}}{365 \text{ days}}$$

It is not practical to use 30-day-month time with accurate interest.

Cancellation Method

To find simple interest by the cancellation method, use the formula $I = Prt$.

Example 12. Find ordinary interest at 30-day-month time on a $900 note at 8 percent interest from September 12 to December 6.

$$I = \$900 \times \frac{8}{100} \times \frac{84}{360} = \$16.80$$

Example 13. In Example 12, find ordinary interest at exact time.

$$I = \$900 \times \frac{8}{100} \times \frac{85}{360} = \$17.00$$

Example 14. In Example 12, find accurate interest at exact time.

$$I = \$900 \times \frac{8}{100} \times \frac{85}{365} = \$16.77$$

In determining the amount of interest by use of the cancellation method, first cancel, if possible, then multiply, and then divide. Also, for accuracy, do not round off until you get your final answer.

Maturity Value

The maturity value of a loan is the sum of the principal and the interest. The symbol for the maturity value is S.

$$S = P + I$$

or

$$S = P + Prt$$

Example 15. Find the maturity value of a $1,000, 9 percent ordinary interest-bearing note due in 75 days.

$$I = \$1{,}000 \times \frac{9}{100} \times \frac{75}{360} = \$18.75$$

$$S = \$1{,}000 + \$18.75 = \$1{,}018.75$$

From *The Wall Street Journal,* with permission of Cartoon Features Syndicate.

Student Review

1. If a note is dated April 20, 1990, and is due on July 7, 1990, determine the number of days the note is outstanding by *(a)* 30-day-month time and *(b)* exact time.

(a) ____________________

(b) ____________________

2. If a note is dated May 18, 1990, and matures on February 5, 1993, determine the number of days the note is outstanding by 30-day-month time, using the compound-time method.

____

3. Find the ordinary interest on a 12 percent $3,000 note due in 100 days.

$____________________

4. Using exact time, find the maturity value of a 10 percent, $2,500 ordinary interest note due in 5 months, if the date of origin is May 5.

$____________________

5. Determine the accurate interest on an 11 percent, $1,800 note dated September 6, 1990, and due on January 28, 1991.

$____________________

Solutions to Student Review

1. *(a)* April 20 to July 20

	3 months
	× 30 days per month
	90 days
Days from July 20 to July 7	− 13 days
Total	77 days

(a) 77 days

(b)

April 20 to April 30	10 days
May	31 days
June	30 days
July	7 days
Total	78 days

(b) 78 days

2.

Year	Month	Day
2	13	35
1993 (3 crossed out)	2 (crossed out)	5 (crossed out)
1990	5	18
2 years	8 months	17 days

(720 days) + (240 days) + (17 days) = 977 days

977 days

3. I = Prt

$$I = \$3{,}000 \times \frac{12}{100} \times \frac{100}{360} = \$100$$

$ 100

4. I = Prt

$$I = \$2{,}500 \times \frac{10}{100} \times \frac{153}{360} = \$106.25$$

S = $2,500 + $106.25 = $2,606.25

$ 2,606.25

5. I = Prt

$$I = \$1{,}800 \times \frac{11}{100} \times \frac{144}{365} = \$78.12$$

$ 78.12

Assignment 21–1

Introduction to Simple Interest

Name ______________________

Date ______________________

A. Find the time, in days, of each of the following notes by 30-day-month time:

1. January 10, 1990, to February 18, 1990 ________

2. March 20, 1990, to April 29, 1990 ________

3. March 6, 1990, to November 15, 1990 ________

4. June 19, 1990, to November 24, 1990 ________

5. May 24, 1990, to September 15, 1990 ________

6. December 31, 1990, to February 28, 1991 ________

B. Find the time, in days, of each of the following notes by exact time:

1. July 8, 1990, to August 21, 1990 ________

2. September 5, 1990, to October 13, 1990 ________

3. November 18, 1990, to March 30, 1991 ________

4. April 6, 1990, to October 20, 1990 ________

5. May 30, 1990, to August 16, 1990 ________

6. June 1, 1990, to December 23, 1990 ________

C. Find the time, in days, of each of the following notes by 30-day-month time, using the compound-time method:

1. January 4, 1987, to September 10, 1991 ________

2. April 16, 1989, to May 24, 1991 ________

3. July 31, 1988, to August 16, 1991 ________

4. December 29, 1989, to May 5, 1991 ________

5. October 9, 1989, to February 7, 1991 ________

6. May 16, 1984, to July 7, 1991 ________

D. Find the due dates of each of the following notes:

	Date of Loan	*Time*	*Due Date*
1.	April 10, 1991	Three months	__________
2.	November 5, 1991	Five months	__________
3.	October 24, 1991	Two months	__________
4.	December 31, 1991	Two months	__________
5.	March 4, 1991	Four months	__________
6.	August 18, 1991	Six months	__________

E. Find the due dates of each of the following notes:

	Date of Loan	*Time*	*Due Date*
1.	April 28, 1991	60 days	__________
2.	January 15, 1991	45 days	__________
3.	July 31, 1991	90 days	__________
4.	November 12, 1991	50 days	__________
5.	October 16, 1991	120 days	__________
6.	February 10, 1991	80 days	__________

Assignment 21–2

Introduction to Simple Interest

Name ______________________

Date ______________________

A. Find ordinary interest to the nearest cent, using 30-day-month time:

	Principal	*Rate*	*From*	*To*	
1.	$1,000	12%	May 10	July 10	________
2.	$ 800	16%	March 20	May 5	________
3.	$2,200	18%	January 10	March 25	________
4.	$ 720	9%	June 4	September 14	________

B. Find ordinary interest to the nearest cent, using exact time:

	Principal	*Rate*	*From*	*To*	
1.	$ 650	18%	January 6	February 5	________
2.	$1,825	12%	March 15	May 14	________
3.	$ 75	15%	July 8	August 13	________
4.	$ 900	$10\frac{1}{2}$%	May 12	July 31	________

C. Find the maturity value at ordinary interest to the nearest cent:

	Principal	*Rate*	*Time*	
1.	$ 800	16%	30 days	________
2.	$1,200	20%	45 days	________
3.	$ 200	$22\frac{1}{2}$%	20 days	________
4.	$ 340	18%	42 days	________

D. Find accurate interest to the nearest cent:

	Principal	*Rate*	*Time*	
1.	$ 900	15%	90 days	______
2.	$ 350	$12\frac{1}{2}$%	73 days	______
3.	$ 80	21%	60 days	______
4.	$1,100	17%	30 days	______

E. Solve the following:

1. Find the ordinary interest on an 18 percent, $5,000 note due in three months, using *(a)* 30-day-month time and *(b)* exact time, if the note is issued on March 5.

(a) $______

(b) $______

2. On May 10, Roland Brooks borrowed $3,000 from his bank at 15 percent ordinary interest. He paid his obligation on August 8. Using exact time, find *(a)* interest and *(b)* maturity value.

(a) $______

(b) $______

3. Donald Quinn inadvertently underpaid his income tax on April 15 by $320. On June 27 he caught the error and remitted the $320 at 13 percent accurate interest. Determine the amount of interest he paid.

$______

4. Find the maturity value of a 16 percent, $750 ordinary interest note, dated July 15 and due October 15, using exact time.

$______

Multiple Sports with Amy Hengst, Accountant

As of December 31, 1990, Multiple Sports had two notes outstanding. Amy asks you to help her determine the accrued interest at year-end, the number of days in the life of each note, and the maturity values of each note.

Note A resulted from a purchase of merchandise on November 1, 1990, for $650. The payment became due on December 1, 1990. Due to the busy season, Multiple Sports asked for, and was granted, an extension of time to pay the debt. Multiple Sports gave a note, dated December 1, 1990, and due March 1, 1991, at 9 percent ordinary interest at exact time.

In addition, Multiple Sports purchased a delivery van on September 10, 1990, for $15,000. A down payment of $3,000 was made, and Note B, at 12 percent ordinary interest, due on July 3, 1992, at 30-day-month time was given for the balance due.

Also, when reviewing the 1989 federal income tax return in getting ready to prepare the 1990 return, Amy discovered that the 1989 deductions were overstated by $1,000, resulting in an under payment of federal income tax by $340. On February 5, 1991, check number 584 was drawn to cover payment in full for the tax due plus 10 percent accurate interest from April 15, 1990, to February 5, 1991. Amy asks you to compute the amount, including interest, to be entered on check number 584.

	Accrued Interest 12/31/90	Total Days of Note	Maturity Value
Note A	$________	________	$________
Note B	$________	________	$________
Check number 584, amount	$________		

Chapter 22

Deriving Other Interest Variables

A consultant is a well-paid expert brought in at the last minute to share the blame.

Learning Goals

Upon completion of this chapter, you should be able to:

1. Calculate simple interest, using a simple interest table.
2. Derive the unknown variable in the formula $I = Prt$ if three of the four variables are known or can be determined.

In some interest problems the amount of interest is known, and determining one of the other interest variables is required. Of the four variables, consisting of interest amount, interest rate, time, and principal, if information on three is given or can be derived from the facts, the fourth variable can be calculated.

The basic formula for interest is as follows:

$$I = Prt$$

If the *principal* is unknown, the basic interest equation can be divided on both sides by *rt*, making the formula read as follows:

$$P = \frac{I}{rt}$$

Example 1. What is the amount of the principal if the interest is $10.50, the rate is 9 percent, and the time is 120 days?

$$P = \frac{\$10.50}{\frac{9}{100} \times \frac{120}{360}} = \$350$$

The problem shown can be simplified for easier cancellation by transferring the denominators of the denominator portion of the fraction to the numerator section. The formula for example 1 could be written as follows:

$$P = \frac{\$10.50 \times 100 \times 360}{9 \times 120} = \$350$$

If the *rate* is unknown, the basic equation can be divided on both sides by *Pt*, making the formula read as follows:

$$r = \frac{I}{Pt}$$

Example 2. What is the interest rate if the principal is $450, the interest is $18.75, and the time is 75 days?

$$r = \frac{\$18.75}{\$450 \times \frac{75}{360}} = 20\%$$

The formula for example 2 could also be written as follows:

$$r = \frac{\$18.75 \times 360}{\$450 \times 75} = 20\%$$

If the *time* is unknown, let *n* represent the number of days that the loan is outstanding, and the basic interest equation would read as follows:

$$I = Pr \times \frac{n}{360}$$

By multiplying both sides of the equation by $\frac{360}{Pr}$, the formula would read as follows:

$$n = \frac{I \times 360}{Pr}$$

Example 3. What is the time in days if the principal is $400, the interest $10, and the interest rate is 12 percent?

$$n = \frac{\$10 \times 360}{\$400 \times \frac{12}{100}} = 75 \text{ days}$$

The formula for example 3 could also be written as follows:

$$n = \frac{\$10 \times 360 \times 100}{\$400 \times 12} = 75 \text{ days}$$

Simple-Interest Table

If interest calculations occur frequently, a simple-interest table may be used as a shortcut in calculating the amount of simple interest due. Use of the table not only saves time but provides greater accuracy—it lessens the chance for error.

Interest tables are available for many different rates and time periods. The following table illustrates how to find interest at 5 percent and 7 percent on one dollar for various time periods. The amounts in the table were carried to six decimal places for greater accuracy in rounding off.

Ordinary Interest Table on $1 Principal

	Rate of Interest			Rate of Interest	
Days	**5%**	**7%**	**Days**	**5%**	**7%**
1	.000139	.000194	19	.002639	.003694
2	.000278	.000389	20	.002778	.003889
3	.000417	.000583	21	.002917	.004083
4	.000556	.000778	22	.003056	.004278
5	.000694	.000972	23	.003194	.004472
6	.000833	.001167	24	.003333	.004667
7	.000972	.001361	25	.003472	.004861
8	.001111	.001556	26	.003611	.005056
9	.001250	.001750	27	.003750	.005250
10	.001389	.001944	28	.003889	.005444
11	.001528	.002139	29	.004028	.005639
12	.001667	.002333	30	.004167	.005833
13	.001806	.002528	31	.004306	.006028
14	.001944	.002722	60	.008333	.011667
15	.002083	.002917	90	.012500	.017500
16	.002222	.003111	180	.025000	.035000
17	.002361	.003306	270	.037500	.052500
18	.002500	.003500	360 (1 yr)	.050000	.070000

Average Monthly Salary	
Professional degree	$3,439
Doctoral degree	2,747
Master's degree	1,956
Bachelor's degree	1,540
Associate degree	1,188
Vocational degree	990
High-school diploma	415

U.S. Census Bureau

To determine the amount of interest by use of the table, find interest for $1 principal for the required number of days at the given percent and multiply that figure by the amount of the principal.

Example 4. Find ordinary interest on $950 for 27 days at 5 percent.

Interest on $1 for 27 days	**=**	**$0.003750**
Principal	**=**	**× 950**
Interest on $950 for 27 days	**=**	**$3.56**

Example 5. Find ordinary interest on $320 for 90 days at 7 percent.

Interest on $1 for 90 days	**=**	**$0.017500**
Principal	**=**	**× 320**
Interest on $320 for 90 days	**=**	**$5.60**

If the exact number of days is not given in the table, the interest of $1 for two time periods added together will give the desired interest.

Example 6 Find ordinary interest on $500 for 72 days at 7 percent.

Interest on $1 for 60 days	**=**	**$0.011667**
Interest on $1 for 12 days	**=**	**+ 0.002333**
Interest on $1 for 72 days	**=**	**$0.014000**
Principal	**=**	**× 500**
Interest on $500 for 72 days	**=**	**$7.00**

Student Review

1. Valerie Lebeaux purchased a diamond necklace for $485. She paid $100 down and 60 days later sent a check for $395.27 as payment in full. What was the rate of ordinary interest to the nearest whole percent?

____

2. John Whitney bought a round-trip plane ticket to Rome, Italy. He paid $200 immediately and agreed to pay the balance in full in 75 days. If the finance charge at 16 percent ordinary interest is $10, determine the cost of the ticket.

$ _______________

3. Anna-Marie Bratton borrowed $750 at 12.5 percent ordinary interest. If she paid $768.75 at maturity, determine the number of days that the loan was outstanding.

____

4. Horace Alexander borrowed $2,100 from Reliable Financial Services at 19 percent ordinary interest. If there is a minimum loan charge of $150, determine the total amount due if payment is made in *(a)* 120 days, *(b)* 150 days.

(a) $ _______________

(b) $ _______________

5. Nobuko Takamatsu purchased a power mower for $310. She paid $60 down and borrowed the balance at 15 percent ordinary interest. Some time later, she mailed a check for $162.50, which included interest to date of $12.50. After another 70 days, she mailed a check for payment in full. Determine *(a)* the number of days from the down payment to the first installment and *(b)* the amount of the second installment.

(a) _______________

(b) $ _______________

Solutions to Student Review

1. $r = \frac{I}{Pt}$

$r = \frac{\$10.27 \times 360}{\$385 \times 60} = .16$

16%

2. $P = \frac{I}{rt}$

$P = \frac{\$10 \times 100 \times 360}{16 \times 75} = \$300$

$\$300 + \$200 = \$500$

\$ 500

3. $n = \frac{360\ I}{pr}$

$n = \frac{360 \times \$18.75 \times 100}{\$750 \times 12.5} = 72 \text{ days}$

72 days

4. (a) $I = \$2{,}100 \times \frac{19}{100} \times \frac{120}{360} = \$133$

Minimum charge is \$150

$S = \$2{,}100 + \$150 = \$2{,}250$

(a) \$ 2,250

(b) $I = \$2{,}100 \times \frac{19}{100} \times \frac{150}{360} = \$166.25$

$S = \$2{,}100 + \$166.25 = \$2{,}266.25$

(b) \$ 2,266.25

5. (a) $n = \frac{360 \times \$12.50 \times 100}{\$250 \times 15} = 120 \text{ days}$

(a) 120 days

(b) $P = \$310 - (\$60 + \$150) = \$100$

$I = \$100 \times \frac{15}{100} \times \frac{70}{360} = \$2.92$

$S = \$100 + \$2.92 = \$102.92$

(b) \$ 102.92

Assignment 22–1
Deriving Other Interest Variables

Name ______________________

Date ______________________

A. Find the principal in the following problems at ordinary interest:

	Interest	*Rate*	*Time (Days)*	*Principal*
1.	$ 7.50	8%	90	________
2.	$ 0.66	22%	30	________
3.	$30.00	10%	45	________
4.	$ 2.00	15%	50	________

B. Find the interest rate in the following problems at ordinary interest:

	Principal	*Interest*	*Time (Days)*	*Rate*
1.	$4,500	$138.75	74	________
2.	$ 420	$ 11.20	120	________
3.	$ 36	$ 4.20	200	________
4.	$8,430	$786.80	240	________

C. Find the time, in days, in the following problems at ordinary interest:

	Principal	*Interest*	*Rate*	*Time (Days)*
1.	$ 960	$10.20	8.5%	________
2.	$ 95	$ 4.75	10%	________
3.	$7,600	$38.00	12%	________
4.	$1,080	$12.60	20%	________

D. Solve the following ordinary interest problems:

1. John Casey invested $1,800 for 210 days and received $94.50 interest. Determine the rate of interest.

____

2. Jack Dokey borrowed $200 and was charged 6 percent interest. If he paid $201.50 at maturity, determine the number of days the loan was outstanding.

____

3. Liz Short purchased a $10,000 90-day treasury certificate at her bank. If the amount of interest earned was $385, determine the interest rate.

____

4. Stephen Fisher paid the bank $12 interest on a 75-day loan at 8 percent. Determine the amount originally borrowed.

____

5. Catherine Lei borrowed $2,100 from the Fast Finance Company at 27 percent interest. If the maturity value of the loan was $2,604, determine the number of days that the loan was outstanding.

____

6. When his 90-day note came due, Leonard Gross paid the bank $525.03, the full maturity value. If the amount of interest was $9.03, determine the interest rate that Mr. Gross was charged.

____

7. Pearl Cohen purchased a gold necklace for $1,400. If she paid $500 down and paid the balance plus $85 interest in a single future payment at 20 percent, determine the number of days of the loan.

____

Assignment 22–2

Deriving Other Interest Variables

Name ______________________

Date ______________________

A. Fill in the blanks in each of the following:

	Interest	*Principal*	*Rate*	*Time (Days)*
1.	$30.00	$3,000	8%	____
2.	$ 4.50	$____	9%	100
3.	$ 5.69	$______	4%	8
4.	$18.75	$ 750	____	75
5.	$ 2.50	$ 480	$7\frac{1}{2}$%	____
6.	$70.13	$3,300	____	90

B. In each of the following ordinary interest problems, find principal to the nearest cent, rate to the nearest tenth percent, or time to the nearest number of whole days.

1. John Levin purchased a sofa for $820. He paid $200 down, and 45 days later he mailed a check for $632.40 to cover the balance due, including interest. What was the rate of interest?

____

2. Tapson Jewelers charges 12 percent interest on past-due accounts. On one customer's account, for $810, the interest charge was $21.06. How many days was the account past due?

____

3. Frank Ross purchased a piano from Player Music Company. If the interest rate is 18 percent and the payment in full, including finance charges of $83.04, is remitted after 91 days, what was the cost of the piano?

____

4. Georgia Morris needs to borrow $1,500 in order to purchase wall-to-wall carpeting. Finance Company A charges 12 percent interest, but has a minimum loan charge of $50. Finance Company B charges 15 percent interest, but has a minimum loan charge of $35.
   (a) If she pays the loan in full after 60 days from which finance company should she borrow the money, and
   (b) how much interest would she save?

(a) ______________

(b) $______________

5. In problem 4, if Georgia Morris pays the loan in full in 90 days, *(a)* from which finance company should she borrow, and *(b)* how much interest would she save?

(a) ______________

(b) $______________

6. Charlie Investor borrowed $2,000 at 9 percent. After 45 days, he paid the interest to date and $500 of principal. Some time later, he sent a check for $1,027.38, which included interest to date and a principal payment of $1,000. The final payment for the balance due, including interest, was made 40 days after the second payment. Determine *(a)* the amount of interest on the first payment, *(b)* the number of days between the first and second payment, and *(c)* the amount remitted to pay off the loan on the third payment.

(a) $______________

(b) ______________

(c) $______________

7. Betty Stern purchased a dishwasher for $420. She paid $78 down and borrowed the balance at 22 percent. Some time later, she mailed a check for $148.36, including interest to date and a principal payment of $140. After another 46 days, she mailed a check for $100, including principal and interest. Subsequently, a check for $110.97 was sent to the seller as a final payment in full. Determine *(a)* the number of days from the down payment to the first installment, *(b)* the principal paid on the second installment, and *(c)* the number of days from the second installment to time of final payment.

(a) ______________

(b) $______________

(c) ______________

Assignment 22–3

Name ______________________

Date ______________________

A. Solve the following ordinary interest problems to the nearest cent by use of the interest tables on page 293.

1. $800 at 5% for 22 days ______
2. $85 at 7% for 60 days ______
3. $220.40 at 7% for 10 days ______
4. $625 at 7% for 180 days ______
5. $475 at 5% for 5 days ______
6. $2,350 at 7% for 31 days ______
7. $95.24 at 5% for 18 days ______
8. $980 at 5% for 24 days ______

B. Solve the following ordinary interest problems at exact time to the nearest cent by use of the interest tables on page 293.

1. $640 at 5%, from June 5 to July 6 ______
2. $80 at 7%, from March 12 to June 10 ______
3. $510 at 7%, from April 7 to October 4 ______
4. $2,500 at 5%, from October 4 to November 2 ______
5. $30 at 5%, from May 29 to June 20 ______
6. $695 at 5%, from December 15 to January 2 ______
7. $93.18 at 7%, from May 20 to February 14 ______
8. $290 at 7%, from August 1 to August 19 ______

C. Solve the following ordinary interest problems at exact time to the nearest cent using the interest tables on page 293.

1. Greg White borrowed $2,300 from the bank on June 1 at 7 percent. If he paid the loan on July 1, determine the amount of interest.

   ____

2. Gary Waters took out a business loan of $650 at 5 percent on January 2. If he paid the loan in full on February 28, determine the amount of interest that Mr. Waters paid.

   ____

3. Jay Scott borrowed $300 from his neighbor on June 30 at 5 percent. He paid the loan in full on December 27. Find the amount of interest paid by Mr. Scott.

   ____

4. Terry Cooke purchased furniture for his home on April 12 for $450. He agreed to pay the loan in full on July 11 at 7 percent. Determine *(a)* interest and *(b)* maturity value.

   (a) ______________

   (b) ______________

Multiple Sports with Amy Hengst, Accountant

On March 20, 1990, Multiple Sports sold $8,800 of football uniforms and equipment to Lincoln High School. Lincoln High School gave a note, dated March 20, 1990, at 9 percent ordinary interest, payable in installments. The first payment was for $2,165, including interest to date of $165. After another 45 days, a check for $3,000, including principal and interest, was received from Lincoln High School. At the end of the football season, Lincoln High School sent a check for $4,001.55 as a final payment in full

Amy asks you to determine *(a)* the number of days from the date of the note to the first payment, *(b)* the amount of interest paid with the second payment, *(c)* the number of days from the second payment to the final payment, and *(d)* the date of the final payment.

(a) ____________

(b) ____________

(c) ____________

(d) ____________

% − × + $ ÷ +

Chapter 23

Bank Discount

My bank balance is so low that my bank sent me last year's calendar.

Learning Goals

Upon completion of this chapter, you should be able to:

1. Differentiate the meaning of the terms *simple interest* and *bank discount.*
2. Understand why a business discounts a note.
3. Discuss why a business has a contingent liability on a discounted note.
4. Define bank discount terminology.
5. Calculate bank discount and proceeds on a noninterest-bearing note.
6. Calculate bank discount and proceeds on an interest-bearing note.

Bank Discount

Simple interest refers to the amount charged by the lender on the principal amount of the loan, payable at maturity. Bank discount occurs when the lender charges interest on the maturity value and deducts this amount at the time of the loan. The term *discount* is differentiated from interest to indicate a slightly higher rate; i.e., 15 percent discount is greater than 15 percent interest.

Though not prevalent today, at one time it was common practice of banks to deduct the interest in advance. For example, assume that a business firm wanted to borrow $4,000 from a bank for 60 days at 12 percent interest. It was common banking practice in the past to deduct the $80 bank discount from the amount of the loan. The borrower would sign a noninterest-bearing note for $4,000 but would receive only $3,920. This was unfair to the borrower in at least two ways. First, the borrower wanted $4,000 but only received $3,920. Second, interest is being charged on $4,000 when the amount borrowed was $3,920.

Nowadays, primarily because of the two objections just noted, a business firm or individual will be able to borrow what is needed and will be charged interest on the amount borrowed.

Discounting a Note

A business will frequently accept a note from a customer on the purchase of merchandise or in settlement of an open account. If the business runs short of cash before the note is due, it can ask the customer to pay early. However, the customer has no legal obligation to do so. At this point, the business could take the note to its bank and, if the bank agrees, discount it. Since the bank does not know the customer of the business, the bank is, in effect, making a loan to the business. Upon discounting the note, the business has made itself contingently liable to the bank. This means that if the customer of the business balks at all in making the payment due at maturity, the business will immediately pay the maturity value. At this time, the business would, once again, have a claim against the customer for the amount due.

If a business can borrow money from the bank, using a note given by its customer, the bank will discount the note, whether it is interest bearing or noninterest bearing. This means that the bank will charge interest on the maturity value of the note, and not the present value, and will deduct this amount immediately.

Example 1 Baker Company sells merchandise to Ron Johnson for $200 and accepts a 60-day, noninterest-bearing note. On the day of the sale, Baker Company discounts the note at the bank at 15 percent. The bank discount is $5, and Baker Company will receive $195. A 15 percent interest charge for 60 days would be $5 on $200. The bank is charging $5 for a loan of $195.

Bank Discount Terminology

The *date of origin* is the date on which the note is written.

The *maturity date* is when the note is due.

The *discount date* is the date when the note is discounted.

The *discount term* is the number of days from the date of discount to the date of maturity.

The *discount rate* is the bank rate charged against the maturity value.

The *discount* is the amount deducted by the bank from the maturity value. It represents the bank's gross profit on this transaction.

The *proceeds* represent the money received from the bank by the seller of the note at time of discount.

Finding Bank Discount on a Noninterest-Bearing Note

When a note is presented to the bank for discounting, the first thing that must be done is to determine the maturity value. The maturity value of a noninterest-bearing note is the same as the principal.

The next step is to determine the discount term. The discount term represents the *exact* number of days from the date of discount to the maturity date, regardless of whether exact time or 30-day-month time was originally specified.

The formula for calculating discount is very much like the one used to compute interest. Since the terms are different, the letters used in the formula will be as follows:

D = dollar amount of bank discount
S = maturity value of note
d = bank discount rate
t = discount term divided by 360
P = proceeds, or the amount of money received from the bank on date of discount

$D = Sdt$
$P = S - D$

Example 2 A $500, 90-day, noninterest-bearing note dated August 15 is discounted at the bank on September 14 at $13\frac{1}{2}$ percent. Determine the bank discount and proceeds.

Since this is a noninterest-bearing note, the maturity value is $500, the same as the principal. The discount term is the exact number of days from September 14 to the maturity date. In this example, the maturity date does not have to be determined, unless the problem requests it, since the discount term of 60 days can be derived by subtracting the 30 days previously elapsed from the 90-day life of the note.

$$D = \$500 \times \frac{13.5}{100} \times \frac{60}{360} = \$11.25$$

$$P = \$500 - \$11.25 = \$488.75$$

Finding Bank Discount on an Interest-Bearing Note

In finding bank discount, the first step is to determine the maturity value. For a noninterest-bearing note, the maturity value is the same as the principal. However, if a note bears interest, it is necessary to compute the interest in order to arrive at the maturity value, since the maturity value on an interest-bearing note is the principal plus the interest. Once the maturity value is determined the steps for discounting an interest- or noninterest-bearing note are the same.

Since most discounted notes are short term, it will be assumed that whether the time on an interest-bearing note is stated in days or in months, if the note is discounted, the actual number of days from date of origin to maturity date is counted in arriving at maturity value. It was previously mentioned that the exact number of days are to be counted in figuring the discount term.

The procedure for discounting an interest-bearing note should involve the following steps:

1. Determine the exact number of days in the life of the note.
2. Determine the maturity value of the note.
3. Determine the discount term, i.e., the exact number of days from the date of discount to the maturity date.
4. Determine the bank discount.
5. Determine the proceeds by subtracting the bank discount from the maturity value.

Example. Assume that the Charles Wong Company sold merchandise for $600 to R. O'Brien on September 5, 1991, and received the following note in exchange.

$600.00 Miami, Florida September 5, 1991

On December 4, 1991, I promise to pay to the order of

Charles Wong Company at 201 Crescent Street, Miami, Florida

the sum of

—Six Hundred and $\frac{00}{100}$ ---------------------------------- Dollars

for value received, with interest at ten (10) per cent per annum.

R. O'Brien

Top Five Radio Advertisers—1987

	($ millions)
Sears Roebuck	$74
Anheuser-Busch	67
General Motors	54
Philip Morris	38
Ford Motor	35

Radio Advertising Bureau

On September 20, 1991, the Charles Wong Company took the note to its bank and discounted it at 12 percent. Determine the bank discount and proceeds.

1. **The exact number of days from September 5, 1991, to December 4, 1991, is 90.**
2. **The maturity value is determined, as follows:**

$$I = \$600 \times \frac{10}{100} \times \frac{90}{360} = \$15$$

$$S = \$600 + \$15 = \$615$$

3. **The discount term covers the period from September 20, 1991, to December 4, 1991. The exact number of days is 75.**
4. **The bank discount is determined as follows:**

$$D = \$615 \times \frac{12}{100} \times \frac{75}{360} = \$15.38$$

5. **The proceeds can then be determined, as follows:**

$$P = \$615.00 - \$15.38 = \$599.62$$

Student Review

1. Francine Foultz loaned $1,500 to a friend on April 30. She accepted a 150-day, noninterest-bearing note. On April 30, she discounted the note at her bank at 13 percent. Find the *(a)* bank discount and *(b)* proceeds.

(a) $ ____________

(b) $ ____________

2. Find *(a)* maturity value, *(b)* bank discount, and *(c)* proceeds on a 90-day, $750, 12 percent note, dated May 18, and discounted at 14 percent on June 2.

(a) $ ____________

(b) $ ____________

(c) $ ____________

3. Determine *(a)* maturity value, *(b)* bank discount, and *(c)* proceeds on a $2,100, 10 percent note, dated September 2, due in 4 months, and discounted on September 2 at 10 percent.

(a) $ ____________

(b) $ ____________

(c) $ ____________

4. Rodent Exterminators charged Charlie Homeowner $2,500 on May 11 for new bathroom walls. Charlie paid 10 percent down and gave a 12 percent note, due in 75 days, for the balance. Rodent Exterminators sold the note to its bank on May 31 at 15 percent bank discount. Find *(a)* bank discount and *(b)* proceeds.

(a) $ ____________

(b) $ ____________

5. Caring Pet Store sold a pedigree Labrador retriever for $400 on August 31. The customer gave a 3-month, 9 percent note. The store discounted the note at its bank on October 25 at 11 percent. Find *(a)* bank discount and *(b)* proceeds.

(a) $ ____________

(b) $ ____________

Solutions to Student Review

1. (a) $D = \$1{,}500 \times \frac{13}{100} \times \frac{134}{360} = \$72.58$

(a) $ 72.58

(b) $P = \$1{,}500 - \$72.58 = \$1{,}427.42$

(b) $ 1,427.42

2. (a) $I = \$750 \times \frac{12}{100} \times \frac{90}{360} = \$22.50$

$S = \$750 + \$22.50 = \$772.50$

(a) $ 772.50

(b) $D = \$772.50 \times \frac{14}{100} \times \frac{75}{360} = \$22.53$

(b) $ 22.53

(c) $P = \$772.50 - \$22.53 = \$749.97$

(c) $ 749.97

3. (a) $I = \$2{,}100 \times \frac{10}{100} \times \frac{122}{360} = 71.17$

$S = \$2{,}100 + \$71.17 = \$2{,}171.17$

(a) $ 2,171.17

(b) $D = \$2{,}171.17 \times \frac{10}{100} \times \frac{122}{360} = \$73.58$

(b) $ 73.58

(c) $P = \$2{,}171.17 - \$73.58 = \$2{,}097.59$

(c) $ 2,097.59

4. $I = \$2{,}250 \times \frac{12}{100} \times \frac{75}{360} = \$56.25$

$S = \$2{,}250 + \$56.25 = \$2{,}306.25$

(a) $D = \$2{,}306.25 \times \frac{15}{100} \times \frac{55}{360} = \$52.85$

(a) $ 52.85

(b) $P = \$2{,}306.25 - \$52.85 = \$2{,}253.40$

(b) $ 2,253.40

5. $I = \$400 \times \frac{9}{100} \times \frac{91}{360} = \$9.10$

$S = \$400 + \$9.10 = \$409.10$

(a) $D = \$409.10 \times \frac{11}{100} \times \frac{36}{360} = \$4.50$

(a) $ 4.50

(b) $P = \$409.10 - \$4.50 = \$404.60$

(b) $ 404.60

Assignment 23-1

Bank Discount

Name ______________________

Date ______________________

A. For the following noninterest-bearing notes, determine the maturity date, discount term, bank discount, and proceeds:

	(1)	(2)	(3)	(4)
Date of origin	June 8	March 20	August 12	July 16
Face value of note	$1,250	$640	$735	$220.60
Time of note	60 days	75 days	4 months	90 days
Date of discount	June 23	March 29	August 12	October 2
Discount rate	16%	15%	12%	18%
Maturity date	________	________	________	________
Discount term	________	________	________	________
Bank discount	________	________	________	________
Proceeds	________	________	________	________

B. Find the bank discounts and proceeds on the following noninterest-bearing notes:

	Date of Origin	*Principal*	*Time*	*Date of Discount*	*Discount Rate*	*Bank Discount*	*Proceeds*
1.	3/25	$ 800	90 days	5/30	18%	________	________
2.	7/18	$1,000	75 days	9/1	20%	________	________
3.	10/20	$ 150	4 months	11/16	9%	________	________
4.	9/1	$4,500	5 months	1/2	$13\frac{1}{2}$%	________	________

C. Solve the following discounted notes:

1. On November 16, John Lippitt discounted a $300, 90-day, noninterest-bearing note at his bank. The note, dated November 4, was discounted at 16 percent. Find *(a)* bank discount and *(b)* proceeds.

(a) $____________

(b) $____________

2. A retailer sold merchandise to a customer for $125 and accepted a 30-day, noninterest-bearing note. The note was immediately discounted at the bank at 12 percent. Find *(a)* bank discount and *(b)* proceeds.

(a) $____________

(a) $____________

3. A manufacturer sold merchandise to a wholesaler on April 18 for $825, accepting a three-month, noninterest-bearing note. The manufacturer discounted the note on June 25 at $7\frac{1}{2}$ percent bank discount. Find *(a)* bank discount and *(b)* proceeds.

(a) $____________

(b) $____________

4. Williams Jewelers accepted a $425 noninterest-bearing note from a customer on July 8. Since the note was not due until November 6, the note was discounted at the bank on July 15 at 15 percent bank discount. Find *(a)* bank discount, and *(b)* proceeds.

(a) $____________

(b) $____________

5. Jim Poley loaned $450 to a friend on July 25. He accepted a 120-day, noninterest-bearing note. On August 30, Mr. Poley discounted the note at his bank at 14 percent. Find *(a)* bank discount and *(b)* proceeds.

(a) $____________

(b) $____________

6. Karen Pfeifer sold furniture for $500 through a newspaper advertisement. The buyer paid $125 down and gave a two-month, noninterest-bearing note on March 20 for the balance. Karen discounted the note at her bank on April 15 at 18 percent bank discount. Determine *(a)* bank discount, and *(b)* proceeds.

(a) $____________

(b) $____________

Assignment 23-2

Bank Discount

Name ____________________

Date ____________________

Find the maturity value, bank discount, and proceeds on the following ordinary interest-bearing notes:

	Date of Origin	Interest Rate	Principal	Time	Date of Discount	Discount Rate	Maturity Value	Bank Discount	Proceeds
1.	3/11	12%	$1,800	60 days	4/10	12%	______	______	______
2.	4/30	12%	$2,400	90 days	5/30	16%	______	______	______
3.	7/25	12%	$ 900	150 days	8/4	10%	______	______	______
4.	11/1	8%	$2,250	60 days	11/16	14%	______	______	______
5.	6/10	16%	$5,400	90 days	8/24	18%	______	______	______
6.	9/5	$13\frac{1}{2}$%	$3,000	75 days	9/20	$13\frac{1}{2}$%	______	______	______
7.	7/31	10%	$1,350	60 days	9/19	14%	______	______	______

8.	12/5	9%	$2,000	75 days	1/4	10%			
9.	8/3	14%	$2,500	3 months	10/22	18%			
10.	6/5	10%	$ 600	6 months	9/21	12%			
11.	3/18	14%	$ 450	20 days	3/23	16%			
12.	9/10	15%	$1,000	40 days	10/14	18%			
***13.**	10/20	12%	$ 935	1 year	12/24	15%			
14.	1/7	$13\frac{1}{2}$%	$ 840	2 months	2/5	12%			
15.	2/25	10%	$2,100	9 months	3/30	14%			
16.	9/6	12%	$1,500	1 month	9/6	12%			

**t* for one year under bank discount is $\frac{365}{360}$.

Assignment 23-3

Bank Discount

Name ____________________

Date ____________________

A. For the following interest-bearing notes, determine the exact number of days in the life of the note, ordinary interest, the maturity value, the discount term, the bank discount, and the proceeds:

	(1)	(2)	(3)	(4)	(5)
Date of origin	October 7	July 11	August 3	Sep. 11	May 6
Face value of note	$690	$3,300	$870	$94.50	$1,350
Time of note	45 days	100 days	3 months	60 days	4 months
Interest rate on note	12%	14%	16%	$7\frac{1}{2}$%	10%
Date of discount	October 22	July 21	October 4	Nov. 4	August 22
Discount rate	16%	12%	18%	7%	16%
Life of note (days)	______	______	______	______	______
Ordinary interest	______	______	______	______	______
Maturity value	______	______	______	______	______
Discount term	______	______	______	______	______
Bank discount	______	______	______	______	______
Proceeds	______	______	______	______	______

B. Solve the following discounted notes at ordinary interest:

1. A wholesaler shipped goods to a retailer costing $255. On March 16, the retailer gave the wholesaler a three-month note, agreeing to pay 10 percent interest. The wholesaler discounted the note on May 2 at 15 percent. Find *(a)* maturity value, *(b)* bank discount, and *(c)* proceeds.

(a) $ ____________________

(b) $ ____________________

(c) $ ____________________

2. Jim Cagnacci loaned an associate $150 on November 21, evidenced by a 10 percent, 90-day note. On December 1, Mr. Cagnacci discounted the note at the bank at 12 percent. Find *(a)* bank discount and *(b)* proceeds.

(a) $____________

(b) $____________

3. Donovan Plumbing did extensive bathroom work for $1,200. The customer paid $200 down and gave a 15 percent, four-month note for the balance. The note dated May 31 was discounted on June 10 at 20 percent bank discount. Find *(a)* bank discount, and *(b)* proceeds.

(a) $____________

(b) $____________

4. Rosalie Wolf discounted a $1,000, 45-day, 9 percent note at the bank on February 2. The note was dated December 31 and was discounted at 13 percent. Find *(a)* bank discount and *(b)* proceeds.

(a) $____________

(b) $____________

5. Joyce Pinney sold her used car to a private party for $2,850. She received $350 down and a 12 percent, two-month note dated December 17. If the note was discounted on January 2 at 14 percent bank discount, determine *(a)* bank discount, and *(b)* proceeds.

(a) $____________

(b) $____________

Multiple Sports with Amy Hengst, Accountant

Multiple Sports has a policy that any customer who cannot pay within 30 days of the invoice date must agree to give an interest-bearing note to cover any extended period before payment is made. Frequently, in order to pay its bills on time, Multiple Sports will discount these notes at its bank. During the month of May, three notes were received from customers to allow an extension of time to pay.

Note A, a $2,400, 75-day, 9 percent note dated May 5, was discounted at the bank on May 11 at 12 percent bank discount.

Note B, a $6,500, three-month note at 10 percent, dated May 18, was discounted at the bank on July 18 at 12 percent bank discount.

On May 31, Multiple Sports received Note C, dated May 29. It was a $3,000, 60-day, 12 percent note which was discounted at the bank on May 31 at 12 percent bank discount.

Amy asks you to calculate the proceeds received from the bank on discounting each of the above notes.

Note A ____________

Note B ____________

Note C ____________

Section 7

Compound Interest and Annuities

% − × + $ ÷ +

Chapter 24

Compound Interest

Credit cards have three dimensions: height, width, and debt.

Learning Goals

Upon completion of this chapter, you should be able to:

1. Differentiate between simple interest and compound interest.
2. Compute compound interest without use of a table.
3. Calculate interest compounded annually by use of a compound-interest table.
4. Calculate interest by use of a compound-interest table if interest is compounded more frequently than once a year.
5. Determine the compound amount from a compound interest table if the number of compoundings exceed the number provided by the table.
6. Derive the compounded amount using a compound interest table if there are several periodic investments of the same or differing amounts.
7. Determine the interest rate or the length of time of an investment if the original investment and maturity value are known.

Simple interest, which has been discussed previously, is the periodic payment of money for the use of money. Sometimes the interest is not paid at periodic intervals. Usually, in such instances, any accrued interest will then be added to the principal. This will then form a new principal which will be subject for the next period to the same rate of interest as the original principal.

This procedure of adding current interest to beginning principal, thus forming a new and larger principal in the following period, is called *compound interest*. The effect is the same as if the accrued interest were paid and then reinvested.

Example 1. Brooks borrowed $500 from a friend for two years at 12 percent with the interest compounded annually. Find the total amount that Brooks owes at the end of the two years.

Original principal	**$500.00**	
Interest for first year	**60.00**	**($500 × .12)**
Principal for second year	**$560.00**	
Interest for second year	**67.20**	**($560. × .12)**
Amount due at end of two years	**$627.20**	

If the interest in example 1 was paid annually, or was not compounded, the total interest would be $120, as follows:

$$I = Prt$$

$$I = \$500 \times \frac{12}{100} \times 2 = \$120$$

Computing Compound Interest for Periods Shorter than One Year

Interest may be compounded on a semiannual, quarterly, monthly, or even daily basis. Savings and loan associations are now trying to entice investors to save with them by offering compound interest on a daily basis, which is easy to calculate using computers. Thus, each day's interest is added to the previous principal balance to form a new principal amount.

If the interest is compounded more than once a year, the periodic interest rate must be reduced proportionately to the number of interest periods in the year. For example, if the annual interest rate is 12 percent, and interest is to be compounded semiannually, the interest computation will be made twice a year at 6 percent, one-half of the annual interest rate.

Selected Starting Salaries—Class of 1988

Petroleum engineers	$33,840
Mechanical engineers	29,388
Electrical engineers	29,316
Computer programmers	25,944
Accountants	23,700
Nurses	23,604
Banking/Finance	21,792

San Francisco Chronicle, 4/25/88

Example 2. In example 1, assume the same facts except that interest is to be compounded semiannually.

Original principal	**$500.00**	
Interest for first semiannual period	**30.00**	**($500 × .06)**
Principal for second period	**$530.00**	
Interest for second semiannual period	**31.80**	**($530 × .06)**
Principal for third period	**$561.80**	
Interest for third semiannual period	**33.71**	**($561.80 × .06)**
Principal for fourth period	**$595.51**	
Interest for fourth semiannual period	**35.73**	**($595.51 × .06)**
Amount due at end of second year	**$631.24**	

From examples 1 and 2 it becomes clear that the more frequently the interest is compounded, the greater will be the maturity value.

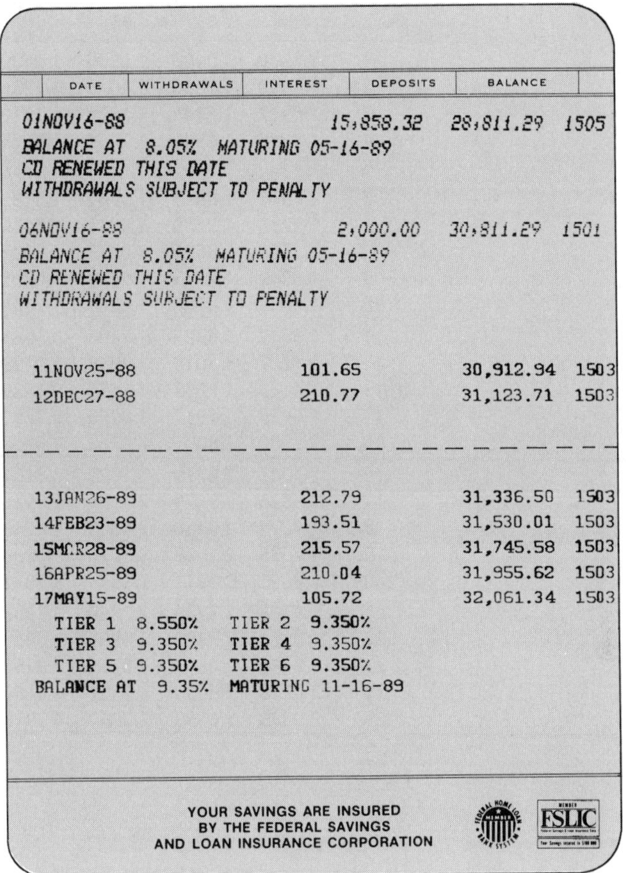

DATE	WITHDRAWALS	INTEREST	DEPOSITS	BALANCE

01NOV16-88 15,858.32 28,811.29 1505
BALANCE AT 8.05% MATURING 05-16-89
CD RENEWED THIS DATE
WITHDRAWALS SUBJECT TO PENALTY

06NOV16-88 2,000.00 30,811.29 1501
BALANCE AT 8.05% MATURING 05-16-89
CD RENEWED THIS DATE
WITHDRAWALS SUBJECT TO PENALTY

11NOV25-88 101.65 30,912.94 1503
12DEC27-88 210.77 31,123.71 1503

13JAN26-89 212.79 31,336.50 1503
14FEB23-89 193.51 31,530.01 1503
15MAR28-89 215.57 31,745.58 1503
16APR25-89 210.04 31,955.62 1503
17MAY15-89 105.72 32,061.34 1503
TIER 1 8.550% TIER 2 9.350%
TIER 3 9.350% TIER 4 9.350%
TIER 5 9.350% TIER 6 9.350%
BALANCE AT 9.35% MATURING 11-16-89

YOUR SAVINGS ARE INSURED
BY THE FEDERAL SAVINGS
AND LOAN INSURANCE CORPORATION

FSLIC

Compound Interest Tables

Since the computation of compound interest for several periods of time is time-consuming and requires a great deal of busy work, compound interest tables have been developed to reduce the mathematical labor. The table on page 324 indicates the compound amount of $1 at various rates of interest for many periods of time. Since all figures shown in the table are based on $1, to find the maturity value of any other principal amount, multiply the appropriate figure derived from the table by the principal. To determine the amount of compound interest, subtract the original principal from the maturity value.

Example 3. In example 1, the amount that Brooks would have to pay after two years could be determined more readily by use of the tables, as follows:

a. **Look down the period column to 2 and move horizontally to the 12 percent column, where the number is 1.2544.**
b. **Multiply 1.2544 by the original principal of $500. The answer of $627.20 is the same as in example 1.**

Amount of $1.00 Compounded Annually to Four Decimal Places

	Interest Rate								
Period	3%	4%	5%	6%	$7\frac{1}{2}$%	8%	9%	10%	12%
1	1.0300	1.0400	1.0500	1.0600	1.0750	1.0800	1.0900	1.1000	1.1200
2	1.0609	1.0816	1.1025	1.1236	1.1556	1.1664	1.1881	1.2100	1.2544
3	1.0927	1.1249	1.1576	1.1910	1.2423	1.2597	1.2950	1.3310	1.4049
4	1.1255	1.1699	1.2155	1.2625	1.3355	1.3605	1.4116	1.4641	1.5735
5	1.1593	1.2167	1.2763	1.3382	1.4356	1.4693	1.5386	1.6105	1.7623
6	1.1941	1.2653	1.3401	1.4185	1.5433	1.5869	1.6771	1.7716	1.9738
7	1.2299	1.3159	1.4071	1.5036	1.6590	1.7138	1.8280	1.9487	2.2107
8	1.2668	1.3686	1.4775	1.5938	1.7835	1.8509	1.9926	2.1436	2.4760
9	1.3048	1.4233	1.5513	1.6895	1.9172	1.9990	2.1719	2.3579	2.7731
10	1.3439	1.4802	1.6289	1.7908	2.0610	2.1589	2.3674	2.5937	3.1058
11	1.3842	1.5395	1.7103	1.8983	2.2156	2.3316	2.5804	2.8531	3.4785
12	1.4257	1.6010	1.7959	2.0122	2.3818	2.5182	2.8127	3.1384	3.8960
13	1.4685	1.6651	1.8856	2.1329	2.5604	2.7196	3.0658	3.4523	4.3635
14	1.5126	1.7317	1.9799	2.2609	2.7524	2.9372	3.3417	3.7975	4.8871
15	1.5580	1.8009	2.0789	2.3966	2.9589	3.1722	3.6425	4.1772	5.4736
16	1.6047	1.8730	2.1829	2.5404	3.1808	3.4259	3.9703	4.5950	6.1304
17	1.6528	1.9479	2.2920	2.6928	3.4194	3.7000	4.3276	5.0545	6.8660
18	1.7024	2.0258	2.4066	2.8543	3.6758	3.9960	4.7171	5.5599	7.6900
19	1.7535	2.1068	2.5270	3.0256	3.9515	4.3157	5.1417	6.1159	8.6128
20	1.8061	2.1911	2.6533	3.2071	4.2479	4.6610	5.6044	6.7275	9.6463
21	1.8603	2.2788	2.7860	3.3996	4.5664	5.0338	6.1088	7.4002	10.8038
22	1.9161	2.3699	2.9253	3.6035	4.9089	5.4365	6.6586	8.1403	12.1003
23	1.9736	2.4647	3.0715	3.8197	5.2771	5.8715	7.2579	8.9543	13.5523
24	2.0328	2.5633	3.2251	4.0489	5.6729	6.3412	7.9111	9.8497	15.1786
25	2.0938	2.6658	3.3864	4.2919	6.0983	6.8485	8.6231	10.8347	17.0001

Compound-Interest Tables for Periods Shorter than One Year

Even if compound interest is calculated more frequently than once a year, the compound interest tables can still be used with the necessary adjustments. The illustrated compound-interest table is based on interest being compounded annually. To compound more frequently than once a year:

1. Divide the annual interest rate by the number of interest periods to be compounded each year to derive the interest rate per period.
2. Multiply the number of interest periods to be compounded each year by the number of years to arrive at the total number of interest periods.
3. Look down the periods column to the number derived in step 2 and move horizontally to the interest rate column determined in step 1 and multiply that figure by the principal.

Example 4. In example 2, the amount Brooks would have to pay after two years could be determined more readily by use of the tables, as follows:

a. **Interest rate per period is 6 percent (annual interest rate of 12 percent divided by 2).**
b. **Total interest periods is 4 (2 interest periods per year times 2 years).**

c. **From the table on page 324, 4 periods at 6 percent is 1.2625.**

1.2625 × $500 = $631.25

The difference of $0.01 is due to the fact that the compound-interest tables are rounded off to four decimal places.

Periods beyond the Tables

When working a compound-interest problem with the use of tables, you might have a situation where there are more periods than the table provides. For example, suppose the table being used only covers 20 periods. You wish to find the compound amount of $1,000 for six years at 20 percent, compounded quarterly. If the table you are using only goes to 20 periods, and you need 24 periods, you can find the rate for 24 periods by multiplying any two of the rates whose periods add to 24. You could take the rate for 17 periods and the rate for 7 periods, and multiply the result by $1,000 to get the compound amount. Hence, using the 5 percent rate, 2.2920 × 1.4071 = 3.2251. $1,000 × 3.2251 = $3,225.10, the compound amount. Note that when you multiply any two rates from the table, your answer must be rounded off to four decimal places *before* you multiply by the investment.

Since the illustrated tables have 24 periods, tracing down to 24 periods and over to 5 percent does give 3.2251.

Several Periodic Investments

The compound-interest tables can also be used if an investor makes several periodic investments of the same or differing amounts. If the investment amounts are the same each period, the compound amount of each investment can be determined or the sum of the factors in the table can be added, with the total multiplied by the periodic investment amount.

Example 5. Barbara Baines invests $400 at the beginning of each year for three years at 16 percent, compound quarterly.

$400 × 1.6010 = $ 640.40 (12 periods)
$400 × 1.3686 = $ 547.44 (8 periods)
$400 × 1.1699 = $ 467.96 (4 periods)
$400 × 4.1395 = $1,655.80

If the investments differ each period, the compound amount of *each* investment must be determined and then added to get a combined amount.

Example 6. **Diane Chan invested $800 in a savings plan at 10 percent, compounded semiannually. The following year she invested $1,000, also at 10 percent, compounded semiannually. Determine her accumulated balance after three years.**

$ 800 × 1.3401 =	$1,072.08	(6 periods)
$1,000 × 1.2155 =	1,215.50	(4 periods)
	$2,287.58	Accumulated balance

Student Review

For partial periods, assume 30-day-month time.

1. Walsh invests $4,200 in a savings program at 8 percent, compounded semiannually, on September 1, 1990. Determine the accumulated amount on March 1, 1993.

$ ________________

2. Hurley invests $375 at 12 percent, compounded quarterly. How long will it take to accumulate a balance of $638.40?

____

3. Joe Thorn invests $1,500 on July 18, 1990, at 10 percent interest, compounded semiannually. Determine his accumulated amount on May 5, 1992.

$ ________________

4. Linda Boyd opened an investment account and began investing $400 semiannually for three years at 12 percent, compounded quarterly. Determine her investment balance at the end of three years.

$ ________________

5. John Wilk opened a retirement investment account. If he deposted $2,000 at the end of year one and $2,400 at the end of year two, determine his investment balance at the end of year five, assuming a yield of 8 percent, compounded semiannually.

$ ________________

Solutions to Student Review

1. Interest rate per period is 4 percent (8 percent divided by 2).
Total interest periods are 5 (2 interest periods per year times $2\frac{1}{2}$ years.)

$$\begin{array}{r} \$4{,}200.00 \\ \times\ 1.2167 \\ \hline \$5{,}110.14 \end{array}$$

$5,110.14

2.

$$\begin{array}{r} \$375 \\ \times\ ? \\ \hline \$638.40 \end{array} \qquad \$638.40 \div 375 = 1.7024$$

Interest rate per period is 3 percent (12 percent divided by 4).
Look down 3 percent column to 1.7024, which is 18 periods.

18 periods $\div$ 4 = $4\frac{1}{2}$ years

$4\frac{1}{2}$ years

3. July 18, 1990 to January 18, 1992 is 3 periods.
Interest rate per period is 5 percent (10 percent divided by 2).

$$\begin{array}{r} \$1{,}500.00 \\ \times\ 1.1576 \\ \hline \$1{,}736.40 \end{array}$$ (Accumulated amount on January 18, 1992)

$$\$1{,}736.40 \times \frac{10}{100} \times \frac{107}{360} = \$51.61$$

$1,736.40 + $51.61 = $1,788.01

$1,788.01

4.

$$\begin{array}{l} \$400 \times 1.4257 = \$\ \ 570.28 \\ \$400 \times 1.3439 = \quad 537.56 \\ \$400 \times 1.2668 = \quad 506.72 \\ \$400 \times 1.1941 = \quad 477.64 \\ \$400 \times 1.1255 = \quad 450.20 \\ \$400 \times 1.0609 = \quad 424.36 \\ \hline \$400 \times 7.4169 = \$2{,}966.76 \end{array}$$

$2,966.76

5.

$$\begin{array}{r} \$2{,}000 \\ \times\ 1.3686 \\ \hline \$2{,}737.20 \end{array} \qquad \begin{array}{r} \$2{,}400 \\ \times\ 1.2653 \\ \hline \$3{,}036.72 \end{array} \qquad \begin{array}{r} \$2{,}737.20 \\ +\ 3{,}036.72 \\ \hline \$5{,}773.92 \end{array}$$

$5,773.92

Assignment 24–1

Compound Interest

Name ______________________

Date ______________________

A. For the following problems, convert the annual interest rate to the interest rate per period and determine the total number of interest periods:

	Annual Rate	*Time of Loan*	*Interest Compounded*	*Periodic Rate*	*Number of Periods*
1.	14%	4 years	annually	________	________
2.	8%	10 years	annually	________	________
3.	10%	6 years	semiannually	________	________
4.	9%	5 years	semiannually	________	________
5.	12%	8 years	quarterly	________	________
6.	17%	10 years	quarterly	________	________
7.	24%	3 years	monthly	________	________
8.	9%	5 years	monthly	________	________

B. Using the table on page 324, solve the following problems:

	Principal	*Annual Rate*	*Time of Loan*	*Interest Compounded*	*Maturity Value*	*Amount of Compound Interest*
1.	$ 5,000	10%	4 years	annually	________	________
2.	$ 2,400	12%	3 years	annually	________	________
3.	$ 8,500	8%	10 years	semiannually	________	________
4.	$ 2,600	10%	12 years	semiannually	________	________
5.	$ 500	16%	6 years	quarterly	________	________
6.	$ 1,200	30%	5 years	quarterly	________	________
7.	$ 6,000	24%	2 years	bimonthly	________	________
8.	$ 1,000	48%	1 year	monthly	________	________
***9.**	$ 3,000	6%	30 years	annually	________	________
***10.**	$ 100	15%	14 years	semiannually	________	________
***11.**	$14,250	16%	10 years	quarterly	________	________
***12.**	$ 3,300	30%	5 years	bimonthly	________	________

* Since the tables are only carried to 4 decimal places, student answers may be slightly different than the given answers.

Assignment 24–2

Compound Interest

Name ______________________

Date ______________________

A. Find the total amount to the nearest cent in each of the following problems by use of the table on page 324:

1. $500 invested for eight years at 8 percent, compounded annually

   ____

2. $350 invested for two years at 10 percent, compounded annually

   ____

3. $2,500 invested for 12 years at 12 percent, compounded semiannually

   ____

4. $180 invested for six years at 15 percent, compounded semiannually

   ____

5. $625 invested for four years at 16 percent, compounded quarterly

   ____

6. $1,250 invested for three years at 12 percent, compounded quarterly

   ____

B. Solve the following by use of the table on page 324.

1. Perlin invests $5,000 at 10 percent, compounded annually for 15 years. Determine the total amount at maturity.

$ ____________

2. Hancock invests $2,500 in a savings plan at 12 percent, compounded quarterly on October 1, 1990. Determine the accumulated amount on April 1, 1992.

$ ____________

3. Nardi invests $1,200 at 16 percent, compounded quarterly for 10 years. Determine the accumulated amount at maturity.

$ ____________

Since the table only goes to 25 periods, the rate for 40 periods can be found by multiplying any two of the rates whose periods add to 40. The above calculation is based on 25 and 15 periods.

4. When Jones's son was six years old, his father invested $500 at 8 percent interest, compounded semiannually. Determine the accumulated amount withdrawn by the son on his 21st birthday.

$ ____________

The rate for 30 periods in the above calculation takes the rate for 25 periods times the rate for 5 periods. The students' answers for this problem and problem 3 (above) may vary slightly with the use of different combinations of periods.

5. If Hightower invests $900 at 16 percent, compounded quarterly, determine how long it takes to accumulate $1,332.18.

____

6. Gresham invests $1,500, compounded quarterly for six years. Determine the annual rate of interest he must get to accumulate $6,073.35 at maturity.

____

Assignment 24–3

Compound Interest

Name ____________________

Date ____________________

In the following problems, for partial periods assume 30-day-month time.

1. Ruth Anderson opened a bank savings account and invested $500 each year at the beginning of the year. If the bank compounds interest semiannually at 8 percent, determine her bank balance at the end of five years.

$ ____________________

2. Elmer Patterson invested $300 semiannually at the beginning of each period at 16 percent interest, compounded quarterly. Determine his accumulated investment balance at the end of three years.

$ ____________________

3. Robert Messman invests $2,000 on November 30, 1990, at 10 percent interest, compounded semiannually. Determine his accumulated balance on June 30, 1991.

$ ____________________

4. On June 15, 1990, Sandy Rubinfeld invested $1,200 at 20 percent interest, compounded quarterly. Determine her accumulated balance on October 10, 1992.

$ ____________________

5. Arthur Frankel received a 6 percent salary increase each year for five consecutive years. If his original salary was $12,800, determine his annual salary for the sixth year.

$ ______________

6. Ezekiel Habersham purchased a home for $45,000. If property increased 5 percent every six months, determine the value of his home after 10 years.

$ ______________

7. Terence Alberigi deposited $1,400 in an I.R.A. savings account at 16 percent, compounded quarterly. Two years later he deposited $2,000, also at 16 percent, compounded quarterly. Determine his accumulated balance after four years.

$ ______________

8. Peggy Vota opened a Keogh plan retirement investment account. At the end of each of the first three years, she deposited $1,800, $3,000, and $7,500, respectively. If the investment yields 10 percent, compounded semiannually, determine her accumulated balance after four years.

$ ______________

Multiple Sports with Amy Hengst, Accountant

On December 31, 1990, Multiple Sports awarded three salespeople a bonus of $2,000 each. However, the money would not be given to the employees until each worked 10 years for Multiple Sports. The three employees will complete their 10 years of employment, as follows:

Jack Morris	December 31, 1993
Arlie Lamb	June 30, 1995
Maryann Hearn	April 30, 1996

The company invested the $2,000 for each employee, as follows:

Jack Morris	12 percent, compounded annually
Arlie Lamb	12 percent, compounded semiannually
Maryann Hearn	12 percent, compounded quarterly

In addition, Ken Paris, the supervisor of the above three employees, was given a bonus of $2,000 on December 31, 1990, and $1,000 on December 31, 1992, payable to Paris on his retirement date, June 30, 2002. This bonus will be invested at 10 percent, compounded semiannually.

Amy asks you to determine the accumulated amount to be paid to the three salespeople when they complete 10 years with the company and the accumulated amount to be paid to Paris on his retirement date, and then submit this information to each employee.

Morris ____________

Lamb ____________

Hearn ____________

Paris ____________

Chapter 25

Present Value

Why do I pay 25 cents on the dollar to borrow a dollar that's only worth 25 cents?

Learning Goals

Upon completion of this chapter, you should be able to:

1. Define the meaning of the *present value* of an investment earning compound interest.
2. Determine the present value of an investment earning compound interest without using a table.
3. Using a present value table, calculate the present value of an investment earning compound interest.
4. Understand how the present value table and the compound interest table are directly related.
5. Derive the present value from a present value table if there are several periodic investments of the same or differing amounts.
6. Determine the present value from a present value table if the number of compoundings exceed the number provided by the table.
7. Using the present value tables, determine the interest rate or length of time of an investment if the original investment and compound interest are known.

Money that you have available at the present time is more valuable than money to be received at some later date. This is so because if you have money to invest now, you can immediately begin to earn interest. The money that you will receive later is not earning any interest now. Therefore, money that is to be received at some future time has a lower value today, known as the *present value*. The present value is the amount of money needed today that, when compounded periodically, will equal a predetermined amount at a predetermined future time period.

As an example, if an individual wanted to put a certain sum of money in the bank, at 8 percent interest, to pay for a trip costing $1,000 two years hence, the present value would be the amount that would have to be invested today. To simplify the computations, if interest were only compounded annually, the value at the end of a year at 8 percent interest would be 108 percent of the value at the beginning of the year. Therefore, $1,000 ÷ 1.08, or $925.93, would be the value at the beginning of the second year. Then, $925.93 ÷ 1.08, or $857.34 would be the value at the beginning of the first year, or in other words, the present value. Another way of saying this is that $857.34 invested today at 8 percent interest compounded annually for two years will have a maturity value of $1,000.

Since it would be quite time-consuming to have to continually divide for several time periods to arrive at a present value, a table showing the present value of $1 at differing interest rates is usually used. The following table shows the present value of $1 with compound interest rates from 2 to 12 percent. The present value of any desired amount can be determined by finding the present value of $1 and multiplying this present value of $1 by the desired maturity amount.

Table 1
Present Value of $1 at Compound Interest (to Four Decimal Places)

Period	Interest Rate 2%	3%	4%	$4\frac{1}{2}$%	6%	8%	10%	12%
1	0.9804	0.9709	0.9615	0.9569	0.9434	0.9259	0.9091	0.8929
2	0.9612	0.9426	0.9246	0.9157	0.8900	0.8573	0.8264	0.7972
3	0.9423	0.9151	0.8890	0.8763	0.8396	0.7938	0.7513	0.7118
4	0.9238	0.8885	0.8548	0.8386	0.7921	0.7350	0.6830	0.6355
5	0.9057	0.8626	0.8219	0.8025	0.7473	0.6806	0.6209	0.5674
6	0.8880	0.8375	0.7903	0.7679	0.7050	0.6302	0.5645	0.5066
7	0.8706	0.8131	0.7599	0.7348	0.6651	0.5835	0.5132	0.4523
8	0.8535	0.7894	0.7307	0.7032	0.6274	0.5403	0.4665	0.4039
9	0.8368	0.7664	0.7026	0.6729	0.5919	0.5002	0.4241	0.3606
10	0.8203	0.7441	0.6756	0.6439	0.5584	0.4632	0.3855	0.3220
11	0.8043	0.7224	0.6496	0.6162	0.5268	0.4289	0.3505	0.2875
12	0.7885	0.7014	0.6246	0.5897	0.4970	0.3971	0.3186	0.2567
13	0.7730	0.6810	0.6006	0.5643	0.4688	0.3677	0.2897	0.2292
14	0.7579	0.6611	0.5775	0.5400	0.4423	0.3405	0.2633	0.2046
15	0.7430	0.6419	0.5553	0.5167	0.4173	0.3152	0.2394	0.1827
16	0.7284	0.6232	0.5339	0.4945	0.3936	0.2919	0.2176	0.1631
17	0.7142	0.6050	0.5134	0.4732	0.3714	0.2703	0.1978	0.1456
18	0.7002	0.5874	0.4936	0.4528	0.3503	0.2502	0.1799	0.1300
19	0.6864	0.5703	0.4746	0.4333	0.3305	0.2317	0.1635	0.1161
20	0.6730	0.5537	0.4564	0.4146	0.3118	0.2145	0.1486	0.1037
21	0.6598	0.5375	0.4388	0.3968	0.2942	0.1987	0.1351	0.0926
22	0.6468	0.5219	0.4220	0.3797	0.2775	0.1839	0.1228	0.0826
23	0.6342	0.5067	0.4057	0.3634	0.2618	0.1703	0.1117	0.0738
24	0.6217	0.4919	0.3901	0.3477	0.2470	0.1577	0.1015	0.0659
25	0.6095	0.4776	0.3751	0.3327	0.2330	0.1460	0.0923	0.0588

Example 1. Mr. and Mrs. Peterson wish to give their son a graduation present of $500 when he graduates in six years. If they can earn 10

percent interest, compounded annually, find the amount Mr. and Mrs. Peterson would have to invest today to realize $500 in six years.

Look down the period column to 6 and move horizontally to 10 percent. This figure, 0.5645, is now multiplied by $500 to arrive at the present value of $282.25. If today Mr. and Mrs. Peterson invest $282.25 for six years at 10 percent, compounded annually, they will have a savings account balance of $500 when their son graduates.

Example 2. Joe Jaegar is planning to take a vacation to Europe in three years. He expects the entire trip to cost him $3,000. Find how much he would have to invest today at 16 percent, compounded quarterly, to have $3,000 in three years.

Since the interest is compounded quarterly, divide the interest rate by 4 and multiply the years by 4. Look down the period column to 12 and move horizontally to 4 percent. This figure, 0.6246, is now multiplied by $3,000 to arrive at the present value of $1,873.80. If Mr. Jaegar would invest $1,873.80 today at 16 percent interest, compounded quarterly, for three years, he would have $3,000 at the end of three years.

Earnings of Top Five Sports Endorsers—1987 (est.)

	($ millions)
Arnold Palmer	$8
Jack Nicklaus	6
Boris Becker	6
Greg Norman	4.5
Michael Jordan	4

Sports Marketing Newsletter

It should be noted that the compound interest tables and the present value tables are directly related. To illustrate this, if in example 2, present value tables were not available, the compound interest tables for 12 periods at 4 percent could be used to find 1.6010. $3,000 divided by 1.6010 is $1,873.83, the same present value as was determined by the use of present value tables adjusted for a rounding off factor of 3 cents.

Example 3. Ron Hidalgo wants to know how much he must invest today in order to withdraw $6,000 in 3 years and $8,000 in 5 years, if his investment can earn 12 percent, compounded quarterly.

Year of Withdrawal	Amount of Withdrawal	×	Present Value of $1	=	Present Value of Withdrawal
3	$6,000	×	0.7014	=	$4,208.40
5	8,000	×	0.5537	=	4,429.60
	Total present value				$8,638.00

Therefore, if Hidalgo invests $8,638 today at 12 percent interest, compounded quarterly, he can withdraw $6,000 in 3 years and $8,000 in 5 years.

If one wanted to withdraw the *same* amount in two or more future periods, a shortcut to determine the present value would be to add the present values of $1 and multiply the result by the amount of withdrawals.

Example 4. If, in example 3, Ron Hidalgo wanted to withdraw $6,000 at the end of the third year and the fifth year, he could save time by adding

the present values of $1 for three and five years, and multiply the sum times $6,000, as follows:

$$\begin{array}{r} 0.7014 \\ +0.5537 \\ \hline 1.2551 \end{array} \times \$6{,}000 = \$7{,}530.60$$

Periods beyond the Tables

In working a present value problem with the use of tables, one might come up with more periods than the table provides. For example, suppose the table being used covers only 16 periods. You are asked to find the present value of $5,000, for five years, with interest compounded quarterly at 12 percent. If the table only goes to 16 periods, you can find the rate for 20 periods by multiplying any two of the rates whose periods add to 20. You could take the rate for 16 periods times the rate for 4 periods, and multiply the result by $5,000 to get the present value for 20 periods. Hence, using the 3 percent column, 0.6232 × 0.8885 = 0.5537. $5,000 × 0.5537 = $2,768.50, the present value. Since the illustrated tables have 20 periods, tracing down to 20 periods and over to 3 percent does give 0.5537.

Example 5. Mary and William Johnson inherited $40,000. They have an 8-year old daughter who, they hope, will go to college in 10 years. The Johnsons believe that it will cost approximately $80,000 to put their daughter through four years of college. If their investment could earn 12 percent, compounded quarterly, determine how much of the $40,000 inheritance would have to be invested today in order to have $80,000 in 10 years.

Select any two periods that add to 40. For example, if 25 and 15 periods are picked, multiply 0.4776 × 0.6419 = 0.3066.

$80,000 × 0.3066 = $24,528

Present Value of a Series of Equal Payments

If the periodic payments or receipts are of equal amount, the present value can be determined from Table 1 by adding the present values of $1 for each period and multiplying the sum by the periodic amount.

Example 6. How much must Dick Robbins invest today in order to withdraw $2,000 a year for four years at 10 percent, compounded annually? From Table 1, the present value of $1 at 10 percent for the first four periods is:

$$\begin{array}{r} 0.9091 \\ 0.8264 \\ 0.7513 \\ 0.6830 \\ \hline 3.1698 \end{array} \times \$2{,}000 = \$6{,}339.60$$

Table 2
Present Value of $1 Received Periodically

Period	Interest Rate 4%	6%	8%	10%	12%
1	0.9615	0.9434	0.9259	0.9091	0.8929
2	1.8861	1.8334	1.7833	1.7355	1.6901
3	2.7751	2.6730	2.5771	2.4868	2.4018
4	3.6299	3.4651	3.3121	3.1698	3.0373
5	4.4518	4.2124	3.9927	3.7907	3.6048
6	5.2421	4.9173	4.6229	4.3552	4.1114
7	6.0021	5.5824	5.2064	4.8684	4.5638
8	6.7327	6.2098	5.7466	5.3349	4.9676
9	7.4353	6.8017	6.2469	5.7590	5.3282
10	8.1109	7.3601	6.7101	6.1445	5.6502
11	8.7605	7.8869	7.1390	6.4950	5.9377
12	9.3851	8.3838	7.5361	6.8137	6.1944
13	9.9856	8.8527	7.9038	7.1033	6.4235
14	10.5631	9.2950	8.2442	7.3667	6.6282
15	11.1184	9.7122	8.5595	7.6061	6.8109
16	11.6523	10.1059	8.8514	7.8237	6.9740
17	12.1657	10.4773	9.1216	8.0215	7.1196
18	12.6593	10.8276	9.3719	8.2014	7.2497
19	13.1339	11.1581	9.6036	8.3649	7.3658
20	13.5903	11.4699	9.8181	8.5136	7.4694

Table 2 can be used if one is looking for the present value of *equal* periodic payments or receipts. In example 6, instead of adding the first four periods of Table 1, the same amount of 3.1698 can be found for the fourth period in the 10 percent column of Table 2. All the amounts in Table 2 can be determined by adding the amounts found in Table 1, allowing for possible slight variations due to rounding.

If the equal periodic payments or receipts are compounded more frequently than once a year, divide the annual interest by the number of compoundings per year, and multiply by the number of periodic payments or receipts.

Example 7. How much must Bob Levin invest today at 8 percent, compounded semiannually, in order to make semiannual lease payments of $1,500 for the next four years.

$1,500 × 6.7327 = $10,099.05.

The same result could have been achieved by adding the first eight periods at 4 percent in Table 1.

Student Review

1. Carol Rockwell will probably need a new roof on her home in about three years. If the cost will be $7,000, how much will she need to invest today at 8 percent, compounded quarterly?

$ ____________

2. Pedro Marino would like to accumulate $9,000 in seven years at 12 percent, compounded quarterly. Determine the amount he would have to invest today.

$ ____________

3. Margaret Ho needs $2,500 in nine years. Determine the annual interest rate she must get if she invests $1,132 today, compounded semiannually.

$ ____________

4. Dennis Middelton wants to pay off his college student loan with payments of $300 quarterly for the next three years. How much would he have to invest today at 8 percent, compounded quarterly?

$ ____________

5. Suzanne Korey has consolidated her debts in one loan. Determine the amount that she must set aside today at 9 percent, compounded semiannually, to pay $500, $750, $1,000, and $1,500, respectively, over each of the next four years.

$ ____________

6. Mary Bogetti expects to make college tuition payments of $5,000 at the end of each of the next four years. Determine the amount she must invest today at 10 percent, compounded annually, to meet the tuition payments.

$ ____________

Solutions to Student Review

1. Interest rate per period is 2 percent (8 percent divided by 4).
Total interest periods are 12 (3 years times 4 compoundings per year).

$$\begin{array}{r} \$7{,}000.00 \\ \times\, 0.7885 \\ \hline \$5{,}519.50 \end{array}$$

$ 5,519.50

2. Interest rate per period is 3 percent (12 percent divided by 4).
Multiply any two periods in the 3 percent column of Table 1 that add to 28.
The suggested solution is based on 25 periods × 3 periods.

$$\begin{array}{r} 0.9151 \\ \times\, 0.4776 \\ \hline 0.4371 \end{array} \qquad \begin{array}{r} \$9{,}000.00 \\ \times\, 0.4371 \\ \hline \$3{,}933.90 \end{array}$$

$ 3,933.90

Note: If the student selects 21 periods × 7 periods, the answer is $3,933.
Any other combination will give the indicated answer, $3,933.90

3.

$$\begin{array}{r} \$2{,}500 \\ \times\, ? \\ \hline \$1{,}132 \end{array} \qquad \$1{,}132 \div \$2{,}500 = 0.4528$$

Total interest periods are 18 (9 years times 2 compoundings per year).
In Table 1, look across 18 periods to 0.4528, which is $4\frac{1}{2}$ percent per period.

$4\frac{1}{2}$ percent per period × 2 = 9 percent

9%

4. Interest rate per period is 2 percent (8 percent divided by 4).
In Table 1, add the first 12 periods in the 2 percent column. Multiple this sum by $300.

$$\begin{array}{r} \$\ 300.00 \\ \times\, 10.5754 \\ \hline \$3{,}172.60 \end{array}$$

$ 3,172.60

Note: Table 2 would be preferable if there was a 2 percent column

5. Interest rate per period in Table 1 is $4\frac{1}{2}$ percent (9 percent divided by 2).

$ 500 × 0.9157 =	$	457.85
$ 750 × 0.8386 =		628.95
$1,000 × 0.7679 =		767.90
$1,500 × 0.7032 =		1,054.80
		$2,909.50

$ 2,909.50

6. Table 2 $5,000 × 3.1698 = $15,849

$ 15,849

Note: In Table 1, the first 4 periods in the 10 percent column add to 3.1698.

Assignment 25–1

Present Value

Name ______________________

Date ______________________

Using the present value table on page 338, solve the following problems:

	Maturity Value	*Annual Rate*	*Time of Loan*	*Interest Compounded*	*Present Value*	*Amount of Compound Interest*
1.	$ 2,000	6%	10 years	annually	________	________
2.	$15,000	8%	3 years	annually	________	________
3.	$ 900	9%	4 years	semiannually	________	________
4.	$ 2,500	8%	$6\frac{1}{2}$ years	semiannually	________	________
5.	$ 350	8%	4 years	quarterly	________	________
6.	$ 1,250	12%	6 years	quarterly	________	________

7.	$10,000	12%	2 years	bimonthly	____________	____________
8.	$ 300	24%	$1\frac{1}{2}$ years	monthly	____________	____________
9.	$ 700	10%	30 years	annually	____________	____________
10.	$ 1,600	8%	20 years	semiannually	____________	____________
11.	$ 5,000	12%	7 years	quarterly	____________	____________
12.	$ 2,000	24%	4 years	monthly	____________	____________

Assignment 25–2

Present Value

Name ______________________

Date ______________________

Solve the following by use of the present value tables on pages 338 and 341.

1. Bill Rouge wishes to have $9,400 in four years to purchase dental equipment when he graduates from dental school. Determine how much he will need to invest now at 10 percent, compounded annually.

   $ ______________

2. Ron Derby intends to pay a $3,000, noninterest-bearing debt in five years. Determine the amount he will need today at 8 percent, compounded annually, to pay the loan.

   $ ______________

3. Gene Moriguchi plans to take his family to the Far East in three years. He expects the trip will cost him $7,000. Determine the amount he will have to invest today at 9 percent, compounded semiannually, to pay for the trip.

   $ ______________

4. Steve Clines intends to give his son a gift of $2,000 in four years. Determine the amount he would have to invest today at 8 percent, compounded semiannually, to accumulate this amount.

   $ ______________

5. Deron Gans intends to buy a new car for $12,500 in two years. Determine the amount he will have to invest today at 12 percent, compounded quarterly, to pay for the car.

   $ ______________

6. Greg Wicks intends to buy a home in five years. He expects the down payment to be $25,000. Determine the amount he would have to invest today at 16 percent, compounded quarterly, to meet the down payment.

   $ ______________

7. Helen Stargell would like to accumulate $8,500 in 10 years at 8 percent, compounded quarterly. To accomplish this, determine the amount she would have to invest today.

   $ ______________

8. Hilda Wolff wants to have $6,000 in 15 years. If she can invest at 12 percent, compounded semiannually, determine the amount she would have to invest today.

$ ________________

9. Ray Kemper wants to invest $3,094.08 today. Determine how long it will take him to accumulate $4,400 at 9 percent, compounded semiannually.

____

10. Alice Denims has $2,121.92 to invest today. Determine the annual rate of interest she must get in order to accumulate $3,800 in five years, compounded semiannually.

____

11. Maria Gonzalez has been working and saving most of her earnings since graduating from high school. She plans to begin college next year and expects her tuition costs to be $1,200, $1,450, $1,700, and $2,000, respectively, over the next four years, payable at the beginning of each year. Determine the amount of savings that she must set aside today at 8 percent, compounded quarterly, to meet her tuition payments.

$ ________________

12. Martha Crosby wants to set up a savings program whereby she can withdraw $1,000 at the end of each of the next 5 years in order to pay for her vacation. Determine the amount she would have to invest today at 10 percent, compounded annually.

$ ________________

13. Mary Kay Beavers joins a golf and country club. The dues are $750 semiannually, payable at the beginning of the period. She pays $750 for the first 6 months and decides to set aside the present value of the dues for the succeeding three years at 12 percent, compounded semiannually. Determine the amount that she must invest today.

$ ________________

14. Robert O'Brien has to pay semiannual child support payments to his ex-wife over the next four years. Determine the amount he would have to invest today at 8 percent compounded semiannually, in order to pay $1,500 semiannually for the next two years and $2,000 semiannually for the following two years.

$ ________________

Multiple Sports with Amy Hengst, Accountant

On January 2, 1990, Multiple Sports signed a five-year lease agreement with Debbie Realty on one building that it occupies. The lease agreement provides for payment of $12,000 at the end of each year, starting December 31, 1990.

On March 15, 1990, Multiple Sports purchased office and store equipment from Selleck Equipment and Supplies Co. Multiple Sports paid $2,500 down and gave a $6,000, noninterest-bearing, four-year note for the balance.

On June 30, 1990, Multiple Sports entered into an agreement to construct a 45-foot yacht to entertain its biggest customers. The yacht will be ready for service in three years. Under terms of the construction and purchase agreement, Multiple Sports can pay *(a)* $100,000 now, *(b)* $125,000 upon completion at the end of three years, or *(c)* $39,000 a year at the end of each of the next three years.

Assuming that Multiple Sports currently can invest its money at 8 percent, compounded annually, Amy asks you to determine the following:

1. The present value of the lease payments on the building.
2. The present value of the office and store equipment if full payment was made on March 15, 1990.
3. The present value of each payment plan on the construction of the yacht.

1. ____________

2. ____________

3.*(a)* ____________

(b) ____________

(c) ____________

% − × + $ ÷ +

Chapter 26

Annuities

Inflation has changed things—now one can live as cheaply as two.

Learning Goals

Upon completion of this chapter, you should be able to:

1. Define an annuity.
2. Differentiate between an *ordinary annuity* and an *annuity due*.
3. Calculate the amount of an annuity without the use of a table.
4. Calculate the amount of an annuity, using the compound interest tables.
5. Determine the accumulated amount from a series of investments by using the ordinary annuity table or the annuity due table.
6. Derive the periodic annuity if the maturity value is known.
7. Determine the amount of an annuity if the last annuity investment earned interest for less than one period.
8. Calculate the amount of an investment at maturity if the interest rate and/or the investment amount changes during the investment period.

An annuity is a series of payments, usually of equal amounts, made at stated intervals for a fixed or contingent period of time. It is paid into a fund that accumulates at compound interest. A company may set up an annuity, in the form of a sinking fund, to pay off a loan at some future date. An individual might set up an annuity to save money for some future obligation. Insurance premiums, retirement plans, and installment payments are other examples where an annuity is used.

Ordinary Annuity

When the series of payments are made at the *end* of each period, this is known as an ordinary annuity. The amount of an ordinary annuity is the sum of the periodic payments and the accumulated compound interest at the end of the annuity period.

The amount of an ordinary annuity can be calculated by the use of compound interest calculations. For example, a series of investments of $500 at the end of each of three years at 8 percent interest would accumulate to $1,623.20 as follows:

$ 500.00	investment at end of first year
40.00	interest, at 8 percent, during second year
500.00	investment at end of second year
$1,040.00	balance at end of second year
83.20	interest, at 8 percent, during third year
500.00	investment at end of third year
$1,623.20	balance at end of third year

The same results, as above, could have been derived by use of compound interest tables.

2 periods at 8 percent =	1.1664	(first investment)
1 period at 8 percent =	1.08	(second investment)
	2.2464	
	× $500	
	$1,123.20	
	500.00	(third investment)
	$1,623.20	

Instead of using the previous two methods, it is quicker and easier to use an ordinary annuity table, as illustrated in example 1.

Ordinary Annuity—Investment at End of Period—Amount of Annuity for $1 Invested at Compound Interest

End of Period	Interest Rate 2%	3%	4%	5%	6%	8%
1	1.0000	1.0000	1.0000	1.0000	1.0000	1.0000
2	2.0200	2.0300	2.0400	2.0500	2.0600	2.0800
3	3.0604	3.0909	3.1216	3.1525	3.1836	3.2464
4	4.1216	4.1836	4.2465	4.3101	4.3746	4.5061
5	5.2040	5.3091	5.4163	5.5256	5.6371	5.8666
6	6.3081	6.4684	6.6330	6.8019	6.9753	7.3359
7	7.4343	7.6625	7.8983	8.1420	8.3938	8.9228
8	8.5830	8.8923	9.2142	9.5491	9.8975	10.6366
9	9.7546	10.1591	10.5828	11.0266	11.4913	12.4876
10	10.9997	11.4639	12.0061	12.5779	13.1808	14.4866
11	12.1687	12.8078	13.4864	14.2068	14.9716	16.6455
12	13.4121	14.1920	15.0258	15.9171	16.8699	18.9771
13	14.6803	15.6178	16.6268	17.7130	18.8821	21.4953
14	15.9739	17.0863	18.2919	19.5586	21.0151	24.2149
15	17.2934	18.5989	20.0236	21.5786	23.2760	27.1521
16	18.6393	20.1569	21.8245	23.6575	25.6725	30.3243
17	20.0121	21.7616	23.6975	25.8404	28.2129	33.7502
18	21.4123	23.4144	25.6454	28.1324	30.9057	37.4502
19	22.8406	25.1169	27.6712	30.5390	33.7600	41.4463
20	24.2974	26.8704	29.7781	33.0660	36.7856	45.7620

The ordinary annuity table shows the amount accumulated from a series of periodic payments of $1 at the designated interest rate. When the periodic investment is an amount other than $1, multiply this amount by the appropriate figure derived from the table.

Example 1. Barry Schulman invests an ordinary annual annuity of $500 for three years at 8 percent. From the table, find the amount of this annuity.

Trace down three periods and move horizontally to 8 percent. Multiply the resultant figure, 3.2464, by $500. The amount of this annuity is $1,623.20.

You will notice that the previous illustrations used the same facts with identical results.

Example 2. Donald Drake invests an ordinary annuity of $200 quarterly for two years at 12 percent. From the table find the amount of his annuity.

First, multiply the years by 4 and take one-fourth of the interest rate.

Trace down eight periods and move horizontally to 3 percent. Multiply the figure derived, 8.8923, by $200. The amount of this annuity is $1,778.46.

Ordinary Annuity—Fixed Maturity

There are many instances where an individual, or a company, has a fixed obligation due at a fixed future date. Because of the difficulty of suddenly raising the money at maturity, this person may decide to set aside an amount each year that, when compounded, will equal the obligation at maturity. To find the amount to be set aside at the end of each period, for a given number of periods, at an expected interest yield, do the following:

1. From an ordinary annuity table, find the amount of $1 at the expected interest rate for the given number of periods.
2. Divide the amount needed at maturity by the amount derived in step 1.

Top Five Network TV Advertisers—1987

	($ millions)
Procter & Gamble	$378
Philip Morris	332
General Motors	273
Kellogg	238
McDonald's	216

The Wall Street Journal, 3/30/88
TV Bureau of Advertisers

Example 3. The Pointer Corporation borrowed $1,000,000 by the issuance of 10-year bonds. Rather than suddenly having to come up with $1,000,000 at maturity, the corporation management decided to set aside a certain amount at the end of each year that, at an anticipated yield of 8 percent, will accumulate to $1,000,000 at the end of 10 years. Find the amount that should be set aside each year.

a. **The amount of $1 at 8 percent for 10 years is 14.4866.**

b. $\frac{\$1{,}000{,}000}{14.4866} = \$69{,}029.31$ **(annual investment)**

In other words, if The Pointer Corporation were to invest $69,029.31 at the end of each year at 8 percent interest for 10 years, it would have accumulated $1,000,000.

Annuities Due

When the series of payments are made at the *beginning* of each period, this is known as an annuity due. Since the first payment is made at the beginning of the first year, the amount of an annuity due will exceed the amount of an ordinary annuity by the compound interest on the first payment for the life of the annuity.

The amount of an annuity due may be found from an ordinary annuity table by taking the amount for one extra period and then subtracting the amount of one payment. To illustrate, assume in example 1 in the ordinary annuity section, that Barry Schulman invested $500 at the beginning of each year for three years at 5 percent. Trace down *four* periods on the ordinary annuity table and move horizontally to 5 percent. Multiply the resultant figure, 4.3101, by $500. From this result of $2,155.05, subtract $500. The amount of this annuity due is $1,655.05.

The amount of an annuity due can be calculated by the use of compound interest calculations. Assume a series of investments of $500 at the beginning of each of three years at 5 percent interest. The amount of this annuity due would be $1,655.05, as follows:

$ 500.00	**investment at beginning of first year**
25.00	**interest, at 5 percent, during first year**
500.00	**investment at beginning of second year**
$1,025.00	**balance at beginning of second year**
51.25	**interest, at 5 percent, during second year**
500.00	**investment at beginning of third year**
$1,576.25	**balance at beginning of third year**
78.81	**interest, at 5 percent, during third year**
$1,655.06*	**balance at end of third year**

***Due to rounding off, there is a difference of $0.01.**

The same result, as above, could have been derived by use of compound interest tables.

3 periods of 5% =	**1.1576**
2 periods at 5% =	**1.1025**
1 period at 5% =	**1.0500**
	3.3101
	× 500
	$1,655.05

Since annuity due tables are provided, as the one illustrated on page 355, it is, again, quicker and easier to use the table.

Annuity Due—Investment at Beginning of Period—Amount of Annuity for $1 Invested at Compound Interest

Value at End of Period	Interest Rates					
	2%	3%	4%	5%	6%	8%
1	1.0200	1.0300	1.0400	1.0500	1.0600	1.0800
2	2.0604	2.0909	2.1216	2.1525	2.1836	2.2464
3	3.1216	3.1836	3.2465	3.3101	3.3746	3.5061
4	4.2040	4.3091	4.4163	4.5256	4.6371	4.8666
5	5.3081	5.4684	5.6330	5.8019	5.9753	6.3359
6	6.4343	6.6625	6.8983	7.1420	7.3938	7.9228
7	7.5830	7.8923	8.2142	8.5491	8.8975	9.6366
8	8.7546	9.1591	9.5828	10.0266	10.4913	11.4876
9	9.9497	10.4639	11.0061	11.5779	12.1808	13.4866
10	11.1687	11.8078	12.4864	13.2068	13.9716	15.6455
11	12.4121	13.1920	14.0258	14.9171	15.8699	17.9771
12	13.6803	14.6178	15.6268	16.7130	17.8821	20.4953
13	14.9739	16.0863	17.2919	18.5986	20.0151	23.2149
14	16.2934	17.5989	19.0236	20.5786	22.2760	26.1521
15	17.6393	19.1569	20.8245	22.6575	24.6725	29.3243
16	19.0121	20.7616	22.6975	24.8404	27.2129	32.7502
17	20.4123	22.4144	24.6454	27.1324	29.9057	36.4502
18	21.8406	24.1169	26.6712	29.5390	32.7600	40.4463
19	23.2974	25.8704	28.7781	32.0660	35.7856	44.7620
20	24.7833	27.6765	30.9692	34.7193	38.9927	49.4229

Example 4. Peter Merkal invests $500 at the beginning of each year for three years at 5 percent. From the table, find the amount of this annuity. Trace down three periods and move horizontally to 5 percent. Multiply the resultant figure, 3.3101, by $500. The amount of this annuity is $1,655.05, the same result as in the previous illustrations.

Example 5. Phyllis Jenkins invests $400 semiannually for five years in an annuity due at 6 percent. From the table, find the amount of her investment.

First, multiply the years by two and take one-half of the interest rate.

Trace down 10 periods and move horizontally to 3 percent. Multiply the figure derived, 11.8078, by $400. The amount of this annuity is $4,723.12.

The general annuity definition is that an ordinary annuity occurs when the series of investments is made at the end of each period, while an annuity due occurs when the series of investments is made at the beginning of each period. These definitions are sufficient when no specific dates are given, such as in example 4. However, when the dates of the investments are given, it should be understood that the series of investments must *begin* sometime. Therefore, a clearer distinction would be that if the *last* investment earns interest for one full period, this is an annuity due, while if the *last* investment earns no interest, or earns interest for less than one period, this is an ordinary annuity.

Example 6. Barbara Bell invests $250 semiannually, compounded at 12 percent, beginning on March 1, 1990. Determine the amount of this annuity on March 1, 1993, if she makes her final $250 investment on March 1, 1993. Since every investment must begin sometime, this is an ordinary annuity for 7 periods because the final investment earned no interest.

In the ordinary annuity table, trace down 7 periods and move horizontally to 6 percent. Multiply the figure derived, 8.3938, by $250. The amount of this ordinary annuity is $2,098.45.

If, in example 6, an investment was not made on March 1, 1993, this would be an annuity due for 6 periods, and the balance on March 1, 1993 would be:

$$\$250 \times 7.3938 = \$1{,}848.45$$

It should be noted that the answer for the ordinary annuity in example 6 is larger by $250 in comparison to the answer as an annuity due. The difference of $250 represents the final installment of the ordinary annuity at no interest.

Example 7. If, in example 6, Ms. Bell withdrew her annuity on April 1, 1993, this would still be an ordinary annuity since the last investment earned interest for less than one period.

Since her annuity amount as of March 1, 1993, was previously determined to be $2,098.45, any partial period would be calculated at simple interest. If 30-day-month time is assumed for partial periods, the additional interest and the amount of the ordinary annuity would be:

$$I = \$2{,}098.45 \times \frac{12}{100} \times \frac{30}{360} = \$20.98$$

$$S = \$2{,}098.45 + \$20.98 = \$2{,}119.43$$

Student Review

For partial periods, assume 30-day-month time.

1. Lorraine Dang invested $300 at the beginning of each quarter at 8 percent, compounded quarterly. Determine the amount of her investment at the end of four years.

$ ____________

2. The Bardaro Corp. borrowed $20,000,000 by the issuance of 6 percent, 20-year bonds. The corporation is required to set up a bond sinking fund. How much will the corporation have to invest at the end of each year at 8 percent, compounded annually, to pay off the bonds?

$ ____________

3. Beginning on August 1, 1990, Ken Crizer invested $600 quarterly at 12 percent, compounded quarterly. If his last investment is on February 1, 1993, determine his accumulated amount on May 1, 1993.

$ ____________

4. Alice Harth invested $750 semiannually, beginning March 1, 1990. If she earns 10 percent, compounded semiannually, determine her accumulated amount on October 12, 1993.

$ ____________

5. Tony Ponce started a savings program, investing $300 at the end of each quarter. For the first three years, his investments earned 8 percent, compounded quarterly. Suddenly, the interest rate on his investment program shot up to 12 percent, compounded quarterly. Determine his accumulated investment balance at the end of six years.

$ ____________

Solutions to Student Review

1. Interest rate per period is 2 percent (8 percent divided by 4).
Total interest periods are 16 (4 years times 4 compoundings per year).

In the annuity due table:

$$\begin{array}{r} \$\ 300.00 \\ \times\ 19.0121 \\ \hline \$5{,}703.63 \end{array}$$

$ 5,703.63

2. In the ordinary annuity table:

$\$20{,}000{,}000 \div 45.7620 = \$437{,}043.84$

$ 437,043.84

3. Since the last investment earns interest for one full period, this is an annuity due.
Interest rate per period is 3 percent (12 percent divided by 4).
Total interest periods are 11.

$$\begin{array}{r} \$\ 600.00 \\ \times\ 13.1920 \\ \hline \$7{,}915.20 \end{array}$$

$ 7,915.20

4. This is an ordinary annuity to September 1, 1993 at 5 percent per period for 8 periods plus simple interest for 41 days.

$$\begin{array}{r} \$\ 750.00 \\ \times\ 9.5491 \\ \hline \$7{,}161.83 \end{array}$$

$$I = \$7{,}161.83 \times \frac{10}{100} \times \frac{41}{360} = \$81.57$$

$\$7{,}161.83 + \$81.57 = \$7{,}243.40$

$ 7,243.40

5. This problem is a combination of ordinary annuity and compound interest.

Ord. Annuity (12 per-2%)	Cmpd. Int. (12 per-3%)	Ord. Annuity (12 per-3%)		
$ 300.00	$4,023.63	$ 300.00	$5,736.49	
× 13.4121	× 1.4257	× 14.1920	+ 4,257.60	
$4,023.63	$5,736.49	$4,257.60	$9,994.09	$ 9,994.09

Assignment 26–1

Annuities

Name ______________________

Date ______________________

A. Determine the final amount of the following *ordinary annuities:*

	Annuity Payment	*Payable*	*Number of Years*	*Interest Rate*	*Amount*
1.	$ 400	annually	10	8%	$ ______
2.	$1,225	annually	7	6%	$ ______
3.	$7,450	semiannually	6	12%	$ ______
4.	$ 900	semiannually	4	16%	$ ______
5.	$ 150	quarterly	3	8%	$ ______
6.	$4,500	quarterly	2	12%	$ ______

B. Solve the following:

1. Grace Burnham invested $500 at the end of each year for 10 years at 8 percent, compounded annually. Determine the amount of her investment at the end of 10 years.

   $__________

2. Loretta Mendelson invested $1,000 semiannually in corporate bonds, beginning March 31, 1986. If the yield is 12 percent, compounded semiannually, determine the amount of the fund on October 1, 1988. (Do not count interest for the extra day.)

   $__________

3. Al Sapiro invests $500 at the end of each half year in a savings account at 8 percent, compounded semiannually. Determine the amount on deposit at the end of seven years.

   $__________

4. Rick Blass invests $300 at the end of each quarter in a mortgage investment program. If the investment yields 16 percent, compounded quarterly, determine the amount of the investment at the end of three years.

   $__________

5. Rosa Perez invested $500 at the end of each year for six years at a minimum guaranteed interest rate of 6 percent, compounded annually. During the first four years, the rate of interest earned was 6 percent. However, during the last two years, the interest rate increased to 8 percent. Determine the amount of her investment at the end of six years.

   $__________

6. Ken Castellino invested $900 at the end of each half year at 10 percent, compounded semiannually. After three years, he increased his semiannual investment to $1,000, and the interest rate was increased to 12 percent, compounded semiannually. Determine the total amount of his investment at the end of eight years.

   $__________

Assignment 26–2
Annuities

Name ______________________

Date ______________________

A. Determine the final amount of the following *annuities due*:

	Annuity Payment	*Payable*	*Number of Years*	*Interest Rate*	*Amount*
1.	$ 700	annually	12	6%	$________
2.	$3,000	annually	15	8%	$________
3.	$ 400	semiannually	6	12%	$________
4.	$ 250	semiannually	4	10%	$________
5.	$ 100	quarterly	2	16%	$________
6.	$ 325	quarterly	3	20%	$________

B. Find the *ordinary annuity* needed to arrive at the desired maturity values:

	Maturity Value	*Payable*	*Number of Years*	*Interest Rate*	*Ordinary Annuity*
1.	$ 1,000	annually	10	8%	$________
2.	$200,000	annually	5	6%	$________
3.	$250,000	semiannually	6	8%	$________
4.	$ 30,000	semiannually	4	16%	$________

C. Solve the following, assuming 30-day-month time for partial periods:

1. The Adler Corporation borrowed $5,000,000 by the issuance of 8 percent, 10-year bonds. The corporation decided to establish a sinking fund to pay off the bonds. Determine the amount it will have to invest at the end of each year, at a yield of 6 percent, to pay off the bonds at maturity.

   $____________

2. Wayne Roget wants to accumulate $14,500 at the end of 10 years to put his son through college. Determine the amount he would have to invest at the *beginning* of each year at 8 percent, compounded annually.

   $____________

3. Joseph Settle is uncertain which investment policy will give him the greater final amount. He could invest $500 today at 8 percent for five years, or he could invest $100 at the beginning of each year for five years at 8 percent. Circle whichever is larger and indicate the amount of difference.

   Compound amount   Annuity due

   $____________

4. Beginning on July 1, 1990, Patricia Madigan invested $300 quarterly at 12 percent, compounded quarterly. If her last investment is made on July 1, 1993, determine her accumulated amount on October 1, 1993.

   $____________

5. Vester Flanagan invested $325 quarterly, beginning March 1, 1990. Determine the accumulated amount on November 1, 1992, if he earns 16 percent, compounded quarterly.

   $____________

6. Mary Hale, wanting to shingle her home, invests $500 semiannually, beginning May 20, 1990. If she earns 12% compounded semiannually, determine her accumulated amount on July 16, 1993.

   $____________

Multiple Sports with Amy Hengst, Accountant

Multiple Sports decided several years ago to set aside equal periodic amounts of money for future purchase of unimproved land for plant expansion. Beginning November 1, 1982, Multiple Sports began investing $8,000 semiannually at 8 percent, compounded semiannually. Beginning with the investment on May 1, 1987, the interest rate increased to 10 percent. In late 1990, Multiple Sports decided it was ready for expansion and found the desired unimproved land in a neighboring town. The purchase arrangements were finalized on December 19, 1990, at a purchase price of $200,000, and the annuity was withdrawn in full to pay the land purchase price.

Construction of the new plant started in February 1991. The contractor gave Multiple Sports the option either to take a $256,000 loan at 10 percent, payable in equal monthly payments over 30 years, or to make a single payment of $400,000 as payment in full on September 1, 1995.

If Multiple Sports decided to pay the $400,000 on September 1, 1995, it would have to set aside equal quarterly installments at 8 percent, compounded quarterly, beginning March 1, 1991, through and including September 1, 1995, in order to accumulate the $400,000 necessary to pay for the construction.

Amy asks you to determine (*a*)* the accumulated amount on December 19, 1990, to pay for the land and (*b*) the amount of each quarterly installment necessary to have $400,000 on September 1, 1995.

(*a*) ____________

(*b*) ____________

*Hint for part (*a*). You can treat the investments before the rate change as an annuity due for 9 periods, and the investments beginning May 1, 1987, as an ordinary annuity for 8 periods; or you can treat the investments before the rate change as an ordinary annuity for 10 periods, with the investments beginning November 1, 1987, as an ordinary annuity for 7 periods.

% − X + $ ÷ +

Section 8

Consumer Purchases

% − × + $ ÷ +

Chapter 27

Installment Sales

If you want to buy a $20,000 car, it's easy—buy an $8,000 car on time.

Learning Goals

Upon completion of this chapter, you should be able to:

1. Differentiate between a *cash sale,* a *credit sale,* and an *installment sale.*
2. Discuss the meaning of *carrying charge.*
3. In an installment purchase, determine the installment cost, the amount of interest, and the amount borrowed.
4. Determine the approximate rate of interest on an installment sale by use of a short-cut installment formula.
5. Calculate the amount of each installment payment if the amount borrowed, the effective interest rate, and the number of periodic payments are given.
6. Find the approximate rate of interest on a personal loan when the borrower makes periodic principal and interest payments.

Installment Payments

Some companies sell on a cash basis only. This means that the buyer has to pay cash immediately at the time of purchase of a product.

Most companies sell on a cash or credit basis. The typical credit situation is when the buyer pays no cash at the time of purchase but will pay the full cash price upon receiving a bill. This is called an open account, and the customer usually has about 30 days to pay.

In certain businesses, sales will be made on an installment basis. This means that the customer makes no down payment, or a small down payment, and then pays a certain amount per week or month over an agreed period of time.

If a customer buys on an installment plan, the total amount to be paid will be considerably larger than if purchasing for cash or on short-term credit. This additional cost is called a *carrying charge* and includes an interest charge for borrowing money for an extended period, a charge for investigating the credit standing of the customer, a charge for additional billing and bookkeeping, and the shared charge to all customers for the greater potential in uncollectible accounts.

To determine the effective rate of interest on an installment purchase, it is necessary to determine the installment total cost, the amount of interest (carrying charges), and the amount borrowed (cash price less any down payment).

Finding the Effective Rate of Interest

Example 1. Assume that a TV-stereo combination is advertised at $600 cash, or $240 down and $45 per month for nine months on an "easy-pay" plan. Find *(a)* the installment cost, *(b)* amount of interest, or carrying charge, *(c)* amount borrowed (cash price less down payment), and *(d)* effective rate of ordinary interest.

(a)	Down payment	$240
	Periodic payments (9 × $45)	+ 405
	Installment cost	$645
(b)	Installment cost	$645
	Cash price	− 600
	Amount of interest	$ 45
(c)	Cash price	$600
	Down payment	− 240
	Amount borrowed	360

(d) The assumption will be made that each periodic payment consists of the same amount of principal and the same amount of interest.

$$\frac{\text{Amount borrowed (from } c)}{\text{Number of payments}} \quad \frac{\$360}{9} = \$40 \text{ principal payment per month}$$

$$\frac{\text{Amount of interest (from } b)}{\text{Number of payments}} \quad \frac{\$45}{9} = \$5 \text{ interest payment per month}$$

Since the principal is not constant, as in previous text units, but decreases by the same amount each month, a single principal balance can be determined by taking the sum of the principal balances at the beginning of each of the nine months and treating this total the same as one purchase with an interest charge of $45 for one month. The following table will illustrate how to arrive at a *single principal amount.*

End of Month	Principal Balance	Principal Payment	Interest Payment
1	360	40	5
2	320	40	5
3	280	40	5
4	240	40	5
5	200	40	5
6	160	40	5
7	120	40	5
8	80	40	5
9	40	40	5
Totals	1,800	360	45

From the above table it should be understood that there is no difference between a single purchase with a net balance due of $360 payable in $40 principal payments, and a series of nine separate purchases, each payable in one month, with a $5 interest charge per purchase. In the latter case, we can assume a combined single purchase of $1,800, payable in one month, with $45 interest charge.

The annual rate of interest can be determined as follows:

$$r = \frac{I}{Pt} = \frac{\$45}{\$1{,}800 \times \frac{1}{12}} = \frac{\$45}{\$150} = 30\%$$

Pt = Payment × time

Formula for the Single Principal Amount

If the installment payments were extended over a longer period of time, the time spent on determining the single equivalent principal amount would be time-consuming and wasteful. A simplified formula can be used to determine this amount.

The symbols for the formula could be as follows:

I = Interest in dollars (total carrying charge)
B = Amount borrowed (cash price less down payment, if any)
r = Effective rate of interest
n = Number of payment periods in one year
p = Number of periodic installment payments
IP = Amount of periodic installment payment

If an amount borrowed is to be paid off on a regular periodic payment schedule, with the same amount paid each time until the balance is zero, the single principal amount may be determined by the following formula:

$$\text{Single principal amount} = \text{Amount borrowed} \times \frac{\text{Number of payments} + 1}{2}$$

In the example:

$$\text{Single principal amount} = \$360 \times \frac{9 + 1}{2} = \$1{,}800$$

Formula for Effective Interest Rate

From the preceding information we can arrive at the formula for the effective rate of interest on an installment purchase as follows:

$$r = \frac{I}{Pt}$$

$$P = B\left(\frac{p + 1}{2}\right)$$

$$t = \frac{1}{n}$$

$$r = \frac{I}{B\left(\frac{p + 1}{2}\right)\left(\frac{1}{n}\right)}$$

and the installment formula is:

$$r = \frac{2\,n\,I}{B(p + 1)}$$

Substituting amounts in the example,

$$r = \frac{2 \times 12 \times \$45}{\$360(9 + 1)} = \frac{3}{10} = 30\%$$

If the principal, \$360, and interest, \$45, were paid in one payment after nine months, then the simple interest formula would be used, as follows:

$$r = \frac{I}{Pt}$$

Substituting amounts in this example,

$$r = \frac{\$45}{\$360 \times \frac{9}{12}} = \frac{1}{6} = 16.7\%$$

Life Expectancy at age 21—in 1985

total	55.1 years
White male	52.3
White female	58.8
Black male	46.5
Black female	54.3

U.S. Bureau of the Census, *Statistical Abstract of the United States:* 1988 (108th edition) Washington, DC.

Therefore, the effective rate of interest is much higher when payments are made in installments instead of making a single payment at the maturity date of the loan.

Note that if the periodic payments were made weekly, n would be 52. If the TV-stereo was sold for \$240 down and \$15 per week for 27 weeks, the installment formula would be:

$$r = \frac{2\,n\,I}{B(p+1)} = \frac{2 \times 52 \times 45}{360(27+1)} = \frac{13}{28} = 46.4\%$$

If the amount borrowed, the effective interst rate, and the number of periodic payments are given, and the periodic installment payment is unknown, first solve for I by transposing in the installment formula, as follows:

$$I = \frac{B(p+1)r}{2n}$$

or, in the example given,

$$I = \frac{\$360(9+1).3}{2 \times 12} = \$45$$

The amount of each installment payment will then be determined by the following formula:

$$IP = \frac{B+I}{p} = \frac{\$360 + \$45}{9} = \$45$$

It should be noted that the effective interest rate derived by the given installment formula is slightly higher than the actual effective interest rate. This is due to the fact that, with fixed equal periodic payments, the amount representing each principal payment is not, in fact, the same each period, but decreases slowly at first and much more substantially during the final installments, with the interest portion having the reverse effect. However, even without the availability of special tables or an appropriate calculator, it is still not too difficult to quickly and easily arrive at a close approximation to the actual installment effective rate.

Personal Borrowing

Personal loans are ordinarily of two types. One is an ordinary note, whereby the borrower agrees to pay the principal sum plus interest in one payment at maturity. These loans are usually made for short periods of time, usually six months or less, and the borrower has reasonably good credit.

The second type of personal loan is when the borrower agrees to pay the principal sum plus interest over a period of time. The interest rate is either applied to the *original balance* or is computed on the *declining principal balance*. These loans usually cover a longer period of time to pay and/or involve borrowers with relatively poor credit.

If a loan is made that requires periodic repayments, the formula to be used for determining the effective interest rate can be the same as used for installment purchases.

Example 1. Irwin Bear purchases a car. He has to borrow $800 from the Friendly Finance Company to pay a portion of the cost, agreeing to pay back $30 a month for 36 months. Determine the effective rate of ordinary interest.

Since the amount borrowed is $800 and the total repayment (36 × $30) is $1,080, the interest is $280.

$$r = \frac{2nI}{B(p+1)} = \frac{2 \times 12 \times \$280}{\$800(36+1)} = 22.7\%$$

Banks and other lenders often charge a set dollar amount per each $100 borrowed per year, chargeable on the *original* balance, with the total of principal and interest to be paid in equal periodic payments.

Example 2. Neal Muira borrows $300 from Akio Inoye and agrees to repay him in 13 equal weekly installments. The interest charge on this loan is $8 per $100 per year on the original principal balance. Find the rate of interest that Mr. Muira was charged.

$$I = \$300 \times \frac{13}{52} \times \frac{8}{100} = \$6$$

$$r = \frac{2 \times 52 \times 6}{\$300(13+1)} = 14.9\%$$

Student Review

1. Eaton Photograpy purchased darkroom photographic equipment for $12,500. The company paid $2,500 down and agreed to pay the balance in 36 equal monthly installments of $325. Determine the effective rate of interest to the nearest whole percent.

____

2. Marlene Stoner borrowed $3,000 from her bank to pay for backyard landscaping. The bank charges $7 per $100 per year on the original balance. If Ms. Stoner pays the loan in 20 equal monthly payments, determine the effective rate of interest to the nearest tenth percent.

____

3. Donald Lundy borrowed $2,100 from the Central Lending Co. to help pay for some dental work. He agreed to pay the loan in 25 equal weekly installments of $90. Determine the effective rate of interest to the nearest whole percent.

____

4. Becky's Tavern purchased several bar stools at a total cost of $8,500. Determine the effective rate of interest to the nearest whole percent if the purchase is paid in 30 equal monthly payments of $320.

____

5. Kreidl Plumbing purchased new plumbing equipment for $2,800. The company paid 15 percent down and agreed to pay the balance in 15 equal monthly payments at an effective rate of 12 percent. Determine the amount of each monthly installment payment.

$____________________

Solutions to Student Review

1.

$$\begin{array}{r} \$12{,}500 \\ -\ \ 2{,}500 \\ \hline \$10{,}000 \end{array} \text{ (amt. borrowed)} \qquad \begin{array}{r} \$\ \ 325 \\ \times\ \ \ 36 \\ \hline \$11{,}700 \\ +\ \ 2{,}500 \\ \hline \$14{,}200 \end{array} \text{ (inst. cost)} \qquad \begin{array}{r} \$14{,}200 \\ -\ 12{,}500 \\ \hline \$\ 1{,}700 \end{array} \text{ (interest)}$$

$$r = \frac{2 \times 12 \times \$1{,}700}{\$10{,}000 \times 37} = 11\%$$

11%

2.

$$I = \$3{,}000 \times \frac{7}{100} \times \frac{20}{12} = \$350$$

$$r = \frac{2 \times 12 \times \$350}{\$3{,}000 \times 21} = 13.3\%$$

13.3%

3.

$$\begin{array}{r} \$\ \ 90 \\ \times\ \ 25 \\ \hline \$2{,}250 \end{array} \qquad \begin{array}{r} \$2{,}250 \\ -\ 2{,}100 \\ \hline \$\ \ 150 \end{array} \text{ (int.)}$$

$$r = \frac{2 \times 52 \times \$150}{\$2{,}100 \times 26} = 29\%$$

29%

4.

$$\begin{array}{r} \$\ 320 \\ \times\ \ 30 \\ \hline \$9{,}600 \end{array} \qquad \begin{array}{r} \$9{,}600 \\ -\ 8{,}500 \\ \hline \$1{,}100 \end{array} \text{ (int.)}$$

$$r = \frac{2 \times 12 \times \$1{,}100}{\$8{,}500 \times 31} = 10\%$$

10%

5.

$$\begin{array}{r} \$2{,}800 \\ \times\ \ \ .85 \\ \hline \$2{,}380 \end{array} \text{ (amt. borrowed)}$$

$$I = \frac{B(p + 1)r}{2n}$$

$$I = \frac{\$2{,}380 \times 16 \times 12}{2 \times 12 \times 100} = \$190.40$$

$$IP = \frac{\$2{,}380 + \$190.40}{15} = \$171.36$$

$171.36

Assignment 27–1

Installment Sales

Name ____________________

Date ____________________

A. Find the installment cost, the amount of interest or carrying charge, and the amount borrowed on the following installment purchases:

	Item	*Down Payment*	*Periodic Payment*	*Number of Monthly Payments*	*Installment Cost (a)*	*Cash Price*	*Interest (b)*	*Amount Borrowed (c)*
1.	Radio	$10	$10	7	$____	$ 75	$____	$____
2.	Washer-dryer	50	15	18	$____	280	$____	$____
3.	Stereo	25	12	30	$____	350	$____	$____
4.	Adding machine	0	8	20	$____	140	$____	$____

B. Using the installment formula, determine, to the nearest whole percent, the effective interest rate of the problems in section A (above)-

Item

1. Radio ____%

2. Washer-dryer ____%

3. Stereo ____%

4. Adding machine ____%

C. The Friendly Finance Company uses the following rate schedule in making some of its loans:

Amount of Loan	*12 Months*	*Monthly Payments 18 Months*	*24 Months*
$100	$ 9.75	$ 7.02	$ 5.45
300	29.10	20.89	15.98
500	48.12	34.07	26.47

From the above table, find the amount of interest and the effective rate of interest to the nearest whole percent charged to each of the following borrowers.

	Amount of Interest	*Effective Interest Rate*
1. $100, 18 months	$______	______%
2. $300, 12 months	$______	______%
3. $500, 18 months	$______	______%
4. $300, 24 months	$______	______%

D. Find the effective rate of interest to the nearest tenth percent on the following personal loans and installment purchases:

1. A student borrowed $350 and agreed to pay the loan back in eight equal monthly installments of $50.

____

2. Don Griffin purchased a new car for $9,600. He paid $500 down and financed the balance through the bank. The bank charged $5 per $100 per year on the original balance. Mr. Griffin paid the loan in 24 equal monthly payments.

____

3. William Funke purchased a vacuum cleaner costing $150. He agreed to pay $30 down and $5 a week for 25 weeks.

____

4. Wayne Durlester purchased a used car, priced at $500. He agreed to pay one-fourth down and the balance at $8 a week for 50 weeks.

____

Assignment 27–2

Installment Sales

Name ______________________

Date ______________________

1. Buttimer Recreation Company sells recreational equipment. George Stewart purchased a new boat for $8,100, paying 10 percent down, with the balance payable in 24 equal monthly payments of $360. Determine the effective rate of interest to the nearest whole percent.

   ____

2. Louis Batmale purchased a summer cabin for $60,000, agreeing to pay $12,000 down, with the balance due in 60 monthly installments of $990 each. Determine the effective rate of interest to the nearest tenth of 1 percent.

   ____

3. Jack Brady sponsored a Little League baseball team. In order to finance a trip to a distant city, he borrowed $1,500 from a local loan company. If he had to repay the loan in 15 equal monthly payments of $110, determine the effective rate of interest to the nearest whole percent.

   ____

4. Ed Davis borrowed $2,600 from his bank in order to pay his personal income and property taxes. The bank charges on the original balance at $6 per $100 per year on the first $2,000 and $5 per $100 per year on any excess. Mr. Davis agreed to pay the loan in 10 equal monthly payments. Determine the effective rate of interest on this loan to the nearest tenth of 1 percent.

   ____

5. Dorian Eunice borrowed $3,500 to remodel her kitchen. She agreed to repay the loan in 18 bimonthly installments of $255 each. Determine the effective rate of interest to the nearest tenth of 1 percent.

   ____

6. Edna Pope borrowed $600 to finance a ski vacation. She agreed to repay the loan in five quarterly installments of $140 each. Determine the effective rate of interest to the nearest whole percent.

____

7. William Pons borrowed $400 in order to pay for minor surgery. He agreed to repay the loan in 25 weekly payments of $17 each. Determine the effective rate of interest to the nearest whole percent.

____

8. James Fulcomer sold his used car to a neighbor for $2,500. He received 20 percent down, with the balance to be paid in 24 equal monthly payments at an effective rate of 12 percent on the unpaid balance. Determine *(a)* the total amount of interest he will receive and *(b)* the amount of each installment payment that he will receive.

(a) $__________

(b) $__________

9. Tom Ayers borrowed $500 from his employer. He agreed to repay the loan through 25 weekly payroll withholdings at an effective rate of 10 percent on the unpaid balance. Determine how much the employer will withhold each week to repay the loan.

$__________

10. Gisela Zander had a new roof put on her house at a cost of $4,200. She paid $1,500 down and agreed to pay the balance in 36 equal monthly payments at an effective rate of 18 percent on the unpaid balance. Determine the amount of each monthly installment payment.

$__________

Multiple Sports with Amy Hengst, Accountant

Multiple Sports has to replace the roof on one of its buildings. Three roofing contractors entered bids. Contractor A charges $9,000 upon completion, or $1,000 down and $375 per month for 24 months. Contractor B charges $8,500 upon completion, or 12 quarterly payments of $875 each. Contractor C quotes $9,200 upon completion, or $1,500 down and $275 semimonthly for 15 months.

In addition, Multiple Sports acquired a pickup truck for $14,000, paying $2,000 down and taking a car loan from North-West Bank for the balance, payable in 36 equal monthly installments. North-West Bank charges $6.40 per $100 on the *original loan balance.*

Amy asks you to determine the approximate interest rate charged by each roofing contractor to the nearest tenth of one percent, as well as the *total cash* to be paid to each contractor under the installment arrangement. Further, Amy asks you to determine the approximate interest rate charged by North-West Bank on the loan for the truck.

	Contractor		
	A	B	C
Interest rate	______	______	______
Total cash paid	______	______	______
		North-West Bank	______

Chapter 28

Rule of 78

I'm suspicious of Rhonda's credit. She always pays in cash.

Learning Goals

Upon completion of this chapter, you should be able to:

1. Determine the prepayment penalty if the borrower pays a long-term installment contract in full before the maturity date.
2. Compare the approximate rate of interest on an installment payment plan, by use of the installment formula, with the effective (real) interest rate, using an amortization table.
3. Define the Rule of 78.
4. Closely approximate by the Rule of 78 the interest included in the prepaid periods when paying an installment purchase balance in full prior to maturity.
5. Calculate by the Rule of 78 the balance due when paying off an installment purchase or loan prior to maturity.

Early Payments on Installment Loans

With a long-term installment contract, such as for the purchase of a home or commercial building, if the borrower elects to pay the balance in full before the maturity date, there is usually a penalty assessed on the unpaid principal balance. The terms of the penalty must be clearly spelled out in the contract of purchase. For example, the contract may specify that the buyer is subject to a 2 percent prepayment penalty on the principal balance due.

World's Five Busiest Airports—1986

	Passengers (in millions)
Chicago (O'Hare)	53.3
Atlanta	45.2
Los Angeles	41.4
Dallas–Fort Worth	39.9
Denver	34.7

San Francisco Chronicle
1987 Universal Press

Example 1. Lori Dung purchased a home at a cost of $150,000. Her original loan was $120,000, payable at 12 percent for 30 years. She decides to pay the loan in full when her principal balance drops to $45,000. If the contract specifies a prepayment penalty of $1\frac{1}{2}$ percent on the remaining principal balance, determine the total amount due, including the last month's interest.

Principal balance due	**$45,000**	
Prepayment penalty	**675**	**($45,000 × .015)**
Interest for one month	**45**	$\left(45{,}000 \times \frac{12}{100} \times \frac{1}{12}\right)$
Total amount due	**$46,125**	

Effective Interest Rate

On a shorter-term installment loan or sale, to quickly approximate the annual interest rate being charged, the following formula can be used:

$$r = \frac{2nI}{B(p + 1)}$$

This is based on the assumption that each payment consists of an equal amount of principal and interest. In fact, since the principal balance decreases with each payment, the amount of interest paid each period also decreases. Therefore, when equal payments are made throughout the loan period, the effect is that each succeeding installment payment consists of an increasing amount of principal and a decreasing amount of interest.

Example 2. Robert Strohmeyer borrows $500 and agrees to repay the loan in three equal monthly payments of $170.85. The installment formula gives an interest rate of 15.06 percent, as follows:

$$r = \frac{2 \times 12 \times \$12.55}{\$500 \times 4} = 15.06 \text{ percent}$$

The real interest rate, based on the unpaid principal balance at the beginning of each month, is 15 percent, amortized as follows:

Beginning of Month	Principal Balance	Monthly Payment	Interest at 15 Percent	Principal Paid
1	$500.00	$170.85	$6.25	$164.60
2	335.40	170.85	4.19	166.66
3	168.74	170.85	2.11	168.74

Rule of 78

If an installment borrower or customer wishes to pay the balance in full prior to maturity, the interest included in the prepaid periods should be deducted from the total balance due. Since the interest decreases with each payment, the amount of excluded interest, without the availability of an amoritization schedule, can be closely approximated by using the Rule of 78. This is based on the sum-of-the-years'-digits concept explained in Chapter 20 on depreciation. If the loan is for 12 months, the sum of the digits is 78, determined as follows:

$$12 + 11 + 10 + 9 + 8 + 7 + 6 + 5 + 4 + 3 + 2 + 1 = 78$$

This is where the Rule of 78 gets it name. However, this rule can apply to any number of periods. If the loan were payable in 8 periods, the sum of the digits is 36.

If an installment loan is paid in full before maturity, the interest included in each unpaid periodic installment must be excluded from the balance due. Under the Rule of 78, the formula to determine the amount of interest exclusion is as follows:

$$\frac{\text{Sum of the digits of unpaid payments}}{\text{Sum of the digits of total payments}} \times \text{Total installment interest}$$

If a 12-month installment loan is paid in full 4 months before maturity, the fraction of the total interest to be excluded is $\frac{10}{78}$. The numerator 10 represents the sum of the remaining unpaid periods, 4 + 3 + 2 + 1. The denominator 78 represents the sum of the periods beginning with 12.

If the payments are spread over many periods, both the numerator and the denominator can be determined by the following formula, assuming n is equal to the number of payments, either unpaid or in total:

Five Leading Causes of Death—1987

	(in thousands)
Heart	763
Cancer	477
Cerebrovascular	149
Accidents	95
Lung	78

San Francisco Chronicle, 8/16/88

$$\frac{n(n+1)}{2}$$

To find 12 payments:

$$\frac{12(12+1)}{2} = 78$$

Example 3. Angela Rodriguez borrowed $600 and agreed to repay the loan in 12 equal monthly payments of $55. Before paying the ninth installment, she inquired about the balance due if paid in full. By using the Rule of 78, Ms. Rodriguez would owe $215.38, determined as follows:

Total interest is $60 ($55 × 12 = $660 − 600)
Sum of the digits for 3 months' early payments is 6 (3 + 2 + 1)

Monthly payment	**$ 55.00**	
Number of months unpaid	**× 4**	
Balance due	**$220.00**	
Less 3 months' interest	**− 4.62**	$\left(\frac{6}{78} \times \$60\right)$
Amount owed in full	**$215.38**	

Note that the final payment covers 4 months, but only 3 months are prepaid.

Example 4. In example 2, assume that Mr. Strohmeyer decides to pay the balance due at the end of the second month. Under both the installment formula and the amortization table, he owes $170.85 for the second month. For the third month, he only owes the principal balance. However, it would be incorrect to deduct $4.18 interest ($12.55 \times \frac{1}{3}$) from $170.85 due the third month, since the amount of interest decreases each month. The amortization schedule shows that he owes $168.74 principal for the third month. However, usually it is time-consuming to prepare an amortization schedule. To quickly approximate what the interest would be for the third month, the Rule of 78 can be used. For one early payment out of 3 total payments, the formula is:

$$\frac{1}{6} \times \$12.55 = \$2.09$$

As can be seen, the $2.09 interest under the Rule of 78 closely approximates the $2.11 interest from the amortization schedule. The balance due at the end of the second month is $170.85 for the second month and $168.76 ($170.85 − $2.09) for the third month, or a total of $339.61.

From *The Wall Street Journal* with permission of Cartoon Features Syndicate.

Student Review

1. Ray Hengst purchased a town house for $140,000. He made a down payment of $28,000 and agreed to pay the balance over 30 years at 12 percent interest. The mortgage agreement states that there will be a prepayment penalty of $1\frac{1}{2}$ percent on the original amount of the loan if paid in full within the first five years of the loan. In the fifth year, when the principal balance is still $110,000, Mr. Hengst pays the loan in full, including the interest for one month on the unpaid balance. Determine the amount of the final payment.

$ ______________

2. Betty Johnson purchased a residence several years ago. The mortgage interest rate is 14 percent, with a prepayment penalty of 2 percent on the unpaid principal balance. When the principal balance is $45,000, the loan, including one month's interest, is paid in full. Determine the amount of the final payment.

$ ______________

3. If the total interest on a 20-month loan is $310, using the Rule of 78, determine the total interest included in the final six installments.

$ ______________

4. Dana Windell borrowed $450 to install a home office bookcase. She agreed to repay the loan in 15 monthly installments of $35 each. Right after paying the ninth installment, she inquired what she owed to pay the balance in full. Using the Rule of 78, determine this amount.

$ ______________

5. Alec Stanculescu borrowed $3,900 and agreed to repay the loan in 30 equal monthly installments of $145. After making 22 payments, using the Rule of 78, determine *(a)* the total amount of interest paid and *(b)* the remaining principal balance.

(a) $ ______________

(b) $ ______________

Solutions to Student Review

1. Principal balance due $110,000
Prepayment penalty 1,680 ($112,000 × .015)
Interest for one month 1,100 $\left(110{,}000 \times \frac{12}{100} \times \frac{1}{12}\right)$
Total amount due $112,780

$ 112,780

2. Principal balance due $45,000
Prepayment penalty 900 ($45,000 × .02)
Interest for one month 525 $\left(\$45{,}000 \times \frac{14}{100} \times \frac{1}{12}\right)$
Total amount due $46,425

$ 46,425

3. $\frac{21}{210} \times \$310 = \$31$

$ 31

4. Monthly payments $ 35
Number of months unpaid × 6
Balance due $210
Less 6 months interest − 13.13 $\left(\frac{21}{120} \times \$75\right)$
Amount owed in full $196.87

$ 196.87

5. *(a)* Original amount of interest due $450
Less 8 months interest − 34.84 $\left(\frac{36}{465} \times \$450\right)$
Total amount of interest paid $415.16

(b) Balance due $1,160 ($145 × 8)
Less 8 months interest − 34.84
Principal balance due $1,125.16

(a) $ 415.16

(b) $ 1,125.16

Assignment 28–1

Rule of 78

Name ______________________

Date ______________________

1. Reynoldo Berrios purchased a residence for $175,000. He made a down payment of $35,000 and agreed to pay the balance over 30 years at 15 percent interest. The mortgage agreement specifies that there will be a prepayment penalty of 2 percent on the original amount of the loan. When the principal balance is $30,000, the loan is paid in full, including the last month's interest. Determine the amount of the final payment.

$ ______________

2. Diana Mah purchased a commercial building for $255,000, giving a down payment of $76,500. She could only get a first mortgage loan from her bank for $110,000 at 15 percent. The balance of the loan was on a second mortgage at 18 percent. The first mortgage had a prepayment penalty of $2\frac{1}{2}$ percent on the remaining principal balance, while the second mortgage had a 3 percent penalty on the original balance. If she pays both mortgages in full when the first mortgage has a principal balance of $36,420 and the second mortgage has a principal balance of $22,800, determine the final payment on *(a)* the first mortgage and *(b)* the second mortgage, including the interest for one month on the unpaid balance.

(a) $ ______________

(b) $ ______________

3. If the total interest on an 18-month loan is $247.50, using the Rule of 78, determine the total interest included in the final nine installments.

$ ______________

4. Nathan Jacobs borrowed $725 to buy carpeting. He agreed to repay the loan in six monthly installments of $125 each. Right after paying the fourth installment, Jacobs inquires what he would owe to pay the balance in full. Using the Rule of 78, determine this amount.

$ ________________

5. Marlene Chavira borrowed $1,500 from her bank to pay for a one-week cruise to Mexico. She agreed to repay the loan in 24 equal monthly payments of $70. After paying the 18th installment, Chavira inquired what she still owes to pay the balance in full. Using the Rule of 78, determine this amount.

$ ________________

6. Debbie Fan decided to consolidate all of her outstanding loans. She borrowed $2,500 from the bank and paid off all her outstanding debts. The agreement with the bank requires that she repay the bank $190 a month for 15 months. When the seventh installment came due, she paid the balance of her loan in full. Using the Rule of 78, determine the amount of the final payment.

$ ________________

7. Masae Staninec decided to paint her house. She borrowed $1,600 and agreed to repay the loan in 12 monthly installments of $150 each. When paying the ninth installment, she decided to pay the balance due on the final three installments. Determine the total amount of interest paid on the loan, using the Rule of 78.

$ ________________

8. Robert Kim borrowed $2,100 and agreed to repay the loan in 16 equal monthly installments of $150. After making 11 payments, using the Rule of 78, determine *(a)* the total amount of interest paid and *(b)* the remaining principal balance.

(a) $ ________________

(b) $ ________________

Multiple Sports with Amy Hengst, Accountant

When Multiple Sports started the new plant construction on February 1, 1991, as discussed on page 363, management elected the option of taking a 30-year, $256,000 mortgage loan, payable in equal monthly installments at 10 percent, beginning March 1, 1991. The mortgage agreement specifies that there will be a $1\frac{1}{2}$ percent prepayment penalty on the remaining principal balance. When the principal balance is down to $75,000, Multiple Sports decides to pay the loan in full, including the prepayment penalty and interest for one month on the unpaid principal balance. Amy asks you to determine *(a)* the final payment on the plant mortgage loan.

On page 379, Multiple Sports received bids from three roofing contractors. Amy asks you to determine how much Multiple Sports would have to pay in full, by the Rule of 78, to *(b)* contractor A *when* paying the 19th payment, *(c)* Contractor B *when* paying the 10th payment, and *(d)* Contractor C *right after* paying the 22nd payment.

Also on page 379, Multiple Sports took out a car loan with North-West Bank. If Multiple Sports pays off the balance in full when the 28th installment comes due, *(e)* determine, by the Rule of 78, the final amount paid.

(a) $__________

(b) $__________

(c) $__________

(d) $__________

(e) $__________

Chapter 29

Loan Repayment

I tried to file for bankruptcy, but my credit wasn't good enough.

Learning Goals

Upon completion of this chapter, you should be able to:

1. Use an amortization table to determine the equal monthly payments necessary to repay a loan over a set number of months at different rates of interest.
2. Prepare a loan repayment schedule when a monthly loan payment has been determined at a given rate of interest.

Various loan repayment methods exist and these are generally determined by agreement between the borrower and lender. The most common way to repay money is to make equal monthly payments during the term of the loan and the process is called *loan amortization* or *loan repayment.* The payment includes principal and interest. A portion of the payment reduces the principal amount borrowed and a portion is interest charged by a lender for use of the money.

Calculating a Monthly Payment

The monthly payment is determined by using an amortization, or loan repayment, table that shows monthly payments necessary to amortize, or repay, a loan in a certain number of years or months at different rates of interest and for different amounts of money borrowed.

Table 29–1 shows the monthly payment necessary to repay $1,000 at different rates of interest for terms of 1 to 40 years. Divide any of these payments by 10 to find the payment necessary to repay $100.

Table 29–1
Table of Monthly Payments to Repay a $1,000 Loan

Term of Years	10%	$10\frac{1}{2}$%	11%	$11\frac{1}{2}$%	12%	$12\frac{1}{2}$%	13%	$13\frac{1}{2}$%	14%	$14\frac{1}{2}$%	15%
1	87.92	88.15	88.38	88.62	88.85	89.08	89.32	89.55	89.79	90.02	90.26
2	46.14	46.38	46.61	46.84	47.07	47.31	47.54	47.78	48.01	48.25	48.49
3	32.27	32.50	32.74	32.98	33.21	33.45	33.69	33.94	34.18	34.42	34.67
4	25.36	25.60	25.85	26.09	26.33	26.58	26.83	27.08	27.33	27.58	27.83
5	21.25	21.50	21.75	22.00	22.25	22.50	22.76	23.01	23.27	23.53	23.79
6	18.53	18.78	19.04	19.30	19.56	19.82	20.08	20.34	20.61	20.87	21.15
7	16.61	16.87	17.13	17.39	17.66	17.93	18.20	18.47	18.75	19.03	19.31
8	15.18	15.45	15.71	15.98	16.26	16.53	16.81	17.09	17.38	17.66	17.95
9	14.08	14.36	14.63	14.91	15.19	15.47	15.76	16.05	16.34	16.64	16.93
10	13.22	13.50	13.78	14.06	14.35	14.64	14.94	15.23	15.53	15.83	16.13
11	12.52	12.81	13.10	13.39	13.68	13.98	14.28	14.58	14.89	15.20	15.51
12	11.96	12.25	12.54	12.84	13.14	13.44	13.75	14.06	14.38	14.70	15.02
13	11.48	11.78	12.08	12.38	12.69	13.00	13.32	13.63	13.96	14.28	14.60
14	11.09	11.39	11.70	12.01	12.32	12.64	12.96	13.28	13.61	13.94	14.27
15	10.75	11.06	11.37	11.69	12.01	12.33	12.66	12.99	13.32	13.66	14.00
16	10.46	10.78	11.10	11.42	11.74	12.07	12.40	12.74	13.08	13.42	13.77
17	10.22	10.54	10.86	11.19	11.52	11.85	12.19	12.53	12.88	13.22	13.58
18	10.00	10.33	10.66	10.99	11.32	11.67	12.01	12.36	12.71	13.06	13.42
19	9.82	10.15	10.48	10.82	11.16	11.50	11.85	12.21	12.56	12.92	13.28
20	9.66	9.99	10.33	10.67	11.02	11.37	11.72	12.08	12.44	12.80	13.17
21	9.51	9.85	10.19	10.54	10.89	11.24	11.60	11.96	12.33	12.70	13.07
22	9.38	9.73	10.07	10.42	10.78	11.14	11.50	11.87	12.24	12.61	12.99
23	9.27	9.62	9.97	10.33	10.69	11.05	11.42	11.79	12.16	12.54	12.92
24	9.17	9.52	9.88	10.24	10.60	10.97	11.34	11.72	12.10	12.48	12.86
25	9.09	9.45	9.81	10.17	10.54	10.91	11.28	11.66	12.04	12.42	12.81
26	9.01	9.37	9.73	10.10	10.47	10.84	11.22	11.60	11.99	12.38	12.76
27	8.94	9.30	9.67	10.04	10.41	10.79	11.17	11.56	11.95	12.34	12.73
28	8.88	9.25	9.61	9.99	10.37	10.75	11.13	11.52	11.91	12.30	12.70
29	8.82	9.19	9.57	9.94	10.32	10.71	11.09	11.48	11.88	12.27	12.67
30	8.78	9.15	9.53	9.91	10.29	10.68	11.07	11.46	11.85	12.25	12.64
35	8.60	8.99	9.39	9.77	10.16	10.56	10.96	11.36	11.76	12.16	12.57
40	8.49	8.89	9.28	9.68	10.08	10.49	10.90	11.30	11.71	12.12	12.53

Example 1. Susan Brown purchases a new car for a total cost of $12,385. She makes a cash down payment of $3,385 and can borrow $9,000 at $11\frac{1}{2}$% interest for 3 years. Calculate her monthly loan payment.

Table 29–1 shows the payment for $1,000 at $11\frac{1}{2}$% for 3 years to be $32.98 per month.

$9,000 ÷ 1,000 = 9

9 × $32.98 = $296.82 per month

Example 2. Jim Travis purchases a light truck for $12,863 with a down payment of $3,163 and a loan for the balance at $13\frac{1}{2}$% interest, and 36 equal monthly payments. Find the amount of each monthly payment.

$12,863 − $3,163 = $9,700 loan

$9,700 at $13\frac{1}{2}$% for 3 years = $33.94 per $1,000

$33,94 ÷ 10 = $3.394 per $100

$9,700 ÷ 100 = 97

97 × $3.394 = $329.22 monthly payment

All-Time Career Pro Basketball Scoring Leaders (Through 1987–1988 Season)

1. Kareem Abdul-Jabbar	37,639
2. Wilt Chamberlain	31,419
3. Julius Erving	30,026
4. Dan Issel	27,482
5. Elvin Hayes	27,313

Example 3. Tim and Mary Coggin purchase a condominium for $92,750. They will pay $18,250 down and can obtain a loan for the balance at $12\frac{1}{2}$% interest for a term of 30 years. Determine their monthly loan payment.

Table 29–1 shows the monthly payment for $1,000 at $12\frac{1}{2}$% for 30 years to be $10.68 per month.

$92,750 − $18,250 = $74,500 loan amount

$74,500 ÷ 1,000 = 74.5

74.5 × $10.68 = $795.66 per month

Loan Repayment Schedule—Equal Monthly Payments

When the monthly loan payment has been established, a loan repayment schedule can be prepared. It will show the number of loan payments, the monthly payment, the amount of monthly loan payment allocated to interest and to principal reduction, and the principal balance of the loan.

Installment Sale Contract

This Agreement made this Fourteenth day of May, 1990, between Eastern Appliance Distributors hereinafter called "seller", and Miranda Appliance Sales hereinafter called "purchaser",

Witnesseth, That:

The seller has this day delivered to and hereby sells to the purchaser, for the sum of Twenty-five thousand & 00/100 dollars, upon the terms and conditions hereinafter set forth, the following described personal property, to wit:

50 Special Electric Frost-Free Refrigerators

30 Poler Freezers

The purchaser acknowledges the receipt of said property, and in consideration of the delivery to Miranda of the possession thereof, hereby grants to seller a security interest in said property pursuant to the California Uniform Commercial Code and agree to pay to the seller therefor the said sum of Twenty-five thousand & 00/100 dollars together with interest on deferred payments until paid at the rate of $11\frac{1}{2}$ per cent per annum, at the times and in the manner following: The sum of Five thousand & 00/100 dollars upon the execution and delivery of these presents, and the sum of at least Six hundred fifty-nine & 60/100 dollars on the Fourteenth day of each and every Month thereafter, beginning June 14, 1990 and continuing until the whole of said sum of $ 20,000 and interest has been fully paid. Each payment shall be credited first to the interest then due and the remainder on the principal sum.

Date of Note MAY 14, 1990 Amount $ 20,000 - Rate 11.5 %

Due MAY 14, 1993 Term 3 YEARS

Monthly Payment $ 659.60 Due

ALWAYS BRING THIS BOOK

DATE OF PAYMENT	DATE DUE	AMOUNT PAID		CREDITED ON INT.		CREDITED ON PRIN.		BAL. OF PRIN. UNPAID		TO WHOM PAID
6/13/90	6/14/90	659	60	191	67	467	93	19532	07	
7/14/90	7/14/90	659	60	187	18	472	42	19059	65	
8/13/90	8/14/90	659	60	182	65	476	95	18582	70	
9/13/90	9/14/90	659	60	178	08	481	52	18101	18	
10/15/90	10/15/90	659	60	173	47	486	13	17615	05	
11/14/90	11/14/90	659	60	168	81	490	79	17124	26	
12/13/90	12/14/90	659	60	164	11	495	49	16628	77	
1/14/91	1/14/91	659	60	159	36	500	24	16128	53	
2/14/91	2/14/91	659	60	154	57	505	03	15623	50	
3/14/91	3/14/91	659	60	149	73	509	87	15113	63	
4/15/91	4/15/91	659	60	144	84	514	76	14598	87	
5/13/91	5/14/91	659	60	139	91	519	69	14079	18	

Figure 29–1 Loan Repayment Schedule

Tim and Mary Coggin
Loan Amount, $74,500
Monthly Payment, $795.66

Interest at $12\frac{1}{2}\%$ per year
Term, 30 years
(360 monthly payments)

Monthly Payment Number	Monthly Payment Amount	Payment on Interest	Payment on Principal	Principal Balance
1	$795.66	$776.04	$19.62	$74,480.38
2	795.66	775.84	19.82	74,460.56
3	795.66	775.63	20.03	74,440.53
4	795.66	775.42	20.24	74,420.29
5	795.66	775.21	20.45	74,399.84

Payment 1	$74,500 × .125 ÷ 12	= $776.04	interest for a month
	$795.66 − $776.04	= $19.62	payment on principal
	$74,500 − $19.62	= $74,480.38	principal balance
Payment 2	$74,480.38 × .125 ÷ 12	= $775.84	interest for a month
	$795.66 − $775.84	= $19.82	payment on principal
	$74,480.38 − $19.82	= $74,460.56	principal balance
Payment 3	$74,460.56 × .125 ÷ 12	= $775.63	interest for a month
	$795.66 − $775.63	= $20.03	payment on principal
	$74,460.56 − $20.03	= $74,440.53	principal balance
Payment 4	$74,440.53 × .125 ÷ 12	= $775.42	interest for a month
	$795.66 − $775.42	= $20.24	payment on principal
	$74,440.53 − $20.24	= $74,420.29	principal balance
Payment 5	$74,420.29 × .125 ÷ 12	= $775.21	interest for a month
	$795.66 − $775.21	= $20.45	payment on principal
	$74,420.29 − $20.45	= $74,399.84	principal balance

Figure 29–1 shows a portion of the loan repayment schedule prepared for Tim and Mary Coggin and the calculations necessary to prepare it.

A fixed monthly payment is generally associated with a loan having a fixed interest rate. In recent years, numerous banks and savings and loan associations have begun to make variable interest rate loans with an interest rate that can go up or down, based on a predetermined index, during the term of the loan. Such a variable interest rate loan will have a monthly payment that will not remain fixed, but will vary in relation to interest rate adjustments.

Loan Repayment Schedule—Equal Principal Payments

Another way to repay a loan on an installment basis is to make equal principal payments each period, along with interest on the previous unpaid principal balance.

Example 4. Michael Kelly borrowed $9,000 to begin a veterinary practice. He agreed to repay the loan in three equal annual principal payments plus interest at 10 percent on the outstanding balance. Calculate his annual payment.

Payment Number	Beginning of Year Principal Balance	Interest Paid	Principal Paid	Total Payment
1	$9,000	$900	$3,000	$3,900
2	6,000	600	3,000	3,600
3	3,000	300	3,000	3,300

Student Review

1. Donald Smith purchased a sports car for $21,000. He paid $3,000 down and will finance the balance at $12\frac{1}{2}$ percent interest for six years. Determine his monthly payment.

$ ____________

2. Clare Thompson has several outstanding loans totaling $62,000. To qualify for the interest deduction on her income tax return, she decides to consolidate her loans under one home equity loan. Rural Bank will charge her 11 percent for 25 years, whereas County Bank will charge her $10\frac{1}{2}$ percent for 30 years. Indicate *(a)* which bank has the lower monthly payment and *(b)* the amount of difference each month.

(a) ____________

(b) $ ____________

3. Lori Kim wants to buy court reporting equipment. The cash price is $1,500, or she can pay 20 percent down, with the balance payable in 24 equal monthly payments at $11\frac{1}{2}$ percent interest. Determine *(a)* the total cash outlay if she purchased on credit and *(b)* the amount of interest paid if purchased on credit.

(a) $ ____________

(b) $ ____________

4. Peter Cistaro needs a real estate mortgage loan of $110,000. Find the monthly payments if he borrows at 12 percent for *(a)* 15 years, *(b)* 20 years, or *(c)* 30 years.

(a) $ ____________

(b) $ ____________

(c) $ ____________

5. Prepare the following repayment schedule for the first two payments of the $75,000 loan.

Loan: $75,000
Interest rate: 13%
Term: 8 years

Payment Number	*Payment Amount*	*Interest Payment*	*Principal Payment*	*Principal Balance*
1	$ ______	$ ______	$ ______	$ ______
2	$ ______	$ ______	$ ______	$ ______

Solutions to Student Review

1.

$$\begin{array}{r} \$\ 19.82 \\ \times 18 \\ \hline \$356.76 \end{array}$$

$ 356.76

2.

Rural Bank	County Bank	
$ 9.81	$ 9.15	$608.22
× 62	× 62	− 567.30
$608.22	$567.30	$ 40.92

(a) County Bank

(b) $ 40.92

3.

$$\begin{array}{r} \$1{,}500 \\ \times .80 \\ \hline \$1{,}200 \end{array} \qquad \begin{array}{l} \$56.84 \text{ (2 yrs. @ } 11\tfrac{1}{2}\%) \\ \quad \times 1.2 \\ \hline \$56.21\text{/month} \end{array}$$

(a)
$$\begin{array}{r} \$\ \ 56.21 \\ \times 24 \\ \hline \$1{,}349.04 \\ +300.00 \text{ (down payment)} \\ \hline \$1{,}649.04 \end{array}$$

(b)
$$\begin{array}{r} \$1{,}649.04 \\ -1{,}500.00 \\ \hline \$\ \ 149.04 \end{array}$$

(a) $ 1,649.04

(b) $ 149.04

4.

(a)
$$\begin{array}{r} \$\ \ 12.01 \\ \times 110 \\ \hline \$1{,}321.10 \end{array}$$
(b)
$$\begin{array}{r} \$\ \ 11.02 \\ \times 110 \\ \hline \$1{,}212.20 \end{array}$$
(c)
$$\begin{array}{r} \$\ \ 10.29 \\ \times 110 \\ \hline \$1{,}131.90 \end{array}$$

(a) $ 1,321.10

(b) $ 1,212.20

(c) $ 1,131.90

5.

Payment Number	(a) Payment Amount	(b) Interest Payment	(c) Principal Payment	(d) Principal Balance
1	$ 1,260.75	$ 812.50	$ 448.25	$ 74,551.75
2	$ 1,260.75	$ 807.64	$ 453.11	$ 74,098.64

(a)
$$\begin{array}{r} \$\ \ 16.81 \\ \times 75 \\ \hline \$1{,}260.75 \end{array}$$

(b) (1) $\$75{,}000 \times \frac{13}{100} \times \frac{1}{12} = \$812.50$ (c) = (a) − (b)

(b) (2) $\$74{,}551.75 \times \frac{13}{100} \times \frac{1}{12} = \$807.64$

(d) (1)
$$\begin{array}{r} \$75{,}000.00 \\ -448.25 \\ \hline \$74{,}551.75 \end{array}$$
(d) (2)
$$\begin{array}{r} \$74{,}551.75 \\ -453.11 \\ \hline \$74{,}098.64 \end{array}$$

Assignment 29–1

Loan Repayment

Name ____________________

Date ____________________

A. Find the necessary monthly loan payment:

	Amount of Loan	Interest Rate	Loan Term	Monthly Payment
1.	$ 9,000	$14\frac{1}{2}$%	5 yrs.	$________
2.	16,000	13%	10 yrs.	________
3.	35,000	$12\frac{1}{2}$%	20 yrs.	________
4.	160,000	10%	180 mos.	________
5.	49,000	13%	120 mos.	________
6.	52,000	$10\frac{1}{2}$%	60 mos.	________
7.	75,000	$11\frac{1}{2}$%	25 yrs.	________
8.	135,000	11%	240 mos.	________
9.	93,000	$14\frac{1}{2}$%	30 yrs.	________
10.	8,000	15%	36 mos.	________

B. Determine the loan amount and monthly payment:

	Purchase Price	Down Payment	Loan Amount	Interest Rate	Loan Term	Monthly Payment
1.	$19,000	10%	$________	12%	5 yrs.	$________
2.	8,300	$2,500	________	14%	36 mos.	________
3.	95,500	20%	________	$12\frac{1}{2}$%	20 yrs.	________
4.	7,200	$500	________	15%	3 yrs.	________
5.	88,000	15%	________	$10\frac{1}{2}$%	15 yrs.	________

6. Jo-Ann Hendricks purchases a classic Packard roadster for $43,500. With a $10,000 down payment, she will finance the balance at $11\frac{1}{2}$ percent for 5 years. Find Jo-Ann's monthly payment.

$ ________________

7. Jim McConnell can obtain a real estate equity loan of $85,000 at $11\frac{1}{2}$ percent interest. Find the monthly payment based on terms of *(a)* 20 years, *(b)* 25 years, and *(c)* 35 years.

(a) ________________

(b) ________________

(c) ________________

8. Carla Smith can purchase a small ranch for $135,000. With a 10 percent down payment, National Bank will finance the balance at $13\frac{1}{2}$ percent for 20 years while City Bank will provide financing at 12 percent for 25 years. If Carla selects the bank loan providing the lowest monthly payment, find *(a)* which bank she should select, and *(b)* the monthly payment.

(a) ________________

(b) ________________

9. A set of dining room furniture can be purchased for $3,000 cash, or on credit for 10 percent down, and the balance at 11 percent interest with 36 equal monthly payments. What will be the set cost if *(a)* purchased on credit, and *(b)* how much is saved by paying all cash.

(a) ________________

(b) ________________

10. Philip can purchase a sport sedan for $23,500 cash, or $3,500 down and 36 monthly payments of $683.60. What is the *(a)* total cost of the car on credit, and *(b)* dollar amount of interest that Philip pays.

(a) ________________

(b) ________________

Assignment 29–2

Loan Repayment

Name ____________________

Date ____________________

A. Prepare the following monthly repayment schedules:

1. Loan: $39,000
Interest Rate: 15%
Term: 10 years

Payment Number	*Payment Amount*	*Interest Payment*	*Principal Payment*	*Principal Balance*
1	*(a)* ________	*(b)* ________	*(c)* ________	*(d)* ________

2. Loan: $63,500
Interest Rate: 11½%
Term: 20 years

Payment Number	*Payment Amount*	*Interest Payment*	*Principal Payment*	*Principal Balance*
1	*(a)* ________	*(b)* ________	*(c)* ________	*(d)* ________

3. Loan: $8,900
Interest Rate: 14½%
Term: 3 years

Payment Number	*Payment Amount*	*Interest Payment*	*Principal Payment*	*Principal Balance*
1	*(a)* ________	*(b)* ________	*(c)* ________	*(d)* ________

4. Loan: $72,800
Interest Rate: 12%
Term: 18 years

Payment Number	*Payment Amount*	*Interest Payment*	*Principal Payment*	*Principal Balance*
1	*(a)* ________	*(b)* ________	*(c)* ________	*(d)* ________

5. Loan: $98,000
Interest Rate: 14½%
Term: 27 years

Payment Number	*Payment Amount*	*Interest Payment*	*Principal Payment*	*Principal Balance*
1	*(a)* ________	*(b)* ________	*(c)* ________	*(d)* ________
2	*(a)* ________	*(b)* ________	*(c)* ________	*(d)* ________

6. Loan Amount: $50,000
Interest Rate: $12\frac{1}{2}$%
Term: 10 years

Monthly Payment Number	Monthly Payment Amount	Payment on Interest	Payment on Principal	Principal Balance
1	(a) ________	(b) ________	(c) ________	(d) ________
2	(a) ________	(b) ________	(c) ________	(d) ________
3	(a) ________	(b) ________	(c) ________	(d) ________

B. Fill in the following loan repayment schedules, assuming equal principal payments:

1. Loan: $20,360
Interest rate: 12%
Term: 4 years
Payable: Annually

Payment Number	Beginning of Year Principal Balance	Interest Paid	Principal Paid	Total Payment
Year 1	(a) ________	(b) ________	(c) ________	(d) ________
Year 2	(a) ________	(b) ________	(c) ________	(d) ________
Year 3	(a) ________	(b) ________	(c) ________	(d) ________
Year 4	(a) ________	(b) ________	(c) ________	(d) ________

2. Loan: $2,100
Interest rate: 9%
Term: 6 months
Payable: Monthly

Monthly Payment Number	Beginning of Month Principal Balance	Interest Paid	Principal Paid	Total Payment
1	(a) ________	(b) ________	(c) ________	(d) ________
2	(a) ________	(b) ________	(c) ________	(d) ________
3	(a) ________	(b) ________	(c) ________	(d) ________
4	(a) ________	(b) ________	(c) ________	(d) ________
5	(a) ________	(b) ________	(c) ________	(d) ________
6	(a) ________	(b) ________	(c) ________	(d) ________

Multiple Sports with Amy Hengst, Accountant

As stated on pages 363 and 389, Multiple Sports began construction of a new plant on February 1, 1991. The company elected the option to take a construction loan of $256,000, payable in equal monthly installments over 30 years at 10 percent interest.

Also, as stated on page 379, Multiple Sports acquired a pickup truck for $14,000, paying $2,000 down. Prior to accepting a bank loan at $6.40 per $100 per year on the original loan balance payable over 36 equal monthly installments, Multiple Sports had considered making 36 equal monthly principal payments along with interest at 10 percent on the previous unpaid balance.

Amy asks you *(a)* to determine the monthly payment on the 30-year construction loan and *(b)* to prepare the monthly repayment schedule for the first two months.

In addition, Amy asks you *(c)* to prepare the loan repayment schedule for the first two months if Multiple Sports had agreed to pay the loan in full on the pickup truck in 36 equal monthly *principal* payments.

(a) ______________

(b)

Monthly Payment Number	Monthly Payment Amount	Payment on Interest	Payment on Principal	Principal Balance
1	______	______	______	______
2	______	______	______	______

(c)

Monthly Payment Number	Beginning of Month Principal Balance	Interest Paid	Principal Paid	Total Payment
1	______	______	______	______
2	______	______	______	______

Chapter 30

Property Taxes

Sure we have some $100,000 homes, but it will cost you $250,000.

Learning Goals

Upon completion of this chapter, you should be able to:

1. Discuss the purpose of property taxes.
2. Differentiate between real and personal property taxes.
3. Define market value, assessed value, and property tax rate.
4. Determine the assessed value if either the market value and the assessed rate are known or the tax paid and the tax rate are known.
5. Find the property tax due when the assessed value and the tax rate are known.
6. Calculate the property tax rate when the revenue required from property taxes and the total assessed valuation are known.

Property taxes, both real and personal, may be imposed by a state, county, or city for the purpose of providing certain governmental functions such as police and fire departments, schools, and public works. **Real** property consists of land and improvements thereon, such as buildings, whereas **personal** property is any property other than real estate and would include such items as cash, stocks and bonds, furnishings, and stock in trade.

Although the amount and degree of various levels of taxation may vary in different locales, the types of mathematical computation involved is generally the same. The three main factors generally considered are the assessed valuation, the tax rate, and the actual amount of tax to be paid by the individual property owner.

Assessed valuation is a term frequently encountered in connection with the levying of taxes and has to do with the value for tax purposes that is placed upon property by the tax assessor. For example, real property is generally assessed for tax purposes using a fixed percentage of the fair market value of the property. The fair market value of a property is what the owner can expect to receive if the property is offered for sale and then is sold. In a county that uses a 25 percent assessed valuation, a piece of property with a fair market value of $160,000 will be given an assessed valuation for tax purposes of $40,000, and it is against this amount that the local tax will be applied in determining the amount of tax to be paid by the owner.

Finding Assessed Valuation

Example 1. What is the assessed value of a building assessed at 35 percent of its fair market value of $125,000?

$125,000 × .35 = $43,750 assessed value

If the amount of tax paid and the tax rate are known, the assessed valuation may be found using the formula:

$$\text{Assessed value} = \frac{\text{Tax paid}}{\text{Tax rate}}$$

Example 2. Barbaix paid a tax bill of $2,736 in an area in which the combined city and county tax rate was set at $7.20 per $100 of assessed value. What is the assessed value of his property?

$7.20 per $100.00 = 7.2% = .072

$$\frac{\$2{,}736}{.072} = 72\overline{)2736000.}\ (38000.) = \$38{,}000 \text{ assessed value}$$

If the assessed value and rate of assessment are known, the fair market value set by the assessor's appraisal may be determined.

Example 3. If a local tax assessor uses a 21 percent assessment rate, what would be the fair market value he has set on a property with an assessed value of $37,800?

$$\frac{\$37{,}800}{.21} = 21\overline{)3780000.}\ (180000.) = \$180{,}000 \text{ fair market value}$$

Finding Tax Due

The following formula is used to find the amount of tax due when the assessed valuation and the tax rate are known:

$$\text{Tax} = \text{Tax rate} \times \text{Assessed valuation}$$

Example 1. Brussell owns a building with an assessed value of $26,000. If the tax rate is announced as 7.25 percent, what tax does Brussell have to pay?

.0725 × $26,000 = $1,885 tax due

or, 7.25% = $7.25 per hundred of assessed value

$26,000 = 260 hundreds

260 × $7.25 = $1,885

Example 2. The total assessed value of the real and personal property of the White Sands Motel is $73,500. If the tax rate is set at $8.12 per $100, and a collection fee of 1.2 percent of the tax is charged by the tax collector, what is the total amount of the tax bill?

$73,500 ÷ 100 = 735 hundreds		
735 × $8.12 = 5,968.20 =	**$5,968.20**	**tax**
$5,968.20 × .012 = 71.6184 =	**+71.62**	**collection fee**
	$6,039.82	**total bill**

Example 3. Buttimer's property is assessed at $85,000 with a combined city and county tax rate of $10.16 per $100. If taxpayers in this area are allowed to pay their taxes in two separate equal installments, what is the amount of each installment due?

$85,000 ÷ 100 = 850

850 × $10.16 = $8,636 ÷ 2 = $4,318 each installment

Finding Tax Rate

When the budgets of the various governmental departments are completed, the amount of tax revenue necessary is known. The tax assessor then submits the total amount of the assessed valuation of taxable property, and the tax rate to be charged is established by use of the following formula:

$$\text{Tax rate} = \frac{\text{Tax revenue required}}{\text{Total assessed valuation}}$$

Example 1. If Martinstown required $315,000 to be raised from property taxes and has a $9,000,000 assessed valuation, what tax rate must be set per $100 of assessed value?

$$\frac{\$315{,}000}{\$9{,}000{,}000} = .035 \times 100 = \$3.50 \text{ per hundred}$$

Example 2. The assessed value of taxable property in the municipality of Plainville is $42,500,000. If taxes to be raised are $170,000 state, $705,000 county, and $230,000 city, what combined tax rate per dollar of assessed value should be established?

Total revenue required =	**$ 170,000**
	705,000
	230,000
	$1,105,000

$$\frac{1{,}105{,}000}{42{,}500{,}000} = .026 = \$.026 \text{ per } \$1.00 \text{ of assessed value}$$

The tax rate can easily be established per $100 of assessed value, as follows:

$$\$.026 \times 100 = \$2.60 \text{ per } \$100$$

States with the Largest/Smallest Population Projections—Year 2000

Largest	(in millions)
1. California	33.5
2. Texas	20.2
3. New York	18.0
4. Florida	15.4
5. Illinois	11.6

Smallest	(in thousands)
1. Wyoming	489
2. Vermont	591
3. North Dakota	629
4. Arkansas	687
5. South Dakota	714

U.S. Bureau of the Census, *Statistical Abstract of the United States*: 1988 (108th edition)

In some areas of the country, the tax rate is expressed in mills. A mill is 1/10 of a cent, or 1/1,000 of a dollar. If a property has an assessed valuation of $73,000, with a tax rate of 39 mills per dollar of assessed value, the amount of tax is calculated as follows:

39 mills = $.039

Assessed value = $73,000

$73,000 × .039 = $2,847

In summary, the following formula should help in determining property tax:

Fair market value
× Assessed rate
Assessed value
× Tax rate
Tax

If working the problem in reverse, substitute division for multiplication.

Student Review

1. Arthur Byrd purchased a condominium for $75,000. If the assessed rate is 30 percent and the tax rate is $9.10 per $100 of assessed value, determine *(a)* assessed value and *(b)* property tax.

(a) $__________

(b) $__________

2. If the property tax on an apartment building is $7,968.75, the property tax rate is $3.75 per $100 of assessed value, and the assessed rate is 25 percent of market value, what is the market value as determined by the assessor?

$__________

3. Quality Supermarket has an assessed value of $180,000 on its building. If the tax rate is $7.74 per $100 and there is a collection fee of 0.7 percent on the tax, determine the total amount of the tax bill.

$__________

4. Patricia O'Connor owns a grocery store. The assessor assigns a fair market value of $310,000, assesses the property at 25 percent, and the tax rate is determined to be $6.24 per $100.
(a) What is the amount of the property tax bill mailed to O'Connor?
(b) If the assessment rate was 50 percent, what would be the amount of the property tax bill?

(a) $__________

(b) $__________

5. If property is assessed at $62,500, what is the amount of the tax bill if the tax rate is 33 mills per dollar?

$__________

Solutions to Student Review

1.

```
    $75,000 (Market Value)
    ×  .30 (Assessed Rate)
(a) $22,500 (Assessed Value)

$22,500 ÷ 100 = $   225
                × 9.10 (Tax Rate/$100)
            (b) $2,047.50 (Tax)
```

(a) $ 22,500

(b) $ 2,047.50

2. $3.75 per $100 = 3.75%
$7,968.75 ÷ .0375 = $212,500 (Assessed Value)
$212,500 ÷ .25 = $850,000 (Market Value)

$ 850,000

3.

```
$180,000 (Assessed Value) ÷ 100 = $ 1,800
                                  × 7.74
$13,932.00                        $13,932 (Property Tax)
   + 97.52                         × .007
$14,029.52 (Total Tax Bill)       $97.52  (Coll. Fee)
```

$ 14,029.52

4.

```
(a) $310,000 (Market Value)       (b) $310,000
     × .25 (Assessed Rate)               × .50
    $ 77,500                          $155,000

$77,500 ÷ 100 = $   775               $155,000 ÷ 100 = $1,550
                × 6.24 (Tax Rate)                    × 3.12
                $ 4,836 (Tax)                        $4,836
```

(a) $ 4,836

(b) $ 4,836

5.

```
 $62,500.00
   × .033
 $ 2,062.50
```

$ 2,062.50

Assignment 30–1

Property Taxes

Name ______________________

Date ______________________

A. Complete the following:

1. Ramirez owns an apartment building with a fair market value of $800,000. If the assessor uses a 25 percent assessment and the combined city and county tax rate is $8.20 per $100 of assessed value, what is the amount of tax?

   $ ______________

2. In the preceding problem, what is the assessed value of Ramirez's property?

   $ ______________

3. The assessed value of Covelli's property is $40,500. If the tax assessor uses an 18 percent assessment, what has the assessor determined to be the fair market value of the property?

   $ ______________

4. The total assessed value of the Williams Apartments is $86,700. If the tax rate is set at $9.21 per $100 and a collection fee of 0.8 percent is charged by the tax collector on the tax, what is the total amount of the tax bill?

   $ ______________

5. The town of Brentville wishes to raise a tax revenue of $7,900,000 based on an assessed valuation of $85,000,000. Rounded off to the nearest cent, what tax rate per $100 should be set?

   $ ______________

6. The fair market value of the Regency Apartments is land $125,000; buildings $758,000; furnishings $93,000. If the tax assessor uses a 28 percent assessment, what will be the total assessed valuation of the Regency Apartments?

   $ ______________

7. Steinberg paid a tax bill of $2,528 in an area in which the combined city and county tax rate was set at $3.16 per $100 of assessed value. What is the assessed value of his property?

$ ______________

8. Young owns a building with an assessed valuation of $21,300. If the tax rate is announced as 6.2 percent, what tax does he have to pay?

$ ______________

9. If a township requires a combined tax revenue of $630,000 from property within the township with an $18,000,000 assessed valuation, what tax rate per $100 should be set?

$ ______________

10. Chester receives a tax bill of $851.20 and is allowed to pay it in two equal installments. If she deducts a $17.08 tax credit for a previous overpayment, what amount should she remit for each tax installment?

1st $ ______________

2nd $ ______________

11. A tax rate is set at 29 mills per dollar of assessed value. If a special fee of $\frac{1}{2}$ percent of the tax due is added to the tax statement, what is the total amount that Young must pay on a property with an assessed valuation of $89,600?

$ ______________

12. What is the tax on a property assessed at $83,500 with a tax rate of 25 mills per dollar?

$ ______________

Multiple Sports with Amy Hengst, Accountant

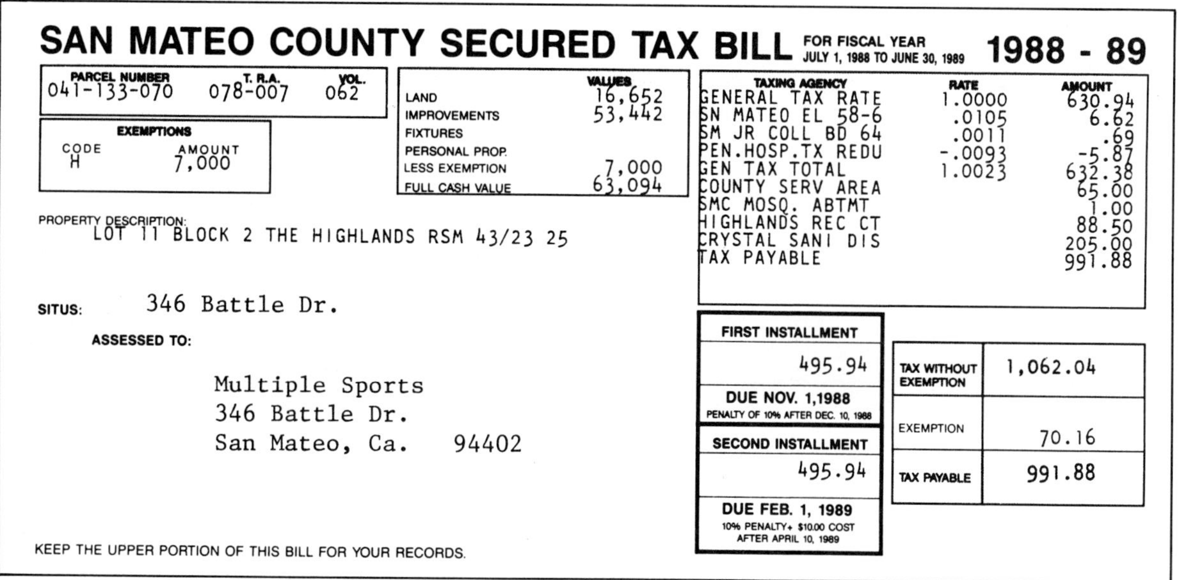

SAN MATEO COUNTY SECURED TAX BILL FOR FISCAL YEAR JULY 1, 1988 TO JUNE 30, 1989 **1988 - 89**

PARCEL NUMBER	T. R. A.	VOL.
041-133-070	078-007	062

EXEMPTIONS

CODE	AMOUNT
H	7,000

	VALUES
LAND	16,652
IMPROVEMENTS	53,442
FIXTURES	
PERSONAL PROP.	
LESS EXEMPTION	7,000
FULL CASH VALUE	63,094

TAXING AGENCY	RATE	AMOUNT
GENERAL TAX RATE	1.0000	630.94
SN MATEO EL 58-6	.0105	6.62
SM JR COLL BD 64	.0011	.69
PEN.HOSP.TX REDU	-.0093	-5.87
GEN TAX TOTAL	1.0023	632.38
COUNTY SERV AREA		65.00
SMC MOSQ. ABTMT		1.00
HIGHLANDS REC CT		88.50
CRYSTAL SANI DIS		205.00
TAX PAYABLE		991.88

PROPERTY DESCRIPTION: LOT 11 BLOCK 2 THE HIGHLANDS RSM 43/23 25

SITUS: 346 Battle Dr.

ASSESSED TO:

Multiple Sports
346 Battle Dr.
San Mateo, Ca. 94402

FIRST INSTALLMENT
495.94
DUE NOV. 1,1988 PENALTY OF 10% AFTER DEC. 10, 1988
SECOND INSTALLMENT
495.94
DUE FEB. 1, 1989 10% PENALTY+ $10.00 COST AFTER APRIL 10, 1989

TAX WITHOUT EXEMPTION	1,062.04
EXEMPTION	70.16
TAX PAYABLE	991.88

KEEP THE UPPER PORTION OF THIS BILL FOR YOUR RECORDS.

Multiple Sports received the above property tax bill on its main location. The land and improvements (building) are shown at the assessed value, which is 25 percent of the market value.

In addition, after the construction was completed on the new plant in neighboring Santa Clara County, a property tax bill was received showing a property tax of $5,555, representing tax of $2,175 on the land and $3,380 on the improvements. The assessment rate in Santa Clara County is also 25 percent, and the property tax rate is $4.12 per $100 of assessed value.

Amy asks you to determine *(a)* the tax rate per $100, *before* exemption, on the San Mateo County property and market value of the *(b)* land and *(c)* improvements of the Santa Clara County property as determined by its assessor.

(a) $__________

(b) $__________

(c) $__________

Section 9

Analysis of Financial Statements

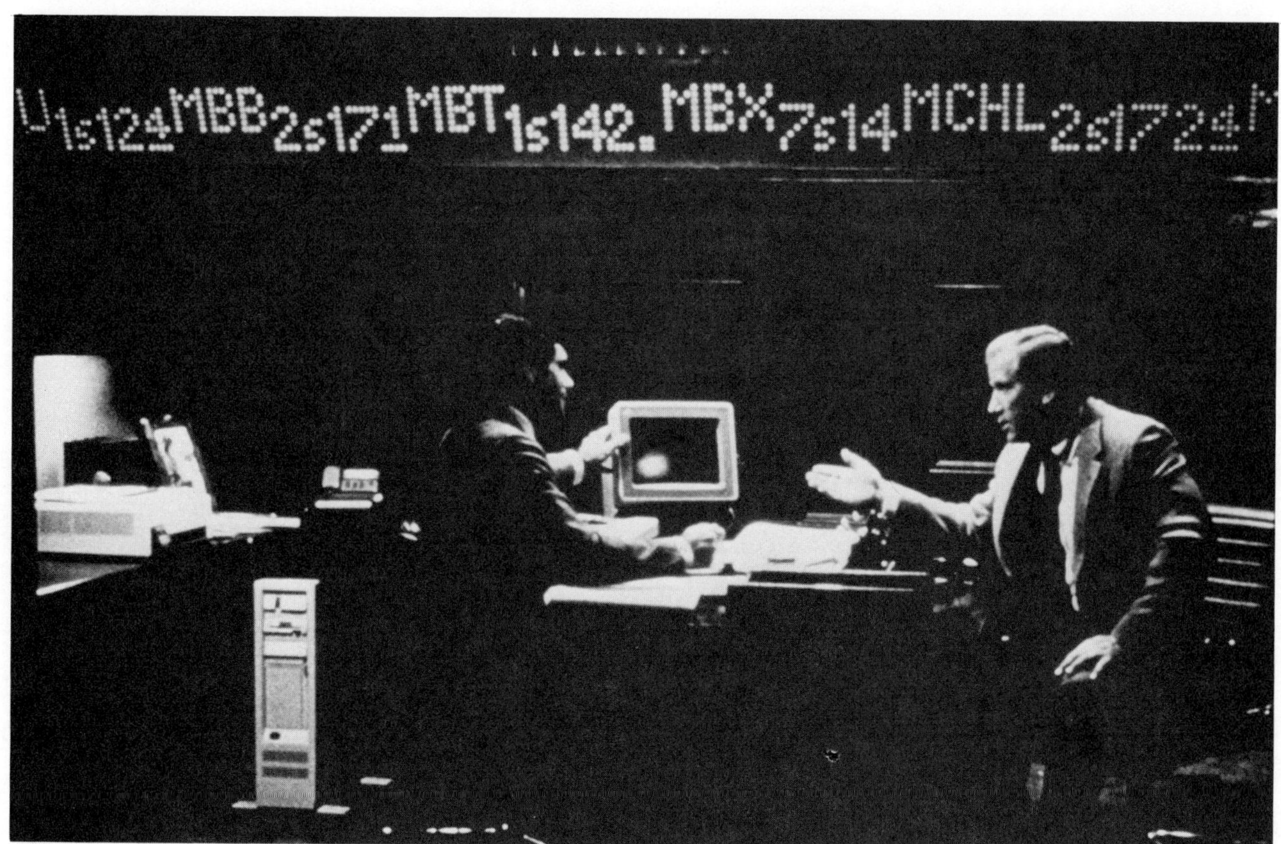

Chapter 31

Balance Sheet

I wasn't affected by the October 1987 stock market crash. I went broke in 1986.

Learning Goals

Upon completion of this chapter, you should be able to:

1. Define a balance sheet.
2. Discuss assets, liabilities, and owner's equity.
3. Explain why the total assets on a balance sheet must always equal the total liabilities and owner's equity.
4. Explain the meaning of contra accounts.
5. Prepare a balance sheet.

Financial Statements

Financial statements represent the accounting language of business. They convey to management, stockholders, creditors, and other interested parties, information concerning the profitability and financial condition of a business. Every company periodically prepares two major financial statements, the balance sheet and the income statement. These statements serve as summary reports of the financial position and results of operations.

Balance Sheet

The balance sheet shows the financial position of a business at a given moment in time. The balance sheet, by classifying similar items into categories, shows types and costs of properties owned, types and amounts of company obligations, and the residual equity belonging to the business.

A balance sheet could be prepared at any time. It is like a photograph, in that one can take a stop-action snapshot of the business whenever it is desirable or necessary. Normally, however, a balance sheet is prepared no more frequently than once a month and no less than once a year.

A balance sheet usually consists of three distinct categories: assets, liabilities, and owner's equity.

Assets

The properties owned by a business are commonly referred to as assets. Assets can be tangible (physical in form) and intangible (nonphysical). Examples of tangible assets are cash, merchandise inventory, land, buildings, furniture, equipment, and machinery. Intangible assets typically include amounts due from customers, investments in securities, patents, and prepayments on insurance, rent, and so on.

Certain assets, such as cash and receivables, either due by note or on open account, are valued at net realizable value. Most other assets are usually valued at cost, the price paid or to be paid to acquire the asset.

Liabilities

Obligations of a company that can be assigned a monetary value are called liabilities. These items represent the debts of a company. The party to whom the money, or equivalent, is owed is called a creditor.

When merchandise or supplies are purchased on open credit, this liability is called an *accounts payable. If a note is given to the creditor, the obligation becomes a notes payable.* A notes payable, a formal written promise to pay a certain amount of money, usually with interest, at a fixed or determinable future date, can also be established when a company borrows money to begin or expand its business. A mortgage payable is a notes payable with the additional feature that certain properties have been reserved as security on the loan. Other unpaid debts of a business on a balance sheet may include taxes, salaries, rent, and interest payable.

Owner's Equity

The business owns the assets of a company. Creditors have dollar claims on these assets. Whatever would be left of the total assets after the claims of the creditors have been satisfied represents the owner's claim. The owner of a business has a residual claim, which represents the difference between the assets and the liabilities.

Example 1. An abbreviated balance sheet might look as follows:

BEAK OFFICE SUPPLIES
Balance Sheet
December 31, 1990

Assets		Liabilities and Owner's Equity	
Cash	$ 4,000	Liabilities:	
Accounts receivable	9,000	Notes payable	$ 3,000
Merchandise inventory	15,000	Accounts payable	10,000
Land	10,000	Wages payable	1,500
Buildings	30,000	Total liabilities	$14,500
Equipment	8,000		
		Owner's equity:	
		A. Beak, capital	61,500
Total assets	$76,000	Total liabilities and owner's equity	$76,000

Balance Sheet Equation

A basic feature of a balance sheet is that the total figure for the assets always equals the combined total figure for liabilities and owner's equity. The two sides must always be equal since they represent two views of the same business. The assets show what the business owns, while the liabilities and owner's equity represent the claims on these assets. The formula can be written in either of two ways, as follows:

Assets = Liabilities + Owner's equity

Assets − Liabilities = Owner's equity

Example 2. The Waters Company has total assets of $240,385 and total liabilities of $118,500. Find the owner's equity.

$240,385 − $118,500 = $121,885

Example 3. Robert Graham is an attorney. On a given date, his law firm had the following assets: cash, $2,100; accounts receivable, $8,000; furniture and fixtures, $5,300; land, $47,000; and building, $78,000. The liabilities of the firm consisted of a note owed to the bank of $9,500 and a mortgage note owed on the land and building of $116,000. Find the owner's equity of the law firm.

Assets		Liabilities and Owner's Equity	
Cash	$ 2,100	Liabilities:	
Accounts receivable	8,000	Notes payable	$ 9,500
Land	47,000	Mortgage payable	116,000
Building	78,000	Total liabilities	$125,500
Furniture and fixtures	5,300	Owner's equity:	
		R. Graham, capital	14,900
Total assets	$140,400	Total liabilities and owner's equity	$140,400

Assets − Liabilities = Owner's equity
$140,400 − $125,500 = $14,900

A number of balance sheet items are frequently reported as gross amounts, with offset, or contra, items deducted in arriving at proper valuations. For example, in arriving at net realizable value, accounts receivable is reported as the gross outstanding amounts to be collected from customers, while an allowance for doubtful accounts is then offset, showing the estimated amount of the outstanding uncollectible accounts. Also, accumulated depreciation is subtracted from the related buildings and equipment balances in order to show the portion of the total cost that has not yet been expensed.

In example 3, if it was estimated that $500 of the outstanding accounts receivable will not be collected, and if the building had already been depreciated by $4,000 and the furniture and fixtures by $2,500, these items might be shown on the balance sheet as follows:

Accounts receivable	$8,000	
Less allowance for doubtful accounts	500	$7,500
Building	$78,000	
Less accumulated depreciation	4,000	$74,000
Furniture and fixtures	$5,300	
Less accumulated depreciation	2,500	$2,800

"This company is smaller than I thought. I'm listed as a major stockholder."

From *The Wall Street Journal*, with permission of Cartoon Features Syndicate.

Student Review

1. The balance sheet items of Burns Escort Service, listed alphabetically, are as follows: accounts payable, $3,825; accounts receivable, $9,640; accumulated depreciation, equipment, $5,350; allowance for doubtful accounts, $525; cash, $7,130; equipment, $12,145; notes payable, ______; owner's equity, $10,960; wages payable, $4,700. Determine the balance of notes payable.

$ ______________

2. Grossman Sign Co. has the following liabilities: accounts payable, $7,380; notes payable, $5,000; wages payable, $2,650; property taxes payable, $675; interest payable, $220. If owner's equity is 40 percent of total liabilities, determine total assets.

$ ______________

3. In problem 2, above, if the owner's equity is 30 percent of total assets, determine owner's equity.

$ ______________

4. The following balance sheet contains several errors. Determine the correct amount of *(a)* total assets, *(b)* total liabilities, and *(c)* owner's equity.

Assets		Liabilities	
Cash	$ 4,790	Accounts payable	$ 7,885
Notes payable	3,850	Allowance for doubtful accounts	910
Accounts receivable	9,115	Wages payable	3,555
Merchandise inventory	12,845	Owner's equity	18,250
	$30,600		$30,600

(a) $ ______________

(b) $ ______________

(c) $ ______________

Solutions to Student Review

1.

Assets:			Liabilities (Excluding Notes Payable):	
Cash		$ 7,130	Accounts payable	$ 3,825
Accts. rec.	$ 9,640		Wages payable	4,700
Less allow.	525	9,115	Total liabilities	$ 8,525
Equipment	$12,145			
Less accum. depn.	5,350	6,795	Owner's Equity	10,960
Total assets		$23,040	Total (Excl. Notes pay.)	$19,485

$23,040
−19,485
$ 3,555 (Notes payable)

$ 3,555

2.

Liabilities:	
Accounts payable	$ 7,380
Notes payable	5,000
Wages payable	2,650
Property taxes payable	675
Interest payable	220
Total liabilities	$15,925
Owner's Equity ($15,925 × .40)	6,370
Total Assets	$22,295

$ 22,295

3. Total liabilities are 70 percent of total assets.

$15,925 ÷ .70 = $22,750 (Total assets)

$22,750 (Total assets)
−15,925 (Total liabilities)
$ 6,825 (Owner's equity)

$ 6,825

4.

(a) Assets:			*(b)* Liabilities	
Cash		$ 4,790	Notes payable	$ 3,850
Accts. rec.	$9,115		Accounts payable	7,885
Less allow.	910	8,205	Wages payable	3,555
Mdse. inventory		12,845	Total liabilities	$15,290
			(c) Owner's Equity	10,550
Total assets		$25,840	Total liab. & own eq.	$25,840

(c) $25,840
−15,290
$10,550

(a) $ 25,840

(b) $ 15,290

(c) $ 10,550

Assignment 31–1

Balance Sheet

Name ______________________

Date ______________________

A. Solve the following:

Assets = liabilities + owner's equity

1. Assets $ 40,000
Liabilities $ 10,000
Owner's equity $ ______________

2. Assets $118,000
Owner's equity $ 41,000
Liabilities $ ______________

3. Liabilities $ 20,000
Owner's equity $ 60,000
Assets $ ______________

4. Owner's equity $ 62,000
Assets $ 91,000
Liabilities $ ______________

5. Liabilities $243,820
Assets 225,641
Owner's equity $ ______________

6. Owner's equity $53,264
Assets 71,817
Liabilities $ ______________

B. Solve the following:

1. Henry Reed runs a small business. His balance sheet shows the following items and amounts: cash, $6,150; account receivable, $10,220; merchandise inventory, $23,700; furniture, $7,400; equipment, $9,800; accounts payable, $11,325. Determine Mr. Reed's owner's equity in this business.

$ ______________

2. Chuck Ohman operates a retail business. His balance sheet shows the following items: cash, $3,700; accounts receivable, $8,245; merchandise inventory, $12,670; land, $39,000; building, $85,000; equipment, $4,200; notes payable, $5,500; accounts payable, $9,120; mortgage payable, $117,490. Determine *(a)* total assets, *(b)* total liabilities, and *(c)* owner's equity.

(a) $ ______________

(b) $ ______________

(c) $ ______________

3. James Seguin operates a sporting goods store. His balance sheet shows the following items: accounts receivable, $7,300; accounts payable, $8,100; allowance for uncollectible accounts (offset to accounts receivable), $540; cash, $5,175; equipment, $8,000; notes payable, $6,200; wages payable, $425. Determine *(a)* total assets, *(b)* total liabilities, and *(c)* owner's equity.

(a) $ ______________

(b) $ ______________

(c) $ ______________

4. Ollie Simpson has his own insurance business. On the current balance sheet, his owner's equity is $12,340. The balance sheet shows he has the following liabilities: accounts payable, $2,400; notes payable, $3,300; mortgage payable, $10,950; salaries payable, $410; interest payable, $225; taxes payable, $95. Determine the amount of the total assets on the current balance sheet.

$ ______________

Assignment 31–2

Balance Sheet

Name ______________________________

Date ______________________________

1. From the following balance sheet items, listed in alphabetical order, determine *(a)* total assets, *(b)* total liabilities, and *(c)* owner's equity: accounts receivable, $6,500; accounts payable, $7,100; accumulated depreciation, equipment, $2,400; allowance for uncollectible accounts, $300; cash, $3,900; equipment, $9,600; notes payable, $5,800.

(a) $ ______________

(b) $ ______________

(c) $ ______________

2. The balance sheet items of Zaro Clothiers, listed alphabetically, are as follows: accounts payable, $19,478; accounts receivable, $24,362; accumulated depreciation, equipment, $4,920; allowance for doubtful accounts, $550; cash ______; equipment, $18,750; merchandise inventory, $17,840; mortgage payable, $11,300; notes payable, $14,500; owner's equity, $24,031; prepaid insurance, $2,100; supplies, $1,242; wages payable, $2,760. Determine the balance of cash.

$ ______________

3. The owner's equity of Factor Company is $24,380. This represents one-fifth of total liabilities. Determine the amount of total assets.

$ ______________

4. The total assets of Growth Company amounted to $84,600 at the end of year 1. By the end of year 2, total assets had increased by $18,300, while total liabilities decreased by $2,600. If owner's equity was $70,000 at the end of year 2, determine the amount of owner's equity at the end of year 1.

$ ______________

5. The balance sheet of Rogers Cement Company before recognizing depreciation on equipment for the current year shows assets of $73,200 and liabilities of $48,690. The equipment cost $6,000, has an estimated life of 5 years, and a salvage value of $400. If depreciation is taken by the straight-line method, determine the balance in owner's equity after recognizing the current year's depreciation.

$__________

6. The following balance sheet contains several errors. Determine the corrected *(a)* total assets, *(b)* total liabilities, and *(c)* owner's equity.

Assets		Liabilities	
Cash	$ 7,500	Accounts payable	$ 8,200
Accounts receivable	4,300	Merchandise inventory	12,640
Owner's equity	9,650	Notes payable	3,800
Equipment	6,300	Accumulated depreciation	3,110
	$27,750		$27,750

(a) $__________

(b) $__________

(c) $__________

7. Ace Parts Company prepared the following balance sheet:

DAVID ACE
Balance Sheet
May 31, 1990

Assets		Liabilities	
Cash	$ 8,420	Notes payable	$12,450
Account receivable	34,961	Accounts payable	33,625
Merchandise inventory	29,648	Allowance for doubtful accounts	2,740
Equipment	18,265	Accumulated depreciation	12,610
Salaries payable	6,225	Supplies	4,350
Total assets	$97,519	Owner's equity	1,744
		Total liabilities	$97,519

Correct the heading and determine the correct *(a)* total assets, *(b)* total liabilities, and *(c)* owner's equity.

(a) $__________

(b) $__________

(c) $__________

Multiple Sports with Amy Hengst, Accountant

Multiple Sports prepares a balance sheet once a year, at the close of business on December 31. Early in February 1991, after the year-end inventory has been physically counted and costs summarized on inventory summary sheets, and after all necessary adjustments for calendar year 1990 have been entered in the books, the December 31, 1990, account balances are up-to-date.

Amy lists all balance sheet accounts and amounts from the accounting records and asks you to prepare a balance sheet, listing assets, liabilities, and stockholders' equity. Unfortunately, the ledger account card for accounts receivable is missing, but all other account balances are available. The list of balance sheet accounts in alphabetical order is as follows: accounts payable, $28,000; accounts receivable, ______; accumulated depreciation, building, $15,200; accumulated depreciation, furniture and equipment, $14,310; allowance for doubtful accounts, $1,227; buildings, $120,000; cash, $18,227; furniture and equipment, $61,725; land, $60,000; merchandise inventory, $51,694; mortgage payable, $145,000; notes payable, $25,000; notes receivable, $22,000; pensions payable, $8,000; prepaid insurance, $542; stockholders' equity, $138,356; supplies, $407; wages payable, $5,120.

Accounts receivable ______________

Chapter 32

Income Statement

The other day we advertised for a night watchman, and that night the safe was robbed.

Learning Goals

Upon successful completion of this chapter, you should be able to:

1. Define an income statement and contrast it with the balance sheet.
2. Prepare a detailed income statement in its three primary sections.
3. Prepare the revenue section for a merchandise business, to arrive at net sales.
4. Determine the total net purchases of a merchandise business.
5. Derive the cost of goods sold if the net purchases and the beginning and ending merchandise inventory amounts are known.
6. Define and prepare the operating expense section of the income statement.
7. Distinguish between the income statement of a service business and a merchandise business.
8. Determine the approximate amount of merchandise lost, stolen, or discarded if a company uses a constant markup on its goods.

The income statement is the other primary financial statement. The income statement is a summary report, covering a period of time, which shows the profitability of a company.

A balance sheet shows the assets, liabilities, and owner's equity of a business at a given moment in time, usually at the close of business on the last day of a month. An *income statement* is the connecting link between two balance sheets to inform the reader as to the primary cause of the change in owner's equity from one period to the next.

The income statement of a merchandising business consists of three primary sections:

1. Revenue from sales of merchandise.
2. Cost of the merchandise sold.
3. Expenses of operating the business.

A simple income statement in abbreviated form might appear as follows:

RICKSON TOYS, INC.
Income Statement
For Year Ended May 31, 1990

Net sales	$120,000
Cost of goods sold	85,000
Gross profit	$ 35,000
Operating expenses	25,000
Net income	$ 10,000

SABRE CONTROLS, INC.
3419 Grand Avenue
OAKLAND, CALIFORNIA 94610

(415) 287-6394

INVOICE

INVOICE DATE: 12/14/90
SALESPERSON: Seehorn
SHIP TO: Same

TO Landowner Apts.
1547 E. 23rd St.
Union City, Ca. 94627

YOUR ORDER NO.	DATE SHIPPED	SHIPPED VIA	F.O.B. POINT	TERMS
09627	12/14/90	Truck	Shipping	2/10, EOM

QUANTITY	DESCRIPTION	UNIT PRICE	TOTAL
3	Strato Electric Range - Model 508	345 00	1,035 00
4	Reliable Microwave - Model 271	210 00	840 00
	Total		1,875 00

ORIGINAL

Thank You

The **net sales** represents the total revenue received or to be received from the sale of merchandise less any sales returns and sales discounts. Uncollectible accounts from sales to customers should also be deducted from gross sales to arrive at net sales. However, in accounting, uncollectible accounts are usually treated as an operating expense.

Cost of goods sold represents the cost to the company of the merchandise that has been sold. If the company is a service business, of course, there would be no cost of goods sold.

Home State of Companies Listed on the N.Y. Stock Exchange

Delaware	45%
New York	8
Ohio	4
California	4
Maryland	4
Pennsylvania	4

The Wall Street Journal, 12/19/87
Delaware Secretary of State's office

In a typical merchandising business, a company does not keep track of the cost of goods as they are sold. Only the selling price is included in the bill and rung up on the cash register. The purpose of this is to save the company time and expense. Therefore, when a company prepares its income statement, the cost of merchandise sold is determined by deduction. For instance, a merchandising company is required by law to take a physical count of its inventory once a year. If a company knows its beginning and ending inventories by taking a physical count of goods on hand times unit invoice cost, and keeps a record of net purchases, the cost of goods sold can be determined as follows:

Beginning inventory	$18,000
Net purchases	80,000
Merchandise available for sale	$98,000
Ending inventory	25,000
Cost of goods sold	$73,000

In the above, net purchases represents gross purchases plus transportation or freight charges in delivering the goods, less any returns or discounts on these goods.

Operating expenses represent the current period costs of running the business. Typical operating expenses include employees' wages, rent, insurance, advertising, depreciation, supplies, and utilities.

If one has a service business, the income statement would be much simpler. Revenue from services rendered would be listed first on the income statement, followed by business expenses. There would be no sales returns or sales discounts, and there would not be a cost-of-goods-sold section.

A more detailed income statement of a merchandising company might appear as follows:

NAIMARK GOURMET SHOP
Income Statement
For Year Ended December 31, 1990

Sales				$134,610
Less: Sales returns and allowances			$ 2,458	
Sales discounts			1,963	4,421
Net sales				$130,189
Cost of goods sold:				
Merchandise inventory, January 1, 1990			$ 12,615	
Purchases		$95,235		
Transportation—in		3,820		
Delivered cost of purchases		$99,055		
Less: Purchase returns and allowances	$1,282			
Purchase discounts	1,860	3,142		
Net purchases			95,913	
Merchandise available for sale			$108,528	
Merchandise inventory, December 31, 1990			14,946	
Total cost of goods sold				93,582
Gross profit				$ 36,607
Operating expenses:				
Salaries			$ 12,750	
Rent			8,164	
Depreciation—equipment			1,856	
Advertising			1,142	
Supplies			1,060	
Miscellaneous			715	
Total operating expenses				25,687
Net income				$ 10,920

Gross profit, or gross margin, is the difference between the net selling price of the goods sold and the cost of these same goods. If a company had regular percent markups on its goods, the gross profit rate, if out of line, might indicate that merchandise has been lost, stolen, or discarded.

Example. Malaster Paint Co. had net sales for the year of $45,000. Cost of goods sold, as derived, was $35,000. If the markup is 33⅓ percent of selling price, find the cost of the unaccounted for goods.

Sales	**$45,000**
Gross profit per markup percent	**15,000**
Cost of goods sold based on markup policy	**$30,000**
Cost of goods sold, as derived	**35,000**
Unaccounted-for merchandise at cost	**$ 5,000**

Student Review

1. Based on the following information about Sullivan Mortuary, determine the net income: advertising expense, $2,175; rent expense, $7,200; depreciation expense, $4,800; revenue, $30,620; salaries expense, $9,500; cash, $4,710; interest expense, $2,125.

$ ________________

2. From the following, determine the gross profit: beginning inventory, $9,730; ending inventory, $11,190; sales, $31,680; net purchase, $21,200.

$ ________________

3. From the following, determine the cost of goods sold: beginning inventory, $18,635; ending inventory, $17,710; purchase discounts, $1,520; transportation-in, $2,295; purchase returns, $1,120; purchases, $83,675.

$ ________________

4. From the following, determine cost of goods sold: net income, $14,400; gross profit, $38,400; operating expenses, 25 percent of sales.

$ ________________

5. Acme Florists sells all of its flowers at a constant markup of 28 percent on selling price. If sales for the year totaled $110,000 and cost of goods sold, as derived, totaled $84,600, determine the cost of the unaccounted-for merchandise.

$ ________________

Solutions to Student Review

1.

Revenue		$30,620	
Expenses:			
Advertising	$12,175		
Rent	7,200		
Depreciation	4,800		
Salaries	9,500		
Interest	2,125	$35,800	
Net income (loss)		($ 5,180)	$ (5,180)

2.

Sales		$31,680	
Cost of goods sold:			
Beg. inventory	$ 9,730		
Net purchases	21,200		
Mdse. avail. for sale	30,930		
Less end. inventory	11,190	19,740	
Gross profit		$11,940	$ 11,940

3.

Cost of goods sold:				
Beg. inventory			$ 18,635	
Purchases		$83,675		
Transportation-in		2,295		
Deliv. cost of purch.		$85,970		
Less: Purch. ret.	$1,120			
Purch. disc.	1,520	2,640	83,330	
Mdse. available for sale			$101,965	
Less end. inventory			17,710	
Cost of goods sold			$ 84,255	$ 84,255

4.

Gross profit	$38,400	
Net income	− 14,400	
Operating expenses	$24,000 ÷ .25 = $96,000 (Sales)	
Sales	$96,000	
Gross profit	− 38,400	
Cost of goods sold	$57,600	$ 57,600

5.

Sales	$110,000		
Cost of goods sold	79,200 ($110,000 × .72)		
Cost of goods sold, as derived		$84,600	
Cost of goods sold, based on markup		− 79,200	
Cost of unaccounted for mdse.		$ 5,400	$ 5,400

Assignment 32–1

Income Statement

Name ______________________

Date ______________________

A. Fill in the missing quantities:

1. Sales $21,600
Cost of goods sold $12,700
Operating expenses $ 6,850
Gross profit $ ______________

Net income $ ______________

2. Sales $ 7,340
Gross profit $ 2,760
Operating expenses $ 1,975
Cost of goods sold $ ______________

Net income $ ______________

3. Cost of goods sold $ 8,920
Gross profit $ 6,450
Net income $ 2,725
Sales $ ______________

Operating expenses $ ______________

4. Operating expenses $ 4,780
Cost of goods sold $ 8,730
Sales $11,910
Gross profit $ ______________

Net income $ ______________

B. Solve the following:

1. From the following, determine the cost of goods sold; beginning inventory, $10,650; net purchases, $71,410; ending inventory, $9,690.

$ ______________

2. From the following, determine the ending inventory: beginning inventory $8,260; net purchases, $54,285; cost of goods sold, $50,915.

$ ______________

3. From the following, determine the beginning inventory: net purchases, $81,725; cost of goods sold, $84,210; ending inventory, $5,640.

$ ______________

4. From the following, determine net purchases: beginning inventory, $2,755; ending inventory, $4,350; sales, $142,700; gross profit, $37,520.

$ ______________

5. From the following, determine net purchases: gross purchases, $74,200; transportation-in, $1,850; purchase returns and allowances, $1,245; purchase discounts, $1,395.

$ ______________

6. From the following, determine *(a)* cost of goods sold and *(b)* gross profit: sales, $192,812; beginning inventory, $7,900; purchases, $161,230; purchase returns, $2,300; purchase discounts, $3,175; transportation-in, $1,850; ending inventory, $3,740.

(a) $ ______________

(b) $ ______________

Assignment 32–2

Income Statement

Name ______________________

Date ______________________

1. Henry Shaver has his own barbershop. Based on the following information, determine his net income: rent expense, $3,600; salary and commission expense, $15,400; payroll tax expense, $1,450; laundry expense, $800; revenue, $31,740; equipment (net), $10,750; depreciation expense—equipment, $2,100.

$ ______________

2. The following information was taken from the accounting records of O'Toole Pharmacy: salary expense, $14,950; beginning inventory, $8,600; rent expense, $7,200; sales, $84,800; transportation-in, $620; sales returns and allowances, $1,125; purchases, $63,400; depreciation expense, $500; ending inventory, $9,500; purchase discounts, $610; miscellaneous expense, $1,250. Determine *(a)* net sales, *(b)* cost of goods sold, and *(c)* net income.

(a) $ ______________

(b) $ ______________

(c) $ ______________

3. From the following, determine purchase returns and allowances: beginning inventory, $8,200; gross profit, $9,090; purchase discounts, $910; ending inventory, $12,400; sales, $48,415; purchases, $45,375.

$ ______________

4. The First-Run Movie Theater incurred the following expenses: rent, $6,300; utilities, $3,200; depreciation—equipment, $1,400; salary, $18,775; film rental, $9,800. If net income is 20 percent of total admissions revenue, determine net income.

$____________

5. From the following, determine sales: operating expenses, $8,500; net income, $1,300; cost of goods sold, 75 percent of sales.

$____________

6. From the following, determine net income: cost of goods sold, $164,200; gross profit, $72,800; operating expenses, 30 percent of sales.

$____________

7. Rattner Appliances had net sales for the year of $58,000. The accounting records show a beginning inventory of $9,000, purchases of $45,000, and an ending inventory of $12,000. If the markup is 30 percent of the selling price on all items, find the cost of the unaccounted-for goods.

$____________

8. The Brennan Company sells one product that it marks up 40 percent on cost. Sales for the period totaled $56,000, and cost of goods sold, as derived, totaled $43,000. Determine the cost of the unaccounted-for merchandise.

$____________

Multiple Sports with Amy Hengst, Accountant

As with the balance sheet, Multiple Sports prepares an income statement once a year. Early in February, 1991, after all necessary adjustments have been entered in the books, the income statement account balances for the year ended December 31, 1990, are up-to-date.

Amy makes a list of all income statement accounts in alphabetical order and asks you *(a)* to prepare an income statement, using the format shown on page 432. In addition, since Multiple Sports has an average markup on merchandise of 30 percent on *net* selling price, Amy asks you *(b)* to determine the approximate cost of the unaccounted-for merchandise.

The income statement accounts are as follows: advertising expense, $5,900; beginning inventory, $47,245; depreciation expense, building, $4,800; depreciation expense, equipment, $4,500; ending inventory, $51,694; insurance expense, $1,200; purchases, $418,607; purchase discounts, $7,916; purchase returns and allowances, $8,411; rent expense, $12,000; salaries expense, $83,600; sales, $574,610; sales discounts, $9,518; sales returns and allowances, $12,742; transportation-in, $5,798; utilities expense, $2,730.

(a)

(b)

Chapter 33

Analysis and Interpretation

If efficiency experts are so smart, why do they work for someone else?

Learning Goals

Upon completion of this chapter, you should be able to:

1. Discuss comparative financial statements.
2. Differentiate between horizontal and vertical analysis of individual items in financial statements.
3. Calculate the dollar amount and percent changes in a company's balance sheet and income statement by both horizontal and vertical analysis.
4. Analyze financial statements by the use of ratios and multiples.
5. Calculate typical ratios used to analyze a company.

Company financial statements are analyzed in an effort to find answers to a variety of practical and important questions. To analyze a statement is to separate the parts of a whole so as to see how they relate to the whole and to each other.

Comparative Statements

The financial statements are frequently analyzed by the use of comparative statements. Comparative statements allow a company to compare the results of one year with another, or to compare company results to industry averages or to the results of other companies. It is important that the analyst develop a basis, or norm, for comparison in order to conclude if something is good, bad, or average. For example, it is not very helpful to know that a firm had net income amounting to 5 percent of sales without knowing that in the preceding three years the rates were 8 percent, 7 percent, and 6 percent, respectively, and that the industry average is 7 percent.

Vertical and Horizontal Analysis

In comparing individual items in the financial statements, two general kinds of analysis may be made, horizontal and vertical. Horizontal analysis is the comparison of an item on one statement to the same item in a preceding or succeeding statement. Vertical analysis is the comparison of a single item in a financial statement to another item in the same statement. The comparisons can be made on a dollar basis or a percent basis.

In the illustrated comparative income statement and the comparative balance sheet, the two middle columns represent horizontal analysis, while the two end columns represent vertical analysis.

When changes in items are shown in both dollars and percents, any large dollar or percent change will stand out and should be easily noted by the analyst.

Comparative Income Statement (Years Ended December 31, 1990, and 1991)

Hwang Supply Company	1991	1990	Increase (Decrease)		Percent of Net Sales	
			Amount	Percent	1991	1990
Net sales	$500,000	$450,000	$50,000	11.1	100.0	100.0
Cost of goods sold	275,000	225,000	50,000	22.2	55.0	50.0
Gross profit	$225,000	$225,000	0	0	45.0	50.0
Operating expenses	125,000	150,000	(25,000)	(16.7)	25.0	33.3
Net income	$100,000	$ 75,000	$25,000	33.3	20.0	16.7

Comparative Balance Sheet (December 31, 1990, and 1991)

Hwang Supply Company	1991	1990	Increase (Decrease)		Percent of Total Assets	
			Amount	Percent	1991	1990
Assets:						
Cash	$ 50,000	$ 80,000	($ 30,000)	(37.5)	6.7	14.5
Accounts receivable	110,000	90,000	20,000	22.2	14.7	16.4
Merchandise inventory	240,000	130,000	110,000	84.6	32.0	23.6
Plant and equipment	350,000	250,000	100,000	40.0	46.6	45.5
Total assets	$750,000	$550,000	$200,000	36.4	100.0	100.0
Liabilities and owner's equity:						
Liabilities	$300,000	$210,000	90,000	42.9	40.0	38.2
Owner's equity	450,000	340,000	110,000	32.4	60.0	61.8
Total liabilities and owner's equity	$750,000	$550,000	$200,000	36.4	100.0	100.0

The dollar amount of any change is the difference between the amount for a base year and for a comparison year. The percent change is computed by dividing the amount of the change between years by the amount for the base year. When comparing data of two or more accounting periods, the base year is usually the first year in the study.

Example 1. In the illustrated comparative income statement, cost of goods sold increased 22.2%, which is determined by dividing $50,000 (percentage) by $225,000 (base).

Example 2. In the illustrated comparative balance sheet, cash is 6.7% of total assets in 1991, which is determined by dividing $50,000 (percentage) by $750,000 (base).

In calculating percent change from one year to the next, there is no problem if positive amounts exist in the base year. However, when the base year is zero or a negative amount, the percent change cannot be calculated. For example, if a company went from net income of $20,000 in 1990 to a net loss of $10,000 in 1991, this would be a decrease of 150 percent. However, if the company went from a net loss of $10,000 in 1990 to net income of $20,000 in 1991, no percent change could be calculated.

Ratios

There are many special measurements that may be developed from financial statements. In addition to analyzing financial statements by vertical and horizontal analysis, the use of ratios may be employed. A ratio is a comparison of one amount to another in relative terms. It shows how many times greater one number is than another and is determined by dividing one amount by the other. If total assets are $50,000 and total liabilities are $20,000, the ratio of total assets to total liabilities can be determined as follows:

$$\frac{\text{Total assets}}{\text{Total liabilities}} = \frac{\$50{,}000}{\$20{,}000} = 2.5 \text{ to } 1$$

In this example, the company has $2.50 of assets for every $1 of liabilities. This ratio indicates the margin of safety to the creditors based on book values.

The following examples of some typical ratios and percents are based on the comparative income statement and balance sheet of Hwang Supply Company illustrated on the previous page. It should be noted in examples 3 through 6 that the balance sheet amounts represent an average balance for the year.

When comparing balance sheet and income statement amounts, since the income statement amount covers a period of time, the balance sheet amount should reflect the average balance during that period. A good method for deriving an average balance would be to add the month-end balances for the last 12 months and divide the sum total by 12. However, to conserve time for classroom purposes, the average amount will be determined as follows:

$$\frac{\text{Beginning-of-year balance} + \text{End-of-year balance}}{2}$$

The following examples are based on the information provided in the comparative income statement and balance sheet of the Hwang Supply Company. Determine each answer for 1991.

Example 1. Ratio of plant and equipment to liabilities.

$$\frac{\text{Plant and equipment}}{\text{Liabilities}} = \frac{\$350{,}000}{\$300{,}000} = 1.2 \text{ to } 1$$

This ratio is especially helpful if the plant and equipment are pledged as security on the creditors' claims.

Composition of the 101st Congress—1989–1990 535 Members, Average Age—52.8 Years

	Number
Lawyers	247
Businessmen and bankers	166
Educators	53
Women	27
Blacks	24
Hispanics	12
Asian Americans	7

San Francisco Chronicle, 11/21/88

Example 2. Ratio of owner's equity to liabilities.

$$\frac{\text{Owner's equity}}{\text{Liabilities}} = \frac{\$450{,}000}{\$300{,}000} = 1.5 \text{ to } 1$$

This ratio shows the relative degree of investment in the business by the owner and by the creditors.

Example 3. Rate of net income to total assets.

$$\frac{\text{Net income}}{\text{Average total assets}} = \frac{\$100{,}000}{\frac{\$550{,}000 + \$750{,}000}{2}} = \frac{\$100{,}000}{\$650{,}000} = 15.4\%$$

This result is useful in comparing with previous years and with the results of competitors. However, it ignores the separate contributions of the owner and the creditors.

Example 4. Rate of net income to owner's equity.

$$\frac{\text{Net income}}{\text{Average owner's equity}} = \frac{\$100{,}000}{\frac{\$340{,}000 + \$450{,}000}{2}} = \frac{\$100{,}000}{\$395{,}000} = 25.3\%$$

This result informs the owner of the rate of return on investment.

Example 5. Accounts receivable turnover.

$$\frac{\text{Net sales}}{\text{Average accounts receivable}} = \frac{\$500{,}000}{\dfrac{\$110{,}000 + \$90{,}000}{2}} = \frac{\$500{,}000}{\$100{,}000} = 5.0$$

This turnover indicates how quickly the credit customers are paying their bills. The greater the turnover, the sooner the average customer is paying. In this example, assuming a 360-day year, a turnover of 5.0 means that the average credit customer is taking about 72 days (360 ÷ 5.0) to pay. If credit terms are 2/70, n/90, this average collection period would appear to be favorable. However, if credit terms are 2/30, n/75, the company probably would want to investigate why many customers are not paying within the cash discount period.

For this turnover, if the information is available, net sales should exclude cash sales.

Example 6. Merchandise inventory turnover.

$$\frac{\text{Cost of Goods sold}}{\text{Average merchandise inventory}} = \frac{\$275{,}000}{\dfrac{\$240{,}000 + \$130{,}000}{2}} = \frac{\$275{,}000}{\$185{,}000} = 1.5$$

This turnover indicates how fast the inventory is moving into and out of the business. The greater the turnover, the shorter the period of time before the goods are sold. In this example, again assuming a 360-day year, a turnover of 1.5 means that the merchandise is on hand an average of 240 days (360 ÷ 1.5) before it is sold.

"And to think all these years you've worried about some boy wonder taking over your job."

From *The Wall Street Journal,* with permission of Cartoon Features Syndicate

Student Review

A. Fill in the missing items in the following comparative financial statements, rounding off percent answers to the nearest tenth.

1.

	1991	1990	Increase (Decrease)	
			Amount	Percent
Sales	$220,000	(c) $______	$______	______
Cost of goods sold	(a) ______	60,000	______	______
Gross Profit	$150,000	$122,000	$______	______
Operating expenses	(b) ______	125,000	______	______
Net income	$40,000	(d) $______	$______	______

2.

	1991	1990	Percent of Net Sales	
			1991	1990
Sales (net)	(a) $______	$840,000	100.0	100.0
Cost of goods sold	605,000	615,000	______	______
Gross profit	$240,000	(c) $______	______	______
Operating expenses	150,000	(d) ______	______	______
Net income	(b) $______	$85,000	______	______

3.

	1991	1990	Increase (Decrease)		Percent of Total Assets	
			Amount	Percent	1991	1990
Assets:						
Cash	$240,610	$195,845	$______	______	______	______
Accounts receivable	457,915	(b) ______	______	______	______	______
Merchandise inventory	809,285	796,740	______	______	______	______
Equipment less depreciation	179,330	190,825	______	______	______	______
Total assets	(a) $______	$1,643,745	$______	______	100.0	100.0

B. **1.** In part A, problems 2 and 3, determine the ratio of net sales to total assets in 1991.

____

2. In part A, problems 2 and 3, determine the accounts receivable turnover for 1991.

____

Solutions to Student Review

A. 1.

(a)	(b)	(c)	(d)
$220,000	$150,000	$122,000	$ 122,000
− 150,000	− 40,000	+ 60,000	− 125,000
$ 70,000	$110,000	$182,000	$(3,000)

(a) $ 70,000
(b) $ 110,000
(c) $ 182,000
(d) $ (3,000)

2.

(a)	(b)	(c)	(d)
$240,000	$240,000	$840,000	$225,000
+ 605,000	− 150,000	− 615,000	− 85,000
$845,000	$ 90,000	$225,000	$140,000

(a) $ 845,000
(b) $ 90,000
(c) $ 225,000
(d) $ 140,000

3.

(a)	(b)	
$ 240,610		$ 1,643,745
457,915	$195,845	
809,285	796,740	
+ 179,330	+ 190,825	−1,183,410
$1,687,140		$ 460,335

(a) $ 1,687,140
(b) $ 460,335

1. (Cont.)

	Increase (Decrease) Amount	Percent
Sales	$38,000	20.9
Cost of goods sold	10,000	16.7
Gross profit	$28,000	23.0
Operating exp.	(15,000)	(12.0)
Net income	$43,000	—

2. (Cont.)

	Percent of Net Sales 1991	1990
Sales	100.0	100.0
Cost of goods sold	71.6	73.2
Gross profit	28.4	26.8
Operating ex.	17.8	16.7
Net income	*10.7	10.1

3. (Cont.)

	Increase (Decrease) Amount	Percent	Percent of Total Assets 1991	1990
Cash	$44,765	22.9	14.3	11.9
Accts. rec.	(2,420)	(0.1)	27.1	28.0
Mdse. inv.	12,545	1.6	48.0	48.5
Equip. less depn	(11,495)	(6.0)	10.6	11.6
Total assets	$43,395	2.6	100.0	100.0

B. 1. $$\frac{\$845{,}000}{\frac{\$1{,}687{,}140 + \$1{,}643{,}745}{2}} = 0.5{:}1$$

1. 0.5:1

2. $$\frac{\$845{,}000}{\frac{\$457{,}915 + \$460{,}335}{2}} = 1.8$$

2. 1.8

*Difference is due to rounding off.

Assignment 33–1
Analysis and Interpretation

Name ______________________

Date ______________________

A. Fill in the missing items in the following comparative income statement. Round off percent answers to the nearest tenth.

Stacey Company Comparative Income Statements for Years Ended December 31, 1990, and 1991

			Increase (Decrease)		Percent of Net Sales	
	1991	1990	Amount	Percent	1991	1990
Gross sales	$206,000	$(4) ______	$ ______	______	______	______
Sales returns	(1) ______	3,200	______	______	______	______
Net Sales	$202,000	$(5) ______	$ ______	______	100.0	100.0
Cost of goods sold	146,000	135,000	______	______	______	______
Gross profit	$(2) ______	$ 53,500	$ 2,500	______	______	______
Operating expenses	(3) ______	46,000	______	______	______	______
Net income	$ 12,000	$(6) ______	$ ______	______	______	______

B. Fill in the missing items in the following comparative balance sheet. Round off percent answers to nearest tenth:

Stacey Company Comparative Balance Sheets, December 31, 1990, and 1991

			Increase (Decrease)		Percent of Total Assets	
	1991	1990	Amount	Percent	1991	1990
Assets:						
Cash	$ 53,700	$ 49,020	$_____	_____	_____	_____
Accounts receivable	81,645	83,518	_____	_____	_____	_____
Merchandise inventory	104,375	101,265	_____	_____	_____	_____
Equipment less depreciation	32,685	33,920	_____	_____	_____	_____
Total assets	$272,405	$267,723	$_____	_____	_____	_____
Liabilities:						
Accounts payable	$ 49,520	$ 42,605	$_____	_____	_____	_____
Wages payable	_____	_____	_____	_____	_____	_____
Total liabilities	$ 50,995	$ 44,665	$_____	_____	_____	_____
Owner's Equity:						
A. J. Stacey, capital	221,410	223,058	_____	_____	_____	_____
Total liabilities and owners equity	$272,405	$267,723	$_____	_____	100.0	100.0

Assignment 33–2

Analysis and Interpretation

Name ______________________

Date ______________________

For the following problems, use the comparative financial statements of the Stacey Company that are presented in Assignment 33–1. Carry each answer to one decimal place. For problems 6 through 10, assume the following balance sheet balances at the end of 1989: total assets, $259,421; accounts receivable, $75,297; merchandise inventory, $93,260; and owner's equity, $219,472.

	1991	*1990*
1. Ratio of total assets to total liabilities	________	________
2. Ratio of net equipment to total liabilities	________	________
3. Ratio of owner's equity to total liabilities	________	________
4. Ratio of cash and accounts receivable to total liabilities	________	________
5. Ratio of cash, accounts receivable, and merchandise inventory to total liabilities	________	________

6. Ratio of net sales to total assets __________ __________

7. Rate of net income to total assets __________ __________

8. Rate of net income to owner's equity __________ __________

9. Accounts receivable turnover __________ __________

10. Merchandise inventory turnover __________ __________

Multiple Sports with Amy Hengst, Accountant

Amy would like to review how Multiple Sports did in 1990 compared to 1989. She asks you to do comparative horizontal analysis of the liabilities and stockholders' equity, based on the following figures and rounding percent answers to the nearest tenth.

	1990	1989	Increase (Decrease) Amount	Increase (Decrease) Percent
Accounts payable	$ 28,000	$ 30,100	______	______
Notes payable	25,000	20,000	______	______
Pension payable	8,000	—	______	______
Wages payable	5,120	6,480	______	______
Mortgage payable	145,000	150,000	______	______
Stockholders' equity	138,356	113,040	______	______
Total liabilities and stockholders' equity	$349,476	$319,620	______	______

In addition, Amy asks you to prepare a comparative vertical analysis of the condensed income statements of Multiple Sports for 1990 and 1989. From the following condensed income statements, complete the percent calculations, rounded to the nearest tenth.

	1990	1989	Percent of Net Sales 1990	Percent of Net Sales 1989
Net sales	$552,350	$526,202	100.0%	100.0%
Cost of goods sold	403,629	381,411		
Gross profit	$148,721	$144,791		
Operating expenses	114,730	119,475		
Net income	$ 33,991	$ 25,316		

Also, Amy asks you to compute the following for 1990:

1. Ratio of total assets to total liabilities.

1. ____________

2. Ratio of stockholders' equity to total liabilities.

2. ____________

3. Rate of net income to total assets.

3. ____________

4. Rate of net income to stockholders' equity

4. ____________

5. Merchandise inventory turnover (see page 439)

5. ____________

---

*Total assets equal total liabilities and stockholders' equity.

% − X + $ ÷ +

Section 10

Business Organization

Chapter 34

Proprietorships and Partnerships

How come all the taxes I pay over a lifetime are spent by the government in less than a second.

Learning Goals

Upon completion of this chapter, you should be able to:

1. Discuss and differentiate three types of business organizations: sole proprietorships, partnerships, and corporations.
2. Determine the distribution of partnership profits if there is no prior agreement.
3. State the three main considerations in the distribution of partnership net income.
4. Calculate the distribution of partnership profits based on the partnership agreement to distribute profits either on the partners' investment ratio at beginning of the year or by their average capital investment ratios.
5. Distribute partnership profits equally after recognizing an interest allowance on capital investments.
6. Compute each partner's share of profits based on a predetermined salary allowance, with the residual divided equally.
7. Distribute partnership profits equally after recognizing a combination of an interest allowance on investment and a salary allowance for personal skills and time.

Types of Business Organizations

There are three types of profit-seeking business organizations: (1) sole proprietorships, (2) partnerships, and (3) corporations.

A *sole proprietorship* is a business owned and operated by a single individual. This individual supplies or acquires all the assets, assumes all the liabilities, and receives the total net income or suffers the total net loss. For business and accounting purposes, the sole proprietor's business assets and liabilities are separated from the personal assets and liabilities. Legally, there is no distinction.

The Uniform Partnership Act, which has been adopted by most states, defines a *partnership* as "an association of two or more persons to carry on, as co-owners, a business for profit." The primary reason to form a partnership is to combine money and expertise. The distinctive features of a partnership include the ease of its formation, the unlimited personal liability, jointly and severally, of each of the partners, co-ownership of partnership property and profits, and the concept of mutual agency, whereby each partner acts as an agent of the partnership, with the other partners and the partnership bound by all normal business agreements made by any partner.

World's Five Largest Public Companies, by Market Value—June 30, 1988

	($ billions)
NTT (Japan)	$277
IBM (U.S.)	76
Sumitomo Bank (Japan)	65
Exxon (U.S.)	63
Dai-Ichi Kangyo Bank (Japan)	62

The Wall Street Journal, 9/23/88
Morgan Stanley Capital *International Perspective*

A *corporation* is a legal entity, separate and distinct from its stockholders. Therefore, the owners of a corporation, its stockholders, are not personally liable for the debts of the corporation beyond the individual stockholder's investment. Partners and sole proprietors are personally liable for all business obligations. Ownership in a corporation is evidenced by shares of stock, which can be transferred without affecting the continuity of the corporation. The corporation continues to exist with the death or withdrawal of a stockholder, and the acts of stockholders, as stockholders, are not binding to the corporation. The primary disadvantage of a corporation is that it faces a double taxation. Earnings of a corporation are taxed in the year earned and are taxed again to its stockholders in the year of distribution. Earnings of a partnership or sole proprietorship are only taxed in the year earned on the personal tax returns of the owners.

Distribution of Partnership Net Income and Loss

In the absence of any prior agreement, all partnership earnings are to be shared equally. This means that if the partnership agreement does not specify how profits are to be distributed, regardless of capital invested or the time or value of services rendered, all partnership profits and losses are to be shared equally.

Any agreement as to the sharing of partnership profits and losses is usually determined at the time the partnership is formed. If partnership profits are to be distributed other than equally, usually consideration is given to the following three elements: (1) salary for personal services rendered by each partner, based on hours of service and individual skills; (2) interest return for the use of invested capital, especially if disproportionate; and (3) reward for the risk assumed by each partner, such as the personal liability if the partnership is unable to pay its debts.

Though any method of distribution mutually agreeable to the partners may be used, subsequent discussion will key on some of the more common methods that are used.

Equal Distribution

If there is no written or verbal agreement as to how profits are to be shared, or if it was agreed that the contribution by each partner to the partnership is the same, then profits shall be shared equally.

Example 1. Aaron Jacobs and Tom O'Toole form a partnership. There is no mention in the partnership agreement as to how profits should be shared. The partnership had a loss of $1,200 in year 1 and a net income of

$8,000 in year 2. Find each partner's share of the partnership net income or loss in year 1 and year 2.

Year 1: $1,200 ÷ 2 = $600 loss to each partner

Year 2: $8,000 ÷ 2 = $4,000 profit to each partner

Investment Ratio at Beginning of Year

The distribution of net income may be based on the relative capital investments of the partners if invested capital is considered to be the primary factor in the production of income. Distribution by this method is often based on the capital account balances at the beginning of each year.

Example 2. Shabazz and Templer form a partnership, investing $12,000 and $8,000, respectively. The partnership agreement stipulates that partnership profits are to be distributed in the ratio that each partner's investment at the beginning of each year bears to the total partnership investment. In the first year net income was $9,000. Shabazz withdrew his entire share of income while Templer did not withdraw any. In the second year, net income was $10,000. Find the profit of each partner for *(a)* the first year, and *(b)* the second year.

$$(a)\ \text{Shabazz} = \frac{\$12{,}000}{\$20{,}000} \times \$9{,}000 = \$5{,}400$$

$$(b)\ \text{Templer} = \frac{\$8{,}000}{\$20{,}000} \times \$9{,}000 = \$3{,}600$$

Since Shabazz withdrew his entire profit, his beginning capital balance for the second year remained at $12,000.

Since Templer had no withdrawals, his beginning capital balance increased from $8,000 to $11,600.

$$(b)\ \text{Shabazz} = \frac{\$12{,}000}{\$23{,}600} \times \$10{,}000 = \$5{,}084.75$$

$$\text{Templer} = \frac{\$11{,}600}{\$23{,}600} \times \$10{,}000 = \$4{,}915.25$$

Average Capital Investment Ratio

The weakness of the preceding method is that a partner could have a large capital balance at the beginning of each year but make major withdrawals shortly thereafter. A more equitable distribution using invested capital would be to distribute profits in the ratio of average capital invested throughout the year. Assume any investment change is computed to the nearest beginning of a month.

Example 3. Reyes and Lufkin enter into a partnership on January 2, investing $8,000 and $7,000, respectively. Reyes makes additional investments of $1,000 on April 28 and $2,000 on November 10. Lufkin withdraws $3,000 on October 18. The net income for the year was $9,300. FInd each partner's share of the net income if it is to be distributed in the ratio of the average capital balances.

Reyes:

$$
\begin{aligned}
\$\ 8{,}000 \times 4 &= \$\ 32{,}000 \\
9{,}000 \times 6 &= 54{,}000 \\
11{,}000 \times \underline{2} &= \underline{22{,}000} \\
12 \quad & \$108{,}000 \text{ (total month-dollars)}
\end{aligned}
$$

Lufkin:

$$
\begin{aligned}
\$7{,}000 \times 10 &= \$70{,}000 \\
4{,}000 \times \underline{2} &= \underline{8{,}000} \\
12 \quad & \$78{,}000 \text{ (total month-dollars)}
\end{aligned}
$$

Reye's share of net income:

$$\frac{\$108{,}000}{\$186{,}000} \times \$9{,}300 = \$5{,}400$$

Lufkin's share of net income:

$$\frac{\$78{,}000}{\$186{,}000} \times \$9{,}300 = \$3{,}900$$

Interest on Capital Investment—Remainder Shared Equally

In some cases, the partners may agree to share profits equally after recognizing interest on capital investments.

Example 4. Assume the same facts as in example 3 except that the partners agree to share profits equally after recognizing an 8 percent interest yield on average investment. To find the average monthly investment, divide total month-dollars by 12.

	Reyes's Shares	Lufkin's Share	Net Income Allocation
Net income			$9,300
Interest allocation:			
Reyes $\left(\frac{\$108{,}000}{12} = \$9{,}000 \times .08\right)$	$ 720		
Lufkin $\left(\frac{\$78{,}000}{12} = \$6{,}500 \times .08\right)$		$ 520	
Total interest allocation			(1,240)
Balance of net income to be allocated equally:			$8,060
Reyes $\left(\$8{,}060 \times \frac{1}{2}\right)$	4,030		
Lufkin $\left(\$8{,}060 \times \frac{1}{2}\right)$		4,030	
Total allocated equally			(8,060)
Partners' net income	$4,750	$4,550	

Salary to Each Partner—Remainder Shared Equally

The personal skills and time devoted to the partnership may vary significantly with each partner. In this case, the partnership agreement may provide that each partner recognize a predetermined salary allowance out of net income, with any residual profits to be shared equally.

Example 5. Lyons and Romo enter into a partnership. It is agreed that they will receive salary allowances of $10,000 and $7,500, respectively, with any residual amounts, plus or minus, to be divided equally. The residual amount is the difference between the total salary consideration and the net income for the period. Find the net income to be distributed to each partner in the first and second year if net income was $12,000 in the first year and $25,000 in the second year.

	Lyons's Share	Romo's Share	Net Income Allocation
Year 1:			
Net income			**$12,000**
Salary allocation:			
Lyons	**$10,000**		
Romo		**$ 7,500**	
Total salary allocation			**($17,500)**
Balance (negative) of net income to be allocated equally:			**($ 5,500)**
Lyons $\left(\$5{,}500 \times \frac{1}{2}\right)$	**(2,750)**		
Romo $\left(\$5{,}500 \times \frac{1}{2}\right)$		**(2,750)**	
Total allocated equally			**5,500**
Partners' net income	**$ 7,250**	**$ 4,750**	
Year 2:			
Net income			**$25,000**
Salary allocation:			
Lyons	**$10,000**		
Romo		**$ 7,500**	
Total salary allocation			**(17,500)**
Balance of net income to be allocated equally:			**$ 7,500**
Lyons $\left(\$7{,}500 \times \frac{1}{2}\right)$	**3,750**		
Romo $\left(\$7{,}500 \times \frac{1}{2}\right)$		**3,750**	
Total allocated equally			**(7,500)**
Partners' net income	**$13,750**	**$11,250**	

In examples 4 and 5, it should be understood that the partners, as owners, are *not* receiving salaries or interest. The interest and salary calculations are only made in order to determine how much of the net income, or net loss, should be allocated to each partner.

Some partnership agreements will provide that partners are to receive interest on capital investment, salary for personal services, with the residual to be distributed in a fixed ratio, consideration being given to personal risk involved.

"Hello, Merrill Lynch, Pierce, Fenner and Beane? This is Carleton Richardson Henderson the third, over at Batten, Barton, Durstine, and Osborne. Hello, are you still there . . . Hello. Hello!"

Student Review

1. Holden and Nokes form a partnership, investing $50,000 and $30,000, respectively. During the first year of operations, the partnership had net income of $24,000. Determine each partner's share of the partnership net income.

Holden: $ ____________

Nokes: $ ____________

2. Kane and Abel form a partnership, investing $24,000 and $30,000, respectively. If partnership profits are to be shared in the ratio of the partners' beginning of the year capital balances, determine each partner's share of the total net income of $13,500 for the first year.

Kane: $ ____________

Abel: $ ____________

3. Aaron and Mays form a partnership, investing $50,000 and $40,000, respectively. The partnership agreement specifies a salary allowance of $900 a month to Aaron and $1,000 a month to Mays, with any residual to be divided equally. If the partnership has net income of $20,000, determine the net income to be distributed to each partner.

Aaron: $ ____________

Mays: $ ____________

4. Gretsky and Howe form a partnership, investing $350,000 and $200,000, respectively. The partnership agreement provides that each partner will recognize a 10 percent interest allowance on the beginning capital balance, a salary allowance of $1,500 a month to Gretsky and $1,800 a month to Howe, with any residual to be divided equally. Determine the net income to be distributed to each partner if the net income is $99,450.

Gretsky: $ ____________

Howe: $ ____________

5. Bird and Johnson form a partnership on January 5, investing $150,000 and $91,000, respectively. Johnson invests another $39,000 on September 12, while Bird withdraws $40,000 on March 29. The partnership agreement states that the partners are to recognize an 8 percent interest allowance on their average capital balances, with any residual to be distributed equally. If the net income is $24,380, determine the net income allocated to each partner.

Bird: $ ____________

Johnson: $ ____________

Solutions to Student Review

1. $\frac{\$24{,}000}{2} = \$12{,}000$

Holden $12,000

Without an agreement, profits are shared equally.

Nokes $12,000

2. Kane: $\frac{\$24{,}000}{\$54{,}000} \times \$13{,}500 = \$6{,}000$

Kane $ 6,000

Able: $\frac{\$30{,}000}{\$54{,}000} \times \$13{,}500 = \$7{,}500$

Able $ 7,500

3.

	Aaron's Share	May's Share	Net Income Alloc.
Net Income			$20,000
Salary allocation			
Aaron	$10,800		
Mays		$12,000	(22,800)
Balance to be allocated equally:			($ 2,800)
Aaron	(1,400)		
Mays		(1,400)	2,800
Partners net income	$9,400	$10,600	0

4.

	Gretsky's Share	Howe's Share	Net Income Alloc.
Net income			$99,450
Interest allocation:			
Gretsky	$35,000		
Howe		$20,000	(55,000)
Balance to be allocated			$44,450
Salary allocation:			
Gretsky	18,000		
Howe		21,600	(39,600)
Balance to be allocated equally:			$ 4,850
Gretsky	2,425		
Howe		2,425	(4,850)
Partners' net income	$55,425	44,025	0

5. Bird:

$150,000 × 3 = $ 450,000
110,000 × 9 = 990,000
12 = $1,440,000

Johnson:

$ 91,000 × 8 = $ 728,000
130,000 × 4 = 520,000
12 $1,248,000

	Bird's Share	Johnson's Share	Net Income Alloc.
Net income			$24,380
Interest allocation:			
Bird: $\frac{\$1{,}440{,}000}{12} = \$120{,}000 \times .08$	$ 9,600		
Johnson: $\frac{\$1{,}248{,}000}{12} = \$104{,}000 \times .08$		$8,320	(17,920)
Balance to be allocated equally:			$ 6,460
Bird	3,230		
Johnson		3,230	6,460
Partners' net income	$12,830	$11,550	0

Assignment 34–1

Partnerships

Name ______________________

Date ______________________

1. Dan Burton and Arnold Jasper form the B & J Specialty Shop. During the first year of operations, the partnership had net income of $9,250. Determine each partner's share of the partnership net income.

Burton: $ ______________

Jasper: $ ______________

2. Schettler and Dierke form a partnership, investing $25,000 and $10,000, respectively. During the first year of operations, the partnership had net income of $5,340. Determine each partner's share of the partnership net income.

Schettler: $ ______________

Dierke: $ ______________

3. Williams and Steiner form a partnership, investing $18,000 and $12,000, respectively. The partnership agreement provides that profits are to be shared according to the partners' investment balances at the beginning of each year, while losses are to be shared equally. The partnership had a net loss of $6,000 during its first year and net income of $8,000 during its second year. Find *(a)* the net loss of each partner the first year, and *(b)* the net income of each partner the second year.

(a) Williams: $ ______________

Steiner: $ ______________

(b) Williams: $ ______________

Steiner: $ ______________

4. Bookspun and Herbel form a partnership, investing $25,000 and $15,000, respectively. The partnership agreement provides that profits are to be shared in the ratio of partners' capital balances at the beginning of each year. The partnership had net income of $10,000 during its first year but incurred a net loss of $4,000 for the second year. Find *(a)* the net income of each partner the first year, and *(b)* the net loss of each partner the second year.

(a) Bookspun: $ ______________

Herbel: $ ______________

(b) Bookspun: $ ______________

Herbel: $ ______________

5. Cowan and Duarte form a partnership, investing $9,000 and $12,000, respectively. The partnership agreement provides that profits are to be shared according to the capital balance ratio of the partners at the beginning of each year. If the partnership net income is $10,500 in year 1, with Duarte withdrawing half his share of the net income and Cowan making no withdrawals, and net income of $14,250 in year 2, find the net income of each partner in *(a)* year 1, and *(b)* year 2.

(a) Cowan: $__________

Duarte: $__________

(b) Cowan: $__________

Duarte: $__________

6. Klemmer and Toler form a partnership, investing $7,500 and $12,000, respectively. The partnership agreement provides that profits are to be shared according to the partners' investment balances at the beginning of each year. The partnership net income was $4,875, in year 1 and $7,162.50 in year 2. If Toler withdrew his entire share of the net income for year 1, and Klemmer made an additional partnership investment of $2,500 at the end of year 1, find the net income of each partner in *(a)* year 1, and *(b)* year 2.

(a) Klemmer: $__________

Toler: $__________

(b) Klemmer: $__________

Toler: $__________

7. Bertram and Mimi form a partnership, investing $28,000 and $25,000, respectively. The partnership agreement provides a salary allowance of $700 a month to Bertram and $850 a month to Mimi, to be distributed out of partnership profits. Any residual is to be divided equally. The partnership had net income of $19,700 for its first year. Determine the net income to be distributed to each partner for the first year.

Bertram: $__________

Mimi: $__________

8. Cameron and Odon form a partnership. The partnership agreement provides that Cameron is to recognize a salary allowance of $900 a month and Odon a salary allowance of $600 a month out of partnership profits. Any residual is to be divided equally. In the first year, the partnership had a net loss of $2,000. Determine the net income or loss distributed to each of the partners.

Cameron: $__________

Odon: $__________

Assignment 34–2

Partnerships

Name ______________________

Date ______________________

1. Williams and Jackson form a partnership, investing $20,000 and $15,000, respectively. The partnership agreement provides that each partner will recognize a 9 percent interest allowance on the beginning capital balance, with any residual to be divided equally. If the total net income for the first year is $7,200, determine the net income distributed to each partner's account.

Williams: $ ______________

Jackson: $ ______________

2. In problem 1, assume that Williams withdraws his entire share of the net income for year 1, while Jackson makes no withdrawals. If the net income for year 2 is $9,500, determine the net income of each partner for the second year.

Williams: $ ______________

Jackson: $ ______________

3. Cope and Lim form a partnership. The partnership agreement provides that, in the distribution of profits, Cope is to recognize a monthly salary allowance of $1,150, while Lim is to recognize a monthly salary allowance of $950, with any residual to be divided equally. Determine the net income of each partner if the total annual net income is $17,418.

Cope: $ ______________

Lim: $ ______________

4. Glick and Hendrick form a partnership, investing $14,000 and $9,000, respectively. The partnership agreement provides that Glick is to recognize a salary allowance of $500 a month and Hendrick a salary allowance of $750 a month out of partnership profits. The agreement further states that each partner will recognize a 12 percent interest allowance on the beginning capital balance, with any residual to be divided equally. Determine the net income to each partner if the total annual net income is $35,000.

Glick: $__________

Hendrick: $__________

5. Murcer and Noren form a partnership on January 10, investing $10,000 and $15,000, respectively. The partnership agreement specifies that partnership profits are to be distributed in the ratio of the partners' average capital balances. Murcer makes an additional investment of $4,000 on September 19, and Noren withdraws $3,000 on May 5. If the net income for the first year is $14,400, determine the amount distributed to each partner.

Murcer: $__________

Noren: $__________

6. In problem 5, assume the same fact except that the partners are to recognize 8 percent interest allowances on their average capital investments, with any residual to be divided equally. Determine the net income of each partner.

Murcer: $__________

Noren: $__________

Name ______________________

Date ______________________

7. John Kreitz and Glen Leiman are in partnership together. Kreitz has a capital balance of $35,000 on January 1. During the year he invests $5,000 on March 20, and $3,000 on November 27. Leiman has a capital balance of $50,000 on January 1. The only change in his capital account during the year is a withdrawl of $12,000 on November 4. If the partnership agreement provides that each partner is to recognize a 10 percent interest allowance on the average capital balance, with the remainder to be divided equally, determine the net income of each partner for the current year if the total net income is $9,000.

Kreitz: $______________

Leiman: $______________

8. Schultz, Todman, and Ulman form a partnership on January 5, investing $15,000, $12,000, and $20,000, respectively. On April 10, Ulman withdraws $4,000, while on October 24, Schultz invests an additional $3,000. The partnership agreement provides that the partners are to recognize monthly salary allowances of $800 for Schultz, $1,200 for Todman, and $500 for Ulman. In addition, the partners are to recognize 8 percent interest allowances on their average capital balances. Any residual is to be distributed equally. Determine the net income of each partner if the total net income for the year is $19,400.

Schultz: $________________

Todman: $________________

Ulman: $________________

Multiple Sports with Amy Hengst, Accountant

After you graduated from college, you took a full-time accounting job with Multiple Sports. However, two of your good friends and fellow graduates, Barbie Bush and Rosie Carter, formed an investment advisory partnership. You have agreed to prepare the year-end financial reports and allocate the profits according to the partnership agreement.

The partnership agreement stipulates that Bush is to recognize a monthly salary allowance of $1,700 and Carter is to recognize a monthly salary allowance of $1,950. In addition, each partner is to recognize an interest allowance at 9 percent on average capital investments, with any residual profits to be divided equally. Bush and Carter had beginning of the year capital balances of $40,000 and $25,000, respectively. Bush withdraw $4,000 on April 27, while Carter invested an additional $6,000 on November 2. The income statement that you prepared shows net income for the year of $46,510, which you will now allocate to each partner. You elect to make all allocations to the nearest dollar.

Bush ____________

Carter ____________

Chapter 35

Corporations

I'll enter the stock market when the IRS goes public.

Learning Goals

Upon completion of this chapter, you should be able to:

1. Discuss the meaning of *common stock* and the basic rights shared by common stockholders.
2. Discuss the meaning of *preferred stock* and the preference rights shared by this class of stockholders.
3. State why the owner's equity of a proprietorship or partnership business combines invested capital and undistributed earnings whereas the stockholders' equity of a corporation lists them separately.
4. Define various terms associated with the stockholders' equity section of a corporation balance sheet.
5. Calculate the book value per share if only common stock is outstanding.
6. Calculate the book value per share of the common stock if both common and preferred stock are outstanding.
7. Calculate the dividend per share to be distributed if only common stock is outstanding.
8. Define cumulative and noncumulative preferred stock.
9. Calculate the dividend per share to be distributed to preferred and common stockholders if the preferred dividend is cumulative or noncumulative.

Corporate Organization

Formation of a corporation requires an application for a charter signed by at least three incorporators and submitted to the corporation commissioner in one of the 50 states. This application is often referred to as *the articles of incorporation.*

Corporate Stockholders

The articles of incorporation specify the number and type of shares that a corporation is authorized to issue.

Common Stock

If a corporation issues only one kind of stock, this stock is called *common stock*. Each share of common stock has the same rights as any other common share. Common stockholders usually have the following basic rights:

1. To vote for the board of directors. The members of the board represent the stockholders in establishing overall company policy.
2. To vote on important corporate actions, such as the incurring of long-term debts, creation of stock option plans, and the election of the external auditors.
3. To share pro rata with the other common stockholders in any profit distributions declared by the directors. This distribution is called a dividend.
4. To purchase additional shares to be issued by the corporation in proportion to present ownership. This is known as a *preemptive right*.
5. To share proportionally in the distribution of assets at liquidation after the creditors have been paid.

Preferred Stock

A corporation may issue more than one class of stock. To appeal to certain stockholders, a corporation may issue a second class of stock known as *preferred stock*. This type of stock does not usually have the rights of the common stockholders, previously described, but it generally has preference rights to dividends and to assets in the event of liquidation. Preferred shares are usually nonvoting and often are callable at the discretion of the corporation. Some corporations issue more than one class of preferred stock, each class designed to appeal to a different type of investor.

Stockholders' Equity

There is no separation of invested capital and undistributed earnings of a sole proprietorship or of a partnership because their business income is only taxed once—on the individual income tax return in the year earned.

The earnings of a corporation are taxed twice. The corporation pays an income tax on the income earned each year. Then the stockholders must report dividends on their individual tax returns when any of the remaining net income is paid to them. Therefore, the stockholders' equity of a corporation must separate the invested capital from earnings retained in the business so the stockholder can be properly informed about whether a taxable distribution of earnings or a nontaxable return of capital has been received. Also, in many states a dividend can only be declared if there are retained earnings.

A condensed, nondescriptive version of the stockholders' equity section of a corporate balance sheet might appear as follows:

Contributed capital:	
Preferred stock	$ 200,000
Common stock	850,000
	$1,050,000
Retained earnings	720,000
Total stockholders' equity	$1,770,000

Stock Terminology

Authorized shares represent the number of shares of a corporation's stock that the corporate charter permits it to use.

Issued shares represent the number of shares issued to stockholders.

Treasury shares represent the number of shares previously issued by a corporation that have subsequently been reacquired with the intention of reissuing them.

Outstanding shares represent the number of shares that have been issued and not reacquired.

Par value is a nominal value assigned to each share of stock to represent the legal capital. It gives no indication as to market value. It is established as a protection to the corporate creditors and prevents distribution of dividends that would reduce stockholders' equity below the total par value. Some corporations issue no-par value stock, while some states substitute stated value for par value.

Five Largest Credit-Card Lenders

	Percent
Citicorp	17%
Chase Manhattan	6
BankAmerica	5
First Chicago	5
Sears Discover	4

The Wall Street Journal, 10/4/88

Book value of a share of stock is determined by dividing the total stockholders' equity relating to a class of stock by the number of outstanding shares of that class of stock. If both common and preferred shares are outstanding, assume that the total book value of the common shares will be the total stockholders' equity minus the total par value of the preferred shares outstanding. Book value does not represent liquidation value since many assets are listed at cost and not current market value.

Market value of a share of stock is the current price at which this stock may be purchased or sold.

Stockholders' equity refers to the net assets of a corporation, the difference, at book value, between the assets and liabilities.

Retained earnings refers to the undistributed earnings of the corporation.

Dividends refers to the distribution of the earnings of a corporation to its stockholders.

Example 1. The Belkin Corporation has assets of $3,500,000 and liabilities of $2,000,000. The corporation has issued only common stock. There are 300,000 shares issued and outstanding. Find the book value per share of common stock.

$$\$3{,}500{,}000 - \$2{,}000{,}000 = \frac{\$1{,}500{,}000 \text{ (stockholders' equity)}}{300{,}000 \text{ (outstanding shares)}} = \$5 \text{ per share}$$

Corporate Dividends

If there is only one class of stock oustanding, the total dividend declared by the board of directors must be allocated equally to each outstanding share of common stock.

Example 2. The D'Angelo Corporation declared a cash dividend of $750,000 to its shareholders. There are 1,500,000 shares outstanding. Determine *(a)* the dividend to be paid per share and *(b)* the total dividend to be received by stockholder Darcy who owns 50 shares.

(a) $\dfrac{\$750{,}000}{1{,}500{,}000} = \$0.50/\text{share}$

(b) 50 shares × $0.50 = $25

When there is more than one class of stock, any dividends declared must first be paid to the preferred shareholders to the extent of their claims. Any excess amounts declared will then be distributed to the common stockholders. The dividend preference to the preferred is often stated as a dollar amount per share, such as $7 preferred. This means that each preferred share outstanding is entitled to a dividend of $7 per share before the common shares will receive any dividend.

Some preferred stocks have their preference rights stated as a percent of the par value. For example, if there is an 8 percent, $50 par preferred outstanding, the yearly dividend preference right to the preferred per share would be $4.

The board of directors has no obligation to declare a cash dividend. Thus, preferred stockholders have no guarantee that they will receive quarterly or annual dividends. They are only assured that they will be paid a dividend before the common shareholders are paid. Before the board declares a dividend, it must determine that there are profits, that cash is available, and that the money is not to be used for other purposes, such as plant expansion.

Most preferred stocks are *cumulative*. This means that if all or any part of a regular dividend on the preferred stock is not declared in the current year, it must be paid in a future year before the common stockholders can be paid. Therefore, if no dividend had been paid to the holders of 6 percent cumulative $100 par preferred stock in the first two years of the corporation existence, an accumulated dividend of $18 per share would have to be paid at the end of the third year before the common stockholders could receive a dividend.

Example 3. The Ziegler Corporation has outstanding 10,000 shares of common stock and 5,000 shares of $4, $50 par cumulative preferred stock. During the first two years of business, no dividend was declared. At the end of year 3, the directors declared a dividend of $80,000. Find the total dividend to be paid *(a)* each share of preferred stock and *(b)* each share of common stock.

(a) 5,000 shares × $4 per share = $20,000 annual dividend

$$\$20{,}000 \times 3 \text{ years} = \frac{\$60{,}000 \text{ accumulated dividend}}{5{,}000 \text{ outstanding shares}}$$

$$= \$12 \text{ per share}$$

(b) $80,000 (total dividend declared) − $60,000 (cumulative preferred dividend) = $20,000 (dividend to common)

$$\frac{\$20{,}000}{10{,}000 \text{ shares}} = \$2 \text{ per share to common}$$

Some preferred stocks are noncumulative. This means that even though a preferred stockholder has preference rights to dividends declared in the current year, any dividend not declared will not carry over to a subsequent year. For example, if a holder of 100 shares of $5, noncumulative preferred stock did not receive a dividend in two successive years, he would only be entitled to a dividend, if declared, of $5 at the end of the third year.

Example 4. In example 3, if the preferred stock were noncumulative, find the total dividend to be paid *(a)* each share of preferred stock and *(b)* each share of common stock.

(a) $4

(b) $80,000 − (5,000 shares × $4 per share)

$$= \frac{\$60{,}000}{10{,}000 \text{ shares}} = \$6 \text{ per share}$$

Student Review

1. The Rockridge Corporation has assets of $5,692,387 and liabilities of $3,826,910. If the corporation has 310,000 shares of common stock outstanding, determine *(a)* total stockholders' equity and *(b)* book value per share of the common stock outstanding.

(a) $____________

(b) $____________

2. Land Development Corporation sold 50,000 shares of common stock for $2,500,000 and 6,000 shares of its $100 par preferred stock for $600,000. If the corporation has year-end liabilities of $1,840,000 and a retained earnings balance of $921,000, determine *(a)* total assets and *(b)* book value per share of common stock oustanding.

(a) $____________

(b) $____________

3. Heavy Metals, Inc., has 825,660 shares of common stock outstanding and declares a cash dividend of $247,698. Determine the total dividend to be received by stockholder McCray who owns 750 shares.

$____________

4. The Reliable Finance Co. has outstanding 40,000 shares of 7 percent, $60 par, noncumulative preferred stock and 92,800 shares of common stock. If no dividend was declared in the first year, $150,000 was declared in the second year, and $197,696 was declared in the third year, determine the dividend paid in the third year to *(a)* each share of preferred stock and *(b)* each share of common stock.

(a) $____________

(b) $____________

5. If in problem 4 the preferred stock is cumulative and a cash dividend of $366,992 was declared in the fourth year, determine the dividend per share in the fourth year to *(a)* the preferred stockholders and *(b)* the common stockholders.

(a) $____________

(b) $____________

Solutions to Student Review

1. *(a)* $5,692,387 − 3,826,910 = $1,865,477

(b) $\frac{\$1{,}865{,}477}{310{,}000} = \$6.02$

(a) $ 1,865,477

(b) $ 6.02

2. *(a)* $2,500,000 + 600,000 + 921,000 + 1,840,000 = $5,861,000

(b) $ 600,000 + 2,500,000 + 921,000 = $4,021,000
− 600,000
$3,421,000 ÷ 50,000 = $68.42

(a) $ 5,861,000

(b) $ 68.42

3. $\frac{\$247{,}698}{825{,}660} = \$0.30$ 750 × $0.30 = $225

$ 225

4. *(a)* $4.20 × 40,000 = $\frac{\$168{,}000}{40{,}000} = \$4.20$

(b) $197,696 − 168,000 = $ 29,696 $\frac{\$29{,}696}{92{,}800} = \$0.32$

(a) $ 4.20

(b) $ 0.32

5.

Year	Dividends Declared	Preferred Dividends	Common Dividends	Pfd. Div. in Arrears
1	0	0	0	$168,000
2	$150,000	$150,000	0	$186,000
3	$197,696	$197,696	0	$156,304
4	$366,992	$324,304	$42,688	0

(a) $\frac{324{,}304}{40{,}000} = \$8.11$

(b) $\frac{\$42{,}688}{92{,}800} = \$0.46$

(a) $ 8.11

(b) $ 0.46

Assignment 35–1

Corporations

Name ______________________

Date ______________________

1. The Thursby Corporation has assets of $2,430,000 and liabilities of $1,626,000. If the corporation has 40,000 shares of common stock outstanding, determine *(a)* total stockholders' equity and *(b)* book value per share of common stock outstanding.

   (a) $ ______________

   (b) $ ______________

2. Financial Planners, Inc., has liabilities of $724,563 and stockholders' equity of $305,924. Determine *(a)* total assets and *(b)* book value per share of common stock. The company has only 200,000 shares of common stock outstanding.

   (a) $ ______________

   (b) $ ______________

3. Home Garden Products has assets of $3,650,000; stockholders' equity of $1,720,000; and 150,000 shares of common stock outstanding. Determine *(a)* total liabilities, and *(b)* book value per share of common stock outstanding.

   (a) $ ______________

   (b) $ ______________

4. Through its charter, Technology, Inc., is authorized to issue 75,000 shares of its $25 par common stock. The company has issued 50,000 shares to the stockholders. Subsequently, however, 3,000 shares were reacquired by the company and are currently being held as treasury shares to be eventually reissued to key employees as a future bonus. If the total stockholders' equity is $1,954,385, determine the book value per share of the common stock.

   $ ______________

5. Insular Energy Systems, Inc., with only a single class of stock outstanding, issued 20,000 shares of its $50 par common stock for $1,500,000. If the company has assets of $3,847,940 and liabilities of $1,692,724, determine *(a)* the book value per share of the outstanding common stock, *(b)* the account title, and *(c)* amount of the noncontributed portion of the stockholders' equity.

(a) $__________

(b) __________

(c) $__________

6. Deluxe Printers Company has assets of $2,963,000 and liabilities of $1,346,000. The company has outstanding 9,000 shares of $30 par preferred and 55,000 shares of common stock. Determine the book value per share of the common stock outstanding.

$__________

7. The Ward Corporation has 2,000 shares of $20 par preferred stock outstanding, total stockholders' equity of $150,000, total assets of $195,000, and 5,000 shares of common stock outstanding. Determine *(a)* total liabilities and *(b)* stockholders' equity per share of common stock.

(a) $__________

(b) $__________

8. Farm Products, Inc., has issued 20,000 shares of its $25 par common stock for $680,000 and 3,000 shares of its $50 par preferred stock for $150,000. The company has $240,000 of retained earnings and liabilities of $725,000. Determine *(a)* total assets, and *(b)* book value per share of common stock outstanding.

(a) $__________

(b) $__________

Assignment 35–2

Corporations

Name ______________________

Date ______________________

1. The Williams Corporation, with 1,250,000 shares of common stock outstanding, declares a cash dividend of $312,500. Determine the dividend paid to each share of common stock outstanding.

$ ______________

2. The Callinan Company has issued only common stock. It has 3,240,000 shares outstanding at the time it declares a cash dividend of $2,430,000. Determine *(a)* the dividend to be paid per share, and *(b)* the total dividend to be received by stockholder Smith who owns 125 shares.

(a) $ ______________

(b) $ ______________

3. The Zarchin Corporation has outstanding 20,000 shares of 5 percent, $50 par, noncumulative preferred stock and 50,000 shares of common stock. If no dividend was declared in the first year of operation, find the dividend paid to *(a)* each share of preferred stock, and *(b)* each share of common stock, if a total dividend of $110,000 is declared in the second year.

(a) $ ______________

(b) $ ______________

4. The Drabkin Corporation has outstanding 10,000 shares of $50 par, $5, noncumulative preferred stock and 100,000 shares of $100 par common stock. The corporation declared no dividend during its first year in operation and $20,000 in the second year. If total dividends of $100,000 are declared in the third year, determine for the third year the dividend per share *(a)* to the preferred stockholders, and *(b)* to the common stockholders.

(a) $ ______________

(b) $ ______________

5. Assume the same facts as in problem 5, except that the preferred stock is cumulative. In addition, another total dividend of $100,000 is declared in the fourth year. Determine the dividend per share in the third and fourth years *(a)* to the preferred stockholders and *(b)* to the common stockholders.

Third year:

(a) $________________

(b) $________________

Fourth year:

(a) $________________

(b) $________________

6. All Clear Cable Company has 280,000 shares of $10 par common, and 75,000 shares of $50 par, 9 percent cumulative preferred stock outstanding. No dividends are declared in the first year of business. Dividends of $420,000 and $900,500 were declared in the second and third years, respectively. Determine the dividend per share in the second and third years *(a)* to the preferred stockholders, and *(b)* to the common stockholders.

Second year:

(a) $________________

(b) $________________

Third year:

(a) $________________

(b) $________________

7. The Xeran Corporation has outstanding 10,000 shares of 6 percent, $100 par cumulative preferred stock and 30,000 shares of $20 par common stock. No dividends were declared during the first three years of business. In the fourth year a dividend of $200,000 was declared, and in the fifth year a dividend of $220,000 was declared. Determine for the fourth and fifth years the dividends per share *(a)* to the preferred stockholders, and *(b)* to the common stockholders.

Fourth year:

(a) $________________

(b) $________________

Fifth year:

(a) $________________

(b) $________________

Multiple Sports with Amy Hengst, Accountant

When you prepared the December 31, 1990, balance sheet of Multiple Sports, as shown on page 427, the balance of stockholders' equity was $138,356. As of December 31, 1990, Multiple Sports had issued 5,000 shares of common stock for $55,000 and 3,000 shares of 8 percent, $20 par cumulative preferred stock for $60,000. There were no preferred dividends in arrears at the end of 1987. No dividend was declared in 1988, $5,000 was declared in 1989, and $10,000 was declared in 1990.

Amy asks you to determine the following: *(a)* the account title and *(b)* the amount of the noncontributed portion of the stockholders' equity; *(c)* the book value per share of the common stock and the 1990 dividend paid to *(d)* each share of preferred stock and *(e)* each share of common stock.

(a) ________________

(b) ________________

(c) ________________

(d) ________________

(e) ________________

Section 11

Insurance

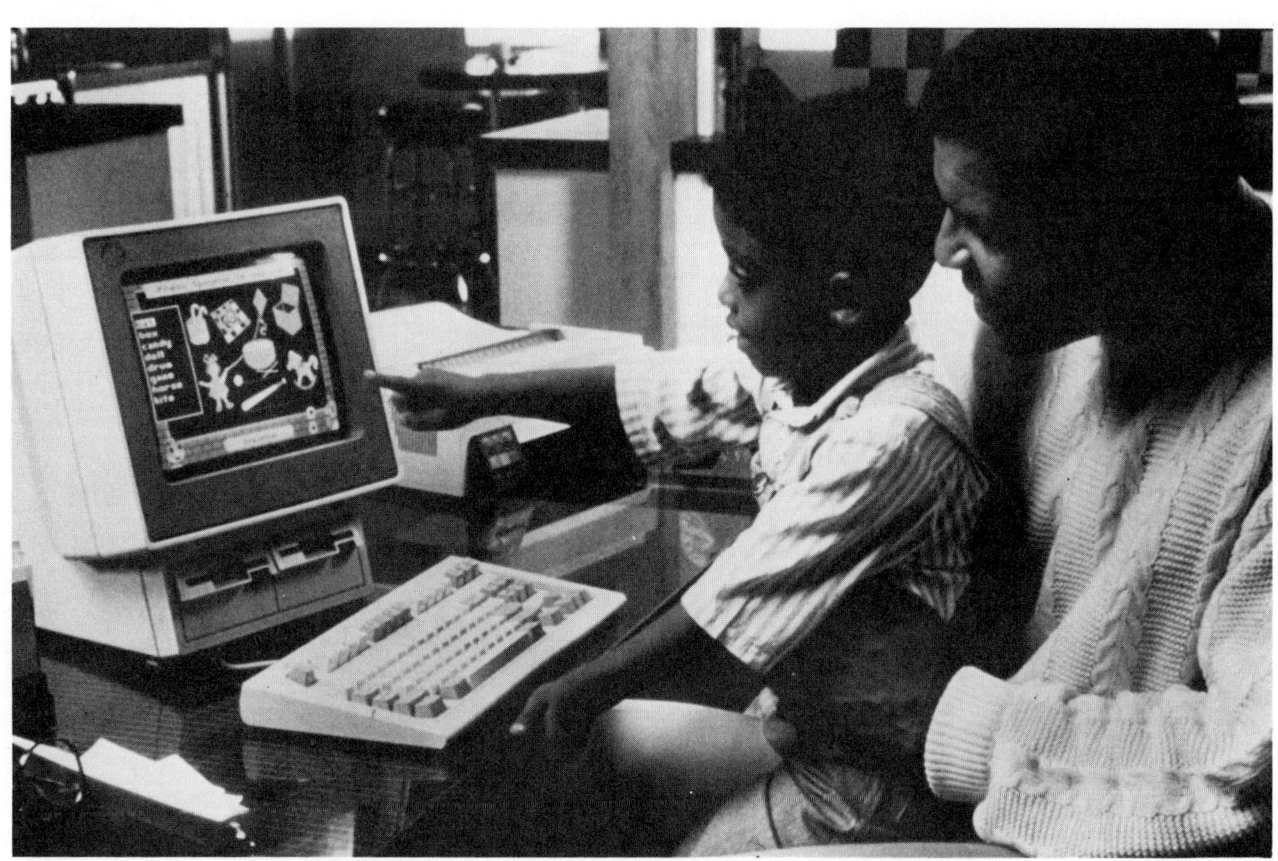

Chapter 36

Fire Insurance

I got nervous when the pilot stood in front of me at the flight insurance counter.

Learning Goals

Upon completion of this chapter, you should be able to:

1. Discuss the reasons for taking out fire insurance.
2. Calculate the annual premium for fire insurance.
3. Calculate the cost of fire insurance if coverage is for more than one year.
4. Determine the amount of premium refund to the insured if either the insurance company or the insured cancels the policy before it expires.
5. Compute the fire insurance premium by use of a short-rate table if the fire insurance policy covers a period of less than one year.

Fire insurance protects against loss or damage resulting from fire. There are many kinds of properties that are insured against fire loss, such as homes, commercial buildings, inventories and equipment.

Fire insurance is taken for the protection of the insured. It is not taken to provide for a profit if a loss from fire should occur. Therefore, the amount paid by the insurance company in the event of a fire loss will be the amount of the loss or the face of the policy, whichever is less.

Example 1. A property is insured for $10,000. There is a loss from fire determined to be $8,000. The insurance company will pay $8,000. If the loss is determined to be $11,000, the insurance company will pay $10,000, the face of the policy.

Fire insurance coverage is taken to protect the insured in the event a fire should occur. Most individuals and businesses take out fire insurance protection, but only relatively few will actually require the benefits. The concept is such that many insureds will pay for the losses of a few. Since none of us knows when, or if, a fire will occur, we are willing to pay a few dollars a year just in case we are one of the unfortunate few.

The annual premium rate for fire insurance is usually stated in terms of dollars and/or cents per $100 of insurance. However, premium tables are often used to determine the annual cost of insurance protection. The premiums are based in accordance with the protection classification and the amount of insurance coverage taken. The protection class is set by an independent fire-rating-bureau evaluation of the fire protection and hazards in the particular area.

Example 2. Bert Kotin purchases a $20,000 fire insurance policy. The annual premium rate is 72 cents per $100. Find his annual premium.

$$\frac{\$20{,}000}{\$100} \times 0.72 = \$144$$

World's Five Largest Insurance Companies—Assets, 1987

	($ billions)
Prudential (U.S.)	$141
Nippon Life (Japan)	123
Metropolitan Life	88
Dai-Ichi Mutual (Japan)	84
Aetna (U.S.)	73

The Wall Street Journal, 9/23/88

If insureds purchase fire insurance for more than one year, they usually receive a reduced premium, such as the following:

Years	Rate
1	Annual rate
2	1.85 times annual rate
3	2.70 times annual rate

Typically, fire insurance is provided for one- and three-year terms. Because of the constantly rising costs of construction, repairs, and replacements, insurance companies generally do not provide fire insurance beyond three years.

Example 3. In example 2, if Mr. Kotin had purchased his policy for three years, find his total premium.

$$144.00 \times 2.70 = \$388.80$$

In recent years, due to high inflation and the rapid increase in property replacement costs, many fire insurance companies will now only insure for one year at a time.

Cancellation of Policy by Insurance Company

In all fire insurance policies, either the insurance company or policyholder has the right to cancel the insurance. If the policy is canceled by the insurance company, most state laws require that the policyholders be given several days' advance notice to give them sufficient time to get coverage from another insurance company. A typical policy might state that the insurance company reserves the right to cancel the policy at any time, but that the policy will continue in force for 10 days after the insured has received written notice of such cancellation.

In most states, if the insurance company prematurely cancels the policy, it cannot retain more than the pro rata portion of the total premium on the policy for the time the policy has been in force. The insured must receive a refund for the balance of the premium. In determining the pro rata portion of the premium that the insurance company will retain, it is the usual practice to use the actual number of days expired and the actual days in the year.

Example 4. Jack Prost purchased a one-year fire insurance policy on December 10, 1990, paying a premium of $90. On March 5, 1991, the insurance company canceled the policy. Find *(a)* the portion of the premium retained by the insurance company and *(b)* the amount refunded to Mr. Prost.

December 10, 1990, to March 5, 1991, is 85 days.

(a) $\$90 \times \frac{85}{365} = \$20.96$

(b) $\$90.00 - \$20.96 = \$69.04$

Example 5. Janice Caine purchased a three-year fire insurance policy on May 15, 1990, paying a premium of $250. The insurance company canceled the policy on July 19, 1991. Find *(a)* the portion of the premium retained by the insurance company and *(b)* the amount refunded to Mrs. Caine.

The policy is for 3 years, or 1,096 days.
The policy has been in effect for 430 days.

(a) $\$250 \times \frac{430}{1{,}096} = \$98.08$

(b) $\$250.00 - \$98.08 = \$151.92$

Short-Term Rates and Cancellation by Insured

Sometimes an insured may want to take a fire insurance policy for a period of less than one year. When this occurs, due to the high initial cost of insurance, the insurance company will short-rate the policy, charging more than what the pro rata portion of the annual rate would be.

A short-rate table, such as the one that is illustrated, is used to determine the premium. To get the short-term premium, find the annual premium and then multiply it by the percent shown on the short-rate table.

Fire Insurance Short-Rate Table

Days Policy in Force	Percent of Annual Premium	Days Policy in Force	Percent of Annual Premium
1	5	147–153	52
2	6	154–160	54
3–4	7	161–167	56
5–6	8	168–175	58
7–8	9	176–182	60
9–10	10	183–191	61
11–14	11	192–200	63
15–18	13	201–209	65
19–22	15	210–218	67
23–29	17	219–228	70
30–36	19	229–237	72
37–43	21	238–246	74
44–51	23	247–255	76
52–58	25	256–264	78
59–65	27	265–273	80
66–73	29	274–282	81
74–80	31	283–291	83
81–87	33	292–301	85
88–94	35	302–310	87
95–102	37	311–319	90
103–109	40	320–328	92
110–116	42	329–337	94
117–124	44	338–346	96
125–131	46	347–355	98
132–138	48	356–360	99
139–146	50	361–365	100

Example 6. Bernice Zarda took out a 60-day, $2,000 fire insurance policy on home furnishings. The annual insurance premium is $30. Find the cost of the short-term policy.

$30 × .27 = $8.10

When the insurance company initiates the cancellation of the fire insurance policy, the insured receives the pro rata portion of the unexpired insurance premium. If the insured should initiate cancellation of the policy before it expires, the insurance company will use the short-rate tables to determine the portion of the premium that is earned. The remainder of the premium is then refunded to the insured.

Example 7. Lene Johnson took out a one-year, $20,000 fire insurance policy dated June 20. On September 8, she canceled the policy. If the annual premium was $110, find *(a)* the amount of the premium retained by the insurance company and *(b)* the amount of the refund paid to Mrs. Johnson.

June 20 to September 8 is 80 days.

***(a)* $110 × .31 = $34.10**
***(b)* $110.00 − 34.10 = $75.90**

Student Review

1. Willie Little purchased a $90,000 one-year fire insurance policy on his summer cabin. If the premium is $0.47 per $100, determine the cost of the coverage.

$ ____________

2. In Problem 1, if Mr. Little took out a three-year fire insurance policy, what premium would he have to pay?

$ ____________

3. Barbary Levy is a student at a community college. During the summer, she rents a storefront to make and sell jewelry and leather goods. Effective on June 2, she buys a $2,500 fire insurance policy on her inventory. If the policy will expire on August 31 and the annual premium rate per $100 is $0.82, determine the cost of the short-term policy.

$ ____________

4. David Wall owns a paint store. He purchased a one-year, $175,000 policy on the building and inventory on March 17, 1990. The insurance company canceled the policy effective July 17, 1990. Determine *(a)* the annual premium paid by Mr. Wall and *(b)* the premium refund paid to him, if the annual rate per $100 is $0.47.

(a) $ ____________

(b) $ ____________

5. Assume the same facts as in problem 4 above, except that Mr. Wall canceled the policy. Determine the premium refund paid to Mr. Wall.

$ ____________

Solutions to Student Review

1. $\begin{array}{r}\$900\\ \times 0.47\\ \hline \$423\end{array}$

$ 423

2. $\begin{array}{r}\$\ 423.00\\ \times 2.7\\ \hline \$1{,}142.10\end{array}$

$ 1,142.10

3. $\begin{array}{r}\$25.00\\ \times 0.82\\ \hline \$20.50\end{array}$ (Annual premium) $\begin{array}{r}\$20.50\\ \times .35\\ \hline 7.18\end{array}$ (90 days)

$ 7.18

4. *(a)* $\begin{array}{r}\$1{,}750{,}00\\ \times 0.47\\ \hline \$822.50\end{array}$

(b) March 17, 1990 to July 17, 1990 is 122 days

$\$822.50 \times \frac{122}{365} = \$274.92$

$\begin{array}{r}\$822.50\\ -\ 274.92\\ \hline \$547.58\end{array}$

or

$\$822.50 \times \frac{243}{365} = \$547.58$

(a) $ 822.50

(b) $ 547.58

5. $\begin{array}{r}\$822.50\\ \times 0.44\\ \hline \$361.90\end{array}$ $\begin{array}{r}\$822.50\\ -\ 361.90\\ \hline \$460.60\end{array}$ or $\begin{array}{r}\$822.50\\ \times .56\\ \hline \$460.60\end{array}$

$ 460.60

Assignment 36–1

Fire Insurance

Name ______________________

Date ______________________

A. Determine the premium on each of the following fire insurance policies:

	Amount of Insurance	*Annual Rate for $100*	*Term of Policy*	*Premium*
1.	$2,200	$0.36	1 year	$________
2.	$30,000	$0.275	1 year	$________
3.	$950,000	$0.384	1 year	$________
4.	$105,000	$0.45	3 years	$________
5.	$1,500	$0.68	2 years	$________
6.	$1,750,000	$0.729	3 years	$________

B. Determine the premium on each of the following short-term fire insurance policies:

	Amount of Insurance	*Annual Rate per $100*	*Term of Policy*	*Premium*
1.	$18,000	$0.29	180 days	$________
2.	$750	$0.67	50 days	$________
3.	$50,000	$0.154	250 days	$________
4.	$1,250	$0.612	110 days	$________
5.	$225,000	$0.73	135 days	$________
6.	$1,350,000	$0.846	218 days	$________

C. The following, one-year, fire insurance policies were canceled by the insured. Determine the amount of refund, assuming a 365-day year:

	Amount of Insurance	*Annual Rate per $100*	*Days of Coverage*	*Premium* Refund
1.	$4,000	$0.375	94	$ ________
2.	$8,600	$0.42	24	$ ________
3.	$22,000	$0.268	192	$ ________
4.	$705,000	$0.47	50	$ ________
5.	$750	$0.31	74	$ ________
6.	$125,000	$0.743	312	$ ________

D. Solve the following:

1. Sandy Lurie took out a 90-day, $5,000 fire insurance policy. If the annual rate per $100 is $0.61, determine the cost of the short-term policy.

$ ________

2. Fred Leonard took out a 68-day, $85,000 fire insurance policy. If the annual rate per $100 is $0.796, determine the cost of the short-term policy.

$ ________

3. Cecil De Loach took out a one-year, $200,000 fire insurance policy on his home on March 5, 1990. The insurance company canceled the policy, effective June 13, 1990. Determine *(a)* the annual premium paid by Mr. De Loach and *(b)* the premium refund paid to him, if the annual rate per $100 is $0.55.

(a) $ ________

(b) $ ________

4. Assume the facts as in problem 3 above, except that Mr. De Loach canceled the policy. Determine the premium refund paid to Mr. De Loach.

$ ________

Multiple Sports with Amy Hengst, Accountant

Multiple Sports acquired its principal building location in 1987 for $210,000, including $70,000 for the land. When the insurance policy came up for renewal in January 1991, the market value of the building, exclusive of the land, had gone up to $225,000. However, the replacement cost on the building was $220,000. The insurance company billed at $0.40 per $100 of replacement cost. The insurance company offered Multiple Sports the option to pay the premium for two years at 1.85 times the annual rate, but the policy was only taken for one year.

Also, on a trial basis, Multiple Sports rented building space across the bay in Alameda County on a six-month lease, from February 1, 1991, through July 31, 1991. The merchandise inventory at this location was insured separately for $50,000. The insurance company charges a premium of $0.60 per $100 per year.

Amy gives you the premium notices from the insurance companies and asks you to verify the premiums prior to payment. You determine the premium on *(a)* the building and *(b)* the merchandise inventory, which agree with the invoices. Also, Amy asks you to determine the refund on the insurance on the inventory if a one-year policy was paid on February 1, 1991, and the policy was canceled on July 31, 1991, by *(c)* the insurance company or *(d)* the insured.

(a) ____________

(b) ____________

(c) ____________

(d) ____________

％ − × + $ ÷ +

Chapter 37

Coinsurance

I just was sold a group health insurance policy—but the whole group must get sick before I collect.

Learning Goals

Upon completion of this chapter, you should be able to:

1. Discuss reasons for taking out more than one insurance policy on the same property.
2. Compute the share of fire loss to be paid by each insurance company if two or more companies provide insurance on the same property.
3. Discuss why many insurance companies have coinsurance clauses.
4. Calculate the liability of the insurance company if the insured incurs a fire loss and does not meet the coinsurance requirements.
5. Calculate the liability of each insurance company if coverage is shared on the same property and there is a loss, with one or more insurance companies having a coinsurance clause.

More than One Insurer

Occasionally, there will be a situation where an insured may take out fire insurance policies on the same property with more than one insurance company. One reason might be that the insured wishes, for business purposes, to share the insurance with different companies. Also, insurance companies might feel that to insure a particular property exclusively would be too large a risk.

When two or more companies provide insurance on the same property, any loss that is incurred, up to the face of the policies, will be borne by the various companies in proportion to the insurance carried by each.

Example 1. The Morro Company carries the following insurance on its buildings: with Insurance Company A, \$20,000; Insurance Company B, \$30,000; Insurance Company C, \$40,000. There is a loss from fire of \$63,000. Determine how much each insurance company will have to pay.

$$\text{Insurance Company A:}\quad \$63{,}000 \times \frac{\$20{,}000}{\$90{,}000} = \$14{,}000$$

$$\text{Insurance Company B:}\quad \$63{,}000 \times \frac{\$30{,}000}{\$90{,}000} = \$21{,}000$$

$$\text{Insurance Company C:}\quad \$63{,}000 \times \frac{\$40{,}000}{\$90{,}000} = \underline{\$28{,}000}$$

$$\text{Total insurance paid}\qquad \underline{\underline{\$63{,}000}}$$

If the loss in example 1 exceeded \$90,000, each insurance company would pay the face of its policy.

Coinsurance

Coinsurance is an arrangement whereby the insurance company and the insured may share fire losses that occur. The insured agrees to bear a portion of a fire loss if the face amount of the insurance coverage is less than a specified percent of the current replacement cost of the property insured.

Why have a coinsurance clause? Most fires do not cause damage to all the property. Usually, only a fractional part of the property is damaged before the fire is put out. Knowing this, many insureds take out insurance on less than the full value of the property in order to save on the premium. In many instances, if policyholders do not take out insurance on a minimum fraction of the total property replacement value, they must agree to share in any losses that might result.

Under coinsurance, the insurance company specifies the minimum rate of insurance coverage that the insured must carry in order to be fully protected. Though any rate may be used, 80 percent is most typical. If the insurance coverage is less than the stipulated percent, the insured must share pro rata with the insurance company for any loss incurred.

If the insured does not carry enough insurance to meet the stated percent, the formula for arriving at the insurance to be collected from the insurance company would be:

Five Leading Causes of Death—1987

	(in thousands)
Heart	763
Cancer	477
Cerebrovascular	149
Accidents	95
Lung	78

San Francisco Chronicle, 8/16/88

$$\text{Insurer's share of loss} = \frac{\text{Insurance carried}}{\text{Insurance required}} \times \text{Actual loss}$$

The limitation on the above coinsurance formula is the face of the policy. The insurance company will pay the lesser amount of either the insurer's share of the loss or the face amount of the policy.

Example 2. David Crane carries $50,000 insurance on his building. There is an 80 percent coinsurance clause. A fire caused a loss of $20,000. The replacement value of the building at the time of the fire was $100,000. Determine the amount recovered from the insurance company.

$$\frac{\$50{,}000}{\$80{,}000} \times \$20{,}000 = \$12{,}500$$

Example 3. If the loss in example 2 were $80,000, determine the amount recovered from the insurance company.

$$\frac{\$50{,}000}{\$80{,}000} \times \$80{,}000 = \$50{,}000$$

Example 4. If the loss in example 2 were $96,000, determine the amount recovered from the insurance company.

$$\frac{\$50{,}000}{\$80{,}000} \times \$96{,}000 = \$60{,}000$$

However, since the face of the policy is only $50,000, that is all that can be recovered.

Coinsurance—More than One Insurer

Sometimes, for reasons stated previously, the insured will carry insurance on the same property with more than one company. It is possible that one, some, or all the companies may have a coinsurance clause, which could be at the same rate, or at different rates.

The formula for determining insurance recovery from loss from each of the insurance companies is as follows:

$$\text{Insurer's share of loss} = \frac{\text{Insurance carried}}{\text{greater of} \left\langle \begin{array}{c} \text{Total insurance carried} \\ \text{or} \\ \text{Total insurance required} \end{array} \right.} \times \text{Actual loss}$$

In the above formula, if the insured meets the coinsurance requirements of the specific insurance company, then that company would use "total insurance carried" as the denominator. If the coinsurance requirements were not met for the specific insurance company, then that company would use "total insurance required" as the denominator. In any case, the maximum coverage is the face of the policy.

Example 5. **Tony Seidl owns a piece of property with a replacement value of $150,000. He takes out insurance with the following three companies: Company A, $60,000, with an 80 percent coinsurance clause; Company B, $30,000, with a 90 percent coinsurance clause; and Company C, $20,000, with a 70 percent coinsurance clause. If there is a fire loss of $60,000, find the amount recovered from each insurance company.**

$$\text{Company A} = \frac{\$60{,}000}{\$120{,}000} \times \$60{,}000 = \$30{,}000$$

$$\text{Company B} = \frac{\$30{,}000}{\$135{,}000} \times \$60{,}000 = \$13{,}333$$

$$\text{Company C} = \frac{\$20{,}000}{\$110{,}000} \times \$60{,}000 = \$10{,}909$$

Mr. Seidl does not meet the coinsurance requirements of Company A and of Company B, but he exceeds the coinsurance requirement of Company C.

Student Review

1. Cerruti Air Conditioning Systems carries the following insurance on its properties: Insurance Company A, $50,000; Insurance Company B, $75,000; Insurance Company C, $60,000. The company incurs a fire loss of $190,000. Determine the amount of insurance paid by *(a)* Company A, *(b)* Company B, and *(c)* Company C.

(a) $__________

(b) $__________

(c) $__________

2. In problem 1, if the fire loss was determined to be $46,250, how much would be recovered from *(a)* Company A, *(b)* Company B, and *(c)* Company C?

(a) $__________

(b) $__________

(c) $__________

3. Retino Electric Co. carries a $450,000 insurance policy on its properties, with a 70 percent coinsurance clause. The company incurred a fire loss of $170,000 when the replacement value of the insured property at the time of the fire was $600,000. Determine the amount recovered from the insurance company.

$__________

4. In problem 3, if the insurance policy had an 80 percent coinsurance clause, what would be the amount recovered?

$__________

5. Squires Aviation has insurance on its property with two insurers: Company A, $60,000, with an 80 percent coinsurance clause; Company B, $100,000, with a 90 percent coinsurance clause. A fire destroys a good portion of the property, causing a loss of $100,000. Determine the amount recovered from *(a)* Company A and *(b)* Company B if the total replacement cost is $200,000.

(a) $__________

(b) $__________

Solutions to Student Review

1. If the fire loss exceeds the total combined insurance carried by the insurers, each insurance company will pay the face of the policy.

(a) $ 50,000

(b) $ 75,000

(c) $ 60,000

2. *(a)* $\frac{\$50,000}{\$185,000} \times \$46,250 = \$12,500$ — *(a)* $ 12,500

(b) $\frac{\$75,000}{\$185,000} \times \$46,250 = \$18,750$ — *(b)* $ 18,750

(c) $\frac{\$60,000}{\$185,000} \times \$46,250 = \$15,000$ — *(c)* $ 15,000

3. There is *no* coinsurance since the insurance policy coverage exceeds 70 percent of the replacement cost.

$ 170,000

4. $600,000
× .8
$480,000 (Insur. req.)

$\frac{\$450,000}{\$480,000} \times \$170,000 = \$159,375$

$ 159,375

5. *(a)* No coinsurance

$\frac{\$60,000}{\$160,000} \times \$100,000 = \$37,500$ — *(a)* $ 37,500

(b) $\frac{\$100,000}{\$180,000} \times \$100,000 = \$55,556$ — *(b)* $ 55,556

Assignment 37–1

Coinsurance

Name ______________________

Date ______________________

Solve the following problems:

1. The Starlite Company carries the following insurance on its properties: Insurance Company A, $30,000; and Insurance Company B, $50,000. The company incurs a fire loss of $90,000. Determine the amount of insurance paid by Company A and Company B.

A $ ______________

B $ ______________

2. The Trenton Corporation incurred a fire loss of $30,800 on its properties. The insurance was carried by the following three companies: X, $15,000; Y, $20,000; Z, $35,000. Determine the amount of insurance paid by each company.

X $ ______________

Y $ ______________

Z $ ______________

3. The Breakers Corp. carries a $30,000 insurance policy on its properties, with an 80 percent coinsurance clause. A fire caused a loss of $20,000. Determine the amount recovered from the insurance company if the replacement value of the insured property at the time of the fire is $35,000.

$ ______________

4. The Hooper Corporation incurred a $30,000 fire loss on its inventory. At the time of the loss the inventory was valued at $50,000. The corporation was insured for $30,000, with an 80 percent coinsurance clause. Determine the amount recovered from the insurance company.

$ ______________

5. Packo Co. holds a $10,000 insurance policy on its inventory, with an 80 percent coinsurance clause. A fire destroys the entire inventory, worth $15,000. Determine the amount recovered from the insurance company.

$____________

6. Fraden Corp. has fire insurance coverage with the following insurance companies: Company A, $80,000; Company B, $100,000. Both insurance companies have a 90 percent coinsurance clause. At the time when the insured property has a replacement value of $250,000, a fire causes a loss of $90,000. Determine the amount of insurance recovered from each insurance company.

A $____________

B $____________

7. Landon Corp. has insurance on its property with two companies: Company A, $20,000, with an 80 percent coinsurance clause; Company B, $30,000, with a 70 percent coinsurance clause. A fire destroys the entire property, valued at $70,000. Determine the amount recovered from the insurance companies.

A $____________

B $____________

8. In Problem 7, assume the same facts except that the fire loss was $28,000. Determine the amount of insurance recovered from the insurance companies.

A $____________

B $____________

Multiple Sports with Amy Hengst, Accountant

When the new plant was completed in Santa Clara County in 1995, the replacement value was estimated to be $400,000. Multiple Sports decided to insure the property with two insurance companies. Multiple Sports took out insurance on the new plant, as follows: Insurance company A, $220,000, with an 80 percent coinsurance clause; Insurance Company B, $60,000, with a 90 percent coinsurance clause. Late in 1995, there was a small fire that caused $18,000 in damages. Amy asks you to determine the amount to be recovered from *(a)* Insurance Company A and *(b)* Insurance Company B.

(a) $____________

(b) $____________

Chapter 38

Life Insurance

I have so much life insurance with this company—when I go, it goes.

Learning Goals

Upon completion of this chapter, you should be able to:

1. Discuss the reasons for carrying life insurance.
2. Differentiate between three basic types of life insurance policies: term, endowment, and whole life.
3. Discuss the dividend options of a participating life insurance policy.
4. Calculate the annual life insurance premium on an ordinary life, 20-payment life, or 20-year endowment policy.
5. Calculate the nonforfeiture value of a whole life policy at the end of each policy year in the event that the insured cancels the policy.
6. Determine the loan value of a whole life insurance policy at any time that the policy is in force.
7. Compute the amount payable to a beneficiary of a life insurance policy under a variety of settlement options.

The primary function of life insurance is to provide financial protection resulting from the loss of human life values. Economic death, whether brought about by death, disability, or old age, can be covered by life insurance. Since the amount of loss is difficult to determine, a typical individual should insure him- or herself for the minimum amount by which the surviving family can live without economic deprivation.

In most types of insurance, the contingency covered under insurance may or may not occur. In life insurance, if the policy is kept in force, payment by the insurer will eventually be made. The uncertainty in life insurance is *when* the insurance must be paid.

Types of Policies

Though there are varieties and offshoots of the basic life insurance contracts, actuarially there are three basic types of life insurance policies: (1) term, (2) endowment, and (3) whole life. In addition, there is the annuity contract, which is, in reality, life insurance in reverse.

Term Insurance. A term life insurance policy is a contract that offers financial protection to the policyholder against the possibility of death during the limited period stated in the policy. There is no protection in case one survives beyond the specified period. Term life insurance is sold for a fixed period of time, such as 1, 5, or 10 years.

The average National Basketball Association (NBA) player is 6′7″, weighs 216 pounds, and is 27 years old

Endowment Insurance. The endowment policy is similar to a term policy in that it offers insurance protection against death for a specified period of time. However, it differs from term in that if the insured survives the endowment period, he or she receives the face amount of the policy, either in a lump sum or in installments. Endowment insurance provides a much lower amount of protection *per premium dollar* than term insurance. Endowment insurance is primarily a means of accumulating funds for a specific purpose, such as meeting a child's college expenses or providing retirement income.

Whole Life Insurance. The term *whole life* is used interchangeably with *ordinary life* or *straight life.* This type of insurance offers protection for the whole life, regardless of the number of years that premiums have to be paid. When premiums are to be paid continuously on a periodic basis throughout the lifetime of the insured, the policy is usually called "ordinary life." When the premiums are to be paid over a limited period of time, such as in one lump sum, or for 10 or 20 years, then the policy is usually called "limited-payment life."

Continuous premium and limited-payment whole life policies offer the insured a combination of premature death protection and the establishment of a retirement fund. Premium payments that exceed costs are used to set up a cash surrender or loan value.

Annuity Insurance. Under an annuity contract, the insured pays the insurance company a specified capital sum, usually in installments, in exchange for a promise by the insurance company to pay, beginning at a certain date, a series of payments as long as the insured lives.

Dividend Options

Life insurance policies are commonly classified as either *participating* or *nonparticipating.* Under the participating plan, the policyholder is usually entitled to a policy dividend. These dividends approximately indicate the difference between the premium payment on the policy and the actual cost experienced by the company. These dividend distributions at year-end are not distribution of income but represent a return of a premium overcharge. The policy contract rarely states the method of calculating the

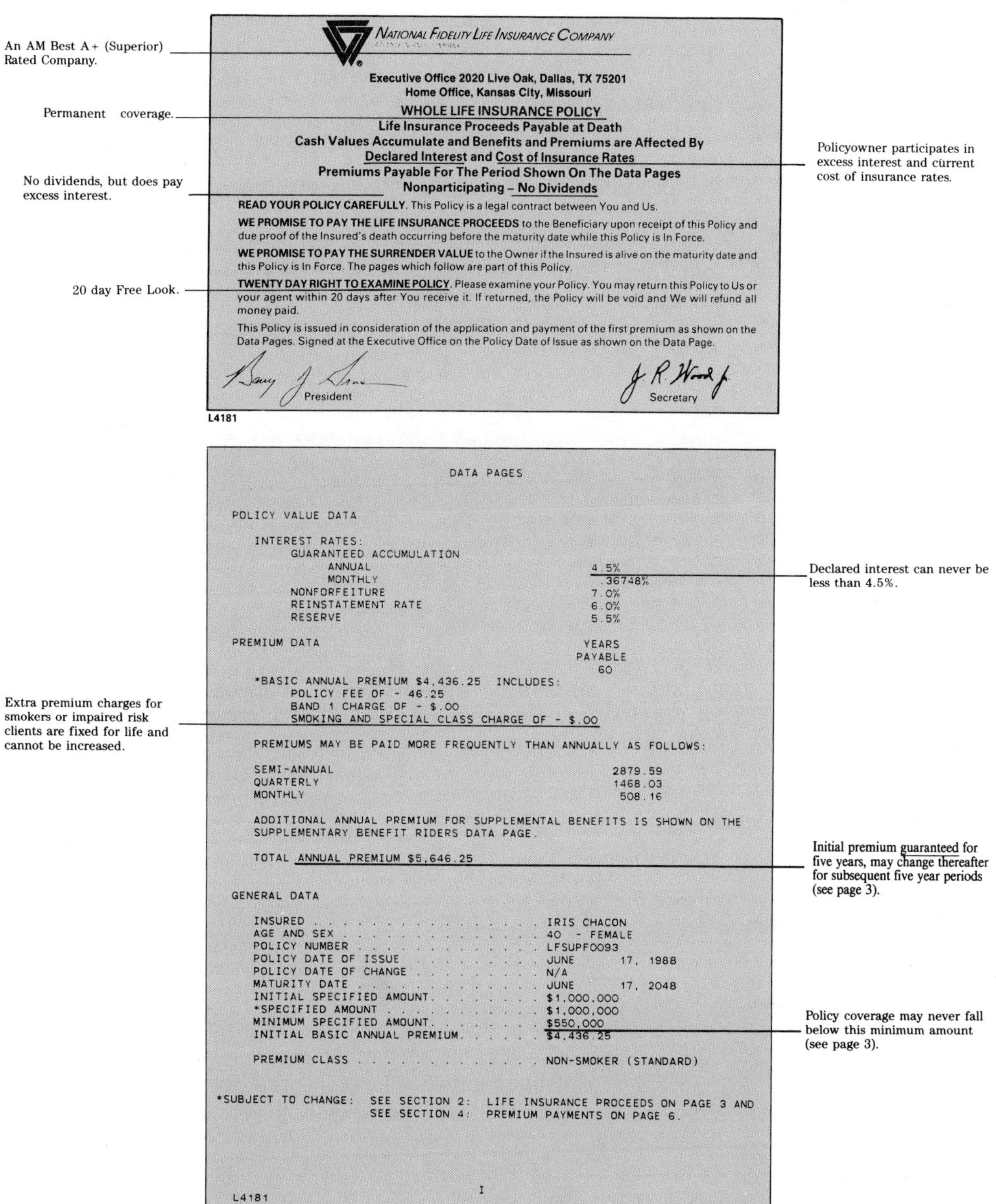

NATIONAL FIDELITY LIFE INSURANCE COMPANY

Executive Office 2020 Live Oak, Dallas, TX 75201
Home Office, Kansas City, Missouri

WHOLE LIFE INSURANCE POLICY
Life Insurance Proceeds Payable at Death
Cash Values Accumulate and Benefits and Premiums are Affected By
Declared Interest and Cost of Insurance Rates
Premiums Payable For The Period Shown On The Data Pages
Nonparticipating – No Dividends

READ YOUR POLICY CAREFULLY. This Policy is a legal contract between You and Us.

WE PROMISE TO PAY THE LIFE INSURANCE PROCEEDS to the Beneficiary upon receipt of this Policy and due proof of the Insured's death occurring before the maturity date while this Policy is In Force.

WE PROMISE TO PAY THE SURRENDER VALUE to the Owner if the Insured is alive on the maturity date and this Policy is In Force. The pages which follow are part of this Policy.

TWENTY DAY RIGHT TO EXAMINE POLICY. Please examine your Policy. You may return this Policy to Us or your agent within 20 days after You receive it. If returned, the Policy will be void and We will refund all money paid.

This Policy is issued in consideration of the application and payment of the first premium as shown on the Data Pages. Signed at the Executive Office on the Policy Date of Issue as shown on the Data Page.

President   Secretary

L4181

DATA PAGES

POLICY VALUE DATA

INTEREST RATES:
GUARANTEED ACCUMULATION
ANNUAL 4.5%
MONTHLY .36748%
NONFORFEITURE 7.0%
REINSTATEMENT RATE 6.0%
RESERVE 5.5%

PREMIUM DATA — YEARS PAYABLE 60

*BASIC ANNUAL PREMIUM $4,436.25 INCLUDES:
POLICY FEE OF - 46.25
BAND 1 CHARGE OF - $.00
SMOKING AND SPECIAL CLASS CHARGE OF - $.00

PREMIUMS MAY BE PAID MORE FREQUENTLY THAN ANNUALLY AS FOLLOWS:

SEMI-ANNUAL	2879.59
QUARTERLY	1468.03
MONTHLY	508.16

ADDITIONAL ANNUAL PREMIUM FOR SUPPLEMENTAL BENEFITS IS SHOWN ON THE SUPPLEMENTARY BENEFIT RIDERS DATA PAGE.

TOTAL ANNUAL PREMIUM $5,646.25

GENERAL DATA

INSURED	IRIS CHACON
AGE AND SEX	40 - FEMALE
POLICY NUMBER	LFSUPF0093
POLICY DATE OF ISSUE	JUNE 17, 1988
POLICY DATE OF CHANGE	N/A
MATURITY DATE	JUNE 17, 2048
INITIAL SPECIFIED AMOUNT	$1,000,000
*SPECIFIED AMOUNT	$1,000,000
MINIMUM SPECIFIED AMOUNT	$550,000
INITIAL BASIC ANNUAL PREMIUM	$4,436.25
PREMIUM CLASS	NON-SMOKER (STANDARD)

*SUBJECT TO CHANGE: SEE SECTION 2: LIFE INSURANCE PROCEEDS ON PAGE 3 AND SEE SECTION 4: PREMIUM PAYMENTS ON PAGE 6.

I

L4181

dividend, and the company annually determines the amount of the dividend.

Participating policies usually offer policyholders several optional ways to receive their refunds. Typical options include (1) payment in cash, (2) application to succeeding premium payment, (3) accumulation with the insurance company at a guaranteed minimum rate of interest, and (4) purchase of paid-up additions to the policy.

The premium on a participating policy is generally larger than on a nonparticipating policy. When comparing the costs of the two types of policies, it is necessary to consider the potential net cost of the participating policy.

Premiums

The following table illustrates a typical annual rate schedule per $1,000 of insurance at different ages for whole life (ordinary), 20-payment life, and 20-year endowment policies. Rates generally vary between insurance companies, based on experience, types of coverage, and dividend participation. In addition, because of their greater life expectancy, rates for females are approximately those of a male five to eight years younger.

Annual Premiums for $1,000 Policy

	Types of Whole Life Policies		
Age at Purchase	**Ordinary Life**	**20-Payment Life**	**20-Year Endowment**
20	16.24	25.72	45.16
30	22.07	32.18	48.91
40	27.12	36.79	50.28
50	41.86	51.22	57.43
60	65.38	76.04	75.10

Example 1. Bill Shreve is 40 years old. What annual premium will he pay for $10,000 worth of *(a)* ordinary life, *(b)* 20-payment life, and *(c)* 20-year endowment?

(a) **$27.12 × 10 = $271.20**

(b) **$36.79 × 10 = $367.90**

(c) **$50.28 × 10 = $502.80**

Nonforfeiture Options

After an initial two- to three-year period to cover selling costs, the life insurance policies, except for term insurance, begin accumulating a gradually increasing nonforfeiture investment for the insured. If an individual took out a life insurance policy each year for one year's protection, such as in term insurance, the premium would automatically increase annually as mortality rates increase with age. Under a whole life policy, with level annual premiums, the policyholder pays more than the actual cost of insurance in the earlier years. Nonforfeiture values occur from these early high premiums and the resultant investment yield on them.

The three most common forms of nonforfeiture options found in policies are: (1) cash surrender value, (2) paid-up insurance, and (3) extended term insurance.

Cash Surrender Value. If a policyholder terminates the policy prior to maturity, the insurance company will have collected more from the insured during the years of coverage than was necessary to cover the cost of the policy while it was in force. If he or she so elects, the policyholder is entitled to a refund for the excess payments.

Paid-up Insurance. If a policyholder terminates the policy prior to maturity, he or she may request paid-up insurance. The insurance company applies the cash value available when the premiums stop to whatever amount of fully paid insurance can be acquired at a single premium rate.

Extended Term Insurance. If a policyholder allows his or her policy to lapse, and does not elect one of the other two nonforfeiture provisions, most insurance companies will give the insured the extended-term option. Under this option, the insurance company converts the cash surrender value of the policy into a single-premium term insurance policy, continuing the full face value of the policy for as long as the single premium will apply.

Cash Surrender Value, Paid-Up Insurance, and Extended Term Insurance for Each $1,000 on Whole Life Policy Issued at Age 21 (Rounded to Nearest Dollar)

End of Year	Cash Surrender Value	Paid-Up Insurance	Extended Insurance	
			Years	Days
1				
2	$ 8	$ 11	1	110
3	15	45	3	121
4	29	79	7	142
5	42	111	10	159
6	50	134	13	70
7	59	157	16	55
8	69	179	18	104
9	79	200	20	296
10	90	221	22	90
11	101	246	22	219
12	112	265	23	15
13	123	284	23	139
14	134	302	23	257
15	145	319	23	363
16	156	336	24	95
17	168	353	24	121
18	180	368	24	157
19	192	389	24	190
20	205	408	24	201

The above table shows the difference in cash surrender value and paid-up insurance, as well as the extended term insurance that may be purchased at the option of the insured if the policy is allowed to lapse.

Example 2. Raymond Dalton purchased a \$12,000 whole life policy when he was 21. He is 32 and decides to terminate the policy. Determine *(a)* the cash surrender value, *(b)* the paid-up insurance, and *(c)* the period of extended term insurance.

(a) \$101 × 12 = \$1,212

(b) \$246 × 12 = \$2,952

(c) 22 years, 219 days

Loan Value

Most life insurance policies have an additional feature that allows the insured to borrow up to the cash surrender value of the policy without reducing the coverage. In the event the insured dies while a loan is outstanding, the insurance company will pay the beneficiary the face of the policy less the amount of the loan and accrued interest outstanding. The insurance company charges a predetermined interest rate on the loan, usually around 8 or 9 percent.

The cash surrender value represents the insured's investment in the life insurance policy at the end of each year. Since the premiums are usually paid at the beginning of the year, the loan value can readily be determined by finding the present value of the cash surrender value on the date of the loan at the predetermined interest rate.

For example, if the cash surrender value at the end of a given policy year is \$2,500 and the loan rate is 9 percent, the insured can borrow \$2,294 at the beginning of the policy year, determined as follows:

$$\text{Loan} = \frac{\$2{,}500}{1.09} = \$2{,}294$$

If the insured wanted to borrow on the policy 120 days before the policy year ends, the amount of the loan would be \$2,428, determined as follows:

$$\text{Loan} = \frac{\$2{,}500}{1 + \left(\frac{9}{100} \times \frac{120}{365}\right)} = \frac{\$2{,}500}{1 + \frac{54}{1825}} = \frac{\$2{,}500}{\frac{1879}{1825}} = \$2{,}428$$

Settlement Options

Proceeds on a life insurance policy are usually paid in a lump-sum amount. However, upon written request of the insured, or by the beneficiary after the death of the insured, the insurance company will agree to pay the proceeds of the insurance contract in accordance with one of several available options. Typical options include (1) a fixed amount paid in regular installments for a fixed period of time, or (2) a fixed amount for a guaranteed number of years, such as 5, 10, or 20, with the same periodic payment to continue thereafter until the beneficiary dies. The installments under the latter options are determined by the age and sex of the payee at the date of payment of the first installment.

The following table illustrates some typical settlement options.

Settlement Options—Monthly Payments for Each $1,000

Option 1		Option 2			
		Age of Payee		Monthly Payment	
Number of Years	Monthly Payment	Male	Female	10 Years	20 Years
6	$14.74	25	30	$3.07	3.04
7	12.76	35	40	3.48	3.42
8	11.26	45	50	4.10	3.92
9	10.09	55	60	5.02	4.49
10	9.18	65	70	6.33	5.01

Example 3. Peggy Vota was the beneficiary of a $15,000 life insurance policy. She elected to receive equal monthly payments for 10 years. Determine her monthly proceeds.

$9.18 × 15 = $137.70 per month

Example 4. Karen Bennett was the beneficiary of a $9,000 life insurance policy when she was 50 years old. She elected to take a life income option, with a fixed guaranteed sum for 20 years. Find her monthly proceeds.

$3.92 × 9 = $35.28 per month

Student Review

1. Richard Uchida, age 30, purchases a $50,000 ordinary life policy. Determine *(a)* his annual premium and *(b)* how much more he would pay during each of the first 20 years if he had taken a 20-payment whole life policy.

(a) $____________

(b) $____________

2. Joan Benjamin purchased a $40,000 whole life policy at age 21. Determine the cash surrender value on the policy if she cancels the policy at age 40.

$____________

3. William Gibson took out a $35,000 whole life policy at age 21. When he reached age 30, he paid his annual premium and decided to borrow on his cash surrender value. Determine the maximum that he could borrow if the loan rate is 8 percent.

$____________

4. Betsy Walsh was the beneficiary of a $60,000 life insurance policy. She elected to receive equal monthly payments for 10 years. Determine her monthly proceeds.

$____________

5. Dennis Middleton was the beneficiary of a $15,000 life insurance policy when he was 45 years old. He elected to take a life income option, with a fixed guaranteed sum for 10 years. Determine his monthly proceeds.

$____________

Solutions to Student Review

1. *(a)* $\$\ 22.07 \times 50 = \$1{,}103.50$

(b) $\$\ 32.18 \times 50 = \$1{,}609.00$

$\$1{,}609.00 - 1{,}103.50 = \$\ 505.50$

(a) $ 1,103.50

(b) $ 505.50

2. $\$\ 192 \times 40 = \$7{,}680$

$ 7,680

3. Cash surrender value is the value at the end of the policy year. Therefore, the cash surrender value at the end of 10 years is:

$\$\ 90 \times 35 = \$3{,}150$

$$\frac{\$3{,}150}{1.08} = \$2{,}916.67$$

$ 2,916.67

4. $\$\ 9.18 \times 60 = \$550.80$

$ 550.80

5. $\$\ 4.10 \times 15 = \$61.50$

$ 61.50

Assignment 38–1

Life Insurance

Name ______________________

Date ______________________

1. Fred Layton is 20 years old. From the premium table provided, determine the premium he will have to pay annually for a $15,000 ordinary life policy.

$ ______________

2. Jennie Robinson, age 40 decides to purchase a $30,000 limited-payment life insurance policy. If she agrees to pay annual premiums for 20 years, determine her annual premium.

$ ______________

3. Mary O'Brien purchased a 20-year, $40,000 endowment life insurance policy at age 30, naming her son the beneficiary of the policy. Determine *(a)* her annual premium payments, and *(b)* proceeds to her son if she dies at age 42, and *(c)* proceeds to Mary O'Brien if she lives to age 50.

(a) $ ______________

(b) $ ______________

(c) $ ______________

4. In problem 3, if Mary O'Brien had purchased a 20-year, $40,000 term life insurance policy at age 30, determine *(a)* the proceeds to her son if she dies at age 42, *(b)* the proceeds that she will receive if she lives to age 50, and *(c)* whether the annual premium will be larger or smaller than with the endowment policy.

(a) $ ______________

(b) $ ______________

(c) ______________

5. Derek Towns, age 30, is unsure about which life insurance policy to take. Determine the annual premium on a $20,000 policy with *(a)* ordinary life, *(b)* 20-payment life, and *(c)* 20-year endowment.

(a) $__________

(b) $__________

(c) $__________

6. James Tipton took out a $5,000, 20-year endowment policy at age 40. He survived the 20-year period. Ignoring interest that he might have received on the premiums, circle whether he received more or less at maturity than the premiums he paid, and by how much.

more
less $__________

7. Reggie Moran purchased a $50,000 life insurance policy at age 30. If he takes the 20-payment life option, determine how much larger his annual premium will be at age 36 than if he had elected the ordinary life option.

$__________

8. In problem 7, indicate how much more (+) or less (−) Mr. Moran will have paid in total premiums with the 20-payment life option compared to the ordinary life option if Moran died at age *(a)* 36, *(b)* 56, or *(c)* 60. In each case, circle the appropriate + or −. Ignore implicit interest that might have been earned on the savings from the lower annual premiums paid in connection with ordinary life.

(a) + − $__________

(b) + − $__________

(c) + − $__________

Assignment 38–2

Life Insurance

Name ______________________

Date ______________________

1. Phil Williams purchased a $20,000 whole life policy at age 21. Determine the cash surrender value on the policy if he cancels it at age 36.

$ ______________

2. Larry Tingall purchased a $12,000 whole life policy at age 21. If he cancels the policy at age 31, determine *(a)* his paid-up insurance, and *(b)* the period of extended term insurance.

(a) $ ______________

(b) ______________

3. If the cash surrender value of a whole life policy is $3,200 at the end of the current year, and the loan rate is 8 percent, determine the amount that the insured can borrow at the beginning of the policy year.

$ ______________

4. Greg Violette took out a $70,000 whole life policy on his 21st birthday. When he reached age 39, he paid his annual premium and decided to borrow on his cash surrender value. Determine the maximum amount he could borrow if the loan rate is 9 percent.

$ ______________

5. In problem 4, if Mr. Violette's premium was paid on March 12, the premium due date, and he borrowed on his cash surrender value on the following May 24, determine the maximum amount that he could borrow.

$ ______________

6. Sam Ziegler was the beneficiary of a $20,000 life insurance policy. He elected to receive equal monthly payments for 8 years. Determine the monthly proceeds.

$ ____________

7. Marie Tumas was the beneficiary of a $5,000 life insurance policy when she was 60 years old. She elected to take a life income option, with a fixed guaranteed sum for 10 years. Determine the monthly proceeds.

$ ____________

8. Myrna Mein was the beneficiary of a $6,000 life insurance policy when she was 50 years old.

(a) Determine her monthly proceeds if she elected a life income option, with a fixed guaranteed sum for 10 years.

$ ____________

(b) Determine her monthly proceeds if she elected a life income option, with a fixed guaranteed sum for 20 years.

$ ____________

(c) If Mrs. Mein lived to age 74, how much more would she have received under option *(a)* than under option *(b)*?

$ ____________

Multiple Sports with Amy Hengst, Accountant

The Board of Directors of Multiple Sports decided to purchase a $200,000, whole life policy on the lives of its chairman and its president. For the chairman, who is age 60, an ordinary life policy was acquired, while for the president, who is only 50, a 20-payment life policy was purchased.

In addition, Multiple Sports has a group life insurance plan whereby every employee of the firm can, at any time, buy a $25,000 ordinary life policy, partially financed by the company. Virginia Lee started working for Multiple Sports at age 21, immediately after graduating from college. At that time, she purchased a $25,000 ordinary life policy. Now that she is 35, with a family, Virginia would like to cut down on her expenses. She is considering several options: canceling the policy and substituting term insurance; converting the policy to paid-up insurance; converting the policy to extended term insurance; paying the annual premium and borrowing the full amount available on the cash surrender value at a loan rate of 7 percent.

Also, Robert Turner, a long-term employee, died recently, and his daughter Rose, age 30, inquires about her settlement options if she decides not to take the $25,000 in a lump-sum amount.

Amy asks you to determine the following: the annual life insurance premium paid for *(a)* the chairman and *(b)* the president; on Virginia Lee's policy *(c)* the cash surrender value, *(d)* the amount of paid-up insurance, *(e)* the length of extended term insurance, or *(f)* the current loan value; for Rose, the monthly amount to be received if she elects *(g)* the settlement option to receive equal monthly payments for 8 years or *(h)* a life income option with a fixed guaranteed monthly sum for 20 years.

Amy also tells you that this will be your final assignment under her direct supervision since she has been promoted to executive vice president of operations, and she congratulates you on your new assignment as the controller of Multiple Sports.

(a) $__________

(b) $__________

(c) $__________

(d) $__________

(e) __________

(f) $__________

(g) $__________

(h) $__________

Appendix

Graphs and Tables

Graphs and tables are used extensively to display statistical data and give an immediate picture of the relationships of selected data without the necessity of extensive study. The student has already encountered examples of tables in connection with the material presented in previous chapters. The basic types of graphs in general use are the *(a)* simple and component bar graph, *(b)* circle graph, and *(c)* line graph.

Simple Bar Graph

A simple bar graph shows the relationship between values that are of the same kind. At the end of the current year, the Richards Manufacturing Company had the following number of employees in its various departments: A, 850; B, 800; C, 520; and D, 120. The bar graph is an excellent method of comparing this data.

In the illustration the bars are placed horizontally, but they could have been placed vertically if desired.

Richards Manufacturing Company, Number of Employees

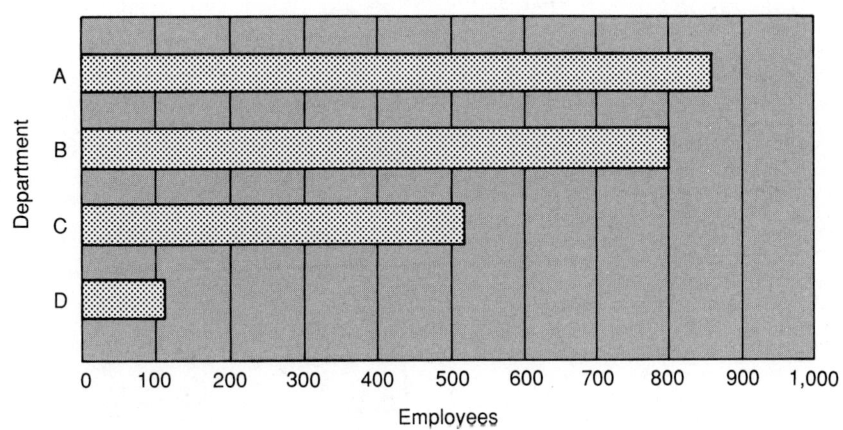

Component Bar Graph

In a component bar graph the individual bars are divided into component parts so that a particular relationship within a given category may be expressed. The illustrated component bar graph below shows the total number of new employees in various departments of the Western Steel Corporation over a given period of time.

Western Steel Corporation, Number of New Employees

Circle Graph

The circle graph, also referred to as a pie chart, is generally used to show the relationship of the parts of a whole in terms of percentage. The circumference of a circle, in a clockwise direction, contains 360 degrees and each percent represents 3.6 degrees of the circle. Thus, 25 percent is $3.6 \times 25 = 90°$ of the circle.

During a certain fiscal period, the Central National Bank reported that for each dollar distributed, 68 percent was paid to savers in the form of dividends, 18 percent went for expenses, and 14 percent was allocated to reserves. After converting the percentage amounts to degrees, the circle graph is illustrated.

$$3.6 \times 68 = 244.8 = 245°$$
$$3.6 \times 18 = 64.8 = 65°$$
$$3.6 \times 14 = 50.4 = \underline{50°}$$
$$360° \quad \text{or } 100\%$$

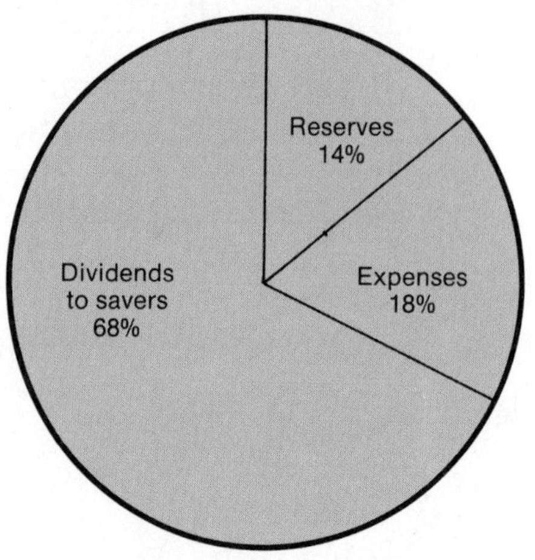

Line Graph

A line graph is generally used to present data in relation to a given period of time. The line graph presented below indicates the dollar amount of sales for the Northwest Publishing Company during the period 1980–1989.

Northwest Publishing Company, Sales 1980–1989

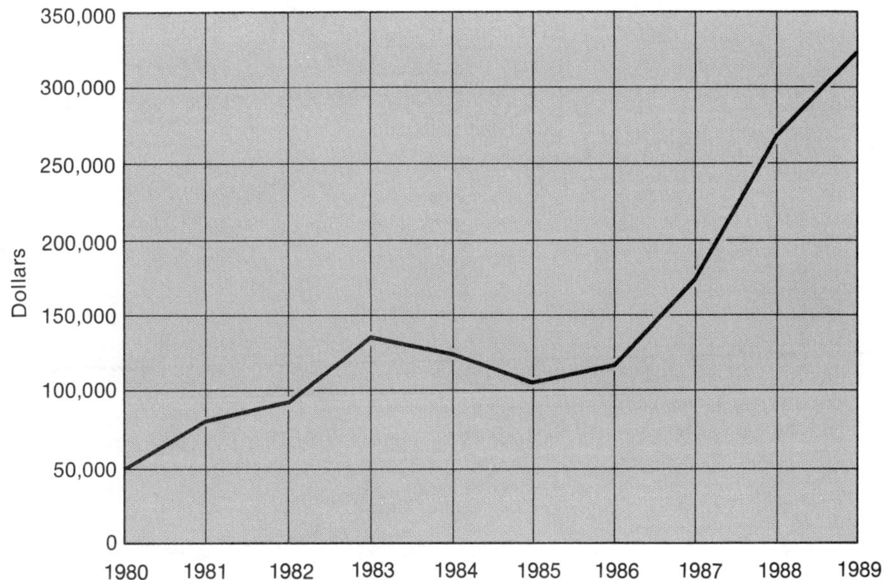

A number of variables may be shown, and are easily compared, on a line graph. An example of this is the line graph comparing the average annual interest rate paid to various depositors at major financial institutions during 1974–1989.

Average Annual Interest Paid on Money Market Accounts at Major Financial Institutions, 1974–1989

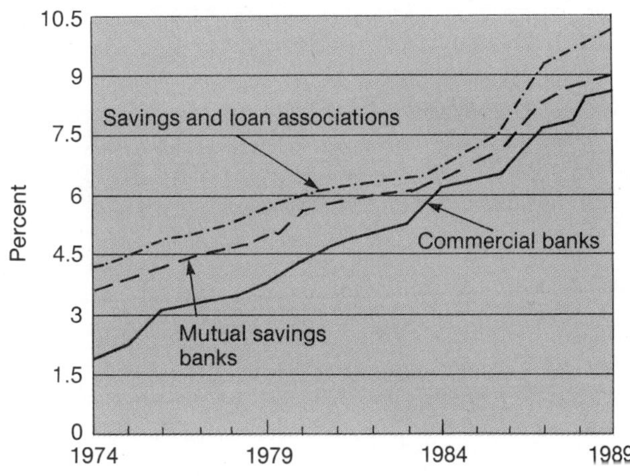

From *The Wall Street Journal,* with permission of Cartoon Features Syndicate.

Appendix

Graphs and Tables

Name ______________________

Date ______________________

1. The yearly sales made by the Alberton Company are shown for 1980–1989. Prepare a bar chart for the purpose of comparing these amounts:

1980	$200,000	1985	$ 570,000
1981	350,000	1986	750,000
1982	500,000	1987	700,000
1983	520,000	1988	820,000
1984	430,000	1989	1,100,000

2. During January 1989, the average sales per employee in the Columbia Department Store's various departments were as follows:

Department	*Average Sales per Employee*
A	$3,700
B	2,300
C	1,600
D	3,200
E	7,300
F	7,500
G	5,300
H	6,100

Prepare a bar chart to illustrate this data.

3. The Best-Bilt Company manufactures truck cabs in standard, deluxe, and custom models. The figures below show production during the four quarters of last year. Prepare a component bar chart.

Quarter	*Standard*	*Deluxe*	*Custom*
I	75	25	10
II	120	50	10
III	230	80	25
IV	170	20	35

4. The Federal Home Loan Bank reported the following as the distribution of outstanding home loans during the second quarter of the current year: savings and loan associations, 43 percent; savings and commercial banks, 26 percent; insurance companies, 12 percent; federal governmental agencies, 9 percent; and private lenders, 10 percent. Prepare a circle graph to illustrate this distribution.

5. The XYZ Company spent a total of $80,000 for newspaper advertising to promote a special sale in various departments. The advertising expenditures were divided as follows:

		Percent of Total
Hardware	$20,000	25
Appliances	25,600	32
Paint supplies	8,000	10
Furniture	16,800	21
Garden supplies	9,600	12

Prepare a circle graph to show the information given.

6. The production figures for the Brown Company during the first 12 weeks of the current year showed the following number of cases shipped to distributors:

Week	*Cases*	*Week*	*Cases*
1	1,200	7	3,500
2	1,250	8	4,260
3	1,300	9	4,700
4	1,550	10	5,530
5	1,820	11	6,200
6	2,100	12	7,920

Prepare a line graph showing the data given.

7. The Merchants Bank of Trade reports the following new accounts opened during the four quarters of last year. Prepare a line graph comparing the data given.

Quarter	*Savings*	*Special Checking*	*Commercial*
I	20	43	75
II	22	57	93
III	32	62	110
IV	50	72	152

Answers to Odd-Numbered Problems

ASSIGNMENT 1–1A

1. 71
3. 69
5. 99
7. MCCVI
9. LXXI
11. Tens
13. Hundredths
15. Thousandths
17. Units
19. Hundreds

ASSIGNMENT 1–1B

1. 780
3. 73.91
5. 1,900.052
7. 70.258
9. 229.2
11. 369.9
13. 62.003
15. 286,003
17. .84
19. .091
21. 3,700.7
23. .093
25. 56,826

ASSIGNMENT 1–2A

1. 270
3. 3,880
5. $1,690.00
7. 31,900
9. $200.00
11. 207
13. 87,257
15. 9,782
17. 33,875,000
19. 93,000

ASSIGNMENT 1–2B

1. .2
3. 6,384.1
5. 2,172.9
7. 372.811
9. 21,874.326
11. 107.84
13. 2.71
15. 3.01
17. .7209
19. .0032

ASSIGNMENT 2–1A

1. 80
3. 37
5. 187
7. 569
9. 317
11. 457
13. 814
15. 1,577

ASSIGNMENT 2–1B

1. 3,122
3. 1,552
5. 3,364
7. $905,492
9. 1,861

ASSIGNMENT 2–1C

1. 18
3. 47
5. 20
7. 433
9. 280
11. 2,385
13. 63,686
15. 549,110

ASSIGNMENT 2–1D

1. 2,780
3. 3,390
5. 3,430
7. 2,451
9. 2,286
11. 5,047

ASSIGNMENT 2–2A

1. 863.863
3. 84.3317
5. 462.474
7. 982.62
9. 24.77

ASSIGNMENT 2–2B

1. 622.2
3. 28.848
5. .0587
7. 190.3584
9. 963.2572

ASSIGNMENT 2–2C

1. $49.03
3. $12,350
5. $133.62
7. $22.44
9. $94,800

ASSIGNMENT 3–1

1. 371
3. 249
5. 459
7. 3,992
9. 5,467
11. 3,100
13. 756
15. 731
17. 1,420
19. 1,548
21. 630,252
23. 478,023
25. 134,724
27. 22,500
29. 246,000
31. 20,300
33. 509,600
35. 72,100
37. 24,920
39. 5,644,830

ASSIGNMENT 3–2

1. $180.00
3. 630
5. $1,044
7. $2,880
9. $173,320
11. $9,660

ASSIGNMENT 4–1

1. 23
3. 4
5. 18
7. 52
9. 2
11. 201
13. 100
15. 486
17. 216
19. 291
21. 28
23. 235
25. 89
27. 11 *r* 56
29. 102 *r* 5
31. 35 *r* 612
33. 61 *r* 143
35. 210

ASSIGNMENT 4–2

1. $2,716
3. $130.50
5. 4,376
7. $21,000
9. 73
11. 80

ASSIGNMENT 5–1

1. 76.44
3. 12,153.6
5. 27.3224
7. 119.9278
9. .59723982
11. 6,334.50636
13. 8.3
15. 2,660
17. 190
19. 1.13
21. 42.60
23. 253.68
25. 31.78

ASSIGNMENT 5–2

1. 60.2
3. $33.12
5. 3.08
7. $1,148.56
9. 42,840
11. $24.48

ASSIGNMENT 6–1

1. $\frac{1}{2}$
3. $\frac{1}{3}$
5. $\frac{1}{7}$
7. $\frac{1}{2}$
9. $\frac{12}{49}$
11. $\frac{11}{24}$
13. $\frac{19}{77}$
15. $\frac{17}{25}$
17. $\frac{37}{180}$
19. $\frac{91}{190}$

1*a*. 9
1*b*. $\frac{1}{9}$
3*a*. 15
3*b*. $\frac{5}{7}$
5*a*. 279
5*b*. $\frac{1}{2}$
7*a*. 93
7*b*. $\frac{3}{5}$
9*a*. 20
9*b*. $\frac{32}{413}$
11*a*. 21
11*b*. $\frac{3}{17}$

ASSIGNMENT 6–2

A. 1. $\frac{98}{112}$
3. $\frac{75}{180}$
5. $\frac{125}{200}$
7. $\frac{56}{60}$
9. $\frac{75}{100}$
11. $\frac{276}{360}$

B. 1. $\frac{5}{2}$
3. $\frac{59}{12}$
5. $\frac{230}{13}$
7. $\frac{352}{15}$
9. $\frac{3,239}{32}$

C. 1. $3\frac{3}{4}$
3. 12
5. 11
7. $75\frac{3}{8}$
9. $3\frac{2}{21}$
11. $5\frac{67}{143}$
13. $17\frac{11}{12}$
15. 18

ASSIGNMENT 7–1

1. 72
3. 60
5. 288
7. $33\frac{17}{20}$
9. $370\frac{37}{84}$
11. $\frac{8}{45}$
13. $\frac{12}{35}$
15. $5\frac{1}{6}$
17. $35\frac{3}{16}$
19. $6\frac{3}{4}$

ASSIGNMENT 7–2

1. $10\frac{3}{8}$
3. $90\frac{1}{4}$
5. $152\frac{1}{3}$
7. $60\frac{3}{4}$
9. $16\frac{1}{8}$
11. $\frac{1}{16}$

ASSIGNMENT 8–1

1. $\frac{33}{175}$
3. 378
5. $149\frac{1}{2}$
7. $5,358\frac{3}{5}$
9. $17\frac{1}{4}$
11. 12
13. $10\frac{1}{5}$
15. $121\frac{1}{3}$
17. $1\frac{1}{8}$
19. $\frac{7}{32}$

ASSIGNMENT 8–2

1. $225
3. $206\frac{3}{4}$
5. 32
7. 224
9. $122\frac{1}{2}$
11. $16,562\frac{1}{2}$

ASSIGNMENT 9–1

1. .75
3. .125
5. 1.4
7. .92
9. .48
11. .8125
13. .26
15. .25
17. .92
19. .71

21. .69
23. .71
25. .32
27. $8\frac{3}{25}$
29. $50\frac{67}{200}$
31. $\frac{1,699}{5,000}$
33. $\frac{199}{1,000}$
35. $67\frac{351}{500}$

21. $\frac{9}{100}$
23. $7\frac{1}{5}$
25. $\frac{93}{500}$
27. $\frac{73}{900}$
29. 20%
31. $33\frac{1}{3}\%$
33. 36%
35. 9%

ASSIGNMENT 10–1

1. .09
3. 1.16
5. 3.8
7. .037
9. .0075
11. 3%
13. 39%
15. 12.8%
17. 1,620%
19. 201%

ASSIGNMENT 10–2

1. $\frac{1}{4}$
3. $\frac{3}{25}$
5. .60
7. $1\frac{3}{5}$
9. $\frac{167}{200}$

11. .17
13. $\frac{3}{20}$
15. $\frac{7}{8}$
17. 12.5
19. $\frac{3}{1,000}$

ASSIGNMENT 11–1

1. $10,879
3. $310.40
5. 918
7. $573.18
9. $875

ASSIGNMENT 11–2

1. 82%
3. 76%
5. 16%
7. $3\frac{1}{2}\%$
9. $11\frac{3}{4}\%$

ASSIGNMENT 11–3

1. $15,600
3. $436
5. $29,000
7*a*. $699.00
7*b*. $559.20
9. 350

ASSIGNMENT 11–4

1. 75%
3. 21%
5. 125%
7. 1,800
9. 200
11. 5%
13. 34
15. 112.5
17. $2,925
19. $260

ASSIGNMENT 11–5

1. $1,920
3. 19%
5. $12,800,000
7. 29,500
9. 7.9%

ASSIGNMENT 12–1

A. Complete the totals and balances on the following check stubs proceeding in numerical order and carrying each balance to the succeeding check stub.

No. 201 $ 175.00
June 1 19
TO Sims Realty
FOR Rent

	Dollars	Cents
BAL. BRO'T. FOR'D.	621.	10
AM'T. DEPOSITED		
TOTAL	621.	10
AM'T. THIS CHECK	175.	00
BAL. CAR'D. FOR'D.	446.	10

NOTICE: Make No Alteration or Change on Any Check, if Error is Made Write New Check.

No. 202 $ 16.23
June 2 19
TO Pacific Gas and
FOR Electric Company

	Dollars	Cents
BAL. BRO'T. FOR'D.	446.	10
AM'T. DEPOSITED		
TOTAL	446.	10
AM'T. THIS CHECK	16.	23
BAL. CAR'D. FOR'D.	429.	87

NOTICE: Make No Alteration or Change on Any Check, if Error is Made Write New Check.

No. 203 $ 6.19
June 7 19
TO City Telephone
FOR Company

	Dollars	Cents
BAL. BRO'T. FOR'D.	429.	87
AM'T. DEPOSITED		
TOTAL	429.	87
AM'T. THIS CHECK	6.	19
BAL. CAR'D. FOR'D.	423.	68

NOTICE: Make No Alteration or Change on Any Check, if Error is Made Write New Check.

(continued)

No. 204 $ 19.70
June 12 19__
TO Cabrillo
FOR Shoe Shop

	Dollars	Cents
BAL. BRO'T. FOR'D.	423	68
AM'T. DEPOSITED	478	00
TOTAL	901	68
AM'T. THIS CHECK	19	70
BAL. CAR'D. FOR'D.	881	98

NOTICE: Make No Alteration or Change on Any Check, if Error is Made Write New Check.

No. 205 $ 52.16
June 19 19__
TO Lincoln Garage
FOR Motor tune-up

	Dollars	Cents
BAL. BRO'T. FOR'D.	881	98
AM'T. DEPOSITED		
TOTAL	881	98
AM'T. THIS CHECK	52	16
BAL. CAR'D. FOR'D.	829	82

NOTICE: Make No Alteration or Change on Any Check, if Error is Made Write New Check.

No. 206 $ 36.10
June 22 19__
TO Superior Market
FOR On Account

	Dollars	Cents
BAL. BRO'T. FOR'D.	829	82
AM'T. DEPOSITED		
TOTAL	829	82
AM'T. THIS CHECK	36	10
BAL. CAR'D. FOR'D.	793	72

NOTICE: Make No Alteration or Change on Any Check, if Error is Made Write New Check.

No. 207 $ 20.00
June 23 19__
TO United Crusade
FOR Contribution

	Dollars	Cents
BAL. BRO'T. FOR'D.	793	72
AM'T. DEPOSITED	26	18
TOTAL	819	90
AM'T. THIS CHECK	20	00
BAL. CAR'D. FOR'D.	799	90

NOTICE: Make No Alteration or Change on Any Check, if Error is Made Write New Check.

No. 208 $ 8.92
June 25 19__
TO Stanley
FOR Record Shop

	Dollars	Cents
BAL. BRO'T. FOR'D.	799	90
AM'T. DEPOSITED		
TOTAL	799	90
AM'T. THIS CHECK	8	92
BAL. CAR'D. FOR'D.	790	98

NOTICE: Make No Alteration or Change on Any Check, if Error is Made Write New Check.

No. 209 $ 35.00
June 29 19__
TO The Emporium
FOR On account

	Dollars	Cents
BAL. BRO'T. FOR'D.	790	98
AM'T. DEPOSITED	12	28
TOTAL	803	26
AM'T. THIS CHECK	35	00
BAL. CAR'D. FOR'D.	768	26

NOTICE: Make No Alteration or Change on Any Check, if Error is Made Write New Check.

ASSIGNMENT 12–2

1. $3,020
3. $11,764

ASSIGNMENT 13–1

		Earnings		
		Standard	*Overtime*	*Total*
A.	Aaron, B.	$ 210.00	—	$ 210.00
	Johnson, B.	184.00	$34.50	218.50
	Travers, D.	272.00	10.20	282.20
	Vernon, P.	308.00	23.10	331.10
	Walters, R.	209.00	16.50	225.50
		$1,183.00	$84.30	$1,267.30

B. 1*a*. $340.00
1*b*. $63.75
1*c*. $403.75
3*a*. $294.00
3*b*. $63.00
3*c*. $357.00
5*a*. $262.20
5*b*. $31.05
5*c*. $293.25
7*a*. $381.82
7*b*. $207.76
7*c*. $589.58

ASSIGNMENT 13–2

		Earnings		
		Regular	*Premium*	*Total*
A.	Bloomer, R.	$181.65	—	$181.65
	Everall, P.	162.36	$ 2.46	164.82
	Jabbar, A.	165.98	15.44	181.42
	Riordan, M.	197.40	—	197.40
	Settle, M.	182.40	7.20	189.60

B. 1*a*. $247.25
1*b*. $23.00
1*c*. $270.25
3*a*. $63.86
3*b*. $10.12
3*c*. $73.98
5*a*. $318.20
5*b*. $14.80
5*c*. $12.73
7. $692.31

ASSIGNMENT 14–1

1. $874.80
3. $696.40
5. $1,430.00
7. $764.00
9*a*. $816.00
9*b*. $1,156.35
9*c*. $953.40

ASSIGNMENT 14–2

1. $380.14
3. $39.20
   $56.00
5. $230.70
7. $5,600

ASSIGNMENT 15–1

A. 1. $26.78
   3*a*. $72.29
   3*b*. $53.78
   3*c*. $3,672.00
   5*a*. $2,264.40
   5*b*. $1,598.85
   5*c*. $191.25
   5*d*. –0–
   7. $130.05

B. Arden $28.69
   Blake –0–
   Carter $24.10
   Dome $61.97

ASSIGNMENT 15–2

A. 1. $1,292.85
   3*a*. $772.65
   3*b*. $1,139.85
   5*a*. $2,832.03
   5*b*. $2,255.99
   7*a*. $33.05
   7*b*. $0.46
   9. $172.94

ASSIGNMENT 16–1

A. 1. $26
   3. $249

	Name	*Deductions* FICA	*Deductions* Federal Income Tax	Net Pay
B.	Bartlett, James	$ 22.21	$ 41	$ 227.15
	Kroner, Peter	49.67	96	503.57
	Murphy, Robert	70.89	229	722.47
	Stollings, Janet	20.51	213	740.61
	Wayne, Darlene	14.05	13	156.59
	Totals	$177.33	$592	$2,350.39

	Name	*Deductions* FICA	*Deductions* Federal Income Tax	Net Pay
C.	Cunningham, D.	$ 92.57	$ 93	$1,024.43
	Gardner, P.	87.98	0	1,062.02
	Lawson, L.	109.01	48	1,267.99
	Riordan, M.	102.51	136	1,101.49
	Tarnopol, L.	118.58	116	1,315.42
	Ward, V.	102.51	61	1,176.49
	Ziegler, S.	118.58	191	1,240.42
	Totals	$731.74	$645	$8,188.26

ASSIGNMENT 16–2

A. 1. $127.51
   3. $408.97
   5. $13.47
   7*a*. $143.00
   7*b*. $143.69

	Name	*Deductions* FICA	*Deductions* Federal Income Tax	Net Pay
B.	Billwiller, J.	$ 3,672.00	$ 7,959.60	$ 38,368.40
	Fraden, J.	2,496.96	3,217.20	26,925.84
	Kirk, W.	1,819.94	2,185.04	19,785.02
	Ohman, A.	1,410.20	2,301.26	14,722.54
	Swanson, S.	1,282.14	2,034.00	13,443.86
	Wells, W.	3,672.00	10,474.62	34,803.38
	Totals	$14,353.24	$28,171.72	$148,049.04

ASSIGNMENT 17–1

A. 1. $551.34
3. $455.52
5. 48.7%

	Final Date of Discount	Amount of Cash Discount	Final Payment Date
B.	1. JAN 19	$ 8.00	FEB 18
	3. JULY 10	$ 99.40	JULY 30
	5. JUNE 19	$ 33.66	JULY 29
	7. AUG 9	$649.90	AUG 29
	9. JULY 14	$ 4.63	AUG 3

ASSIGNMENT 17–2

1. $80.25
3. $86.40
5. $1,531.72
7*a*. APRIL 10
7*b*. MAY 15
7*c*. APRIL 13
9*a*. AUG 15
9*b*. $2,425
9*c*. SEPT 4
11. $5,200.75

ASSIGNMENT 17–3

1. $294
3. $54
$66
$132
5. $167.84
7. $243.46
9. $237.00
11. $118.39

ASSIGNMENT 18–1

1*a*. 25%
1*b*. $13.75
3*a*. $63.84
3*b*. 32%
5*a*. $300.00
5*b*. $186.00
7*a*. $428.80
7*b*. 16%
9*a*. $45.72
9*b*. $9.72

ASSIGNMENT 18–2

A. 1*a*. $800
1*b*. $880
3*a*. $125
3*b*. $625
5*a*. $246
5*b*. $164
7*a*. $360
7*b*. $480
9*a*. $1.40
9*b*. $0.35
9*c*. 25%
11*a*. $40
11*b*. $50

B. 1. $320
3. $0.71 (or $0.72)
5. $8.45
7. 121%
9. $1,156.25

ASSIGNMENT 18–3

A. 1. $300.20
21%
79%
3. $4.90
$30.10
86%
5. $396
$205.92
52%
7. $915
$173.85
81%
9. $186.84
$332.16
36%

B. 1. $442
3. $199.39
5. $187.50
7. $62.50

ASSIGNMENT 19–1

1. $43,500
3*a*. $7,560
3*b*. $12,220
5*a*. $96,370
5*b*. $86,350

ASSIGNMENT 19–2

1. $2,192,100
3*a*. $135,550
3*b*. $363,925
5. $6,400.32
7*a*. $28,150
7*b*. $29,800
7*c*. $28,878.75
7*d*. $28,425

ASSIGNMENT 20–1

A. 1. $180
3. $3,124

B. 1. $3,040
3. $1,171

C. 1*a*. $725
1*b*. $725
3*a*. $88
3*b*. $525
5*a*. $390
5*b*. $520

ASSIGNMENT 20–2

A. 1. $1,750
3. $400

B. 1*a*. $2,500
1*b*. $1,667
3*a*. $1,200
3*b*. $3,120
5*a*. $557
5*b*. $35

ASSIGNMENT 20–3

A. 1. $540
3. $620

B. 1*a*. $1,800
1*b*. $1,500
3*a*. $4,200
3*b*. $6,675
5*a*. $1,750
5*b*. less
5*c*. $150

ASSIGNMENT 20–4

A. 1. $3,660
3. $2,218
5. $821

B. 1. $7,211
3. $6,254

C. 1. $3,124
$4,998
$2,999
3. $409
$204
5. $2,232
$1,339
7. $4,318
$5,454
9. $1,072
$2,858

ASSIGNMENT 21–1

A. 1. 38
3. 249
5. 111

B. 1. 44
3. 132
5. 78

C. 1. 1,686
3. 1,095
5. 478

D. 1. July 10, 1991
3. December 24, 1991
5. July 5, 1991

E. 1. June 27, 1991
3. October 29, 1991
5. February 13, 1992

ASSIGNMENT 21–2

A. 1. $20.00
3. $82.50

B. 1. $9.75
3. $1.13

C. 1. $810.67
3. $202.50

D. 1. $33.29
3. $2.76

E. 1*a*. $225.00
1*b*. $230.00
3. $8.32

ASSIGNMENT 22–1

A. 1. $375.00
3. $2,400.00

B. 1. 15%
3. 21%

C. 1. 45
3. 15

D. 1. 9%
3. 15.4%
5. 320
7. 170

ASSIGNMENT 22–2

A. 1. 45
3. $6,401.25
5. 25

B. 1. 16%
3. $1,825.05
5*a*. Company A
5*b*. $6.25
7*a*. 40
7*b*. $94.32
7*c*. 50

ASSIGNMENT 22–3

A. 1. $2.44
3. $0.43
5. $0.33
7. $0.24

B. 1. $2.76
3. $17.85
5. $0.09
7. $4.89

C. 1. $13.42
3. $7.50

ASSIGNMENT 23–1

A.		*1*	*3*
	Maturity date	August 7	December 12
	Discount term	45	122
	Bank Discount	$25.00	$29.89
	Proceeds	$1,225.00	$705.11

B.		*Bank Discount*	*Proceeds*
	1.	$9.60	$790.40
	3.	$3.60	$146.40

C. 1*a*. $10.40
1*b*. $289.60
3*a*. $3.95
3*b*. $821.05
5*a*. $14.70
5*b*. $435.30

ASSIGNMENT 23–2

	Maturity Value	*Bank Discount*	*Proceeds*
1.	$1,836.00	$ 18.36	$1,817.64
3.	$ 945.00	$ 36.75	$ 908.25
5.	$5,616.00	$ 42.12	$5,573.88
7.	$1,372.50	$ 5.34	$1,367.16
9.	$2,589.44	$ 15.54	$2,573.90
11.	$ 453.50	$ 3.02	$ 450.48
13.	$1,048.76	$131.10	$ 917.66
15.	$2,259.25	$210.86	$2,048.39

ASSIGNMENT 23–3

	1	*3*	*5*
Life of note	45	92	123
Ordinary interest	$ 10.35	$ 35.57	$ 46.13
Maturity value	$700.35	$905.57	$1,396.13
Discount term	30	30	15
Bank discount	$ 9.34	$ 13.58	$ 9.31
Proceeds	$691.01	$891.99	$1,386.82

B. 1*a*. $261.52
1*b*. $4.90
1*c*. $256.62
3*a*. $65.38
3*b*. $985.45
5*a*. $45.65
5*b*. $2,506.02

ASSIGNMENT 24–1

A.		*Periodic Rate*	*Number of Periods*
	1.	14%	4
	3.	5%	12
	5.	3%	32
	7.	2%	36

B.		*Maturity Value*	*Amount of Compound Interest*
	1.	$ 7,320.50	$ 2,320.50
	3.	$18,624.35	$10,124.35
	5.	$ 1,281.65	$ 781.65
	7.	$ 9,606.00	$ 3,606.00
	9.	$17,230.20	$14,230.20
	11.	$68,411.40	$54,161.40

ASSIGNMENT 24–2

A. 1. $925.45
3. $10,122.25
5. $1,170.63

B. 1. $20,886.00
3. $5,760.96
5. $2\frac{1}{2}$

ASSIGNMENT 24–3

1. $3,182.80
3. $2,573.87
5. $17,128.96
7. $5,359.40

ASSIGNMENT 25–1

	Present Value	Amount of Compound Interest
1.	$1,116.80	$ 883.20
3.	$ 632.88	$ 267.12
5.	$ 254.94	$ 95.06
7.	$7,885.00	$2,115.00
9.	$ 40.11	$ 659.89
11.	$2,185.50	$2,814.50

ASSIGNMENT 25–2

1. $6,420.20
3. $5,375.30
5. $9,867.50
7. $3,849.65
9. 4 years
11. $5,143.39
13. $3,687.98

ASSIGNMENT 26–1

A. 1. $5,794.64
   3. $125,680.76
   5. $2,011.82
B. 1. $7,243.30
   3. $9,145.95
   5. $3,591.27

ASSIGNMENT 26–2

A. 1. $12,517.47
   3. $7,152.84
   5. $958.28
B. 1. $69.03
   3. $16,638.05
C. 1. $379,339.65
   3. $101.06
   5. $4,499.96

ASSIGNMENT 27–1

		Inst. Cost (a)	Interest (b)	Amount Borrowed (c)
A.	1.	$ 80	$ 5	$ 65
	3.	$385	$35	$325

B. 1. 23%
   3. 8%

		Amount of Interest	Effective Interest Rate
C.	1.	$ 26.36	33%
	3.	$113.26	29%

D. 1. 38.1%
   3. 16.7%

ASSIGNMENT 27–2

1. 18%
3. 15%
5. 19.7%
7. 25%
9. $20.50

ASSIGNMENT 28–1

1. $33,175
3. $65.13
5. $407.40
7. $184.62

ASSIGNMENT 29–1

A. 1. $211.77
   3. $397.95
   5. $732.06
   7. $762.75
   9. $1,139.25

		Loan Amount	Monthly Payment
B.	1.	$17,100	$380.48
	3.	$76,400	$868.67
	5.	$74,800	$827.29

7*a*. $906.95
7*b*. $864.45
7*c*. $830.45
9*a*. $3,482.40
9*b*. $482.40

ASSIGNMENT 29–2

A. 1*a*. $629.07 3*a*. $306.34
1*b*. $487.50 3*b*. $107.54
1*c*. $141.57 3*c*. $198.80
1*d*. $38,858.43 3*d*. $8,701.20

	Payment Amount	*Interest Payment*
5.	*(a)* $1,209.32	*(b)* $1,184.17
	(a) $1,209.32	*(b)* $1,183.86

Principal Payment	*Principal Balance*
(c) $25.15	*(d)* $97,974.85
(c) $25.46	*(d)* $97,949.39

	Beginning of Year Principal Balance	*Interest Paid*
B. 1.	*(a)* $20,360	*(b)* $2,443.20
	(a) $15,270	*(b)* $1,832.40
	(a) $10,180	*(b)* $1,221.60
	(a) $5,090	*(b)* $610.80

Principal Paid	*Total Payment*
(c) $5,090	*(d)* $7,533.20
(c) $5,090	*(d)* $6,922.40
(c) $5,090	*(d)* $6,311.60
(c) $5,090	*(d)* $5,700.80

ASSIGNMENT 30–1

A. 1. $16,400
3. $225,000
5. $9.29
7. $80,000
9. $3.50
11. $2,611.39

ASSIGNMENT 31–1

A. 1. $30,000
3. $80,000
5. $(18,179)
B. 1. $45,945
3*a*. $19,935
3*b*. $14,725
3*c*. $5,210

ASSIGNMENT 31–2

1*a*. $17,300
1*b*. $12,900
1*c*. $4,400
3. $146,280
5. $23,390
7*a*. $80,294
7*b*. $52,300
7*c*. $27,994

ASSIGNMENT 32–1

A. 1. $8,900
$2,050
3. $15,370
$3,725
B. 1. $72,370
3. $8,125
5. $73,410

ASSIGNMENT 32–2

1. $8,390
3. $940
5. $39,200
7. $1,400

ASSIGNMENT 33–1

A. Fill in the missing items in the following comparative income statement. Round off percent answers to the nearest tenth.

Stacey Company Comparative Income Statements for Years Ended December 31, 1990, and 1991

	1991	*1990*	*Amount*	*Percent*	*1991*	*1990*
Gross sales		(4) 191,700	14,300	7.5	102.0	101.7
Sales returns	(1) 4,000		800	25.0	2.0	1.7
Net sales		(5) 188,500	13,500	7.2		
Cost of goods sold			11,000	8.1	72.3	71.6
Gross profit	(2) 56,000		2,500	4.7	27.7	28.4
Operating expense	(3) 44,000		(2,000)	(4.3)	21.8	24.4
Net income		(6) 7,500	4,500	60.0	5.9	4.0

B. Fill in the missing items in the following comparative balance sheet. Round off percent answers to nearest tenth.

Stacey Company Comparative Balance Sheets, December 31, 1990, and 1991.

	Amount	*Percent*	*1991*	*1990*
Assets:				
Cash	4,680	9.5	19.7	18.3
Accounts receivable	(1,873)	(2.2)	30.0	31.2
Merchandise inventory	3,110	3.1	38.3	37.8
Equipment less depreciation	(1,235)	(3.6)	12.0	12.7
Total Assets	4,682	1.7	100.0	100.0
Liabilities:				
Accounts payable	6,915	16.2	18.2	15.9
Wages payable	(585)	(28.4)	0.5	0.8
Total liabilities	6,330	14.2	18.7	16.7
Owner's Equity:				
A. J. Stacey, capital	(1,648)	(0.7)	81.3	83.3
Total liabilities and owner's equity	4,682	1.7		

ASSIGNMENT 33–2

	1992	*1991*
1.	5.3 to 1	6.0 to 1
3.	4.3 to 1	5.0 to 1
5.	4.7 to 1	5.2 to 1
7.	4.4%	2.8%
9.	2.4	2.4

ASSIGNMENT 34–1

1. $4,625
   $4,625

3*a*. $3,000
   $3,000

3*b*. $5,000
   $3,000

5*a*. $4,500
   $6,000

5*b*. $6,750
   $7,500

7. $8,950
   $10,750

ASSIGNMENT 34–2

1. $3,825
   $3,375
3. $9,909
   $7,509
5. $6,600
   $7,800
7. $4,050
   $4,950

ASSIGNMENT 35–1

1*a*. $804,000
1*b*. $20.10
3*a*. $1,930,000
3*b*. $11.47
5*a*. $107.76
5*b*. Retained earnings
5*c*. $655,216
7*a*. $45,000
7*b*. $22

ASSIGNMENT 35–2

1. $0.25
3*a*. $2.50
3*b*. $1.20
5. Third year:
   a. $10.00
   b. -0-
   Fourth year:
   a. $8.00
   b. $0.20
7. Fourth year:
   a. $20.00
   b. -0-
   Fifth year:
   a. $10.00
   b. $4.00

ASSIGNMENT 36–1

A. 1. $7.92
   3. $3,648.00
   5. $18.87
B. 1. $31.32
   3. $58.52
   5. $788.40
C. 1. $9.75
   3. $21.82
   5. $1.61 (or $1.60)
D. 1. $10.68
   3*a*. $1,100
   3*b*. $798.63

ASSIGNMENT 37–1

1A. $30,000
1B. $50,000
3. $20,000
5. $10,000
7A. $20,000
7B. $30,000

ASSIGNMENT 38–1

1. $243.60
3*a*. $1,956.40
3*b*. $40,000
3*c*. $40,000
5*a*. $441.40
5*b*. $643.60
5*c*. $978.20
7. $505.50

ASSIGNMENT 38–2

1. $2,900.00
3. $2,962.96
5. $12,537.31
7. $25.10

ASSIGNMENT APPENDIX

Problem 1
Alberton Company, sales (1980–1989)

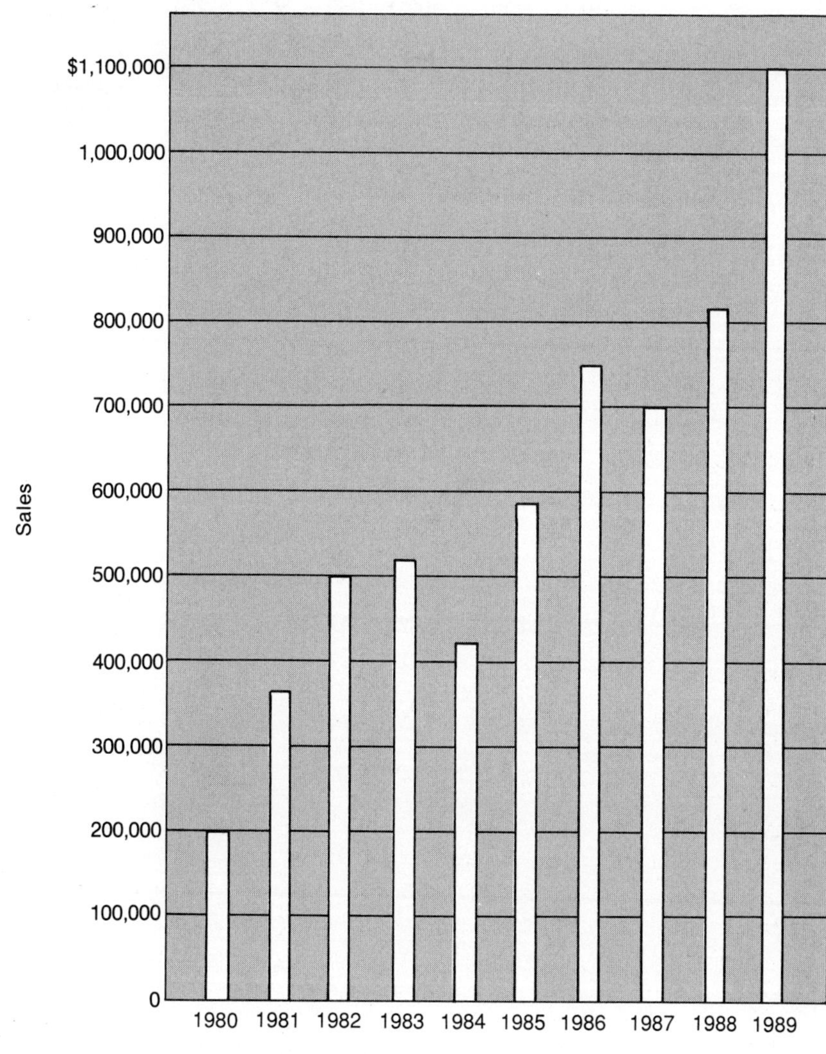

Problem 3
Best-Bilt Company, quarterly production of cabs—19—(standard, deluxe, and custom models)

Quarter
I
II
III
IV
0 50 100 150 200 250 300 350
NUMBER OF UNITS
S D C

Problem 5
XYZ Company, Distribution of $80,000 advertising budget expressed as percent of total

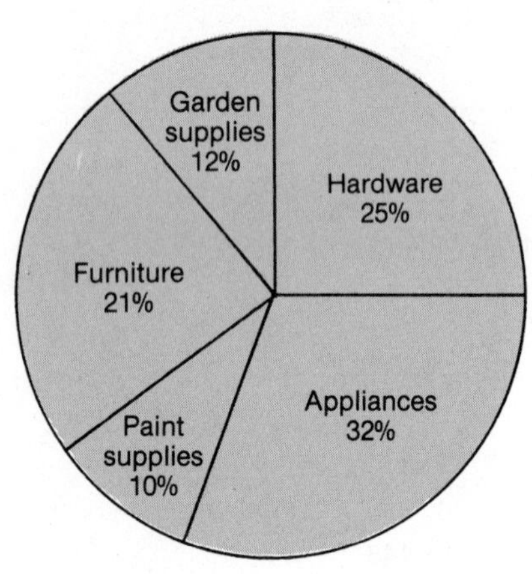

Problem 7
Merchants Bank of Trade, new accounts (four quarters, 19—)

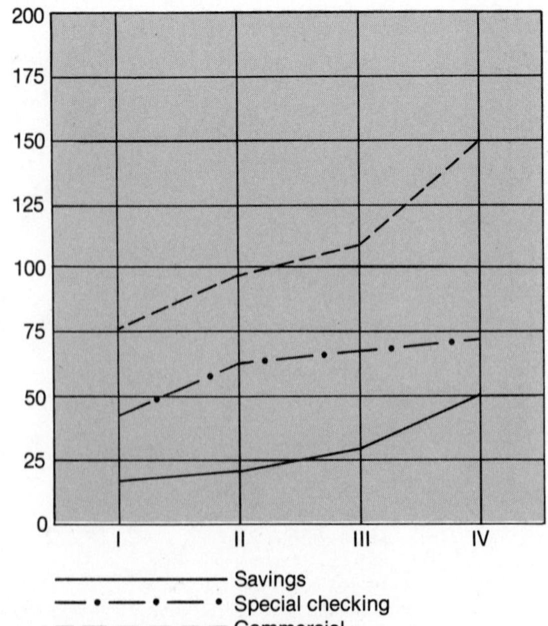

Index